CW00550089

The Life of R. H. Tawney

Socialism and History

Lawrence Goldman

B L O O M S B U R Y

LONDON • NEW DELHI • NEW YORK • SYDNEY

Bloomsbury Academic
An imprint of Bloomsbury Publishing Plc

50 Bedford Square	1385 Broadway
London	New York
WC1B 3DP	NY 10018
UK	USA

www.bloomsbury.com

Bloomsbury is a registered trade mark of Bloomsbury Publishing Plc

First published 2013
This paperback edition published 2014

© Lawrence Goldman, 2013, 2014

Lawrence Goldman has asserted his right under the Copyright, Designs and
Patents Act, 1988, to be identified as Author of this work.

All rights reserved. No part of this publication may be reproduced or transmitted
in any form or by any means, electronic or mechanical, including photocopying,
recording, or any information storage or retrieval system, without prior
permission in writing from the publishers.

No responsibility for loss caused to any individual or organization acting on or
refraining from action as a result of the material in this publication can be
accepted by Bloomsbury or the author.

British Library Cataloguing-in-Publication Data
A catalogue record for this book is available from the British Library.

ISBN: HB: 978-1-7809-3704-5
PB: 978-1-4725-7742-9
ePDF: 978-1-7809-3612-3
ePUB: 978-1-7809-3828-8

Library of Congress Cataloging-in-Publication Data
A catalog record for this book is available from the Library of Congress.

Typeset by Deanta Global Publishing Solutions, Chennai, India
Printed and bound in Great Britain

A=9820.

The Life of R. H. Tawney

I Dafydd Elystan —
oddi wrth

Jane + Xerec

Brynawr wella.

18. iii. 15

To Henry Mayr-Harting, Henrietta Leyser
and Mark Whittow

Contents

Acknowledgements

My interest in R. H. Tawney is personal as well as scholarly. As a junior research fellow in Cambridge in the 1980s I sometimes found myself taking lunch or dinner next to the former diplomat and historian Michal Vyvyan, then emeritus fellow of Trinity College, who was Tawney's nephew and one of his two literary executors, and whose reminiscences of his uncle and correspondence feature in this book. I barely knew who Tawney was at that stage but Vyvyan's conversation and recollections of him interested me greatly. Then I left Cambridge and discovered that I had been appointed to 'Tawney's job' as it was described to me, teaching adult students as the History and Politics lecturer at the Department for Continuing Education in the University of Oxford. Tawney had held this position – in fact, he had invented it himself – between 1908 and 1913. Like Tawney, I taught four extra-mural evening classes a week and summer schools as well, and like Tawney I spent five years in the job. The experience was formative, as it had been for Tawney, and it led me to a scholarly interest in the history of adult and workers' education in England, published as a book, *Dons and Workers: Oxford and Adult Education Since 1850* in 1995.[1] Tawney emerged from that study as the most deep-thinking, skilled and radical tutor in the educational movement which, from the Edwardian period, sent university tutors to the towns and cities of Britain to teach tutorial classes, as they were called, to working men and women. The idea of writing his biography began to take shape, and a first attempt was published in the *Oxford Dictionary of National Biography* in 2004.[2] Not long after Tawney died the other of his literary executors, Sir Richard Rees, commented that 'the problem of finding someone capable of doing justice to the different aspects of Harry's personality and life is not a simple one.'[3] Though my personal connections with Tawney may be considered slight and coincidental, they may go some small way towards an understanding of certain aspects of his career.

While there are many extant summaries of his life and several books which provide good accounts of his biography, restrictions on the use of Tawney's papers, including the amount that could be quoted directly from them, have deterred a full-scale study of the man up to now. Our knowledge not only of

Tawney himself but of British socialism, education and historiography in the first half of the twentieth century have been the poorer for this, and I hope this book goes some way to make amends. To be able to read Tawney in his own, often magnificent words, whether in letters, speeches, lectures or unpublished articles, is one of the aims of this book.

My primary thanks are to Tawney's great nephew and current literary executor, Major General Charles Vyvyan, for his interest in the project of writing Tawney's life from scratch, for making available to me those items of Tawney's personal papers then in the possession of the family, and for permission to quote in full and at length from the Tawney and Tawney-Vyvyan collections held in the archives of the British Library of Political and Economic Science, London School of Economics. I am especially grateful to Sue Donnelly and her admirable team of archivists at the LSE who made my days there working on Tawney's papers and associated collections so pleasant and profitable. Their help with queries and their general consideration for scholars is exemplary. I would also like to record my thanks to the staff of the British Library; the National Archives; the London University Institute of Education library; the Lambeth Palace Library; the London Metropolitan Archives; the Oxford University Archives; Rhodes House Library, Oxford; the Cambridge University Library; the libraries of Trinity College and King's College in Cambridge and the libraries of Christ Church, Balliol College and St. Peter's College in Oxford; Toynbee Hall, Whitechapel; Rugby School Archives and Tameside Local Studies Library.

For permission to quote from the collections in their ownership or care, I am grateful to the London School of Economics; London University Institute of Education; London Metropolitan Archives; the Trades Union Congress Library of London Metropolitan University; the Trustees of Lambeth Palace Library; the Literary Estate of Lord Dacre of Glanton; the Economic History Society; the Master and Fellows of Trinity College, Cambridge; the Master and Fellows of Balliol College, Oxford and Rugby School.

Chapter 3 of this book, which is about Tawney's experience teaching workers between 1908 and 1913, is an adapted and expanded version of chapter 3 of my earlier book *Dons and Workers. Oxford and Adult Education Since 1850* (Oxford, 1995). I am grateful to the Delegates of Oxford University Press for permission to use the material in an altered form in this book.

I am grateful to Rugby School for permission to reproduce three photographs of Tawney as a schoolboy. The remaining photographs are items held in the Tawney collections at the British Library of Political and Economic Science at the London School of Economics, and are reproduced with the permission of Charles Vyvyan. I acknowledge Mr Alan Chappelow MA, FRSA, of Downshire Hill, Hampstead, London, whose photograph of 'Tawney in old age' appears in this book. I am grateful to *The Times* for permission to publish the photo of the unveiling of Tawney's blue plaque in Mecklenburgh Square in November 1980. In all other cases, including images taken by Flemons of Tonbridge ('Tawney as a boy') and Ellen Macnaughton of South Kensington (portrait of Jeanette Beveridge), every effort has been made to trace, inform and acknowledge those who own the rights to the photographs used.

I was fortunate to be elected to a Visiting Fellowship in the History Department of the Australian National University, Canberra, where a first draft of this book was written in early 2012. I'm especially grateful to Pat Jalland and Melanie Nolan, my opposite number as the editor of the *Dictionary of Australian Biography*, for the warmth of their welcome and hospitality during a most enjoyable academic term in Australia. Barry Smith's recollections of Tawney in Australia in 1955 and Frank Bongiorno's written account of Tawney's experience of Australian electioneering were received with much gratitude. At Oxford University Press my close colleagues on the *Oxford Dictionary of National Biography*, Philip Carter, Mark Curthoys and Alex May have shared their many insights into the craft of the biographer with me in a tutorial lasting fully nine years. I am grateful for their patience, advice and interest, and for the support of the other members of the *Oxford DNB* team – Robert Faber, Jo Payne, Laura Dawkins, Ryan Kidd, Katie Raymond, Martha Skipper and the late Ralph Evans – as well. I have relied for some years on the help of younger historians to take up the slack in my college while I have been working at the *Oxford DNB* and thinking about Tawney, and I gratefully acknowledge the contributions of Holger Nehring, Tim Johnston, Edmund Neill, Daniel Gerrard and Graciela Iglesias-Rogers in teaching and organizing History at St. Peter's. I thank the Master and Fellows of St. Peter's College, Oxford for granting me a year of leave for research and writing. Without the support of Dr Nicholas Cole during my absence this book would have been impossible. He has, in addition, provided inspiration, friendship and great good humour for the past 6 years.

Others who have provided advice, answers to my questions or just encouragement include: Sir Brian Harrison, Jose Harris, Ross McKibbin, William Whyte, Ben Jackson, Matthew Grimley, Janet Howarth, Philip Waller, Michael Freeden, David Feldman, Frank Bongiorno, Kynan Gentry, David Grylls, the late Colin Matthew and Rusty MacLean at Rugby School. Tony Corley sent me the drafts of two unpublished essays concerning Tawney's friend and historical mentor, George Unwin. I am grateful to Dr A. C. Lynch of Potters Bar for providing extracts from the unpublished autobiography of his father, Mr A. J. Lynch, who was the liaison officer between Tawney and the South Tottenham Labour Party in 1922–3. Adam Sisman, the biographer of Hugh Trevor-Roper, used his knowledge of recent historiography and of 'the gentry controversy' in particular in a most helpful reading of my chapter on Tawney's historical writings. Jane Whittle was kind enough to share with me the draft of her introduction as editor of a volume of essays marking the centenary of the publication in 1912 of Tawney's first major historical work, *The Agrarian Problem in Sixteenth Century England.* Tony Wright, another of Tawney's biographers, generously read and commented on the whole manuscript. I take full responsibility for the interpretations advanced, and for the mistakes.

For hospitality during my research trips to London I would like to thank Richard Lander and Sarah Barclay pre-eminently, and also David and Suzy Herman, David Cesarani and Dawn Waterman, and Ruth and Ben Whitby. Harry Swinton lent technological support at a crucial moment. My sixth-form History teacher, Roger Knight, was kind enough to advise on the compilation of an index. Tony Morris was the editor who first commissioned this book many years ago. I am grateful also for the continuing support I have received from Claire Lipscomb and the editorial staff at Bloomsbury.

My greatest appreciation is for my colleagues in History at St. Peter's College, Oxford over the past 23 years to whom this book is dedicated. We made a great team.

List of Illustrations

Abbreviations used in the Text

ASB	Annette Susannah Beveridge
BBC TRANSCRIPT 1963	Transcript of interviews made by the BBC for a radio biography of Tawney, broadcast on the Home Service, 12 May 1963, Lena Jeger papers, London School of Economics
BEV	Beveridge papers, London School of Economics
BLPES	British Library of Political and Economic Science, London School of Economics
CB	*R. H. Tawney's Commonplace Book* (eds J. M. Winter and D. M. Joslin) (Cambridge University Press, Cambridge, 1972)
CHT	Charles Henry Tawney
CJP	Creech Jones Papers, Rhodes House, Oxford
EHR	*English Historical Review*
EcHR	*Economic History Review*
HBC	Henry Beveridge Collection, British Library
IOE	Institute of Education Archives, University of London
JB	Jeanette Beveridge
JT	Jeanette Tawney
LJP	Lena Jeger Papers, London School of Economics
LMA	London Metropolitan Archive

LMU	London Metropolitan University: Trades Union Congress Library Collections
LSE	London School of Economics
ODNB	*Oxford Dictionary of National Biography*
OUA	Oxford University Archives
PD	*Parliamentary Debates, 4th series*
RHT	R. H. Tawney
T	Tawney Papers, London School of Economics
T.ADD	Tawney Additional Mss, London School of Economics
TRANSCRIPT 1982	Transcript of an interview with J. M. K. Vyvyan conducted by Signora Capodivento of Barletta, Bari, Italy, Lena Jeger papers, London School of Economics
TSF	Tawney Staff Files, London School of Economics
TV	Tawney-Vyvyan Collection, London School of Economics
WEA	Workers' Educational Association
WHB	William Beveridge
WT	William Temple

Introduction

A gentleman once said to Archbishop William Temple during the Second World War, 'We need more men like Tawney'. The Archbishop, who had been Tawney's close friend since schooldays, apparently replied, 'There are no men like Tawney'. Tawney's singularity is the rationale of this book. He was the leading economic historian of his generation whose book, *Religion and the Rise of Capitalism*, sold more copies than any other history book in the interwar period; he was a notable political thinker of whom it has been said that he, 'more than any other single individual, gave socialism in Britain a coherent creed';[1] he was also a leading educationist who designed and implemented in person new and enduring forms of adult education, and then became the most vocal and persistent advocate of the reform of the British secondary education system. Each of these achievements on its own might be enough to merit Tawney a biography; taken together they make him one of the most important and compelling of academic and political figures in recent British history. As one of his severest critics admitted, 'when the historian comes to write . . . an intellectual history of the early twentieth century, Tawney will be one of those figures he will really have to concern himself with.'[2] Though this biography pays full attention to his achievements, it has been written not only because the story of Tawney's life adds context and detail to each major element of his work, but also because his life is intrinsically more interesting, more varied and more influential than might be imagined.

When the first of various studies of Tawney's thought was published some 12 years after his death in 1974, the historian A. J. P. Taylor welcomed a book 'about Tawney's ideas rather than about his life. This was the right choice. To outward appearance Tawney's life was much like that of any other professor of history'.[3] Taylor evidently knew little about Tawney. Professors of history do not usually begin their careers as social workers in London's East End. Relatively few of them go out to teach history and economics to workers. They do not usually fight at the Somme; they rarely devote themselves for several years to the interests of the Miners' Federation of Great Britain and to the wider cause of industrial justice. Few of them are parliamentary candidates or sit on royal commissions of enquiry; even fewer write a general election manifesto for one of the two major political parties in modern British politics, or, if they are historians of England, write a classic work on the economy and society of modern China. They tend not to know prime ministers and leaders of the Labour Party, or to find themselves in the British embassy in Washington DC at the time of the attack on Pearl Harbor. Their closest friends tend not to be the Archbishop of Canterbury, Temple, or the man who did most to design the British welfare state, William Beveridge, whose sister Tawney married. Tawney was, and did, all these things and more. He was no ordinary professor of history but one who believed that scholarship and the service of society should go together. He was, indeed, no ordinary great man.

Those who have written about Tawney since the 1970s have maintained the focus on his ideas, specifically his political ideas. His contribution to the history of British socialism and his relevance to contemporary socialism have been the subject of considerable interest and the flow of books and articles on these questions has been steady. They have been based largely on Tawney's published works for two reasons: first, because this is the normal practice of political science, and second because Tawney's papers, which are held at the London School of Economics where he taught for more than 30 years, are voluminous and, until now, have carried certain restrictions limiting their use. This has not only deterred biographers but also obscured an accurate appreciation of his various contributions. Tawney's best-known political works, *The Acquisitive Society* (1921) and *Equality* (1931) have attracted much attention. But the argument of this book is that equally revealing sources for an appreciation of his thought can be found in his pamphlets, articles, unpublished lectures and papers, memoranda and letters.

This is a familiar justification for biography – that a published life, based on archival sources, is intrinsically revealing in itself and provides necessary background and context for other academic work. But in Tawney's case the claim for biography may be taken further in the form of a challenge or corrective to an undue concentration on the study of his texts. For Tawney never saw such texts as either systematic or timeless: they were not statements designed to endure, but the best sense he could make of a specific situation or historical conjuncture. Generalizing from them must be done with care, therefore. Twenty-two years after *Equality* was published, Sir Stanley Unwin, his publisher, wrote to ask him if he would bow to the requests of many of his readers for an entirely new, fourth edition of the work.[4] But in a book consisting of a series of closely argued policy prescriptions ranging from the nationalization (or state ownership) of British industries to the abolition of fee-paying schools, that was not easily achieved. Tawney replied that 'the book has been overtaken by events. A good many of the evils mentioned in it, if they have not wholly disappeared, no longer exist on the same scale.' The statistics were all out of date and the 'arguments and conclusions based on them, would require to be changed throughout'. It was, replied Tawney, 'a historical document . . . a base-line by which one can judge how the tide has risen.'[5] He could not rewrite it, he explained, though he was persuaded to add a further preface to a new edition, and also a new concluding chapter in which he set out some of the welcome social changes in Britain since he wrote the book.[6] To Tawney, its topicality at a moment in time was not a handicap or a weakness: as he wrote elsewhere, 'It is of the nature of political thought that much of its best work is topical. It achieves immortality not by eschewing the limitations of time and place, but by making them its platform.'[7]

Not long after his correspondence with Unwin, Tawney explained in a lecture that 'political thought worthy of the name' was neither to be found in abstract philosophy nor in the practical applications and measures supposedly influenced by that philosophy, but in an 'intermediate region, where abstractions and practice meet'.[8] This may be why Tawney is not widely read in courses on the history of political thought, which tend to focus on the more abstract of texts where close analysis in the attempt to reconstruct an author's intellectual intentions is both possible and fruitful. But Tawney himself always inhabited the 'intermediate region' between principle and practice in a career spent seeking to apply knowledge and intellect to policy-formation and the business of government. Biography is arguably the most suitable genre for the analysis of this type of social activism and of the writing to which it gives rise, for in a biography the development and implementation of ideas can be related to the development of all aspects of a life, and books and articles can be treated not as abstract statements in themselves but as the products of specific experience and context.

But not too specific! In his famous address in 1945 about two people he knew well and respected deeply, *The Webbs and Their Work*, Tawney reminded his listeners that

> In the library of hell a special stack is reserved for those biographies – a vast and dreary host – of great men and women, which throw light on every aspect of their victims' personalities from their taste in dress to their second cousins' Christian names, except the characteristics in which their greatness consisted.[9]

This book will have to discuss Tawney's dress sense, or rather, the lack of it, because it was a genuine issue in his relationship with the woman he married. But in the manner of articles in the *Oxford Dictionary of National Biography*, my aim is to provide an overall architecture for Tawney's life rather than a mass of detail, and I hope thereby to do justice to the nature of Tawney's greatness. Articles in the *Oxford DNB* take a chronological approach to their subject, as does this book, but also try to establish the key themes and issues in each biography, and organize the essay around them. This has been my approach here. Rather than an unbroken narrative I have divided Tawney's life into a series of periods and phases, each of which has a thematic unity. I have also brought together discussion of his political thought, historical work and educational activism in single and separate chapters devoted to each. This is designed to make it easier to understand the development of the main branches of his work; it should also assist in relating the different elements of his political, social and historical thought to each other and to the whole.

With the exception of the chapters that focus on Tawney's courtship and marriage, and his service in the British army during the First World War, where, in both cases, it has been possible to recreate his experiences on something like a monthly and weekly, if not a daily basis, this biography does not give details on where he was and what he was doing at any and every stage in his life. It used to be said at the London School of Economics that were one to open any cupboard in the School, 'a bit of Tawney was sure to fall out'.[10] But even an archive as large as this one cannot provide details on all aspects of his life and, for example, there are relatively few archival sources on his early years up to and including his time as an undergraduate at Oxford. Nor, unfortunately, are there abundant materials relating to the drafting of all his major published works. I have, however, made ample use of many of his unpublished lectures which do form part of the collection. These are often very revealing of his attitudes, which may be one of the reasons why Tawney and his literary executors did not seek to publish them during his life or after his death, though volumes of his essays did appear in 1953 while he was still alive, and in 1964, 2 years after his death, respectively.[11] Not to have used unpublished lectures would have been to neglect an important and authentic source which at the moment of delivery represented Tawney's views on an issue. But whether these lectures should be taken as seriously as those that Tawney did publish is a valid question, and one that has no easy answer. My instinct has been to use this material in the hope of getting closer to the essential Tawney.

While most notable men and women are celebrated and memorialized because of their achievements, the pattern, nature and components of some people's lives are arguably as significant as their specific contributions. No one could diminish or ignore Tawney's achievements as a scholar and also as a contributor to the modern politics and welfare of Britain, but the view taken in this study is that the nature of Tawney's life matters as much as, if not more than, those specific contributions. This is because much of his influence was derived from deep resources of character, and a remarkable personal authority that came from his wide experience, his learning, his facility with language and his physical appearance and bearing. Together these seem to have impressed all those who met or dealt with him such that one of the commonest words used to describe him in life and in death was 'nobility'. As this biography shows, however, Tawney was not an easy man in private and his marriage was fraught with problems, some of which were of his making. I hope I have not flinched from judging him, and, in a phrase common among those who have worked for the *Oxford DNB*, I hope that in those judgments I have been 'wise, liberal and just'.

In so far as there can be an argument in a biography, in this case it is that Tawney as a young man was committed to an ethical and spiritual socialism which was centred on individual behaviour above all. He sought to make socialists by education and conviction; he judged policy not by its utility and outcome, but by its moral intentions. He rejected as morally unworthy versions of socialism which simply sought to materially enrich workers and their families. It was an outlook shared by many who helped to make the Labour Party in the Edwardian period, but this is now largely forgotten. In many personal contexts Tawney remained committed to this outlook, but after the First World War, as he was drawn into the formal politics of the Labour Party, and particularly as a result of his membership of the 1919 Royal Commission on the Coal Mining Industry, he adopted in public the more conventional state-socialist views that had become the party's official doctrine under its 1918 Constitution. These ideas form the basis of *Equality*, which is a type of programme or blueprint for the Labour Party in power. The tension between these two positions was acknowledged by Tawney but never resolved. Arguably, the same tension can be seen today in the contrast between those styles of socialism that focus on personal conduct and behaviour, and those that place faith and authority in the hands of the state. To understand Tawney's political development is to thus understand something of the history of socialism in Britain in the twentieth century. In many ways he has been the most representative (as well as the most admired) of British socialists.

Tawney's life also helps in understanding the peculiar identity and place of intellectuals in British history between about 1850 and 1950.[12] Tawney never described himself as an intellectual nor used the word much at all, no doubt because 'intellectual' and, even more, the word 'intelligentsia' suggest the separation of an elite from the rest of society of which he disapproved.[13] Tawney, on the other hand, spent his life creating and sustaining educational and political relationships with workers through the Workers' Educational Association and the trade union movement. Yet his family background – he was the son of a notable orientalist and Cambridge 'Apostle' – and his education made him a member of the late-Victorian 'intellectual aristocracy' and he moved easily within the overlapping worlds of the British intellectual elite.[14] Writing in 1955 the American sociologist Edward Shils emphasized the unique integration and social status of British intellectuals since the reform of Oxford and Cambridge in the mid-nineteenth century. Their union 'with the Civil Service, the Church, the Houses of Parliament, the Press, and the leadership of the political parties, through the ancient universities principally, but also through kinship and through the social and convivial life of London upper-class society, constituted a bond from which few could escape and which no other country could then or has since matched'.[15] Tawney kept his distance from the salons of the upper classes, distrusted any type of conspicuous consumption (as he distrusted any type of conspicuous or self-conscious intellectualism) and lived frugally. However, his relations with all the other institutions of English life mentioned by Shils were close and warm.

In other societies – Germany and the United States, for example – it would have been impossible for a radical of Tawney's type to have maintained his social and political credentials and enjoyed acceptance, let alone influence, among the power elites of these nations.[16] But Tawney knew prime ministers and cabinet secretaries, corresponded with archbishops and bishops, wrote memos for the Treasury and leaders for the *Manchester Guardian*, served on Royal Commissions and became a British diplomat, if only for a single year in 1941–2. During that year he found himself drawn into an alliance with the ambassador in Washington DC, the former Foreign Secretary, Lord Halifax, in a joint manoeuvre to deflect, of all people, the General Secretary of the Trades Union Congress whose grasp of international affairs was not the best. Tawney demonstrates that British intellectuals of his era could comfortably retain their place at the heart of the culture even while espousing unorthodox politics. Socialism in Britain did not involve displacement beyond polite society, and that was the case in very few other countries.[17] Yet this assured social position did not imply or lead to a diminution of radicalism, for those, like Tawney, who were already within the fold were well placed to undertake the conversion of the establishment. Tawney was a son of Oxford, for example, who spent much of his youth and early middle age signing public letters and writing critical essays calling for the university's reform. After his death he was accused by another leading British historian of the twentieth century, Geoffrey Elton, of subverting and undermining British society. It may be some measure of Tawney's fair-mindedness and balance as a reformer that, as explored in the conclusion to this book, he was also criticized by those further to the left than he, who were innately suspicious of Tawney's relations with British elites.[18]

Tawney took every opportunity to put his case whether in the press, lecture hall or public meeting but he was always more of a tutor than a self-conscious intellectual, never more comfortable than when in the informal company of his students. He taught and learnt from the workers simultaneously, respecting their experience and noting down anecdotes and details of working-class life in his journal. His familiarity with workers, whether in the classroom, the trade union headquarters or in the trenches on the Western Front, gave him authority as a public advocate for their interests and as a scholar of their history. Few figures have moved so easily between the different arenas and levels of British politics, education and scholarship in modern times, a feat that owed much to the relatively open and accommodating attitude of British elites and workers both, and something also to Tawney's personal qualities and patent integrity. Even his severest critics like Elton and another very notable historian, Hugh Trevor-Roper, sympathized with the general respect in which he was held.

In the past generation Tawney's work has been discussed and analysed in a very large number of academic books and articles from a wide range of academic disciplines, as befits a man who, as this book shows, enjoyed a healthy contempt for the strict disciplinary structures of English academic life. As the publications multiply, and as they focus more insistently on a few of Tawney's texts without reference to the details of his life and wider interests, there is a danger that he will be reified and abstracted into a set of generalized political principles, pigeon-holed as this or that type of socialist, this or that type of thinker, this or that type of historian in a manner 'that feel[s] foreign to the felt experience of reading Tawney's prose'.[19] The purpose of this book is to capture again the essence of the man and establish a workable account of his life for all to use. One of his admirers, and another economic historian, W. H. B. Court, observed in 1970 that 'we are faced with a great lack of knowledge about his thoughts and feelings in his early years, which will not be supplied until a proper life of him has been written.'[20] This book contains new information and detail on Tawney's life up to the First World War, but it must be admitted that, as is often the case when writing biography, the sources are far more plentiful when reconstructing Tawney's life in maturity, by which time he was famous, than in his youth. I have quoted liberally from Tawney's letters, lectures, pamphlets and papers in the belief that to recover his own view of his life and times in his own remarkable words is what is most required at this stage. I have tried to work from the voluminous papers Tawney left behind rather than from secondary sources about him. Establishing the details and pattern of his life has taken precedence over disputes regarding points of interpretation with other academic writers. In this I have followed Tawney's example, for he was not disputatious by nature: he spoke his mind, sometimes vehemently, but never resented or sought to silence alternative points of view. In the famous historical controversy over 'the rise of the gentry' it was other historians who picked a fight, and readers will be able to judge Tawney's response for themselves.

That said, I readily acknowledge the labours of several historians and political scientists who have done so much already to explain Tawney's work. Jay Winter provided working texts of many of Tawney's lesser known but crucial essays and journals in the 1970s and drew attention to the significance of Tawney's early political and historical thought.[21] Ross Terrill provided the first biography and interpretation at roughly the same time and thereby shaped all subsequent work on Tawney.[22] Tony Wright's elegant study brought to bear on Tawney's life and thought the insights of a practising politician, reminding us that Tawney was often very close to parliamentary politics.[23] Norman Dennis and A. H. Halsey located Tawney in a distinctive English tradition of socialism.[24] Marc Stears and Ben Jackson have applied approaches drawn from political science to Tawney, placing him in association with other thinkers in Britain and the United States.[25] More recently Gary Armstrong and Tim Gray have drawn attention to the changes and inconsistencies in Tawney ideas, though Tawney himself would have been the first to admit that he was not a systematic social thinker and that the construction of a philosophical system was never his aim.[26] Probably the best work of all, the meticulous study of Tawney's educational thought and activism by J. R. Brooks, remains unpublished.[27] I owe a debt to these authors and many others who have gone before, for establishing the major themes in Tawney's life and pointing towards the issues that require attention.

After he died, in a remarkable public debate on his legacy and his location in British politics which occurred in 1981–2 as a consequence of the secession of Labour MPs and party members to form the centrist Social Democratic Party (SDP), Tawney was claimed by many different people representing many different positions on the left of British politics, most of whom had little inkling of his original and personal views on the nature of British socialism. Tawney himself was never in any doubt that he was a Labour Party man and the attempt to capture the aegis of this lifelong socialist for the short-lived SDP was rightly bound to fail.[28] But Tawney was and remains a singular figure in British political history. The fact that he was a patriot; that he volunteered to fight for his country in 1914 in a war he always believed necessary; that he always rejected pacifism and pacifists; that he opposed communism at every stage of his career and also opposed Marxism as an ideology and philosophy of history; that he believed in the retention of nuclear weapons and an Atlantic alliance with the United States; that he supported academic selection for secondary education and the existence and retention of grammar schools; that he did not conceive of public expenditure and material fulfilment as the solution of social ills; and that he was a Christian above all things with a profound personal faith – all these aspects of his life and thought make him rather different from some of those who might invoke him today in the name of their socialism. The details of his life and thought should, in fact, be a caution against easy or comfortable assumptions that he can be assimilated or employed in any contemporary context. What may strike a reader is how different he was from today's variants of socialism.

There are too many partisan accounts of Tawney already, and it is not intended to add another to the list by approaching his biography through the ideas and issues of the present, or by giving ammunition to any cause or faction. This is, I trust, a properly historical and contextual account of Tawney's life, and that life was always beyond the reach of faction or sect. More than half a century after his death he belongs to no one: 'now he belongs to the ages'.[29]

1

Calcutta, Rugby, Oxford, Whitechapel

Richard Henry Tawney, known to the world as R. H. Tawney, to his intimates as Harry, and to some of his comrades in the First World War as Dick, was born on 30 November 1880 in Calcutta, the son of Charles Henry Tawney (1838–1922) and his wife Constance Catherine Fox (1841–1920).[1] She was the daughter of Charles J. Fox, a physician from Brislington in Somerset, and they married in India in 1867 where Charles Tawney was then teaching.

Some of Tawney's ancestors had apparently fought for Parliament and Cromwell in the English Civil War, providing a familial link with the period which, as a historian, he made his own and with a cause for which he had strong but ambivalent feelings. In the eighteenth century the various branches of the Tawney family were prosperous provincial capitalists, involved in banking, brewing and building with interests and land in Oxfordshire and Warwickshire. There is a memorial in Binsey Church to the west of Oxford to two generations of Tawneys who were buried there between 1717 and 1800. Those commemorated include Richard Tawney (1684–1756), boatmaster, brewer and mayor of Oxford in 1748–9, and his two sons, also brewers, Richard Tawney (1721–91) who was three times mayor of Oxford (1764–5, 1778–9 and 1790–1) and who was knighted in 1787, and his younger brother Edward Tawney (1735–1800), also mayor of Oxford on three occasions (1772–3, 1784 and 1797–8). These three Tawneys owned extensive property in the St Thomas's district of Oxford, and were the founders there of what is today Morrell's Brewery, one of the best-known Oxford businesses. They also owned several pubs in and around the city.[2] The brewery was purchased by the Morrell family at Edward Tawney's death. The Tawney family were among the first subscribers to the Oxford Canal Company in the 1770s and another Richard Tawney was its agent (general manager) from 1795. He, in turn, purchased the Banbury New Bank in 1819.[3] Two of R. H. Tawney's later ancestors followed in the family tradition and were also mayors of Oxford. Charles Tawney held the office in 1837–8 and 1840–1, and Lily Sophia

Tawney (1867–1947) was the first woman mayor of the city, though much later in 1933–4. She was R. H. Tawney's cousin, the daughter of a brother of Tawney's grandfather called Archer Robert Tawney who had been a banker and legal scholar.[4]

R. H. Tawney's great-great grandfather, Henry Tawney, was born in Oxford in 1746 and was a successful builder and timber merchant there. One of Henry Tawney's sons, Richard, was Tawney's great-grandfather. He was born in 1774, owned land in Warwickshire and died and was buried in Dunchurch in that county in 1832. He fathered 11 children, including 5 sons. The eldest of the five, Tawney's grandfather, also Richard, who was born in 1801, was educated at Rugby School and then at Trinity College, Oxford. At least two of Richard's brothers were undergraduates at Oxford as well. Richard became a fellow of Magdalen College there in 1824, and was successively dean of arts and bursar at the college. He then took a parish and was rector of Willoughby in Warwickshire from 1835 until his death in 1848. Richard's wife, Susannah James Bernard, died young at 30 years of age in 1846, but by then the couple had five children of whom the eldest, Charles Henry Tawney, born in Clifton, outside Bristol, in 1838, was R. H. Tawney's father. If not quite 'the rise of the gentry', the title of R. H. Tawney's most famous and controversial academic article, this was a family history based on the careful accretion of wealth and local status from relatively humble origins. Like many entrepreneurial families who came to prominence during the Industrial Revolution, later generations purchased landed estates and were enabled by inheritance to divert from business and commerce to scholarship and the church.

R. H. Tawney's father, Charles, was educated first at a day school in Redland, Bristol known as Bishop's College. He then proceeded to Rugby School where many of the Tawney family were educated.[5] From Rugby he went to Trinity College, Cambridge, matriculating in 1856, where he won all the honours open to an undergraduate reading classics: he was Bell university scholar in 1857, and Davies university scholar and scholar of Trinity in the following year. He graduated Senior Classic in 1860. He was then elected to a prize fellowship of his college – an academic honour granted to the cleverest young scholars – in that year. Throughout his childhood, early manhood and beyond as well, Charles was a close friend of the great Victorian moral philosopher, Henry Sidgwick, who overlapped with him at Bishop's College, Rugby and Trinity as well, arriving in Cambridge a year ahead of C. H. Tawney.[6] Henry secured Charles's membership of the elite academic society in Cambridge, the Apostles, which also included in this period the physicist James Clerk Maxwell, the historian Oscar Browning and a future Master of Trinity, Henry Montagu Butler.[7] Sidgwick, whom C. H. Tawney described as 'such a cordial and sincere friend', continued to correspond with him during his long sojourn in India and they would meet on Charles's occasional returns to Britain.[8] To the line of brewers, bankers and gentlemen in R. H. Tawney's past was thus added a connection to the highest intellectual achievements of the Victorian era. Though he saw his father only intermittently, he would have been aware through him of some of the finest minds of the mid-Victorian generation, and familiar also with the academic culture from which they came and for which R. H. Tawney was himself destined.

While Sidgwick remained at Trinity for the rest of his life, dying in 1900, Charles joined the Bengal Education Department and went to India in 1864, largely, it is believed, out of a sense of educational mission and purpose and from an interest in oriental languages, though also on grounds of health, for he had suffered from tuberculosis and required a warm climate.[9] India apparently also agreed with Constance Tawney's constitution and at first, before her family grew in number, she spent long periods in India with her husband, enjoying the summers in Simla and Darjeeling in the traditional manner. Charles was an assistant professor and then professor of History in the University of Calcutta from 1866 to 1872. In his first years the vice chancellor of the university was Henry Maine, the jurist and author of the famous comparative and historical study, *Ancient Law*, published in 1862.[10] From 1872 Charles held a chair of English. Four years later he became Principal of Presidency College in the university. He combined his teaching and research with three periods as Registrar of Calcutta University and also intermittent spells as Director of Public Instruction in Bengal.[11] The suggestion made by at least one biographer that R. H. Tawney's socialism was a reaction to his father's imperialism was contested by Tawney's nephew, literary executor, and another fellow of Trinity College, Michal Vyvyan.[12] Charles was never a member of the Indian Civil Service and no imperialist by nature, becoming, in fact, a very notable scholar and translator of monumental Hindu epics.[13] As for his son, though Tawney occasionally expressed the conventional anti-imperialism of progressive opinion in the early twentieth century, notably when addressing audiences outside Britain, he was always much more focused on domestic politics and society. Tawney's socialism did lead to disagreement with his father, but its roots were in England rather than in reaction to British India.

Charles Tawney's life in India can be traced through correspondence with one of his undergraduate friends from Cambridge, Cecil James Munro (1833–82), whose family owned estates at Hadley Wood to the north of London. Munro was educated at Harrow and read classics and mathematics at Cambridge but, like Charles Tawney, was consumptive and spent long periods in hot climates, corresponding from there with his contemporaries on issues of history, theology and philology. To Charles he wrote about classical texts, the Aristotelian origins of the first lines of John's gospel, and the philosophy of the nineteenth-century French sociologist, Auguste Comte, known as positivism.[14] Both men were interested in the 'comparative method' as it was known, of which Comte was the prime exponent and prophet. This was the cutting-edge idea of mid-Victorian scholarship which was applied equally, though with different outcomes, to the study of social structures, national histories, cultures, mythologies and languages. Charles's interests in Sanskrit emanated from an interest in the linkages between classical and oriental languages and the comparisons that might be made between them.

Charles taught English language, literature and history to Indian students, among whom he was deservedly popular. He was a notable scholar of Shakespeare, though he published little on him. In his spare time he 'threw himself' into learning the local languages and translating from Sanskrit. In addition to this language and several European classical and modern languages, he knew Hindi, Urdu and Persian. His teaching duties could be taxing and unremitting: he complained of 'sitting in a chair for 3 weeks and looking over 500 papers on Shakespeare' when he wanted to be travelling, researching and translating: 'I have been thinking of going up country. I want if I can get an appointment to tackle the real Hindi in Hindustan speaking natives.'[15] He admired the local cultures and, if he grew slightly cynical about native behaviour, stoutly defended the Bengalis on occasion. When, against the wishes of the inhabitants, it was proposed to replace an English education with a 'vernacular education in the three Rs', Tawney led a successful public campaign to oppose the change.[16] Later he complained about the treatment of Afghans who thought the British had taken their Amir and came to rescue him. General Roberts had them hanged, much to Charles Tawney's disgust and that of other British liberals and humanitarians as well.[17] He remarked that 'the empire is too big already in my opinion – But I believe I am "intemperate and disloyal"', to which Munro replied that he was 'glad you are so unpatriotic and disloyal: but I expected you would be, so I am delighted that, even at the front, some carry their vices to the degree of not approving the sight of a gibbet with prisoners of war on it'.[18]

Far from looking down on his students and charges in some figuration of Victorian cultural superiority, Charles Tawney devoted his life to making their cultures accessible in the west. 'He genuinely loved India through its learning and literature' and at the unveiling of his portrait in the University of Calcutta, another professor there described him as 'an ideal teacher who combined in himself the best of the East and the best of the West'.[19] His greatest achievement was his translation of Sanskrit classics into English, including plays, stories, philosophy, works of religion and ethics. His initial publications, in 1874 and 1875 respectively, were prose translations of two plays: *Uttara-rāma-carita*, concerning the later life of Rama, avatar to the Hindu god Vishnu, by the eighth-century Sanskrit playwright Bhavabhūti, and the *Mālavikāgnimitra* of Kālidāsa, the greatest of Sanskrit writers, who probably lived in the fifth-century AD. The latter work concerned the affairs of King Agnimitra who reigned in northern India in the second-century BC. Charles Tawney is most famous for his translation of the extensive compilation of wondrous fables and legends, 'the mirror of the Indian imagination', *Kathā-sarit-sāgara*, or the *Ocean of the Streams of Story*, compiled in the eleventh century by Somadeva Bhatta, the poet (about whom little is known) at the court of King Anantar in Kashmir. Tawney's English edition in two volumes appeared in the early 1880s, published by the Asiatic Society of Bengal and annotated by him with parallels drawn from folklore in a wide range of cultures. It was subsequently republished in a limited and private edition of 10 volumes in 1924, 2 years after his death. He was also an acknowledged expert on Jainism and the translator of several works in this tradition, notably the *Kathākośa*, an anthology of religious stories, in 1895[20] and Merutunga Suri's narrative poem from the fourteenth century, *Prabandha-cintāmani* (1899–1901), a classic of Gujarati literature.

R. H. Tawney was one of three sons and five daughters in the family. His elder brother Charles (b. 1870) died in 1925 in Canada. His younger brother Stephen Edward (1882–1965?) followed R. H. Tawney to Rugby but was later institutionalized: Tawney visited him regularly until an old man himself.[21] Of his five sisters, one became a nurse and another was working for the Chelsea Furnishing Company in Sloane Square around 1906.[22] Only two of them married: Constance (1868–1938) and Mildred (1878–1947). Agnes (1869–1959), Margaret (1873–1948) and Mary (1875–1957) lived beyond the Second World War by which time their aged brother had become responsible for their welfare. With the exception of Mildred, mother of Michal Vyvyan, whom he saw regularly and with whom he corresponded through his life, Tawney was not especially close to his family. As a young man he visited them dutifully but their impact on him seems to have been slight.

Charles Tawney certainly disapproved of his son's growing commitment to socialism; meanwhile it has been suggested that his son had no sympathy for his father's high and pure academic scholarship, lacking in social purpose and relevance.[23] Yet Tawney was clearly the product of an upper middle class and academic background on both sides of his family that he never rejected and from which he derived an inner confidence that was noted by all who knew him well. According to his pupil, colleague and friend, the economic historian M. M. ('Munia') Postan, 'For all his socialist views and humble personal tastes Tawney preserved throughout his life the outward manners – not only the tone of voice, but also the *façon d'agir* – of an Edwardian and even Victorian gentleman with family roots in the English countryside, the Church, and the Indian Civil Service (*sic*).'[24] There was indeed a solidity, rootedness and Englishness in Tawney's family background; previous generations were the epitome of the lesser English gentry and the professional middle classes.

When Tawney was 5 years old Constance brought her children back to England leaving Tawney's father in India. At the end of 1892 Charles retired from the Education Service and took a job for which he was eminently fitted as the librarian of the India Office in London. He retired from it in 1903. The young R. H. Tawney moved with his family to several places in southern England, including Clifton, Tonbridge, Godalming and Weybridge in Surrey, before being sent to Rugby School in September 1894 where he was in Whitelaw's House. Though he became a noted critic of private, fee-paying education later in life and referred very rarely to his formal schooling, there can be little doubt that Rugby left its mark on him. His mature philosophy and commitment to social service owed much to Rugby's distinctive traditions of broad-church Anglicanism, altruism, social activism and cultural high-mindedness.

Tawney's headmaster was the stern and moralistic John Percival, until a few years before the President of Trinity College, Oxford. Tawney remembered him as 'a very impressive figure, the sight of whom when I was a little boy always frightened me to death. I think as headmasters go, he was probably rather better than most'.[25] In Oxford, Percival had played an important role in the encouragement of women's higher education, serving as chairman of the committee which founded Somerville College. He was also a supporter of the educationist Michael Sadler, another slightly earlier product of Rugby, in the development of Oxford's first courses in adult education.[26] Later, as Bishop of Hereford in the Edwardian period, Percival was a keen early patron of the Workers' Educational Association (WEA) and a supporter, with Tawney, of a campaign begun in 1907 to reform Oxford and Cambridge.[27] Robert Whitelaw,

Tawney's housemaster, 'belonged to the old type of scholar . . . to whom scholarship was a religion' and his teaching 'inspired so many generations'. He was also a fine English stylist.[28] Tawney was taught classics in the sixth-form at Rugby by Frank Fletcher who had been educated at Balliol College, Oxford and who was later headmaster of Marlborough and Charterhouse. Fletcher thought that Tawney was one of 'the two finest minds' that he had ever encountered, the other being the Balliol tutor, R. L. Nettleship.[29] Another classics master at Rugby, J. L. Paton, who taught the Sixth Form lower bench at Rugby, was noted for his puritanical habits, informal dress and manners, and for his democratic sympathies, organizing classes locally for working men. Just such habits and predilections were characteristic of the later Tawney.[30] Paton was successively headmaster of University College School, London and High Master of Manchester Grammar School. He remained in contact with Tawney and helped secure him an appointment as a leader-writer on the *Manchester Guardian* in 1908.[31]

At Rugby, Tawney won a hatful of prizes for classics: Latin verse in 1896 and 1898, Latin prose in 1897 and 1898, Latin hexameters in 1899 and Greek iambics in the same year. In 1897–8 he was head boy of his house probably on the strength of his intellect alone. His obituary in the school magazine, *The Meteor*, so many years later described his career at Rugby as 'unobtrusive'.[32] Tawney took no part in the school debating society, for example. In the absence of any reports of his academic progress at Rugby we depend upon accounts of his sporting prowess. He only managed to make fly-half in the House second rugby fifteen in 1898.[33] At cricket he was better. Though many of his scores for Whitelaw's were in single figures he was occasionally mentioned in reports of house matches. In a match against School House, 'Greenside was out to a very fine catch in the deep by Tawney (R. H.).'[34] His best match came at the very end of his time at Rugby in the summer of 1899 when Whitelaw's House beat Brooke's House and Tawney contrived to make 39 runs and take three wickets in his opponents' second innings.[35] More revealing than his scores are the photographs in the school archive. They show a thin and physically immature youth, much smaller than many of his contemporaries. He grew in height and girth and did not lack a physical presence in later life, but Tawney left Rugby with some growing still to do. His facial expression, however, is determination personified. Sitting next to his housemaster for the annual house photo, it is the great Mr Whitelaw who looks uncomfortable while Tawney stares resolutely into the camera.

There is an oft-rehearsed story that Tawney met his lifelong friend and coadjutor, William Temple, later Archbishop of Canterbury, on the platform of Rugby station on their first day at the school. But Tawney came to Rugby a year ahead of Temple, the boys were in different houses – Tawney in Whitelaw's House and Temple in School House – and Tawney recollected that they became friends outside school during the summer holidays of 1896 when they were aged 15 and 16, respectively. 'I happened to be spending several weeks at Ambleside, where his parents had taken a house for the summer. I took some long walks with him and his brother, and spent afternoons with him on a boat on Windermere, he reading Kant's *Critique of Pure Reason*, while I dabbled in the water or fished.'[36] This description may not simply reflect Tawney's later modesty; by all accounts he enjoyed typical boys' pursuits, recalling much later that 'I made quite a good collection of [butterflies] when I was young.'[37] Tawney was at Rugby with Ted Scott, the son of the great editor of the *Manchester Guardian*, C. P. Scott, who later gave him a job and began Tawney's lifelong association with that newspaper.[38] He was also at Rugby with the uncles of R. A. Butler, the Conservative politician with whom Tawney collaborated over the 1944 Education Act. Decades later 'RAB' remembered that fact, though it would have been ironic indeed if the 'old boys network' had played a part in the reform and extension of state education for which Tawney worked all his adult life.[39] Arthur Ransome, sometime spy and author of *Swallows and Amazons*, transferred to Whitelaw's House in the summer term of 1899 and was Tawney's 'fag' (servant) at Rugby for a matter of months. On writing to congratulate Tawney on his 80th birthday, Ransome described Tawney as 'a very good employer of labour'. Tawney replied that 'it was not due so much to innate virtue as to the fact that I was much more afraid of [fags], including yourself, than they could possibly have been of me.'[40] In another letter written at this time Tawney recollected 'that I hated my first term and most subsequent terms, but I ultimately became more reconciled to it.'[41] He seems to have had almost no contact with Rugby after leaving in 1899, but in old age, when he could ill-afford it, he was a subscriber to the school appeal and even allowed his name to be publicized as such *pour encourager les autres*.[42]

Tawney followed his teacher, Frank Fletcher, to Balliol in 1899 to read classics – Classical Moderations followed by Literae Humaniores, known as 'Greats' – apparently winning the top classical entrance scholarship to Balliol of the year. To mark the transition from boyhood, on arrival in Oxford he grew a beard, much to his family's amusement and derision. In due course the beard went but the moustache stayed for the rest of his life.[43] It was a mark of his standing and potential that he should have gone to Balliol, then in its heyday as the most influential of Oxford's colleges, famed not only for its scholarship, but also for its ethic of public service and collective social conscience. His tutors there were the philosopher John Alexander Smith, notable for his expertise in Aristotle; H. W. C. Davis, historian and later Regius Professor of Modern History in Oxford; and the Latinist F. de Paravicini.[44] Arguably of greater influence on him in view of his later career was the then Master, Edward Caird, and the History tutor with whom he would collaborate in many different projects in adult education, A. L. Smith, later another Master of Balliol.

Tawney fitted in very well. He seems to have moved easily between different undergraduate circles and was something of a social lion in Oxford, at least at first. Though not suited to the sporting ethos of his school, he contrived to be secretary to both the hockey XI and tennis VI, and even played rugby for the college; no doubt standards were not so exacting at Balliol.[45] In his first weeks in college Tawney befriended another Balliol fresher who had come up from Charterhouse, William Beveridge, and the two were much in each other's company for the next four years at Oxford.[46] This was to be another of Tawney's lifelong relationships. Both men were members of a group that revolved around a young aesthete, Arthur Collings Carré, also at Balliol, who was the acknowledged leader of the college's intellectuals, but whose life ended in obscurity and suicide some years after they all left the university. The group included R. C. K. Ensor, the historian; Alfred Zimmern, a pioneer in the study of international relations; Richard Denman, later a Labour MP; Arthur Pickard-Cambridge, Oswald Falk and William Temple.[47]

Relations within the group were intense, precious, probably flirtatious. After Tawney had gone down Temple wrote to him in this style: 'I wish you would come back; when you are here your cynicism repels me & keeps me optimistic: when that constraining force is withdrawn, you see what happens!' and 'I wish you were here to argue & discuss & make fun of all things sacred & were vehement over all things trivial! & lie in bed past breakfast time till I come to smack you!'[48] But any hints of homo-eroticism did not lead to active homosexuality. The sheer proximity of these young men within closed male institutions encouraged such associations and this kind of banter.[49] As Tawney wrote of Temple after the latter's death, 'Like all wise men, he recognised that – fortunately for mankind – nonsense forms a large part of life, and welcomed it when it came his way.'[50] A year or two later and Temple was writing a quite different sort of letter to his friend – eight pages of philosophy and theology on 'the good of the universe' in which Temple discussed some of the central doctrines of Christianity, including the virgin birth, which, he said, he did believe in, just about.[51] That it was essentially horseplay, however, is not the same as saying that it was uninfluential. Tawney, like so many men of his era and education, was more comfortable with men than with women, and had male friends almost exclusively. When he wrote, the subjects on whom his political ideas were premised were working-class men almost without exception. Tawney had little experience and understanding of women and this may explain some of the difficulties he encountered in his marriage. Indeed while they were courting, his fiancée wrote to him to berate his circle of Balliol friends for being so supercilious and superior in their manner.[52] Perhaps because of Jeanette's criticisms, a year later Tawney was very keen that she meet a very different kind of man, Albert Mansbridge, a clerk from Ilford and the founder of the WEA: Mansbridge along 'with Will [Beveridge] and William Temple is the man who has been most to me'.[53]

Tawney befriended Jimmy Palmer, a tutorial fellow of Balliol, the college chaplain and later a bishop. He also approved of a notorious Balliol character of this era, Francis or 'Sligger' (as from 'sleek one' through 'slicker') Urquhart, the first Roman Catholic tutor in Oxford since the Reformation, a sociable and snobbish rather than a scholarly don, who lived in the college for 40 years and who Tawney recollected 'as a civilising influence'.[54] Among students from other colleges, Tawney was close to two in particular with whom he would later collaborate in the WEA and the general cause of educational reform: J. L. Stocks, who had also been at Rugby, went up to Corpus Christi College, and who became an Oxford philosopher, and A. D. (Sandy) Lindsay, who studied at University College after his education in his native Scotland and who became Master of Balliol in the 1920s.[55] Tawney and Lindsay would share a passion for workers' education in North Staffordshire, where Lindsay much later became the founding vice-chancellor of the University College of North Staffordshire, later Keele University. Tawney also came into contact with students influenced by the social teaching of the Anglo-Catholic theologian, Charles Gore, later Bishop of Oxford and a mentor to Tawney.[56]

Tawney was not a member of Balliol's Arnold Society and rarely attended meetings of the college's Brackenbury Society. With Beveridge, whom Tawney and his friends referred to as 'Drink' (probably because he didn't), he shared a growing interest in social and economic issues, and together, early in 1902, they founded their own society. As Beveridge explained to his mother,

> Tawney and I are going (if we can) to add one to the unnumbered crowd of societies at Oxford; I don't think it has a name but its object is to be the writing of papers on social questions from a matter of fact and as far as possible practical point of view. Theories are in fact to be eschewed while facts (in theory at least) are to abound in the society. It has only two members at present but hopes to expand; the only way to turn about things is to write about them so we shall try.[57]

Tawney read a paper on the 'Taxation of Site Values' at its only recorded meeting in June 1902, no doubt killing-off the group as soon as it was founded by the sheer tedium of the subject.[58] But Tawney was by now in earnest on social questions and it was while he was at Oxford that he joined the Independent Labour Party, which had been founded by industrial workers in the North of England in 1893 and was a forerunner to the Labour Party, created from a different set of constituents in the following decade.[59] He was also a member in Oxford of the Christian Social Union, founded in 1889: its basic principle that economic and social life must be organized and conducted in accordance with Christian principles was to be fundamental in everything Tawney said and did for the rest of his life.[60]

Tawney undoubtedly enjoyed Oxford and was never at rest with socializing, sport, long walks and also long talks into the night. His letters are full of the latest college news and gossip. But there was a shadow over his time there in the form of his younger brother Stephen who had followed him to Rugby. As Tawney explained to Dick Denman, 'He is 19, and was low down in the school when he left'. Their parents thought Stephen should take a junior administrative position in Africa. Tawney thought this entirely unsuitable and asked Denman if he could help find Stephen, whose interests were literary if anything at all, a position on a newspaper.[61] Tawney also encouraged Denman to befriend the lost soul, which he did for his friend, inviting Stephen to stay with him and join him in London.[62] Stephen's letters in reply to Denman's betray an entire absence of self-confidence, much self-recrimination and excruciating immaturity: 'I gabbled an immense amount of drivel . . . I made myself a pretty ass . . . Do not tell Harry that I have been talking rot. I fear his wrath'.[63] The doctor decreed that Stephen was not strong enough for university.[64] In July 1902 Tawney was unable to join his friends in Switzerland because he had to look after his brother who had had some sort of unspecified breakdown. At some stage in 1905 or

1906 he reported to Denman that 'my brother has got to go to a nursing home'.[65] Stephen's psychological problems would later, and at a singular moment, affect Tawney's prospects.

Oxford ended unhappily for Tawney. Regarded as of surpassing brilliance, he took a first class in Classical Moderations after 2 years and was *proxime accessit* (runner-up) for the university's Craven Scholarship. At one point he had declared that he 'hate[d] the sight of Greek and Latin . . . but I don't want to get a 2nd. I don't think I shall', and he was right.[66] Expected to graduate with a first-class degree in Literae Humaniores ('Greats') as well, which included courses in Greek philosophy, ancient history, logic and moral and political philosophy, he took a second in the summer of 1903. His father was dismayed and apparently wrote 'How do you propose to wipe out this disgrace?' Edward Caird, the then Master of Balliol, suggested more charitably to Fletcher that, though Tawney's 'mind was chaotic . . . the examiners ought to have seen that it was the chaos of a great mind'.[67] But an entry in the journal of Clement Webb, philosophy tutor at Magdalen College,[68] suggests that the examiners had reached a firm and clear view of Tawney's merits on this occasion:

> Walker of Queen's[69] dined with Cowley[70]. Benecke[71] interviewed him as to our fellowship candidates he [Walker] having examined in Lit Hum this year. They [the examiners] considered Tawney a "fraud": who wrote long essays on what in *viva* he was proved not to have read at all. This getting up of a common notebook the vice of Balliol men this year.[72]

If this was correct, and as senior common room gossip it may not have been, it would seem that Tawney had not worked hard enough and had cut some academic corners.

Tawney was in Broadstairs on the Kent coast, tutoring a likely applicant for Balliol, when he received the news of his degree. He tried to shrug it off, claiming 'to feel a kind of sympathy for examiners': the feeling was not mutual, it would appear.[73] Replying to a letter from Will Beveridge, who *had* been awarded a first, he feigned some of that 'effortless superiority' for which Balliol men of this generation were famed:

> Thank you for your letter. It was a pleasant relief from the effusions which have been addressed to me as one on whose corpse they are depositing a wreath & a mourning card. My only grief at present is that I am not more distressed: my conscience is seared, or something unpleasant and unchristian has happened to me, for I assure you that after a single explosion against the *perfidium genus*

examinatorum I relapsed in to the perfect self-satisfaction of him who neither runs nor swings his arms but does all things as, when & where they should be done.[74]

Tawney had hoped that with a first-class degree he would find his way rapidly to a college fellowship in Oxford. This was now impossible and in the weeks following the publication of the results he cast around for things he might do in the time-honoured fashion of new graduates. He rejected 'the English Civil' – the home civil service. He went up to Liverpool in September 'to see a man about an educational post' but nothing came of it.[75] He thought he might join the Charity Organisation Society (COS), a voluntary organization that, since the late 1860s, had pioneered new forms of social work in London and other cities, but admitted 'that money is rather a difficulty'.[76] Then, through Beveridge, came the suggestion from Canon Samuel Barnett, the Warden of Toynbee Hall, the university settlement in Whitechapel in the East End of London, that he take on the role of secretary of the Children's Country Holiday Fund (CCHF) based at Toynbee. He 'jump[ed] at it'. The CCHF organized holidays in private homes for children from the inner parts of London. Tawney preferred this to joining the COS, 'firstly because the pay is double & secondly because I think to get anything worth learning out of the COS I should have to stick it longer than I am prepared to do'.[77] In fact, Tawney had thought of going on to Toynbee while still an undergraduate and in the summer of 1902 had visited the settlement 'as the Toynbee people think it advisable that I should see how the jobs run before embarking on it'.[78]

A week later, at the end of October, he went travelling on the first of several trips to Germany to improve his German. It was an obvious thing to do on the part of a young man without a clear sense of his future: for educated and progressive young Britons in the Edwardian age, German culture and German social innovations at municipal and national level were magnets that drew them to learn from what seemed to be a higher and better-ordered society. Tawney also admired the scenic countryside.[79] He took German lessons, first from two elderly ladies in Freiburg and then from a man who kept interrupting his studies with 'diatribes against Chamberlain, accompanied with graphic representations of what he conceives to be the typical Englishman. I am in danger of returning home as an imperialist & protectionist'.[80]

Beveridge had taken the post of sub-warden at Toynbee Hall, combining it with an Oxford fellowship, and when Tawney returned at the end of the year he followed his friend to London's East End, joining him as a resident there, and devoting himself like the other 'settlers' to civic leadership, education and uplift in a notorious Victorian slum neighbourhood – as well as the organization of summer holidays for local children. He was elected Jenkyns Exhibitioner by Balliol for 3 years in 1904 which provided him with some financial support while in London, but an exhibition – a relatively small grant of funds – was not a college fellowship.

Tawney may have tried to feign insouciance but his failure to get a first and begin an academic career in Oxford hurt him profoundly. His closest friends, Beveridge and Temple, achieved what eluded him and both went on to Oxford fellowships, Beveridge at University College, and Temple at Queen's College.[81] Some sense of Tawney's mood can be gathered from an undated letter sent to him by Temple, evidently written to encourage him after he had given up some unspecified opportunity for a university award or position. Temple wanted Tawney to stay in the academic hunt and also to rebuild his confidence:

> I want to talk to you: because you are sometimes foolish!! Though you may just now be sensible. Do you intend to give up – if you ever had – any idea of going in for a fellowship? The point is that if you refuse offers now, they won't go on. Very likely you are quite clear on the subject; but our dons are still wearying their friends with your praises, & some of them want to know whether you have really made up your mind or not. You see the thing will settle itself if you leave it alone; so if you ever want or are going to want to be a don, you must not throw away chances now ... Keep your body well – it looked rather run down at Oxford – and I will see to your soul![82]

Had he been successful like his friends and become a don, Tawney might have taught classics for the rest of his life and enjoyed a comfortable existence in a North Oxford villa. Instead, in behaviour that suggests the depth of his disappointment, thereafter he studiously refrained from using or even signalling his classical education: 'He came to think that scholarship was a vanity; I do not remember him ever using a Greek quotation and rarely a Latin one. If I used one he looked at me quizzically.'[83] Perhaps it was his failure at this stage that also explains his reputation as a very generous examiner: much later he was to tell his former pupil and colleague at the London School of Economics, Sir Arnold Plant, that 'one ought to take a chance on giving lots of firsts. They might give a good chap a running start and if one made mistakes they would soon show up and little harm would be done in the long run.'[84] But by closing off one very obvious route, and pitching Tawney first into the life of the urban poor, and then into contact with the respectable working class, this failure was the making of him: it not only brought him experience but it turned an immature man with a social conscience into a social activist with personal experience of urban poverty and the labour movement, and it turned a classicist into an economic historian. On this occasion, as on others, the assessment of Oxford examiners was for the best. Some years later he received a letter from the economist E. J. Urwick begging forgiveness 'for a certain sensation of relief at the news that you also secured a second in Schools. At all events it proves that such a failure is not incompatible with good work in the world of economics.'[85]

The post of Secretary of The Children's Country Holiday Fund was no sinecure. The CCHF had been founded in 1884 'to provide fresh air for ailing London children'.[86] In the early twentieth century it sent approximately 40,000 needy children aged between 5 and 14 from London for holidays in the country every summer, and if the focus of activity was just a few weeks in July and August there was year-round organization and preparation to attend to. The CCHF was chaired by Samuel Barnett, patronized by the aristocracy and bishops, and its council included many well-to-do citizens. Funds were raised by local voluntary committees in the London boroughs. Workers in London visited families, ensured that the children came from clean and respectable homes, selected the children on grounds of their needs and health, and calculated the amounts that each family should contribute towards the cost 'in proportion to the family's circumstances'.[87] Meanwhile agents in the field, 'local visitors' as they were called, had to sign up potential host families for the children and inspect their homes, transmitting the details to Tawney in the London office, which was located in Buckingham Street, off the Strand. The children were sent to more than a thousand villages where it was hoped they would benefit from fresh air and 'country objects and pursuits' – 'the full pleasures of field and hedgerow and country walks'.[88] There were rules for hosts – 'no more than two a bed; no mixing of the sexes in the same bedroom' – and for the children as well: if found to be dirty or guilty of serious misconduct they could be sent back to London.[89] The cost of a child's holiday was estimated to be 14 shillings; the Fund paid 'cottagers' as they were called five shillings per week for taking a child. Parents were asked to make a contribution if they could, but two-thirds of the funds were raised by the committees or were donated by well-wishers.[90]

The work was not without its problems and controversies. In 1904 there was a smallpox scare in London and the CCHF had to allay fears that infected children might be sent out from the capital by promising to ensure that only healthy children would be chosen, and all the children would be vaccinated, or, if over the age of 10, re-vaccinated.[91] In the following year there was correspondence in

The Times concerning the activities provided for the children and the educative value of their experience. The Rev Lucius Fry of the rectory in Upper Edmonton on the fringes of London wrote to bemoan the absence of planned activities for the children and the consequent nuisance they could make of themselves and to insist on their being accompanied to the country by a tutor or responsible adult. Other correspondents drew attention to successful schemes of this sort which might be emulated. Tawney replied by defending the children and their country hosts, and provided details of the things they did, including writing 'brief accounts of the animals and plants which they see'.[92] But the CCHF took the point and promised more structured activities in the future.[93] A charming vignette describing those days when the children were sent out to the countryside from London was contributed to the *Toynbee Record* in the summer of 1906. Almost certainly by Tawney – the style gives it away – it presents the scene at Toynbee Hall which was used as the assembly point for many thousands of the holidaymakers.

> The Quadrangle is filled from eight in the morning with bundles and children and parents, upon a small group of whom, from time to time, a visitor comes down, attaches labels (to the children) and marches off with them, if possible minus the parents and not without the bundles, to the railway station.[94]

Tawney remained at Toynbee Hall for the best part of 3 years and during this time he grew very close to Samuel Barnett who became a genuine mentor to him. He returned as a resident for periods in the latter half of 1908 and in the spring of 1913 when he was between different employments. His work for the CCHF, however, took him away from Whitechapel on a daily basis, and was exacting at times, requiring extensive correspondence. Whether for this reason or for another, he seems to have become detached from the daily life in Toynbee Hall and does not feature as one of the key figures there in this period. He wrote only a single signed article for the monthly *Toynbee Record*, for example, and his name occurs only rarely in its pages. How great an impact the CCHF had on him is difficult to assess: like many young graduates he needed a period in which to determine his life's direction and the CCHF provided an interlude in which to take stock and reflect. Having no children of his own, it was also the only period when he was directly associated with them and their welfare, and it may have concentrated his mind on the educational needs of the young, which became the dominant campaign among the many that he took up in later life.

Arguably of greater significance than his formal employment at Toynbee Hall were the lectures Tawney gave there in the evenings. In October 1904 a Toynbee

Hall Enquirers' Club was started that was focused on social institutions and their reform.[95] Tawney began lecturing with Beveridge on 'Social and Industrial Questions', followed by a course in early 1905 on 'British Political Institutions'. Later in 1905 he lectured on his own on the subject of 'Social Aspects of Industry'. The report on the first set of lectures in 1904 described 'animated' discussions in which most of the speakers from the floor 'started with a strong bias towards some kind of socialism'. Nevertheless, the men – and it was overwhelmingly a male audience – 'wanted to discuss matters upon their minds' and there was a 'diversity of opinion' when it came to assessing the value of different methods and social institutions. 'Many of the facts mentioned had come within the experience of some member of the audience, and a good deal of really suggestive information was forthcoming.'[96] This was Tawney's first experience of lecturing to an adult audience and what he described – for this brief report was almost certainly written by him – is a model of the type of adult tutorial class that he was to make into such a potent educational and social force in the coming years.

Tawney would have been conscious that he was himself following the example of Arnold Toynbee after whom the Hall was named. Toynbee had been a young Oxford don, not unlike Tawney in type, who combined lecturing to working-class groups in the late 1870s and early 1880s with the writing of an original and influential book on economic history, *Lectures on the Industrial Revolution in England* (1884), published in the year after his early death.[97] All Tawney's life he pursued historical scholarship alongside social and political advocacy in a similar pattern, the two reinforcing each other. His historical interests may also have been encouraged by making contact with the most notable social reformers of the era, Sidney and Beatrice Webb, in 1905 or 1906, around the time of the Liberal election victory of that era. Much later Tawney recalled his first visit to their home at 41 Grosvenor Road. He walked off with the hat of John Burns, a Liberal minister, and was seriously admonished by Beatrice on the following day: 'The episode confirmed her conviction of incorrigible incompetence, unreliability, moral laxity and mental imbecility of most products, however insignificant, of the older universities, and took some time to live down.'[98]

Yet for all their efforts, both Beveridge and Tawney could see that the educational and social impact of Toynbee Hall was very limited. It was excellent at introducing clever Oxford men to the realities of poverty and squalor, but nothing like as good at relieving these features of urban life. Tawney reflected on his lectures that 'the direct educational value of such a series is, no doubt, not very great'.[99] Both young men studied social problems while living in the East End, and Beveridge wrote on this basis his famous study of *Unemployment:*

A Problem of Industry (1909) and developed his idea of labour exchanges, both of which were remarkable intellectual and practical achievements. If Toynbee Hall could do little good as a civic centre in the slums, it did at least facilitate serious engagement with urban problems among some of its residents. Thus Tawney was one of the earliest members of the National Anti-Sweating League, formed in 1906 and drawing together people from diverse political and religious backgrounds to combat low wages, long hours and unsafe and insanitary working conditions, the basic features of what was known colloquially as 'sweating'. Its headquarters were soon located in Mecklenburgh Square, Bloomsbury, where Tawney would later live. Its campaigns led to the establishment of Trade Boards under the 1909 Trade Boards Act to regulate remuneration and conditions in so-called 'sweated trades', many of them exploiting child and female workers as well as male employees, like tailoring, box-making and chain-making.[100] The anti-sweating campaigns also introduced Tawney to another of his lifelong friends, James Joseph ('Jimmy') Mallon, from 1906 a resident at Toynbee Hall and later its Warden, with whom he would continue to collaborate in educational and social causes for the rest of his life.[101]

Tawney was a confirmed and sincere advocate of Trade Boards, which comprised representatives of workers, owners and managers, and also independent members who together negotiated standards for each sweated industry. They had been introduced into selected trades under the terms of the 1909 Trade Boards Act. He opposed the imposition of a national minimum wage as advocated since the 1890s by Sidney and Beatrice Webb as an alternative solution to the problem of low wages. He was especially opposed to any national minimum calculated on the basis of a subsistence level due to all: 'It means that people are not paid what they are worth, but what is necessary to keep them working. That is how a horse or slave is paid.'[102] He feared that a minimum wage would become a ceiling above which remuneration could not rise; that it would encourage skilled workers to restore their differentials and hence stoke wage inflation; and that some industries might not be able to afford the minimum and be rendered uncompetitive.[103] Conversely, he was attracted to the idea of trade boards because workers would be actively involved in bargaining for their income. From this early stage in his career as a social reformer it is evident that he preferred social institutions in which workers were engaged on their own account and placed in control of their own destinies, rather than having solutions imposed on them by their employers or by the state. In any case, trade boards were in the tradition of free collective bargaining prized by the British trade union movement since the mid-nineteenth century. Though Tawney has been criticized recently for taking these positions, especially for his distrust of the minimum wage, and described as 'disappointingly circumspect and conventional' and 'a very moderate socialist indeed', it is not self-evident that a model of collective self-regulation in which workers bargain for themselves is any the less radical than having a level of remuneration imposed on them by government, the character and policy of which could easily change at the next election or over time.[104] Tawney favoured a functioning example of industrial democracy in which workers were to be party to crucial decisions affecting them, and which would have an educative function for them, teaching them the details of their industry and techniques of bargaining within it. It was an early example of a style of independent and voluntary social action to which Tawney was always attracted.

Tawney wrote about problems of poverty, presenting a paper, for example, to the Sociological Society in 1909 on pauperism which, like the contemporaneous minority report of the Royal Commission on the Poor Laws, rejected the assumptions about poverty as a problem of character which had underpinned the treatment of pauperism since the New Poor Law of 1834.[105] He was genuinely interested in all the issues of the East End, including unemployment, casual labour, homelessness and overcrowding. But he could intuit that 'the social question' in Britain was changing from a concern for the unskilled and *lumpen*, which had dominated social discussion since the 1880s and which had been focused on the problems of 'Outcast London',[106] to an interest in the affairs of the newly powerful organized working class in the cities of the industrial north. The new Labour Party of 1906 was a creation of the mill towns of Lancashire and Yorkshire where a much more cohesive and self-conscious working class of men with craft skills was capable of asserting itself. When the young David Marquand interviewed Tawney at the time of his 80th birthday he asked him what had made him a socialist and Tawney replied 'Going out into the world and meeting working people. But not the working people in the East End: they were a subservient lot. The working people in Rochdale: they were proud and they told you what they thought.'[107] Tawney reflected deeply on these differences at this stage in his life. According to an entry he made in 1912 in his *Commonplace Book*, a journal he kept for 3 years before the First World War,

> One whole wing of social reformers has gone, it seems to me, altogether astray. They are preoccupied with relieving distress, patching up failures, reclaiming the broken down. All this is good and necessary. But it is not the social problem,

and it is not the policy which would ever commend itself to the working classes. What they want is security and opportunity, not assistance in the exceptional misfortunes of life, but a fair chance of leading an independent, fairly prosperous life . . . It is no use devising relief schemes for a community where the normal relationships are felt to be unjust.[108]

A year later in his lecture on 'Poverty as an Industrial Problem' he contrasted the two places he had come to know best: 'It is in Lancashire, where Labour is protected by factory acts and trade unions, not in East London, where it is not, that factory life, co-operation, friendly societies, education, social institutions for a hundred different purposes, find their fullest development.'[109] Tawney was describing two different groups here, one that he had met in the slums of London which required support and another group who sought not assistance but the means to help themselves by their own efforts and through their own skills. It was this latter group that interested Tawney: he could establish a relationship of equals with communities composed of respectable, independent, self-sufficient and skilled workers who wanted to study their own history as part of a process of individual and communal self-discovery and self-realization. Tawney had discovered, meanwhile, that he had no aptitude for the distribution of soup and blankets or the task of uplifting people who lacked the capacity to be uplifted. To use his intellectual resources to educate and also liberate serious-minded people on terms of social equality, however, was a very different and much more appealing concept. As another biographical appreciation of Tawney put it, he 'encountered in Lancashire, with its Nonconformist chapels and strong trade unionism, the normal working class life which he had missed in London, and which few other historians have ever sought. This was the cast in which his mind took shape; since then his beliefs have changed little.'[110]

Spending time at Toynbee Hall helped Tawney find his vocation elsewhere. As he wrote to Beveridge in September 1905 while on holiday in the Lake District, 'teaching economics in an industrial town is just what I want ultimately to do.'[111] The reply he received, while characteristically big-headed, was another challenge from a friend to stop drifting and set a course: 'The CCHF doesn't lead naturally to positions of lecturing on economics in a University town. You haven't specialised as I have; you are not in a position to write an original book, as I am. You are not even advertising yourself by Oxford lecturing, as I am.'[112] Tawney was offered a lowly position at the University College of South Wales and Monmouthshire in Cardiff in the autumn of 1905 which would have involved delivering nine lectures a week on subjects he had yet to master. Beveridge could see some advantages in the position: 'It does at least have the very distinct merit of being teaching (which you must live by) in a district (unlike Oxford) where you can still learn and observe industrial conditions. Isn't that in some ways your ideal?'[113] Tawney turned it down, however. But in the following year he took another and similar position: 'I have gone . . . to Glasgow, to be extra assistant in economics, while Smart is busy with the Poor Law Commission. Time 5 months to end of March with a break at Xmas. Salary £50. There's glory for you.'[114]

William Smart, Adam Smith Professor of Political Economy at Glasgow University since 1896, was the member of the Royal Commission on the Poor Laws who drafted the majority report, in fact, and while he was doing that in London, Tawney stood in for him as best he could in Glasgow. Smart welcomed him in appealing style: 'I am delighted to hear from Mr Jones that you are coming to be one of us . . . I think you will find the Department a very good place for work, experience, and afternoon tea . . .'[115] The 'Jones' referred to was Tom Jones, later the assistant secretary to the cabinet under Lloyd George and Baldwin, who was a lecturer in Smart's department. Jones was Senior University Assistant in Political Economy and Tawney the Junior Assistant. In the event, because the poor law enquiry took so long, Tawney spent 2 years teaching in Glasgow and also assisting Smart with a massive and unfinished project that came out of his work for the Royal Commission – an economic history of the nineteenth century – leaving Glasgow in the summer of 1908.[116]

While there Tawney carried on with social investigation, especially into the education of working-class children in the city and the relationship of defective education to adolescent unemployment and casual labour. He could see that the 'social problem' had to be solved when men were young or not at all. As he wrote to Beveridge in April 1907 from Glasgow, 'Personally when I survey the class of men who applies here [for relief] I am rather hopeless about doing anything with them now that they have grown up.'[117] From this early stage he advocated raising the school-leaving age to at least 15 and ensuring 'continuation education' for those leaving school at 14, none of whom should work more than 30 hours a week while they also learnt a skilled trade.[118] He presented a distillation of this research to the Poor Law Commission himself in 1907 in two papers, one on the problem of 'boy labour' in Glasgow and the other on the method of poor relief used in Strasbourg, which Tawney had investigated in person and found to be efficient and humane, without the stigma attaching to poor relief in Britain.[119]

Tawney's work in Glasgow centred on boys who left school at 14 or less and were taken-on in unskilled occupations as 'a messenger, a milk boy, or a van boy' throughout their adolescence, only to be sacked on reaching adulthood.[120] Poorly educated and without skills, they were doomed to irregular, casual labour for the rest of their lives and were frequently pauperized. He was questioned intensively by members of the Royal Commission on both aspects of his research. Among his interlocutors was the famous mid- and late-Victorian housing reformer, Octavia Hill, who was incredulous that relief was offered in Strasbourg without reference to suitability and character. When she referred to unemployment as 'a personal thing', Tawney contradicted her: 'No, it is caused by the industrial system'. When she placed emphasis on 'the personal characteristics of the boy', Tawney blamed something much bigger: 'The general system degrades the whole class of boys, and puts an incentive in the way of all boys, good and bad, to make a mess of their lives'.[121] These brief exchanges captured the essential difference between those wedded to the Victorian poor laws who placed emphasis on individual responsibility, and those who sought their reform, if not their total abolition, on the grounds that poverty was a social rather than an individual failing.

In the summer of 1908 Tawney proposed marriage to Jeanette Beveridge, Will's sister. She at first declined him and then relented. After 3 months of intense emotional upheaval amounting to a genuine personal crisis, Tawney went on a short walking-holiday with his future brother-in-law in August 1908. From North Wales he wrote back to Jeanette to explain that

> One of the things I want to do (the world permitting) is to make myself a real master of some parts of economics and history . . . The ideal life has always seemed to me a mixture of scientific study and practical business, one helping the other; books without things make Oxford dons, and things without books make borough councillors, between whom the world goes to the devil.[122]

In a matter of weeks he would take up a new position – new in the sense that he was the first to hold such a job – which enabled him to be a scholar and activist simultaneously and to make himself a pioneer in the study of economic history in Britain. The job took him to places like Rochdale, Chesterfield, Wrexham and Longton in the Potteries of North Staffordshire, small industrial towns where he was enabled to teach workers what they wanted to learn and to establish himself as an educationist, historian and reformer.

Tawney wrote and said little about his childhood and youth. If his reticence on the subject of Rugby was influenced by his later politics, his silence over

Oxford was more likely the result of disappointment. At the end of his life the ghost was laid to rest and amends made on both sides by the award to him of an honorary degree by the university, which evidently delighted him.[123] But his silence is unfortunate because by the time he graduated he was already some sort of socialist, though how and why he had reached this position is obscure. No doubt a combination of his reading, his friends, his teachers and the powerful sense of social responsibility and service which defined both institutions that framed him was at the root of it. Many who attended the same institutions were touched in similar ways and went into progressive politics, the civil service, education and social reform because of it. Indeed Tawney, in his confidence and assurance, struck one of those who knew him best, his personal friend and joint literary executor, Sir Richard Rees (who was also George Orwell's literary executor), as a representative figure, 'one of the last representatives of an older and less insecure generation'.

> I was continually being impressed by the depth and wisdom and brilliance of Tawney's insight. And then from time to time, I'd be somehow baffled by what seemed to me an almost unnatural fixity of outlook, and an almost unrealistic confidence which he never lost. But I suppose what I'm really saying is, that this was the psychological attitude [of one] who felt his feet were always on solid ground, and that is an attitude – er – a feeling, which is much less familiar to people born in this century than in the preceding one.[124]

Whether from his education, or from membership of this generation, or from his own inner resources, Tawney seems never to have known doubt: this made him a brilliant advocate and polemicist, unafraid to take a lead, but it led him to underestimate alternative or opposed arguments, and to overlook the requirement to justify to others those positions that he himself took to be axiomatic.

Courtship and Marriage

The marriage of Richard Henry Tawney to Annette Jeanie Beveridge, known as Jeanette, in 1909 seems outwardly to have been an utterly predictable upper middle class Edwardian union. They had met at Oxford, where he had read Greats (classics) and she had studied French. She was the sister of his best friend while he was at the university, and both the bride and the groom came from families with strong and recent experience of India. Both families had even settled in Surrey. But an outwardly perfect alliance brought together two young people with different temperaments and ambitions. The marriage was always known to have been a difficult one with the suggestion that Tawney was unfulfilled in it. Jeanette has been presented as feckless, disorganized, mercenary and eccentric.[1] Though her recurrent illnesses undoubtedly complicated and probably undermined the marriage, the prevalent view of their relationship at the time and since has not been sufficiently generous to Jeanette nor sufficiently sceptical of Tawney as a lover and husband. Jeanette had much more depth and colour to her than has been recognized and Tawney's emotional immaturity – without doubt the product of an upbringing lacking in contact with girls and women – has been obscured. The couple found a *modus vivendi* in time and were genuinely devoted and attached to each other for decades. But it was not the relationship that either had really wanted: Jeanette had desired to be loved and cared for, and Tawney had wanted a partner in his social endeavours. Neither was to be satisfied with the compromise they struck.

Jeanette was born in India. She was known as 'Tutu' or just 'Tu' to her family. Her father, Henry Beveridge, was then a judge in the Indian Civil Service; remarkably, he supported Indian nationalism and the Congress party. Her mother Annette Susannah, nee Akroyd, was a highly intelligent and strong-willed woman who had gone out to India on her own to educate Hindu women in a secular curriculum. She married her husband in 1875 and they had four children, but Will and Jeanette, the middle pair, were the only ones to reach maturity, losing their younger brother Hermann in 1890 and elder sister, Letty, in 1893, both to influenza contracted in England.[2] Annette was a gifted linguist, translator and orientalist, reading among other languages German, Hindi, Persian and Chagatai Turkish.[3] George Bernard Shaw described her as 'the cleverest woman of my acquaintance and the wickedest in her opinions' and both elements of this summation emerged in her dealings with R. H. Tawney.[4] Annette brought the family back to England in 1890 and they settled in a large and comfortable home, 'Pitfold', in Shottermill near Haslemere, Surrey. Jeanette went up to Somerville College, Oxford in 1899 to read French after a period at a Swiss finishing school. Her brother Will was also studying there and 'my Mother believed in certain aspects of the equality of the sexes, of which this was one'. Jeanette had never written an essay before and was immediately discouraged by her college tutor. But she was also tutored by the distinguished medieval scholar and socialist, Frederick York Powell, the then Regius Professor of History, whom she liked and admired, not least because he 'marked my outpourings with alphas'.[5] She led a lively undergraduate existence of punting and tennis and, like Tawney, experienced what she called the 'mediocre success' of a second-class degree.[6] After Oxford and 6 months in Florence learning Italian and studying music, she returned to the family home. Her letters from Somerville suggest that she was spontaneous in manner and fun loving. Her first extant note to Tawney sets the tone: 'By the way I fell into the River on Monday. You can't imagine how proud I feel – The worst of it is it wasn't my fault for I even attempted to prevent the catastrophe, but it was fun to be splashing about'.[7] She wrote to relations and friends in an easy, unaffected and chatty style, a mixture of thoughts, feelings and news. In one of her early letters to Tawney she informed him 'that mine is a very peculiar typewriter and has that way of writing pure gibberish on occasion, so please accept it as best you can'.[8] She was playful, girlish and gay. Though no great beauty, she was 'tall and of good physique' with what she described as 'fresh colouring'.[9]

The couple met in June 1902 at the end of Tawney's penultimate year in Oxford. As Tawney recalled 6 years later: 'I can't honestly say that I fell in love with you at first sight, for I have only hazy recollections of that river picnic' but after an excursion of friends to the Birmingham City Art Gallery that summer, 'I knew I wanted you'. But there was no declaration of intent or whirlwind romance, for as Tawney continued: 'It seems to me that instead of falling in love with you, I've crawled into love with you, and wasted a good deal of time in the process. You must have thought me a cold-blooded villain, as I suppose I seem to most people'.[10] Certainly they seemed to develop an understanding; sometime before Tawney left Balliol in June 1903 he had sent 'a note to give you my love, and to say (though I can't) how much I enjoyed our time together . . . You know we understand each other, and nothing else matters. Ever your lover, Harry'.[11] For the rest of her life Tawney signed off his letters to Jeanette in that manner. Later that year they corresponded while Tawney was in Germany for the first time. She wrote to him asking for an explanation of the tariff reform controversy then dominating British politics and Tawney replied at length. He favoured free trade, he said, above all because protection would create powerful vested interests behind tariff barriers. But perhaps surprisingly he declared an admiration for the tariff reformer in-chief, Joseph Chamberlain, who 'is the only man in the country with an idea & he deserves to win, even by lying'.[12]

Yet the affair remained lukewarm as Tawney tried to make his way in the world. Jeanette recalled that they shared 'common interests from Spinoza to dogs' and that his first act of courtship was to take her to Bach's St Matthew Passion at St Paul's Cathedral.[13] She also recalled an awkward passage on a sofa together after friends had gone out and left them alone; nothing happened, and Tawney then discovered 'an unexpected pressing engagement which would prevent him staying to dinner after all'.[14] He would 'occasionally send a picture postcard and occasionally he would leave a book with me'. Though Tawney could not dance he gallantly attended social functions in Surrey to make up the numbers: he confessed to Jeanette that 'every partner suggested supper to him after a turn or two' on the dance floor.[15] Tawney was sharing a flat with her brother south of the river in London in this period, so he and Jeanette interacted frequently. In 1905 Jeanette also volunteered to help organize the Children's Country Holiday Fund (CCHF) in Surrey which she did for some years, finding willing homes in the vicinity whose owners would take in children for 2 weeks in the summer. As she then wrote to her brother, 'I have been thinking about the CCHF . . . I wrote to Harry to know if he had any list of people who used to take children & if he could give me any regulations to help me'.[16] No doubt this was valuable and satisfying voluntary work for a young woman with time on her hands. Jeanette also ran a club for the working girls from a local factory whose only recreation up to that point had been sex with the local men.[17] Years later, with tongue in cheek, she recalled 'the agreeable correspondence of the Secretary of the Children's Country Holiday Fund' who 'had a jocular way of treating dilemmas which encouraged me to confessions'.[18] She corresponded often with him over private homes she had signed up for the scheme and children sent down for vacations to fill spare bedrooms, and when they met, whether in the London flat or the Beveridge family home in Surrey where Tawney was a frequent and, at this stage, a welcome guest, they talked business as well as pleasure. But 'there was nothing in his manner to encourage me or my family to hope that my future might be secured'.[19]

Jeanette had had her admirers. Her first love was a student engineer at Edinburgh University with whom she played lieder on the piano: 'we realised in time . . . that we cared each of us for the love songs, but not each of us for the other'.[20] An older man, 'a north country businessman' proposed to her in 1906 and soon after her refusal he married his landlady's daughter.[21] A regular army officer offered his hand in 1907 and was refused.[22] Every year Annette packed off her daughter to the capacious home in South Wales of one of Annette's college friends who had married very well and had five sons: nothing came of it.[23] And nothing came of the relationship with Harry Tawney either until a crisis occurred between them in May and June 1908. This was a difficult time for Tawney for other reasons: he had begun teaching tutorial classes on an experimental basis but was still unsure whether Oxford would endorse the idea, fund the classes and set up a programme of education in alliance with the Workers' Educational Association (WEA). Whether he would have a job in the autumn was obscure, therefore. At this very point it would seem that Jeanette received yet another proposal of marriage. Some months after the crisis, when Tawney had won her back, he found it 'odd, my darling, to think of you having been on the point of marrying someone else, and it gives me a shiver down the back to think what a near thing it was'.[24] This other proposal from an unknown suitor galvanized him into declaring his love for her, but almost too late, and in a form that she found difficult to accept. The crisis and its subsequent resolution tells us much about Tawney.

Tawney seems to have declared his love for her in a meeting they had on 14 May 1908. Jeanette rejected him and he sat down that evening to write her the love letter he should have sent years before:

> I can honestly say that I love you with every power I possess and to the best of my knowledge have loved you since we went to the Birmingham picture gallery . . . it seemed to me that the only way of winning you was to make myself a better man with greater weight and influence and if possible better in other ways too and I determined that instead of trying to make money I would fight for some cause, however small. I ought to say it was not only my love for you which made me determine this but also that I felt what some people call "a call" to try and do something in connection with the Labour movement, and what was really I

suppose, ambition. You & this were so mixed up together that whenever I have done anything useful even in a small way I hoped that you would hear of it and feel pleased . . . I do so want you to see that in my sheepish way I have tried to be what I thought might be more worthy of you. It seems now that I have thrown away the end in looking after the means. But please try to believe that it was not because I loved you less but because I loved you more that I never told you of my love before today . . . My absence from you in Scotland taught me two things, that love is a much bigger thing than I am, and that I could not get on without seeing you. I vowed after seeing you in Glasgow that I would tell you that I loved you as soon as ever I got a decent job.[25]

Ambition, preoccupation with social causes and worldly success, his sense of his inferiority until he had something to show for himself, and the repression and shyness that afflicted British men of this background and education, all conspired in his silence over several years.

Jeanette's reply was devastating. She had been confused by his lack of ardour, had imagined that he did not love her and had 'resolved to see you as little as possible & discourage any attempts to have you here':

You puzzled me so & I somehow never guessed that you really knew your own mind but thought you liked me quite a lot . . . I know you'll swear when I say that I'm not really capable of caring properly for you . . . honestly Harry – I don't feel as though you'd ever make me love you – I say this because I ought [to] let you know my feelings. All I can give you is friendship – a sorry substitute but I can do no more. Forgive me if I seem to write callously. I do grieve more than I can say to cause you pain & I only want to help you.[26]

In letters that followed over the next days she repeated herself:

I want to love you because I can't help it not because you are a fine character or a practical man or have loved me for so long – You deserve a better fate & I could not allow you to have me now as I am. Somehow all my powers for caring seem to have gone & that is why I am unhappy . . . If you could only see how much easier it would be to say "yes" & not worry but I can't feel as though I can give you ¼ even of what you give me & that's a waste & a bad bargain.[27]

She felt it best to be as direct with him as she could be: 'I know I don't love you now & honestly don't feel I ever shall'. She wanted time to herself and knew that a meeting would be painful for him, and asked that they not see each other: 'You know me well enough to know that I really hate being alone & going about alone & love to be taken care of so that it's not on my own account that I say you mustn't come. I half hoped in the beginning that you'd see my weaknesses and scorn me but I fear you won't so good bye for the present. Try & think kindly of me & forgive me.'[28] She asked for 'three or four weeks of quiet . . . you cannot understand the relief it has been to me to be left alone these few days.'[29]

Tawney acceded, of course. In his replies he was soothing, sympathetic, but also evidently frightened that she would reject him outright if she reached a decision quickly and so he gave her the time and space she requested.

> You must try not to let yourself be worried more than is inevitable, and above all not to rush your feelings, or to make up your mind, instead of letting it make itself up . . . It is better to be troubled now than to hurry oneself and make a mistake. I do so want you not to be *hurried*, or to feel that anything, even a wrong decision, is better than the pain of uncertainty, and so to make up your mind before it is ready . . . If you would rather not consider this matter until you have got through this summer's work I shall be content to wait . . . You are not causing me pain and you will not do so by waiting . . . If you ever should care for me, we shall be the better for having seen all round ourselves.[30]

In a slightly later letter he counselled her to think of him 'as a companion in misfortune, and don't resort to drastic measures and absolute irrevocable decisions to clear up a matter which will manage itself if it is left alone, one way or another'.[31]

While Jeanette waited and reflected, Harry continued to write to her in letters that were designed to be persuasive, praising her qualities in passages which contained as well some honest self-analysis:

> But you can't understand what you have done and are doing for me to make me better, less censorious, and hard, more kind and patient with everybody. Nobody can say why a person does inspire them in this way . . . And I can honestly say that one reason I love you is that you have helped me so much, and do help me every time we meet. By nature I'm egotistical and self-centred with ready-made criticisms of people from whom I differ. You showed me without meaning to do so probably that it is worthwhile to try and see people from their point of view, instead of only from my own, and by showing me that you have opened a new world to me . . . I don't think I'm doing wrong in telling you quite plainly how you have made a man of me, not much of one, but less narrow than I should have been but for you.[32]

This was more than tactical: indeed it was probably true, and it explains why Jeanette's 'friends say we are not suited to each other'.[33] Indeed, the most important figure in the couple's lives, Tawney's friend and Jeanette's brother, also had his reservations: Will 'thinks that you and I have not mixed with the same sort of people, or had the same interests, that you are a society lady, and I a rather ineffective mixture of a student and a "social worker." Therefore we shan't get on, because we shall never understand each other.'[34] Jeanette's aunt apparently said much the same thing: 'she thinks because you get on with people and like seeing them, and I'm a stick, that therefore I should hamper your pleasure, and you would worry me.'[35] Tawney contested this of course, but in the spring and early summer of 1908 Jeanette was fully conscious of his weaknesses and was weighing their likely effects upon any marriage. Tawney was too much the dedicated and humourless young reformer, driven by politics and public concerns, rather too prone to the moral judgment of others, and lacking in humanity and sensitivity. As Jeanette would remind him a few months later in a very accurate assessment of his weaknesses:

> By the way you have a very narrow point of view about those that care for things you don't care for. For goodness sake don't be too sure you are right. It's fatal to be as critical & intolerant as you are. What you do is not only no good but harm. It always grieves me to see the way that those who take life seriously so often succeed in making life & themselves ridiculous. If you should see a good thing, why not be content with that & not make virtue foolish by some narrow expression of opinion [?][36]

On 17 June he pleaded for another chance:

> I know that if we were married I should not force my opinions on you, or think myself wiser than you, but should thank God for your being different from what I am (sic) . . . I know I seem hard and flippant and incapable of tenderness, and I cannot expect you to think me other than I seem. But give me a chance, and I will show you that there is in me something besides a bag of theories and moral maxims, and that I have a heart.[37]

She did give him that chance, though whether in doing so she made the right choice is an open question. Two days later the crisis, which had lasted a month or so, was over. Tawney received another letter from Jeanette (which is not extant) and now felt 'a bit overwhelmed. I never dared to hope that you would care for me so soon. In fact, after your last two letters I pretty well despaired and committed my soul into the hands of the Almighty.'[38] His prayers had been answered.

But what had Jeanette committed *herself* to? Now assured that he had won her heart, in letters later that summer Tawney wrote to her about marriage.

Finding happiness and fulfilment with another person had nothing to do with it, apparently:

> The fact is that it's probably the wrong way to look at marriage as a pleasure, or a relaxation or a consolation or a comfortable nest into which the blasts of the working world do not penetrate. My own experience is that directly one says "Now I'm going to be happy," and does a thing merely for the sake of happiness, one isn't happy at all . . . To personify one's happiness in a person is degrading to the person and I believe it is the death of real love . . . when married people find marriage a disappointment I suspect in some cases it is because they have made happiness an end in itself, and having got it find that it is not really an end i.e. a complete satisfaction at all.[39]

Perhaps personal happiness was unfulfilling for Tawney, but Jeanette had already made it clear that she liked and wanted to be cared for. These comments betray an immaturity in human relations in Tawney. He may have believed that he knew the facts of love from his experience, but that experience was limited and shallow, and he was dogmatizing here without insight or sympathy.

In a subsequent letter he went further: having explained what was wrong with conventional concepts of marriage, he now explained his idea of wedlock:

> I did want to explain that marriage means more to me than merely living with a person whom one loves. It has often seemed to me, when I have considered other married people that they have failed by not trying to realise each other's interests or facing the fact that one cannot live for pleasant moments without life being a long disappointment. I should be quite miserable (I think) without some kind of cause, however insignificant, to work for, and I wanted you to understand that before marrying me. What I want us to be able to do is to live for something more important than ourselves; if one can do that incidental unhappiness doesn't count; if one doesn't do it I should be inclined to say that other happinesses don't count either.[40]

A fulfilling relationship with another – the desire of most people in most times – was not enough for the young Tawney, or perhaps more accurately, was not fully appreciated and understood by him. 'People do not always think rightly about love', he told her. 'Many think of it as a passion or a feeling. But it is a way of life that swallows up our individual eccentricities. I do want us to live that way together, feeling that we belong to a cause and are members of an army'.[41] That made Jeanette into some sort of camp follower.

In many of the letters he wrote that summer he was evidently torn between public causes and his private devotion to her. Alarmingly in a lover, private devotion was not the stronger of the two forces: 'I always felt that it might come to my having to choose between you & doing what I thought right in the way of work, and I know that, if it did, I should have to give you up. Now I've got both . . .' – or so he hoped.[42] His letters are seeded with expectations about her role in his work and about their companionate marriage. He wanted her, he wrote, 'because I believe you will make me a better and more effective man in my work and all that belongs to it . . . I want us to work together as well as live together'. He retained just enough self-knowledge to ask her for another service: 'don't let me become more of a didactic prig than I am already'.[43] When away from her, teaching one of the first tutorial classes in Rochdale, he expressed the tension between personal love and service once again: 'I did so enjoy seeing you last week, and I can't imagine now how I ever got on without you. I don't feel a bit [that] our love for each other was making us slack or self-centred; but I feel more keen to be of some real use in the world if possible'.[44] On the very eve of their wedding he was still pontificating on the same theme: 'It is good that we understand each other. You must not be annoyed with me for having talked to you so much about our duty to work in a small way at social questions, or of speechifying about them. When we were first engaged I felt some regret lest I might let my love for you make me choose what was easy & safe'.[45] But if he sometimes preached to Jeanette, he also wrote with youthful sincerity and enthusiasm which deserves respect:

> That is what is so delightful in the socialist movement. We are working for a cause & you & I will do our little bit together . . . what more can any of us wish than to be used up and worked out in such service? . . . I feel so sure that there is no happiness except in service ("he that will be first among you, let him be servant of all") that I can wish nothing better for those whom I love than to feel what I do.[46]

For her part Jeanette, who, by background and temperament had undoubtedly expected something rather different from married life, tried to keep up and agree. In one letter that reveals her doubts and confusions she wrote to tell him 'in plain black and white that I fully agree with what you say about marriage . . . I've never felt satisfied with living for oneself & I crave the Crusade idea of living for other things. Somehow I get muddled and find myself thinking conventional things which I don't believe. It's a sort of association I can't get free from. Now I begin to see more clearly . . .'[47]

He wanted an alliance in social reform and failed to see how being personally unfulfilled might corrode a marriage. She was trying desperately to go along with him, despite her own instincts, no doubt out of love and regard. Tawney could not appreciate that Jeanette might be different from him and require something more from a marriage than a partnership: she did not have the strength or confidence to challenge his immaturity. The word partnership conjures up the marriage of Sidney and Beatrice Webb; Beatrice entitled the second volume of her famous memoirs 'Our Partnership'.[48] The Webbs were committed socialists whose marriage was devoted to the cause of social progress, and a couple whom Tawney had met already, whom he came to admire absolutely, and whose friendship in later life was one of the most important influences on him. Beatrice had married Sidney acknowledging that their marriage would be a partnership rather than a romance. But Jeanette needed and wanted something rather different: she 'love[d] to be taken care of' she had told him. If supportive of social reform, she was not a political animal committed to causes in the manner of Beatrice Webb, or indeed of R. H. Tawney. In the years that followed there were to be no children to give another aspect to the marriage; Jeanette fell ill and was often convalescing away from home; meanwhile Tawney was active in a range of campaigns to which he gave himself wholeheartedly. He was always solicitous and caring, but as he built a public career Jeanette was neglected and lost confidence. It is no great surprise that her memoirs convey a sense of regret and a lack of fulfilment. They hint also at the absence of a physical relationship within their marriage, though the prose is deliberately obscure at this juncture and there is no other evidence to substantiate the point.[49]

In the days and weeks following their reconciliation and Jeanette's acceptance of Harry's proposal, they faced a more immediate problem than differing conceptions of wedded bliss in the shape of Annette, Jeanette's mother. She was combative, possessive, especially where her children were concerned, manipulative, and unwilling to marry off her daughter to a man with no money, few prospects and a foul temper. Though Annette had welcomed Tawney to the family home on many occasions as Will's friend, and though they had swapped books and discussed points of philosophy together, Tawney was unacceptable as a son-in-law. For some months therefore, the young couple's lives were bound up in a struggle to win her approval of the match, or at least prevent her from undermining their plans. When Jeanette told her parents of her engagement she encountered immediate opposition. They were shocked and complained that she had told others of their plans before telling them. This prompted Jeanette to assert her deep affection for Harry: 'Honestly, mother, my heart is in this & has never been in anything else – I can understand what a surprise it was to you both though I always felt you had guessed my secret years ago but I was too uncertain of Harry's feelings to speak of it to you.'[50] As Jeanette recalled years later:

> Contrary to expectation my immediate family regarded our engagement in the light of a major misfortune. My parents had hoped that I would marry a rich man . . . They deplored the undefined educational work on which my husband was to be employed, which gave no annual increment such as appertain in the civil service. The proposed marriage became to me, at any rate, more satisfactory through opposition.[51]

His mother's unreasonableness also provoked Will to write 'one of the sharpest letters he ever wrote to Annette' in which he defended Tawney's character, ability and social status:

> You have not had a pair of children to deal with but a pair of absolutely determined grown people. The parents cannot surely under any circumstances refuse assent because of their own personal likes or dislikes or on any ground except absolutely definite ones of health or character . . . I do entreat you to consider for a moment how you would regard any lady of your acquaintance who treated my proposal for her daughter's hand as you have been treating Harry's . . . I quite realise that announcements of this sort appear at first rather as shocks. I was much surprised myself when the possibility of feeling between Harry and Tutu was first suggested to me some time ago. But such doubts as I have had on the matter have been entirely the opposite of you i.e. whether she was the person to make *him* happy – In view of his long determination – and really in view of hers – there is no room left for doubting by third parties.[52]

For much of this period Annette would not see her aspiring son-in-law: as Tawney lamented, 'I believe if I could see your parents, I could show them that I am not the futile youth whom they knew two years ago but a man who knows his own mind and can hold his own in the world.'[53] Jeanette's father, Henry, relented quite quickly, acted as an intermediary and was 'reasonableness itself, especially on the subject of money.'[54] But Annette conducted affairs by correspondence only for some weeks. She began in a provocative manner, drawing Jeanette's attention to the case of Tawney's brother and thus to 'mental illness' in the Tawney family with all its supposed implications for the raising of a family. This may appear now to have been underhand and beyond reason, but the influence of eugenics – and thus of the idea of the inheritance of mental characteristics – on Edwardian liberals (and not just conservatives) was powerful.[55] Annette did not raise this objection again directly – though she did tell her relations of Tawney's 'invalid brother' to the annoyance of both Jeanette and her brother – but it evidently troubled Tawney who also felt he must admit to Jeanette that an elderly aunt in her 'seventies was suffering from "softening of the brain".[56]

On 12 July 1908 Annette set out her further objections to the marriage in a letter to Tawney. He had limited professional experience; she was dismissive of his qualifications in economics; the post he was hoping for, teaching tutorial classes, was not certain, and was at best, merely 'an experiment'. It would only pay £400 or £500 a year, and he had no reserves of capital to fall back on. Jeanette could not be kept in the manner to which she had become accustomed, nor retain her previous class position: 'I fear your marriage because it involves rupture with my daughter's past preferences, habits and tastes. Time & fit arrangements might give some assurance that she can readjust herself to greatly changed conditions'. She wrote that she would never be able to 'sanction your marriage to my daughter. It is best for me to tell you this, though I judge that you attach little value to parental sanction', but she was not resolutely opposed: 'If the serious difficulties of finance have been removed or placed in a more hopeful position & if you are both of the same mind now, I will arrange the wedding in a quiet manner and will settle on my daughter a sum of money to come after our deaths & of which the amount will depend on what you can do. At best it will be a small sum'.[57] This was more an act of deterrence than of outright hostility and on the following day Henry Beveridge wrote to Tawney to interpret: 'There is no objection to your putting a notice into the *Morning Post*.'[58]

Annette's opposition continued, though at the lower level of guerrilla warfare, and she picked fights in letters of icy disdain over essentially trivial matters from Tawney's written style to his plans for the wedding.[59] As Tawney wrote to Jeanette from Longton in October 1908, no doubt with her accusations of insanity in mind, 'We must regard your mother's attitude as a kind of illness, which she can't help, and for which she is hardly responsible'.[60] At least Tawney's parents were in favour, his father playing a supportive and soothing role throughout: 'It is my firm belief that everything will come all right. I have told you in my previous letter . . . that your conduct has in my opinion been quite correct.'[61] Tawney's formal engagement that autumn as a teacher of tutorial classes not only answered one of his future mother-in-law's objections but also provided the couple with an income, however modest. In the months before the wedding Jeanette tried her best to be that companion in social causes that Harry required and she struggled through a text on political economy by the American, Henry Seligman: 'There is a sort of satisfaction in reading Seligman for I feel we are perhaps both thinking on similar lines! . . . I find his chapters on value and price very stiff. Still I take in something & what I don't I shall re-read later on'.[62] Perhaps not unnaturally she was rather more keen 'to talk to you about *The Room With a View* which I was finishing on Sunday'.[63] But as the appointed day came nearer Harry's temper exploded over the issue of the groom's attire. To him such things were trivial: to Jeanette, his appearance and his general untidiness were genuine issues that irked her all their lives together. Aware, no doubt, of all the adverse comments and reflections on their marriage – that she was throwing herself away on a man without position and prospects – she probably wanted him to at least look the part on this occasion. Tawney's abject apology for losing 'his accursed temper again' and writing her a 'wretched letter' at least suggested self-knowledge: 'Oh my dear, do put up with me in these things. I know in my heart that I'm not half good enough to marry you, and I do thank God for my happiness. Yet when I get worried by things, as I was on Thursday, I behave like a spoiled baby'.[64]

Two weeks later, on 28 June 1909 they were married at St Stephen's, Shottermill, close to Haslemere. It was an Oxford/ WEA /Toynbee Hall affair: the Reverends William Temple and Samuel Barnett officiated; the WEA's treasurer, Tawney's friend from Toynbee Hall, T. Edmund Harvey, was best man; Albert Mansbridge and Will Beveridge looked on. Given their many difficulties in getting to the altar they chose two very apposite hymns: 'Lead us, Heavenly Father, lead us/ O'er the world's tempestuous sea' and 'God our help in ages past'. As Jeanette recalled with some irony and perhaps also some resentment, 'After a year of strain we were united by Canon Barnett (assisted by the present Archbishop of Canterbury) with an exhortation to make each other spiritually uncomfortable through life. Thus and only thus could we avoid the smug contentment which spells ruin to all marital happiness'.[65] Their honeymoon consisted of 3 months in Germany, 2 of them spent in Freiburg, with visits also to Manheim, Munich and Nuremburg. It conformed in some ways to Tawney's idea of a partnership: They 'saw a good many cathedrals & pictures . . . and I got introductions to a certain number of municipal authorities who told me about town administration, and let me ask questions [of] them in very shaky German. They are a long way ahead of us in some of these matters'.[66]

Married life began at 24 Shakespeare Street, Chorlton-on-Medlock, Manchester, where they lived for 5 years, a good location from which to reach tutorial classes in Lancashire and the Potteries. Tawney recalled that 'their rent was supposed to be £26 per year, but the landlord actually took less "under an illusion . . . that our respectability was so conspicuous as to raise the tone of the neighbourhood and the prospective value of his property".[67] Tawney took four evening classes each week through the autumn and winter, staying overnight in two of the towns where he taught. In the summer he spent periods in Oxford, teaching on the WEA summer school there and researching in the Bodleian Library. Jeanette did a variety of things at first: she was 'a self-appointed liaison officer between factory workers and the Factory Inspectorate' and she was trained by Maude Royden, the feminist teacher and leading woman-Anglican, as a speaker for the suffrage movement. On one occasion Jeanette's social research led her to spend the night in a lodging house for vagrant women: her stylish undergarments led them to suspect her of being a prostitute.[68] In feminist circles in the city Jeanette was outspoken in her support for a reformed divorce law allowing 'complete equality of divorce facilities for rich and poor'. She could, she explained 'imagine the hell it must be to live in cramped conditions when out of tune'.[69] In her manuscript autobiography, admittedly written much later in the 1930s, Jeanette added a chapter on marriage and its tribulations in general which, while not quite descending to the particulars of her own state, struck a tone of disillusion, resignation and unhappiness. She contrasted the 'idyllic pictures' of newly-wedded bliss with the reality:

> Who before marriage could begin to guage (sic) the pre-bath male mood? Who recognise his telephone manner, so disconnected with his tea-party voice? Who could measure the extent and location of his smoking propensities? Who would dream of his dislike of the Monday laundry collection? ... Who would guess that he would always dislike breakfast chat and prefer his newspaper to one's silvery tones?[70]

It was deeply unfortunate that within a year of their marriage Jeanette fell seriously ill, waking up one summer morning in their Oxford lodgings to 'a leg double its girth'.[71] Though never named or explained this was probably the first of several bouts of oedema that she suffered through her life. She had been ill for a period after studying at the university but from 1910 onwards she was often afflicted by poor health. There were periods of remission but she required many operations, hospitalization and convalescence and she suffered from many different ailments and conditions. In 1910 it wasn't just a swelling of the leg but colitis and uterine problems as well, and what the doctors called 'internal poisoning'.[72] She had periods during 1910, 1911 and also in 1912 in a clinic in Harrogate. In the latter year she required an appendectomy and the removal of varicose veins from her 'bad leg'.[73] She made the best of it, as she could: 'Harry has supplied me with much frivolous literature which is one of the great consolations of operations as one really has to put up with being mindless for a little time.'[74] The winters of 1910–11, 1911–12 and 1912–13, when they should and would have been building the foundations of their marriage were spent by Jeanette alone, convalescing in Italy, at, respectively, San Remo, the Bay of Naples and finally in Sicily. Her first letter home in December 1910 told of problems and disagreements and the hope that they might put it all behind them: 'Dear, does it not strike you that we wasted our opportunities very much when we were together [?] We were sometimes cross & now I'd give anything to have that time back again to spend with you.'[75] Subsequent letters reflected on their troubled marriage and hoped for better in the future; frequently Jeanette blamed herself for those troubles though the suspicion must be that in this way, bearing all the responsibility rather than arguing over the distribution of blame, she could more easily counsel a new start. Evidently they had sought advice and help for their relationship from Samuel Barnett:

> we must try to deserve each other's company by being really nice – I have a feeling that if one plays at not caring or squabbling it has a way of making one really care less – I think we must remember when next we want to spar how we felt apart. The Canon told us at difficult moments to see the Christ in each other. He is right – we will try.[76]

Two weeks before Tawney came out to San Remo at the end of March 1911 Jeanette wrote to voice her growing concern that when they met again all the old difficulties might recur. She could not refrain from reverting to his habits and dirtiness which she found so troublesome; she reminded him of the frequency of their bickering and arguments – every four and half minutes she claimed. 'I do hope' she wrote, 'you have some hope that when we are together we shall not want to be apart again!'[77] A lonely and sick young woman in a clinic in Italy might be expected to worry a little about the imminent arrival of her husband after months apart. But there is a deep sadness to these letters in early 1911, reflecting Jeanette's gloom about their relationship and its chances for the future. While her letters home in the subsequent winters of convalescence do not discuss their marriage, the replacement of this subject by the uncontroversial discussion of the places she had visited and the books she was reading seems to suggest a growing distance between them, as if they were once more living single lives, as in a sense they were. Their separation would only continue during the first half of the Great War between 1914 and 1916.

After Tawney died his friend and literary executor, Sir Richard Rees, spoke of the harmony between the private and public Tawney: 'his public life, and his

public activities were a direct and natural expression of his personal humaneness
and his personal idealism – there was absolutely no sense of strain, or conflict
and inconsistency, between his private personality and his public life and public
work'.[78] Rees was referring to the consistency of Tawney's views and his attitude
towards his fellow men. He would have known nothing about the troubled
history of Tawney's early relations with his wife, having met the couple much
later. In private, as this history of their relationship shows, there was unhappiness,
insensitivity, incompatibility and also sheer bad luck in their early years together.
To tell this story is not designed to depreciate Tawney in any way. Not to have
told it would have been to exclude a crucial element in his life's history, though
one obscured to almost everyone else, then and since. And to have omitted this
passage in their lives would have perpetuated the historians' injustice towards
Jeanette, who emerges as a lively, kind and unfortunate woman who made a
mistake – the wrong choice in June 1908 – and came, I think, to regret it. Tawney
would not be the first great man to have made a bad marriage; nor, *pace* Richard
Rees, is he alone in a disjunction between his public reputation and his private
life. But Tawney's bad marriage was, in large part, of his own devising. It is not
uncommon to find figures in history who have thrown themselves into public
work to salve or evade an unhappy personal life: the remarkable creative feats
of one of Tawney's early heroes in the socialist movement, William Morris, can
be explained in this way. Those made unhappy through immature or selfish
conceptions of personal and marital relations are less common and perhaps less
sympathetic figures.

   No argument is being advanced here, and certainly not one which would
undermine Tawney as a public figure because he was an immature lover and
an irascible husband. Indeed, we might argue that what emerges from this
story is the simple fact that Tawney was much more suited to education and
politics than to matrimony – and he probably recognized that, which is why he
always wanted his marriage to be a partnership and a crusade. Moreover, the
reasons for his ineptitude with Jeanette and with women more generally can
probably be traced to his upbringing and early institutionalization as much as
anything else: too many late-Victorian and Edwardian men were emotionally
stunted in this way.

   Tawney recognized his ignorance and inexperience, at least. In October 1916
he wrote to Lawrence Hammond, his friend and fellow historian, now also in the
army, though with a commission, to commend those he'd met in the sergeants'
mess of the 22nd Battalion of the Manchester Regiment. 'There are some quite

nice men among them. But I feel terribly old. I never could take much interest in "girls" & often have cause to wish that side of my education had not been neglected'.[79] Years before in a letter to his friend Dick Denman at the end of 1902 while both were at Balliol, Tawney had asked if he had any 'views on the female franchise?' Tawney explained that he was 'plagued with old ladies who ask me mine, which are that women are all fools, that all women over 30 are damned fools, & that anyhow injustice is the best policy'.[80] This was knockabout student stuff, a display of bravado and self-mockery, and probably of no consequence in a political context, though one historian has asked why Tawney took no part in the struggle for women's suffrage before 1914.[81] But men despise and deride what they don't know, and Tawney knew little about women when he wrote this or when he was courting Jeanette, or when he was in the sergeants' mess. Tawney, in his naivete, was apt to moralize about his marriage; the case being advanced here is that we should not moralize and judge in our turn, but should accept it as one element in a complex life.

3

Workers' Education, 1908–13

> Not the least noteworthy of the developments to strike the future historian of the twentieth century will be . . . the emergence, among the rank and file of the working-class world of the conviction that education may be used as an instrument of social emancipation, and a determination to build up, both through and in addition to the ordinary machinery of public education, an educational movement which is stamped with their own ideals, and the expression of their own experience.[1]

In this way Tawney, writing in 1924, explained the developments in workers' education before the First World War in which he played a leading role. While the part played by workers themselves was indeed a crucial determinant of what occurred, the origins of the Workers' Educational Association (WEA), its partnership with Oxford and then other British universities, and the development of the tutorial classes movement so-called, is a complex story of institutional experimentation and development in which the demand for education from working-class communities was but one of several factors. It is also a story which had considerable implications for the strategy of the British working-class movement at the time and which was formative for Tawney himself. He emerges not only as the central figure in these negotiations and experiments, but also as the movement's greatest teacher, its deepest thinker and its most impatient reformer.

The first of several contexts in which to situate the developments after about 1903 is the wider political and social development of the working class itself. The founding of the Labour Representation Committee in 1900, the election of 29 Labour MPs in 1906 and the doubling of trade union membership among British workers from approximately 2 to 4 million between 1900 and 1914 were only the most obvious signs of the maturity and growing independence of the labour movement in this period. The point was appreciated in the famous report on *Oxford and Working-Class Education* in 1908 which will figure prominently in this account and which was drafted by Tawney. As he expressed it there,

> The genius of English workmen for organization has covered some of the districts of northern England (for example, Lancashire) with a network of institutions, industrial, social, political and religious . . . There are certain towns in which almost every adult appears to a stranger to be connected with half a dozen different associations. It is obvious that the common atmosphere thus created is favourable, like that of an Oxford college, to the dissemination of ideas.[2]

Whether or not the comparison to Oxford was a good one, it was clear to many that this rich associational culture could sustain educational initiatives if of the right sort. As the *1908 Report* (as it became known) went on, 'If a class is formed under the control of members of working-class societies, its influence filters through a hundred different channels, and may leaven a whole town.'[3] As Arthur Greenwood, later deputy leader of the Labour Party, and another of the central figures in workers' education of this period, explained, 'The time was ripe for a development of adult education. A generation of compulsory education had begun to bear fruit, and working-class organisations, no longer struggling for mere existence, had become an integral part of the background of working-class life.'[4]

It was out of this mature working-class culture at this particular stage that the WEA emerged. As a member of one of the first tutorial classes, and a pupil of Tawney's, was to put it much later: 'The more one thinks of the early nineteen hundreds the more strongly one realizes that there was a something "in the air" of which the Association was the culmination and became the rallying point.'[5] Albert Mansbridge, the founder of the WEA, talked of 'the stirring of a vast multitude. Something was happening on all sides of us to the democracy of England. Wherever we went we found this spirit. People were hungry for something. They were reaching out for something.'[6] The Association was not just a means of developing working-class interest in higher education and satisfying it, but an organization, with authentic roots in this culture, with which socially conscious university men and the universities themselves could collaborate.

The WEA was founded in May 1903 as the 'Association to Promote the Higher Education of Workingmen': its name was changed 2 years later at its second annual meeting in Birmingham. Its founder, Albert Mansbridge, who became one of Tawney's closest friends, was an archetypal lower middle-class scholar who had been involved for some time in the educational activities of the cooperative movement. Born the son of a carpenter in Battersea, he grew up in a family closely involved with the chapel and with cooperation. Mansbridge's own experience illustrated very well the waste of talent in late-Victorian and Edwardian society: though he won a scholarship to Battersea Grammar School he was forced to leave at 14 because his father would not countenance giving his fourth son the privilege of an education denied to his three elder brothers. Mansbridge eventually became a clerk in the Co-operative Wholesale Society and then, in 1901, a cashier in the Co-operative Permanent Building Society.[7] Here was an example of one sort of man – intelligent, but educationally frustrated, and locked into low-grade white-collar employment – who Tawney had in mind as he laboured to develop adult education in Edwardian England.

The new organization was launched in Oxford at a conference held on 22 August 1903, and 'attended by a large gathering of representatives of cooperative societies, trade unions, and university bodies'.[8] In addition to these, it also depended upon a variety of religious groups, 'particularly adult schools and educational societies attached to churches and chapels'.[9] It rapidly developed into a loose federation of different working-class institutions and individuals. By 1912 it had 110 local branches, 1,879 affiliated societies and over 7,000 individual members.[10] That the WEA met an obvious need and spread so rapidly was the result of another contextual change in this period: the effects of the Education Act of 1902. This provided state funds for secondary education for the first time and established local educational authorities with considerable powers which might act as partners in worthwhile voluntary initiatives. The Act opened up the possibility of more than an elementary education for bright working-class children who might progress to the secondary level, and even beyond, on scholarships. More to the point, it ensured the development of a type of student who perhaps stayed on in school to the age of 15 or 16 and then took employment in a manual or skilled position. Such a person had frequently developed the requisite skills and the desire for the type of higher education that would be offered in the new tutorial classes. Many people with some form of secondary education would find their way into adult education in the course of the next generation.[11]

Another context for these developments in working-class education after 1900 was the perceived failure of the earlier movement of university extension to reach the working class and provide a sustained and challenging educational experience. University extension lecturers had been going out from Cambridge, Oxford and London Universities since the 1870s and 1880s to lecture and take classes in dozens of locations across the country. The movement drew in many students – Oxford's programme in the 1890s catered for almost 20,000 students every year, many of them women – and enjoyed considerable success and recognition, but its finances and aims did not support the sort of serious-minded and intensive work at university standard that many tutors and reformers wished to encourage, and the movement had not been very successful at reaching working-class men and thus educating the coming political force in Britain. It was this that interested Tawney, of course, and he was in a singular position to take it forward. He had joined the WEA in 1905 and had quickly been advanced to a seat on its executive committee. He was part of the circle of Oxford reformers who saw this particular project as a way of promoting the wider social mission of the university. And he had come to understand that educating workers, as equals, in economics and history was his vocation, what he most wanted to do. In consequence, Tawney's hand was behind much of what was written and done to establish this new movement in 1908 and beyond. Because he lacked a base in Oxford he was not able to lead the initiatives, though all parties seem to have deferred to his judgement. But when it came to choosing the pioneer tutor, he was the obvious candidate. Meanwhile in London a new format for the education of adults in smaller classes had been tried out at Toynbee Hall where Samuel Barnett also wanted something that would provide far more thorough and systematic teaching than was possible in a course of lectures. What was now required was the construction and direction of a coalition of forces to introduce these changes and link together formally the universities and working-class education.

The final context was internal to Oxford itself: the movement, of which Tawney was a key member, of a group of young dons to reform the university and make it more accessible to working-class scholars. This movement was an important episode in itself in Tawney's life, but it is best understood as a part of his growing involvement in workers' education in this era. The two movements linking Oxford's reform to its role in the provision of adult education were fused together in his mind and his educational outlook from about 1906 until the First World War. Tawney wrote the chapter on adult education in Henrietta Barnett's biography of her husband and he there made it clear that the inspiration for the movement was provided by Samuel Barnett, a mentor to the most socially minded of the younger generation of Oxford graduates and no stranger to the arts and skills required to lead unobtrusively a public campaign from a vicarage. The Barnetts' home 'became a centre to which all proposals were brought and where all plans of action were laid'.[12]

United in and around the 'Catiline Club' in Oxford, the younger members of the group included William Temple at Queen's College, Alfred Zimmern of New College, Richard Livingstone of Corpus Christi, J. L. Myres and W. H. Fyfe. Tawney was an equal member and lent important assistance from outside: indeed, being outside Oxford gave him greater latitude to make radical arguments against the university. Livingstone eventually became President of Corpus Christi College and vice-chancellor of Oxford.[13] Fyfe, another classicist, was a fellow of Merton College and eventually Principal of Aberdeen University.[14] Myres, a classical archaeologist and historian who had worked with Arthur Evans in his youth, was a Student of Christ Church until 1907, and after a brief spell at Liverpool University, returned to the Wykeham Chair of Ancient History in Oxford in 1910, which he held until his retirement.[15] Zimmern was an ancient historian; later, under the impact of the Great War, his focus changed to the cause of international peace and from 1930 until 1944 he was the first incumbent of the Montague Burton Chair of International Relations in Oxford.[16] Zimmern was the closest to Tawney and they exchanged many private letters on the reform of Oxford, discussing issues and tactics. Barnett also sent him dozens of documents – 53 in all – which he had collected or could get access to and which had reference to the governance and finances of the university and its colleges.[17] The group also received help from J. A. Spender, editor of the liberal *Westminster Gazette*, which became the organ of the reformers, and Bishop Gore of Birmingham. Gore was a product of Balliol, a former fellow of Trinity, Oxford, a leading Anglo-Catholic, and successively Bishop of Worcester, Birmingham and Oxford. As the first principal of Pusey House in Oxford (1884–93) he had exercised a profound influence on the religious life of the University; as a Canon of Westminster he had inspired Mansbridge, and Tawney would later become his protégé and friend.[18]

In a memoir of William Temple, Tawney provided a recollection and summary of the Oxford reform movement in the years 1905–7:

> Owing chiefly to Canon Barnett, then Warden of Toynbee Hall, the subject received from 1905 onwards, some attention in the press. The development of secondary education which the act of 1902 was designed to promote, and the change of government in 1906, made the issue appear a more live one than might otherwise have been the case. A group of young dons at Oxford was formed to press for reform from inside. It included Sir Richard Livingstone, Professor Myres and several other persons ... Temple ... was an active member of the group. It may fairly be said to have played an important part in setting on foot the movement which led ... later, on conclusion of the War, to the appointment of the Royal [Asquith] Commission on Oxford and Cambridge.[19]

The aim of the group, in essence, was to raise academic standards in the University and simultaneously broaden its social range and intake. They contended that Oxford and Cambridge were wasteful of resources, inaccessible and therefore failing in their national duties, poorly managed and constitutionally ungovernable. Higher research was to be encouraged; the curriculum was to be modernized to include the social sciences; the university was to be subsidized by the colleges (which were to lose much of their autonomy); and clever students from humble backgrounds were to be admitted at the expense of the notorious 'idle pass men'. Entrance examinations to the university were to be reformed to enable a wider range of applicants; scholarships should be awarded to the needy rather than those from privileged backgrounds who had already benefited from private education. Their objectives were expressed by Tawney (under the pen-name 'Lambda') in a series of articles in the *Westminster Gazette* in February and March 1906 which were inspired by Barnett.[20] Several more anonymous pieces were published in the same newspaper a year later, though these were written by Zimmern, Temple and Livingstone as well as Tawney.[21] And within a few weeks a third series appeared in *The Times* under the title 'Oxford and the Nation'.[22]

Tawney's articles began with the familiar cry of all university reformers that unless Oxford changed 'she will have abdicated the leadership of English education' within a generation. For Tawney, change meant broadening the social composition of the university and using all funds responsibly to that end. He sought 'a National University . . . accessible to men of humble means' and purged of 'the rich and idle'. He aimed to show that the time had arrived for another 'impartial review of the resources and opportunities of Oxford, such as might be made by a Royal Commission'.[23] In subsequent articles on college finance, the relationship of the colleges and the university, the scholarships system, the entrance examination and on scholarly research, which Tawney wanted to support more actively, he exposed the obstacles that prevented the admission of poor students. And he developed an argument that was to have influence in Oxford over the subsequent initiatives in working-class education: that a university which had always been 'foster mother to the class which had been dominant in politics, education, and business' now had a duty to 'fresh sections of the community, on whom the responsibilities of education or administration are now devolving'.[24]

Zimmern wrote to Tawney to tell him of the effects of his pieces in Oxford:

> Your articles have been an immense draw; everyone is discussing them and
> most people are aggrieved, though at Univ[ersity College] they pay you the

immense compliment of saying you're "not grossly unfair." I fear you'll not be able to preserve your anonymity: I hear you are suspected both at Balliol and Merton . . . I am rather surprised at the resentment shown at criticism: but of course it comes from our thinking of Oxford as a national and most people here as a private corporation. . . . At present they are scared, rather irritable, and don't quite see what you're driving at beyond swearing at their incomes. Put in something somewhere to show that you realize the good side of corporate college feeling, but only think it too expensive a luxury.[25]

In his next letter Zimmern reported that 'they take us for agitators . . . an impression I find it rather exhilarating to encourage in the Common Room'. But he suggested that Tawney take the paradoxical line in his articles 'that it is we who are the true Conservatives', seeking to reform Oxford so that the university would be even better placed to provide national academic leadership.[26] The Oxford jurist, Sir William Markby, also wrote with congratulations:

I think your articles excellent. They are temperate + forcible + quite deserve the prominent place given to them by the W[estminster]G[azette] for which, by the way, I think we are greatly indebted to Spender. The answers to them in the W.G. + in the Ox[ford] Mag [azine] are nothing more than attempts to palliate – they do not answer the substance of the charges . . . it will be easy to show that there is a large surplus available after all reasonable needs of education have been satisfied . . . On the whole I think you are to be congratulated on having made an excellent start.[27]

By the end of the year Tawney's identity as the external ringleader of the group was common knowledge in the university, as a playfully supportive letter from Jeanette Beveridge makes clear:

Have just been to Oxford where I heard much of your articles that was sufficiently uncomplimentary even to satisfy me – It is really splendid that you are so unpopular though I am sorry that Oxford cannot judge impartially or rather impersonally. Your offence in holding the Jenkins (sic) (of which I was ignorant) is black indeed – If you like to furnish me with a logical justification for the obviously right I will try to make some use of it against future onslaughts.[28]

The second series of pieces in the *Westminster Gazette* made essentially the same points as the first. While much space in the third series of articles in *The Times* was devoted to internal reform of the procedures and constitution of the university and colleges, the context of developing national aspirations was not forgotten. As the authors wrote in their first article, 'The educational ideals of the country are in course of rapid growth. It is in essence a movement towards completer employment of human gifts and natural resources for national well-being, and it involves profound changes of method and organization. In this movement Oxford should have a share worthy of her best past.'[29]

Bishop Gore also raised the issue of university reform in a question in the House of Lords in July of the same year, calling for the appointment of a new royal commission 'to inquire into the endowment, government, administration, and teaching of the Universities of Oxford and Cambridge and their constituent colleges, in order to secure the best use of their resources for the benefit of all classes of the community'.[30] The reformers hoped that the threat of an enquiry would force Oxford into voluntary changes: as Gore explained, 'there is a desire that the Government should intimate an intention of appointing a commission but at the same time should delay its actual appointment for a year or two to give the Universities, as it were, a period of time to reform themselves'.[31] Similar arguments were set down in a letter in *The Times* on the same day that was signed by several of the reformers.[32]

These arguments were repeated for the best part of 6 years, during which time Oxford and Cambridge were threatened once more with outside investigation by the state. Internal attempts at constitutional reform *were* made, though many of the most controversial aspects of the ancient universities' arrangements remained intact on the eve of the First World War. Partisans for adult and workers' education in Oxford certainly employed the spectre of a commission to extract support for their initiatives out of the university. And Tawney, for one, remained faithful to root-and-branch reform of Oxford. But by 1912 the moment had passed and the idea of an enquiry and legislative reform faded, to be revived at the end of the First World War.[33]

The process that led Tawney to Rochdale and Longton in Stoke-on-Trent as the first teacher of tutorial classes under the joint auspices of Oxford and the WEA began at a special 'Joint Conference on Education of Workpeople' held in the Examination Schools in Oxford on 10 August 1907, which over 400 delegates attended, representing over 200 organizations.[34] The point of the conference was to win support for the establishment of a 'joint committee' of university figures and representatives of the working class to devise a new type of extramural education. The conference was to give its blessing to this, and solidify the coalition favouring reform of workers' education. The meeting was led-off by two papers from Walter Nield of Oldham, the President of the North Western Co-operative Education Committees' Association, on 'What Workpeople Want

Oxford To Do' and from Sidney Ball, a tutor at St John's College, Oxford and Fabian Society member, on 'What Oxford Can Do For Workpeople'. That they bore a resemblance may have had something to do with the fact that Tawney provided suggestions for both authors.[35] As Tawney explained in a note at the bottom of Ball's address, Samuel Barnett had sent a draft of Ball's remarks to Tawney in Glasgow: 'I wrote (i) suggestions for Ball (ii) suggestions for Nield. Both used them at the conference from which Tut[orial.] Classes started. Ball, not knowing the source of his and Nield's papers, commented with surprise and gratification on the similarity of their tone.' Nield concentrated on the provision of scholarships by which 'the best sons of workmen should proceed to Oxford easily' and on the organization of 'reasonably sized classes (under University conditions)' in working-class communities. Responding, Ball set out a scheme for such classes: 'One or two thoroughly qualified men might be selected for a period of three or five years to organise, in cooperation with local working-class associations, workmen's classes within a certain area: the classes themselves being arranged on a principle of a graduated and continuous curriculum of an Oxford type.'[36]

The Joint Committee was subsequently established under a statute passed by the University's Convocation. The seven Oxford members who sat on it were Thomas Strong, Dean of Christ Church; Herbert Turner, Savilian Professor of Astronomy from New College; Hastings Lees Smith, Professor of Economics at University College, Bristol; John Marriott, then in charge of the university's extension lectures' delegacy; and the three chief protagonists of working-class education in the university, Zimmern, Ball and A. L. Smith, a historian and later Master of Balliol. The seven nominated by the WEA included two Labour MPs, C. W. Bowerman and David Shackleton; W. H. Berry from the cooperative movement; Richardson Campbell representing the friendly societies; Alfred Wilkinson, a Labour councillor from Rochdale; J. M. Mactavish, a Scottish shipwright who had made a brilliant speech at the 1907 meeting and who would follow Mansbridge as General Secretary of the WEA, and Mansbridge himself.[37] In the event, the Committee's report, *Oxford and Working-Class Education*, often called the *1908 Report*, was written by Tawney with some help from Zimmern, while the final draft was perfected by Strong who was 'sure to phrase it right for Oxford reading'.[38] Tawney worked on it during the summer of 1908 while undergoing the agonies and ecstasies of rejection and acceptance by Jeanette Beveridge. As he wrote to her at one stage in jest, 'Did I tell you that the Labour People and the Oxford People are meeting on Saturday? I am rather excited about it as I filled the report with revolutionary sentiments and don't want them to be cut out.'[39] The report was published in November 1908. As Zimmern wrote to him having worked through Tawney's draft, 'I have paragraphed the Report as you wished: there are 144 sections. The more I read it the more I like it. We are all immensely in your debt. I only wish you would get the credit.'[40] With or without acclaim, it was a singular success for the reformers that their most effective penman had, behind the scenes, drafted the university's response to criticism of its exclusivity.

In *Oxford and Working-Class Education* Tawney reviewed the whole field of adult education, considered the current commitment to it on the part of Oxford, and presented the case made by working people for access to the university and its educational resources. He outlined the desired programme of tutorial classes, considering such matters as the curriculum and methods of study to be adopted. The report considered the admission of working people to the university and in its final chapter it even gave attention to 'the after career of working-class students'. It was hardly an investigative report given that the main recommendations were already clear to the Joint Committee before its work began. Indeed, it reads rather more as Tawney's manifesto for the educational rights of working people and as a plan of action that might be adopted by other voluntary bodies in the future. It was recommended that Oxford university extension should develop a new emphasis on class work; that each class should meet regularly for at least 2 years; that classes concentrate on advanced academic work with regular essays and final examinations. The management of the classes was to be the responsibility of local working-class organizations which would choose the subject and the tutor, and, to an extent, negotiate over the syllabus.[41] 'We have no fear at all' ran the *Report* 'that were the classes placed, as we recommend, under the direct control of workpeople, in co-operation with University men, they would be used for any but the highest educational ends.'[42] The tutors from Oxford were to be full-time appointees mixing tutorial class teaching with internal university instruction. In addition, the *1908 Report* emphasized that tutorial classes were not a substitute for study at the university, but a preparation for it: 'in the future qualified students from the tutorial classes should be enabled regularly and easily to pass into residence at Oxford, and to continue their studies there.'[43] It was to prove the most difficult of the various recommendations to realize.

Much later Tawney explained the document in his own words:

Oxford and Working-Class Education which appeared in 1908, was a document of considerable importance in the history of Adult Education in this country. It gave an account of the forces, which had produced the working-class demand for Adult Education; explained why the existing University Extension Movement failed to satisfy it; stated the conditions which must be met if a vigorous system of Adult Education for workers was to be created, and set out in detail the machinery required in order that such a system might develop. The proposals of the Report were accepted, not only in Oxford, but, with some modifications of detail, by other Universities. The development of the Tutorial Classes Movement, in which all English and Welsh universities now take part, and more recently of less exacting forms of adult education, has been largely the result of the work then done by the Oxford Committee.[44]

The first tutorial classes did not wait upon the publication of *Oxford and Working-Class Education*. At the end of 1907 Tawney had been invited to begin teaching two experimental classes and in January 1908, while the Joint Committee was sitting, they began in Longton and Rochdale in response to the representations received from both places to move beyond the constraints of university extension lectures.[45] After the 1908 Report had been published and the university had agreed to its recommendations, Tawney was formally appointed as the first tutor of the new movement – a crucial step not only in his academic career but also in his private life, as it partially answered the misgivings of his mother-in-law towards the marriage. He spent most of the summer of 1908 in states of impatience about a job, and despair and then relief about his relationship with Jeanette, and the two issues were interrelated. As he wrote to his fiancée at the end of June,

> I'm a bit worried about the future – not the ultimate future but the date of our marriage. Those wretched Oxford people are so slow in getting things carried through that, though they are nearly certain to offer me a fairly decent job, they may not actually make a "firm offer" till October when the colleges can be squeezed for the necessary money – That means that I shall be working on the [Glasgow] Post till then, and shall have to give up a great deal of time preparing lectures for October to March at very short notice . . . I don't want when I marry you to be overwhelmed with work in the first few weeks . . . As it is I sometimes feel qualms lest the new life should seem horribly strange and hurried to you after what you've been used to . . . I want you to be let down gently![46]

At the first meeting of the Tutorial Classes Committee in November 1908 it was resolved: 'That Mr R. H. Tawney, B.A., Balliol, be appointed as a teacher under the Committee, to take, if possible, 5 classes; the Committee to be responsible for £200 annual payment to Mr Tawney, and for Mr Tawney to reside and lecture in Oxford in the summer term'.[47] Tawney's relief was immense. He had stood out for a permanent position teaching Oxford's tutorial classes all year. Letters to Mansbridge in early 1908 suggest how cussed and demanding he could be in the pursuit of secure university employment and status.[48] He wanted to teach tutorial classes and also to be given an official position within the university; he would not be fobbed off delivering 'lectures in Oxford of an unofficial kind'.[49] All Souls College made a grant to the WEA for 3 years in the first instance with which they made up Tawney's salary to a more respectable level.[50] Indeed, Tawney was officially 'All Souls Teacher in Political Science' and delivered a course of lectures in the college each Trinity (summer) term for four consecutive years. But no college was willing to offer a fellowship to the tutor of these new classes: at Magdalen, for example, the idea was shot down by the fellows who 'simply say that College money oughtn't to be used for such a purpose'.[51] Perhaps this explanation from Zimmern to Tawney was designed to shield him from the truth. If so, Tawney was wise to it and under no illusions: as he wrote to Jeanette, 'Bad news! The Magdalen fellowship is off: they are so sick with me for attacking Oxford that they will not elect me. I am very sorry for the disappointment it will cause my people, and also because I should have liked to present you with it . . .'[52]

Tawney taught tutorial classes for Oxford for the next 5 years. Most were on economic and industrial history, but he also gave classes on seventeenth-century political history, economic theory and local government. A great deal of material about the first two Oxford tutorial classes has survived, both of which were taught by Tawney and both of which helped to establish his reputation as a university teacher and public figure. Tawney was still living in Glasgow when the classes began and he would leave the city on a Friday morning to arrive at Longton for a class that evening. He would stay the night and then go on for a Saturday afternoon class in Rochdale, returning home on Sunday.[53] Later, after their marriage, Tawney moved to Manchester to be closer to the districts where he was teaching.

Both classes were in 'Industrial History', specifically 'The Social, Industrial and Economic History of England, with Special Attention to the Seventeenth, Eighteenth and Nineteenth Centuries'. Economics and economic history were central to the curriculum of the new movement because, above all, the workers 'wanted to know something of the forces which had made them what they were'.[54] Tutorial classes were an exercise in understanding where working-class communities had come from, and also in thinking about where they might be

going. As Tawney put it in 1931, 'the problems of the future . . . are most likely
to be faced with success by workers who are familiar with the past history of
their industries, and who have studied the process of development by which the
trade union movement has reached its present position.'[55] A later report by the
education inspectorate into Oxford's programme of tutorial classes noted that
working class students 'have been willing to read "economic" history, or "social"
history, or "industrial" history in the belief that such special studies would throw
light on immediate problems of social life.'[56]

Tawney later described a tutorial class as 'the nucleus of a University
established in a place where no University exists'.

> Thanks to the fact that they are small, tutor and students can meet as friends,
> discover each other's idiosyncrasies, and break down that unintentional system
> of mutual deception which seems inseparable from any education which relies
> principally on the formal lecture. It is often before the classes begin and after
> they end, in discussions round a student's fire, in a walk to and from his home,
> that the root of the matter is reached both by student and tutor.[57]

At Rochdale, Tawney met a class 'almost, if not entirely, made up of "workmen"
in the strictest sense of the term' in the words of the class secretary, L. V. Gill.[58]
Another student, T. W. Price, then working at a local bleaching works, was more
precise:

> There are in the class 12 iron workers, 8 skilled and 4 unskilled, and 3 joiners.
> All the chief branches of the cotton industry are represented, spinning, weaving,
> bleaching and finishing. There are also 2 carpet weavers, a wool-sorter, a
> spindlemaker, a shuttlemaker, a printer, a housepainter, a picture-framer, an
> accountant's clerk, a cashier, a teacher, 2 journalists, and an insurance agent. Of
> the lady students one is a clerk, one a dressmaker, one a schoolmistress, and the
> fourth is a working-man's wife.[59]

Gill wrote to Mansbridge after the first class that 'Tawney captured them right
away'. He wrote again, after the second class, to explain that 'it is a case of love
at first sight on both sides. His lectures are brilliant, illuminating, simple, lucid,
eloquent'.[60] Price apparently 'went home as if I were walking upon air & was so
exuberant that my wife wanted to know what was the matter with me'. It was
not just that Tawney was 'the right man for teacher . . . we [also] have the right
kind of men and women in the class . . . men and women in earnest'. After only
2 weeks there could be no going back: 'None of us, now that we have become
acquainted with Mr Tawney & his methods, will be contented any longer with

the ordinary University Extension lecture; we want lectures that will stimulate us to work, not lectures that are half popular entertainments.'[61] J. W. Henighan, a general labourer, was wonderfully expressive:

> At nearly half-past two Gill entered the room followed closely by a young man wearing the gown; he was the much debated tutor . . . Briefly, Tawney stated his opinion of what the class should be, and without more ado delved deep into his work. My first impression was of surprise, first at his youth, and secondly at the sweet affable charm of his presence. There was none of the academic manner about him; none of that air which is so inclined to freeze; he was one of us. We had expected the frigid zone; we were landed at the equator. Tawney is not a teacher: he is a man with a soul.[62]

One of the students had taken a Bachelor of Commerce degree from the Victoria University, and he ended a long and reflective letter to Mansbridge with the judgment that 'from the teaching point of view and seriousness of students, I think our class compares favourably with real University work.'[63] But difficulties were inevitable when it came to the contribution that students could make. Henighan advised preparatory instruction in composition before future classes: 'In the case of workmen, essay-writing is the greatest difficulty, so few being able to express their thoughts in writing.'[64]

After the last class of the session, Alfred Wilkinson, a member of the Joint Committee, wrote to Mansbridge to sum up: 'Tawney has captured not only the heads but the hearts of his scholars; if you can get [another] don like him, we can turn England upside down in a few years' time.'[65] Tawney, for his part, also wrote a report on the first session of the Rochdale class which was printed in the local press. He noted the great improvement made by the students over the term and the excellence of the 'first five or six' of them whose work 'was on a level with that in the honour schools of the only universities with which he is acquainted'. He also took the opportunity to call for improved secondary education on general grounds and so that tutorial class students would have the necessary skills of composition, and for a reduction in overtime so that students would have leisure for study.[66] In his confidential report to the Delegates in Oxford, Tawney emphasized the quality of the best students whose 'power to grasp general ideas and to write forcibly and fluently was most striking'.[67] It is doubtful if he exaggerated their talent: Gill went on to become Secretary of the WEA's North West District and Price became Secretary of the Midlands District and the Association's first (and best) historian. And one of the two journalists in the class was A. P. Wadsworth, who went on to edit the *Manchester Guardian*, write distinguished histories of the cotton industry and become another of Tawney's lifelong and closest friends. Tawney recalled Wadsworth in an obituary as 'an alarmingly precocious youth of seventeen – Alfie as we called him – whose impish sallies, backed by formidable batteries of recondite information, ensured that the Saturday gatherings of which in the opening decade of the present century he and I were members, should at any rate be kept awake'.[68] So precocious was he that Tawney set him to work on papers in the cellars of the Rochdale Town Hall researching trade union organization, remuneration and living standards in early nineteenth-century Rochdale.[69] For his part Wadsworth used to say that 'Tawney made me'.

When A. L. Smith wrote to one potential donor to solicit funds for the new tutorial classes he praised the 'remarkable work' produced by the Rochdale students in their first months and offered to show copies of their essays as proof.[70] When Zimmern paid a visit to Rochdale in April 1908 he received 'a royal welcome': 'Price gave me the finest tea I ever had in my life, and we spent a jolly evening at the Club. I was really impressed with the class . . . and Tawney's treatment of the subject is masterly. It was an Oxford lecture in conception and treatment, not a popular lecture at all'.[71] The examination of students in the Longton class in 1908 was undertaken by L. L. Price, who, long before, had given Oxford extension lectures. He commented that 'the work sent in was of good quality for the most part, showing considerable knowledge . . . It was evident that great interest had been taken and much pains bestowed by the students. Some of the papers were remarkably full and accurate and most exhibited distinct signs of independent thought on the subject'.[72]

The Longton Class was rather different in social composition from that at Rochdale 'being representative of all sections of . . . the middle and working classes' and as such was undoubtedly more like the majority of tutorial classes to follow.[73] It comprised 'a gardener, a plumber, a potter's thrower, a potter's decorator, a basketmaker, a miner, a mechanic, a baker, several clerks, a librarian, a grocer, a miller's agent, a railway agent, a clothier, insurance collectors, and elementary school teachers'.[74] In fact there were 17 among the last category among a total of 38 in the class. One of the students later described the class as 'a cross-section of many callings and activities'.[75] The *1908 Report*, in reproducing the report of the class secretary, referred to this mix as 'ideal', reinforcing the perception that some of those who were ostensibly investigating specifically 'working-class education' also favoured the integration of the social classes through adult education.[76] Certainly the Longton class was unrepresentative of the local employment and class structure, but, as Tawney himself explained, the social divisions within the class were more apparent than real: 'Teachers, elementary and secondary, are often the children of work-people and marry them; while their salaries are so low as to place them, at any rate at first, in an economic position inferior to that of many artisans.'[77] A similar point was made in the first report of the Tutorial Classes Committee by Mansbridge and Temple: the clerks and shop assistants enrolled in the earliest classes were 'not usually classified as "workpeople"' but the majority of them still 'belonged to working-class families.'[78] The presence in the class at Longton of a knot of seasoned campaigners from the local branch of the Social Democratic Federation (SDF) is also noteworthy. As Tawney explained to Jeanette after one session,

> My class went off pretty well tonight: they've started a reading circle on Wednesday evenings to read Toynbee's "Industrial Revolution"; there's enthusiasm for you. But I'm afraid the ladies, mainly school teachers, feel rather left out in the cold, as the discussion after the class is usually dominated by enthusiastic socialists.[79]

To his amusement, Tawney found himself the object of political suspicion all round. The group from the SDF 'had been ordered by their secretary to resign on the grounds that the purity of their faith would be contaminated by contact with a heretic like myself'. On the other hand he 'was informed by the Chairman of the Education Committee that we could not have a room in which to meet because my weekly visits to the town would reduce it, as he said, to a den of anarchy'.[80] In classes Tawney himself would not be drawn: as Emery later recalled 'we were always speculating whether he was a member of the ILP or the Labour Party, but he never gave himself away'.[81]

At Longton, as in Rochdale, Tawney won universal acclaim: 'The lecturer was the right man in the right place and is evidently experienced in dealing with audiences of workpeople. He was lucid and eminently pure-minded in his treatment of the subject, and possessed the faculty of being able to capture and hold the interest of the class.'[82] Frank Emery recalled that Tawney was 'was not too particular about his dress'. Despite this,

> It was the man's face, the man's eyes, the way the man handled his subject which enthralled us. And for the first time in our lives we were brought into contact with the real teacher . . . For the first, say, twenty minutes you had the presentation of all the factual detail, all the stuff requisite for the understanding of what the discussion was likely to become later. Then for the following twenty minutes he

would give you the case for and against. And here you got a masterly analysis of all the sources because Tawney always taught wherever he could from the sources . . . And then during the third twenty minutes he would sum up and his summaries were always masterly. But you never could find where Tawney stood politically if he was dealing with any economic subject, or social or political subject as the case may be . . . he never gave himself away . . . at the end of each lecture there was an hour's discussion . . . they used to go for Tawney just like bulls at gates, and he used to enjoy it . . . the members – young members of the ILP and the young members of the old SDF, and there were quite a number of SDF members in those days, you know . . . well they used to ask Tawney these questions and he used to revel in his replies.

Reinforcing Emery's recollections, another student recalled that

From our varying standpoints we fired loaded questions at our tutor designed if possible to extract from him support for our own interpretation of events. But Tawney was not to be drawn in that way. With that slight twinkle in his eye . . . he would endeavour to give us a truly balanced outlook on the course of history . . . He had the virtue of all great teachers, in that he widened our minds and influenced us to read and think for ourselves.[83]

The surviving sources on the Longton class also provide information on the problems encountered. The class secretary, Edward Stuart Cartwright, wrote candidly to Mansbridge in November 1909 to explain them:

We are trying hard here to keep the class up to a high level. There are several of the newer members who find the subject very stiff owing to their defective preliminary education . . . One thing this has brought home to me, personally – how very difficult and distasteful the mere physical act of writing is to a miner or a potter. I can see this is a very big initial obstacle to surmount. I felt weary in spirit last night when it was brought home to me what spade work had to be done before the Tutorial Classes movement can begin its work proper.[84]

Because most of the students 'had little practise in composition' Tawney himself did not 'think it wise to press them too hard to write papers'.[85] A few months later Cartwright identified the greatest difficulty as 'the unstable conditions of life of the ordinary industrial student, with sometimes long and sometimes irregular hours of work, and the uncertainty of employment'.[86] Zimmern, writing about workers' education in North Staffordshire in 1914, itemized 'the ravages of overtime, the anxieties of unemployment, the suspicions of foremen and managers, the difficulties of obtaining quiet for reading and writing' as enemies of the working-class student.[87] Nevertheless, one of the students, Frank Emery, recalled Tawney's commitment to the highest standards: 'He never came down. He set the standard so high that sometimes you had to climb just like an Alpinist, you see, climb the mountain to follow Tawney. Always on the Olympian heights.'[88]

One of the students in Tawney's class in Wrexham expressed the frustrations of worker students in a letter written to Mansbridge asking to withdraw from the group:

> Having had practically no education I am handicapped at every point, the rules of grammar, composition, punctuation, and the sequence of historical persons and events are so absent from my knowledge as though they did not exist; for instance, I could not at the present moment say who was Queen Victoria's father, nor who preceded her in the monarchy and when I hear such names as William of Orange, Pitt and Sir Walter Raleigh, I don't know until I search for their history whether they were Primates, Pirates, Peers or Premiers. Of course, until I joined the Economics class I had never found it necessary to know anything about them because my life had been spent in a sphere in which the only important thing seemed to be the devising of some scheme whereby one could escape from what seemed to be the inevitable end of one's fellow workers, viz., poverty and that old British institution, the workhouse.[89]

Another student, already a member of one of Tawney's classes and painfully conscious of his educational handicaps – 'being raised in a drunken home and always travelling from town to town' – wrote for help: 'Having noticed the keen interest you have in the students under your charge it has given me courage to write asking your advice as to the best method of self-education; hoping that you won't regard this communication as impudent or insincere, Yours Joseph Walker.'[90] Yet another wrote with the sort of dilemma that inspired Tawney to become the champion of free secondary education for all in the interwar period. His daughter had won a scholarship to the local technical school but he still couldn't afford to send her.

> I should like to give her the advantage of a good sound education. But I am not in a possition (sic) to do so financially & I have to seriously consider how I should keep her while going through . . . Very little possibility of getting more & don't see how I ought to take on more than I can reasonably fulfil. You see I don't know how or where to turn to increase my income & my wife will not listen to her excepting (sic) the scholarship on my present wage . . . so if you could advise me I'd should be glad.[91]

We can imagine Tawney's reply, and it may well have influenced the outcome. A month later John Bailey wrote again to explain that he had 'come to the conclusion that she shall go & if things go worse, well I shall have done my best'.[92] A decade later this episode may have been in Tawney's mind when, in his famous book *Secondary Education for All*, he gave the following example of the sort of dilemma that afflicted parents:

> Shall I let my child accept the scholarship he has won at the secondary school? If I don't it is unfair on him. If I do, it is unfair on his younger brothers and sisters, who will go short of food.

Such situations led Tawney to advocate the introduction of maintenance allowances for children attending secondary schools from poor backgrounds.[93]

Reports on the first Oxford tutorial classes give a graphic insight into the disabling effects of fatigue, unemployment, poor housing, illness and poverty that disfigured working-class life in the first years of the century. The initial annual report on Oxford's tutorial classes gave an example of a student in Tawney's Longton class who worked for 626 hours in 9 weeks between February and April 1909, and concluded that 'the long hours of labour' was the 'greatest single obstacle to the extension of adult education'.[94] Tawney's own reports on his classes in 1909–10 inveighed against the 'systematic misuse' of overtime by some employers: 'A very promising student in one of my classes has worked from 6 a.m. to 9 p.m. every day from October to March, with the result that even when he can attend the class he is too worn out to read or do the requisite number of essays.'[95] At Longton in 1908, eight students ceased to attend the class between the beginning of the term in October and Christmas, and 'the chief reason was unemployment'.[96]

Nor was Tawney's life especially easy in these years: 'I've got to leave for Wrexham tomorrow by the 9 am train, in order to meet my class at tea in the afternoon and have a several hours wait at Cheltenham on the way. I find the trains so bad in this neighbourhood that I shall be sleeping away from [home] four nights in the week.'[97] Those who knew him well, or who travelled with him, marvelled at 'his amazing capacity for work' on the move, on station platforms, or in trains.[98] 'Sloth was to him a mortal sin.'[99] The discomforts were offset by the mutual support, camaraderie and sheer enthusiasm which usually developed. At Rochdale, for example, after the Saturday afternoon class, Tawney used to have tea and spend the evening at the home of one of the students 'and on these occasions other members of the class would crowd into the house to the limits of accommodation – and even beyond – and the discussion would often go on until the early hours of the morning.[100] It was the same at Longton. Cartwright recalled a particular scene:

> The class meeting is over, and we sit at ease, taking tea and biscuits . . . Talk ranges free and wide – problems of philosophy, evolution, politics, literature. Then R. H. T. reads to us Walt Whitman's "When Lilacs Last in the Dooryard Bloom'd"; this moves a student to give us his favourite passage from the same source: "Pioneers! O, Pioneers!" Another follows, quoting from a poem from Matthew Arnold that evidently has bitten him . . . And for some of us as we sit listening, a new door opens.[101]

That was written in 1929 and it echoes what Cartwright wrote in a report after 3 years of work in Longton in 1911: 'The tutorial class has made for something more than mental training, it has made for the development of the human spirit; and for many of us opened the door to a wider and deeper life.'[102] He wrote in a similar vein in a personal letter to Tawney:

> In our talks around the fire, in our long walks in the country, there has been a spirit of comradeship, a sense of the unity of all knowledge, which has prevented any narrowness or intolerance of outlook. It is not only economics in which we are interested but in all branches of art and thought. The class has broken bonds which kept us from a fuller and freer life. We are not so much possessed of a few more facts, but are changed. The effect of the class has been a development of the spirit rather than the mind . . .[103]

It is only the language of personal transcendence and idealism that can capture the experience of learning for these adult scholars. Tutorial classes may have provided the tools for the social emancipation of a class; they continued to offer students personal and emotional liberation, as well. As another student wrote to Tawney after the experience of studying for a fortnight in Oxford at the WEA summer school in Balliol, 'My outlook is wider. I think . . . I shall be able to get more pleasure out of life and I feel there are other spheres of usefulness to society besides those I acknowledged before I went to Oxford in 1910.'[104]

　　To the very end of his life Tawney was reminded by his students from these and other tutorial classes of his personal impact on them. 'I feel a sense of great indebtedness to you,' wrote one: 'I am one of a goodly number who look upon *our* Tawney as a "brick".'[105] Another contacted him after some hesitation:

> I have often wished to write to you, for often do I think of the pleasant hours I've spent in your company and with the class; and I am beginning to realize what

a great influence your teaching and personality has had on my life. And I want you to know these things, and, well, I want you not to forget an old student and his wife. . . .[106]

At the very end of his life came a letter from old Fred Rudge, one of the original Longton class, now eighty-one and still living in Stoke-on-Trent

> to thank you for all you did for me in those far off days at [the] Longton Class. I often wonder if in all your experience you have had a much tougher piece of raw material to try & educate . . . my interests had been . . . Horse Racing etc., the only writing I had ever done was to my mother & of course my girl . . . I still treasure the exercise books we used to write our essays in.

'I recollect your name very well,' replied Tawney. 'As soon as I saw it it carried my mind back to the Longton Class which was one of the most enjoyable experiences of my life.'[107] To another he wrote that he 'enjoyed such classes more than any other teaching work which I have done.'[108] Frank Emery was struck as much by Tawney's personal as by his scholarly qualities:

> He impressed us at once by his humility, and let me say this quite humbly, his nobility. I don't think I've ever met a more humble but yet at the same time a more noble creature. He was the type of man with whom his students never could become familiar, because he was too much the friend to become familiar with, and at the same time so aloof from the academic and scholarly point of view as to make you realise that here was true greatness . . . it's the man that impressed us, it was the impact of this man on the whole life of the district.[109]

Although students wrote of their own personal experiences, there was no contradiction in these classes between personal enrichment and the social project that was intended by this new movement. *Oxford and Working-Class Education* had insisted that a general elevation of the working class was the movement's goal. The WEA named its magazine *The Highway* to emphasize its mission to construct a broad path 'along which the average man and woman can travel towards a larger life' rather than an 'educational ladder' by which the lucky or talented few could escape their origins.[110] The early students rejected the idea that 3 years of study in a tutorial class should end in individual qualifications and certificates for the successful. The students in the original tutorial classes were also resistant to the idea that some of their number might qualify for scholarships to study at Oxford, even though this was an explicit aim in *Oxford and Working-Class Education*. The Rochdale class rejected the idea of three of its members going to the university in 1910. One of the class members wrote to

Tawney with their objections. They wondered how the students would be chosen
if the movement was opposed to competitive examinations: 'The fact is Tawney
I am afraid of the competitive. I can't see how we can avoid this & I can't imagine
competition as a beneficial influence in the kind of education we are after. Can
you?' They feared a change in the relationships within the class if a handful of
students might qualify for some sort of scholarship. They worried that Oxford
might turn the head of a Rochdale student: it would be a good idea 'if only the
members of the tutorial classes were cultured enough to see things in their true
proportions but that is not the case . . .'

> You say "we ought not to regard the Tutorial Classes as an end in themselves", no
> I don't think we ought – but we ought to regard them as a means to an end & that
> end should be the creation of a strong desire, a strong public opinion, in favour
> of a truly democratic system of education. That desire can be largely assisted, I
> think, by extending the tutorial class idea & the kind of education *Ideal* created
> by contact with Tutorial Classes will be healthy and pure if the scholarships are
> left out altogether.[111]

Opinion at Longton had been more divided, however, and in 1913 the class
wrote to the Tutorial Classes Committee in Oxford to endorse the idea of
scholarships, though only under specific conditions. Longton students remained
against the idea of prizes for the few in principle, but they 'would not have the
same objection to a student proceeding to the university with the definite object
of becoming a Tutorial Class teacher'.[112] Even this was controversial, however,
and met with 'vigorous opposition within the WEA'.[113] Nevertheless, funds were
found to bring three students to Oxford in October 1913, one of whom, (Albert)
Frank Emery, returned to the Potteries to follow a career in adult education, and
remained in contact with his former tutor to the end.[114]

Perhaps the finest example of the camaraderie and the collective endeavour
of the early tutorial class students was the North Staffordshire Miners' Higher
Education Movement, started in 1911 by the students of the Longton class. It
was intended to bring adult education to the isolated mining communities to the
north and west of the Potteries.[115] As Zimmern explained in 1914,

> These villages are for the most part difficult to reach and are thus removed from
> all contact with the ordinary opportunities of civilization. The university tutorial
> class students three years ago discerned in these semi-industrial villages a great
> field for missionary work, and as this coincided in point of time with a demand
> for higher education which came from the miners themselves, the two parties
> were quickly brought together and a new educational movement set on foot.[116]

It started with a meeting at the Stoke School of Mining in May 1911 which brought together members of the Longton tutorial class and representatives from some 20 neighbouring mining villages. Tawney gave an address on 'Higher Education Considered Apart From Industrial Training'.[117] The Longton tutorial class students organized it and were themselves the tutors, passing on the knowledge and insight they were gaining from Tawney to other workers.[118] After the first year students from other tutorial classes that had started or were in process in the Potteries shared the work. It was not successful in all locations, but the first classes reached approximately 200 students, and by 1916–17 the Movement was serving 650 students in 27 centres.[119] In 1921 NSMHEM merged into the newly established North Staffordshire District of the WEA. Seven years before that Zimmern related that he had attended a lecture given to 'an audience of miners in a village schoolroom on one of the ridges overlooking this vale of smoke'. The lecturer, 'a distinguished student of sixteenth century England' (and hence almost certainly Tawney) had apparently mused that if Erasmus himself had returned to Britain 'to meet his fellow scholars' and to 'investigate the revival of humanism in the England of today' he would have been directed to visit the Potteries.[120]

At one of the meetings of the Joint Committee responsible for *Oxford and Working-Class Education*, Mactavish had 'raised the question of the character and standpoint of the teachers. He said they must be men capable of approaching the subjects they taught from the working-class point of view . . . there was too little common language and sympathy between lecturers and working-class audiences.'[121] It was Tawney's achievement that he was able to find the common language and the sympathy to make the first classes so successful and thus set a standard and a model for the movement to follow. Beatrice Webb, who came to know Tawney very well, described him as 'a scholar, a saint and a social reformer'.[122] But that was written in the 1930s. In the Edwardian period Tawney was also among the more militant and impatient of the leaders of working-class education. While others put their energies into building the infrastructure and spirit of this movement, Tawney did not deviate from the position he set out in 1906 when writing anonymously in *The Westminster Gazette*: that provision for working-class students and communities was to go hand in hand with the reform of the ancient universities. He continued to press for a Royal Commission to investigate the finances and social composition of Oxford and Cambridge, and, as some remarkable letters to Mansbridge in the autumn of 1912 demonstrate, he took it upon himself to goad the WEA to pursue this course in parallel with its strictly educational work.

Tawney wanted the WEA 'to take risks' and 'to be willing to face anger at the Universities'. He wanted to see the Association 'stepping boldly forward and not merely asking for a Commission to inquire, but specifying in outline the abuses which need inquiry'. The Association's annual meeting should pass a resolution decrying such attempts at reform as had so far been made in Oxford; the *Highway* should 'commit itself to a forward policy'. To Tawney, the object of the WEA was 'not to be popular with all parties but to speak for those who can't speak for themselves, and the more unpleasant that is, the more readily it should do it'. It was necessary to take the initiative because, in Tawney's view,

> Oxford at least is sinking back into the bad old ways. Class prejudice is as strong there as ever (naturally it is not shown to you). Workpeople who go there for the summer school accept kindness when they ought to demand justice. Can you honestly say you think that the great system of educational and social privilege of which Oxford is the symbol is nearer being shaken than it was when the Oxford Report was presented? I cannot.[123]

The real object for Tawney was to open Oxford so that working people could study within the walls. Even while teaching tutorial classes and extolling their virtues in public, he regarded them as insufficient for the educational needs of the workers and as all too easily provided by a university that remained fundamentally unchanged by their existence. In a subsequent letter to Mansbridge he reminded him of the recommendation of the *1908 Report*: 'that Tutorial Classes were only a step towards throwing open the University & not a substitute for it'. Oxford was content to 'throw crumbs to labour in the shape of Tutorial Classes' and the annual Summer School: the initiatives since 1907 were 'a sort of "fire insurance"' for the university. (Zimmern had called the 1908 Report the university authorities' 'trump card in Reform from Within').[124] Indeed, it was 'becoming a settled doctrine at the Universities that Tutorial classes exhaust their responsibilities'. Hence the Oxford Joint Committee should demand a reduction in the cost of student living and a reform of the scholarship system to channel assistance to poorer students.[125] As he explained in a third letter, calling on the WEA to press the prime minister, Asquith, for a Royal Commission, 'directly we let educational authorities think we are almost satisfied, our day is over'.[126] Conciliation, as Tawney called it, had not succeeded. Pressure should be applied because Oxford was vulnerable. As he wrote to Mansbridge in exasperation, 'Don't you yet understand that Oxford started Tutorial Classes because it was *afraid?*'[127]

The accuracy of this comment may be open to some doubt. These letters had a purpose: Tawney was trying to stiffen the sinew of a man noted for his gentleness and emollience, and who was, as Tawney hinted in his first letter, rather too easily impressed by Oxford's charm and 'good manners'.[128] The evidence does not suggest that fear alone inspired Oxford's patronage of the new movement; indeed, a better word might be prudence. The enthusiasm of a minority met with the enlightened self-interest of considerably more dons, who recognized the merit in being seen to support the educational democracy, but showed no very great willingness to change the settled structures of the university and devote considerable resources to the project. Moreover, as we have seen, Tawney's own students in the first tutorial classes were suspicious of scholarships to Oxford for just a few of their number: the movement was feeling towards a collective ethic of education, which in other respects Tawney supported. And Tawney's putative assault upon his own university would have alienated Oxford from the movement for working-class education at a time when university and college finance, as well as good will, were crucial to it.[129]

Tawney's impatience, as expressed in these letters, and his continued campaign for extensive institutional reform of the universities, mark him out from many of his colleagues in the movement who seemed somewhat more willing to accept and use what was offered. Later images of him as a benign and statesman-like intellectual father-figure to the labour movement have tended to obscure the impatient radical of the Edwardian period. But Tawney's criticisms of Oxford and the relationship of the new movement to the university, which he had helped to construct, must be differentiated from those articulated at Ruskin College, Oxford, and in other parts of the labour movement from 1909. Ruskin, which had been founded in 1900 as a college for working men specifically and which was independent of the university, experienced the secession of some of its students and tutors in 1909 over the relationship of the college to these wider developments in adult education. The secessionists, who formed the Plebs League, explicitly rejected the tradition of 'liberal adult education' in association with universities and partially funded by the public purse that was being established at this stage, and developed instead a Marxist-inspired variant of workers' education that became the Labour Colleges movement and which sparred with the WEA for the next half century.[130] Tawney refrained from criticizing a parallel if essentially different educational movement which was also seeking to educate workers. But he did not approve of the mixing of educational with ideological aims. The point of a 'democratic education' was just that – it should be thoroughly democratic and provide students with the means to make up their own minds.

Late in his life, in 1953, at a time when the issue of alleged political bias in adult education was once more causing difficulties for the movement, Tawney recalled that, 'as a teacher of Tutorial Classes, I never felt tempted to engage in propaganda. A doubtless very improper conceit persuaded me that the world, when enlightened, would agree with me. I thought, therefore, that the longest way round was the shortest way home, and that my job was to promote enlightenment.'[131] In fact, to many in the movement, 'enlightenment' implied socialism, for a fair and dispassionate analysis of society and economy must inevitably result, they believed, in the acceptance of socialism, not only as a more just social system but as an economically more efficient one also.[132] The tutor did not have to indoctrinate, merely explain. On his 80th birthday the general secretary of the National Council of Labour Colleges, J. P. M. Millar, wrote to him with his congratulations and Tawney replied with recollections of their breakfasts together at a London hotel during the Second World War: 'In spite of the fact that we were supposed to be embittered antagonists, I think we found that we had more in common than might have been expected, remembering the official denunciations launched from both sides in which I, at any rate, usually refused to participate.'[133]

Mansbridge and Tawney tried to meet similar types of criticism from an influential antagonist in London, George Lansbury, with similar styles of emollience. They went together in the autumn of 1908 to a meeting in Poplar, Lansbury's political headquarters, where they expected 'to be attacked by hot socialists'. Lansbury was intending 'to oppose [the WEA] in Poplar'. Mansbridge wrote to him to explain the movement's aims:

> Our plan has been to go to any locality and at once to attempt, always with extraordinary success, to federate all working-class and educational organisations for purely educational purposes in an unsectarian and non-party organisation which must not deal with measures before Parliament, or likely to be before it – but must seek for labour all the education that can be got under the law, and to stimulate a real demand amongst those who at present make no demand.[134]

But such candour was never likely to have succeeded because it was the WEA's politically unaligned position which was the problem among 'hot socialists'. They feared a manoeuvre on the part of Oxford, reformist dons and liberal-minded collaborators from the working class to take the workers away from their true interests and consciousness. Lansbury's opposition endured and Tawney was still trying to win him round after the December 1910 general election, when he was returned for the constituency of Bow and Bromley. Tawney then invited him to the WEA's offices in London to see for himself, and explained that

> the backbone of the movement consists of men who are working at the politics side of the labour & socialist movement. Socialists predominate in all the classes I teach and I believe that this is so elsewhere, because it is they who know best what education can do for labour. Many a man has told me that the WEA has helped him to be of use in the trade union & labour movements. And none of them object to the WEA for being non-political in the sense of trying to aid students of all political views.[135]

The approach does not seem to have succeeded because 2 years later Lansbury took issue in the House of Commons with a suggestion apparently made by Tawney 'that the Labour Party ought to get and train its young men':

> I don't altogether agree: I'm very much afraid of taking them away from their work. They tend to become superior and "intellectual". I know it's difficult for them to do propaganda and other things without leisure. But they must fight it out somehow. I think the only "intellectual" in our party has not been good for it.[136]

This difference between them was to re-emerge much later when, after the division and defeat of the Labour Party in the 1931 election, Lansbury was its leader and Tawney was once more calling for intellectual leadership in the party and the careful planning of a political strategy. If Lansbury was suspicious of the politics of the WEA, Tawney was equally critical of Lansbury's anti-intellectualism and the wider failure to grasp the need for the training of the future leaders of the working class which he represented.

To Tawney, the process of political change depended on education: only by education could the moral reformation of society be achieved. But the change was not worth having if not arrived at freely and openly and without dictation or bias. Indeed, we can go further: it was in adult education specifically that Tawney met and helped shape an example of the good society – the tutorial class. The class was a functioning example of fellowship, equality and democracy and it also gave to its members the opportunity for spiritual self-realization. The experience of adult education gave Tawney 'his model of the socialist society'.[137] As Jay Winter has put it, 'These classes were voluntary groupings of men and women who came together out of their belief in a moral principle – the pursuit of knowledge, which was in Tawney's view one of the gifts of God.'[138] Indeed,

Tawney wrote in his *Commonplace Book* that people should 'think of knowledge, like religion, as transcending all differences of class and wealth . . . in the eye of learning, as in the eye of God, all men are equal because all are infinitely small'.[139] Teaching tutorial classes helped fix Tawney's convictions and suggested a lifelong vocation as teacher, therefore. According to his nephew 'the WEA was the greatest and most practical interest in Tawney's life'.[140] The classes themselves gave him insight into the values and organization of the kind of society he was seeking to create. They also provided an education in the life of the working class for the tutor himself. The *Commonplace Book* contains anecdotes and details about the employment and the attitudes of his students. And Tawney pressed his students to provide him with information on wages, piece-rates, hours, conditions and household budgets.[141] He, in turn, peppered his reports to Oxford with details of their difficulties and their exploitation.

The *Commonplace Book* was not the only book to emerge out of the early Oxford tutorial classes, nor was Tawney the only tutor to have learnt as he taught. In a textbook on economics published in 1916 Henry Clay also paid tribute to his students' 'wide and diverse industrial experience' and to their criticisms of the views he put before them.[142] Late in his life Tawney reflected that if he 'were asked where I received the best part of my own education, I should reply, not at school or college, but in the days when as a young, inexperienced and conceited teacher of Tutorial Classes, I underwent, week by week, a series of friendly, but effective deflations at the hands of the students composing them'.[143] He not only learnt from his students, but managed also to achieve that personal integration into working-class communities that had eluded him in a very different social context at Toynbee Hall. As Gill wrote in his class secretary's report from Rochdale in 1910, their tutor had 'established for himself a position in the town especially among Labour men, and his withdrawal from Rochdale would be looked upon as a calamity by a far larger circle than the members of the class'.[144] Later he would be invited back as Labour parliamentary candidate in the constituency. Learning from his students was all part of the essential equality of tutor and student in the tutorial class. It also appealed to a man who was an instinctive democrat and who looked forward, in the words of the *1908 Report*, to 'the development of a democratic education and of an educated democracy'.[145] As Tawney told the people of Rochdale in 1910, 'In the past, education had been supplied too much by churches, philanthropic institutions, and a group of benevolent officials at Whitehall. It should be supplied by the people for the people.'[146]

4

The Somme

In 1913 Tawney gave up full-time tutorial class teaching to take up a position in social research as the first Director of the Ratan Tata Foundation attached to the London School of Economics. According to his wife, who had been seriously ill since 1910, 'we had no wish to come south except for feebleness on my part which seemed to prevent my acclimatizing myself to the grey sunless northern climate.' After 5 years of intensive teaching perhaps Tawney was ready for a change, nonetheless – and the advantages of a move to London which would allow him access to the political and intellectual life of the capital were obvious. In 1912 when C. P. Scott offered him a more senior position on the *Manchester Guardian* as a leader writer specializing in 'labour subjects' it was evidence that Tawney was winning recognition and reputation and becoming a public figure.[1] Harry and Jeanette took a flat in Mecklenburgh Square, between Bloomsbury and Holborn, which, on and off, would be the location of their homes for the rest of their lives and which, with the dedication of a blue plaque in 1980 outside no. 21, their last home, will be associated with Tawney in perpetuity. For his part, Tawney was very comfortable in Bloomsbury, but made a clear distinction between the geographical area and 'Bloomsbury' used as shorthand for the literary circle and lifestyle of the Woolfs and their friends, which was, he wrote, a 'mental disease'.[2]

The Ratan Tata Foundation was established to undertake research into the prevention and relief of poverty.[3] Ratan Tata was the second son of the Indian industrialist Tata, and he pledged funds for the initiative when he met Sidney and Beatrice Webb, the founders of the London School of Economics (LSE), in Bombay in 1912.[4] Tawney began work at the start of 1913, adopting as the first project a review of the trade boards established in 1909. He recruited a group of young and talented researchers and reformers, and over the next 3 years a series of their monographs was published, each of them a distinguished work in its own right. Arthur Greenwood, later a Labour Minister of Health, investigated the health of schoolchildren in a book that utilized the reports of elementary school medical officers on 800,000 children.[5] The Foundation's secretary, M. E. Bulkley, added two further studies on the provision of school meals (and, more generally, the nutrition of schoolchildren) and on the effects of the Trade Board Act in the box-making industry.[6] This established that the minimum rates being paid under the terms of the legislation were actually below those already being paid in many parts of that industry. A. L. Bowley, later a very notable social statistician, led a comparative study into working-class living conditions in four English towns, Northampton, Warrington, Stanley and Reading, which concluded that 'permanent, as distinct from occasional, poverty exists in certain places on a scale which is really appalling.'[7] A final study based on interviews with nearly 900 tailoresses and more than 300 boxmakers in Stepney and Bethnal Green in 1913–14 examined the impact of homework on women.[8] Tawney himself added two similar studies on the effect of minimum rates in the chain-making industry and in tailoring in London.[9] Several of these books were published during the First World War, the last as late as 1916, and Tawney contributed introductions to them all, some almost certainly written from army camps and depots in England.

Worthy as this work may seem – and it certainly amounts to an important and overlooked contribution to the study of poverty in England in the wake of the revelations of Charles Booth and Seebohm Rowntree a generation earlier – it may appear to have been a step backwards for Tawney. In 1908 he had substituted the study of industrial conditions and the teaching of industrial workers in the north for the study of poverty among the casual poor of London's East End, a change of focus that not only led him towards a vocation as a teacher but also changed the nature of his politics by bringing him into contact with self-sufficient and skilled working men. Why, then, return to the study of sweated labour in the capital? The answer may be found in Tawney's inaugural lecture as Director of the Ratan Tata Foundation in October 1913 at the LSE entitled 'Poverty as an Industrial Problem'. Here, he set out an original and unorthodox approach to poverty which substituted a focus on the many in regular work for the traditional concentration on casual workers and the unemployed. Poverty, argued Tawney, was not about exceptional need but about ensuring that in normal circumstances the normal man received a normal remuneration sufficient to meet his normal requirements.

> The problem of poverty, as our generation understands it, is not primarily why certain persons fall into distress. It is why the product of industry is distributed

in such a way that, whether people fall into distress or not, large groups among them derive a meagre, laborious and highly precarious living from industries from which smaller groups appear to derive considerable affluence.

Other social investigators had related poverty to low wages: Henry Mayhew writing in the middle of the nineteenth century was one of the first. But Tawney was going further in calling for a redirection of intellectual effort to think first about the majority when conceptualizing poverty. He complained that for too long poverty had been understood in terms of its effects, not its causes. It was treated at the point of manifestation rather than at the point of origin, which was in work itself. It was in this sense that he now understood the problem of poverty as 'an industrial one' located in mills and mines but 'not in casual wards and on the Embankment', the traditional location for those sleeping rough in London. He traced the shifting 'centre of interest' since the New Poor Law of 1834 'from pauperism to poverty, from poverty to the distribution of wealth, from the distribution of wealth to the control of industry' which was the emerging issue of the early twentieth century. Now, he contended, the student of social conditions had to investigate 'the low normal standard' rather than 'the man below the margin'.[10]

Tawney's approach was obviously coloured by his 5 years in the north, living and working within industrial communities and observing a different sort of need and want. The 1913 lecture was self-consciously unorthodox, an attempt to shake up an audience used to thinking about social deprivation as a problem located among a definable unskilled minority in a particular place. It might have spawned a new line of urban and social research. It certainly registers the change in Tawney himself between 1908 and 1914. He left London disillusioned by charity and good works among the East End poor; he returned with respect for the industrial working class and for the political culture they had created. But Tawney's radical approach to the problem of poverty, if this it was, was cut short by war. When he emerged from the fighting at the end of 1916 the subjects on which he then concentrated were different from those of his youth. The reorganization and control of industry had usurped the problem of poverty because industrial reform and, through it, the construction of a more equal society, would, Tawney hoped, alleviate if not abolish gross deprivation. As he wrote in 1920, 'Prior to the war students and reformers were principally occupied with questions of poverty. To-day their main interest appears to be the government of industry'.[11]

In early August 1914 Jeanette and Harry watched from their window overlooking Mecklenburgh Square in London as young men in uniform drilled

below. Tawney then went on a walking holiday with his former student from
Longton and close friend, E. S. Cartwright, only to be arrested when Cartwright
relapsed 'into his native patois' from the Potteries and they were mistaken for
spies! 'It took some labour to convince a rural policeman in a benighted Southern
county that when the authentic Hun set out to spy he was better equipped than
with fishing rods and a lurcher.'[12] Harry and Jeanette next went with friends on
an extended holiday to Wharfedale in the Yorkshire Dales but it 'was rather a
poor-spirited affair' as events in Flanders 'pulled [them] up with a jerk'.[13] Tawney
was initially disinclined to join up: 'Harry is feeling very strongly that he must
not go & I really think he is right', wrote Annette Beveridge to Will.[14] But as
friends, academic collaborators like P. A. Brown, a WEA lecturer with whom he
had edited a selection of historical documents for use in the Association's classes
that was published in 1914,[15] and WEA staff members enlisted, he became
'thoroughly restless with his academic work'. He tried first to join the Artists'

Rifles but realized that he would not be comfortable in a corps of made up of
conventional public school and university men. 'He then decided to enlist as
a private in a North country regiment. As the profession was quite unfamiliar
to him, he was not ashamed to learn it from the bottom.'[16] On 26 November
1914 he signed up for the 7th City Battalion of the Manchester Regiment as
a private.[17] The battalion had been formed 5 days earlier by the Lord Mayor
of Manchester and the major cotton manufacturers in the city (which would
surely have brought a rueful grimace to Tawney's face).[18] In time this became the
22nd Manchester Battalion in which Tawney served up to the Somme offensive.
It was one of seven so-called 'pals battalions' raised in Manchester (the 16th,
17th, 18th, 19th, 20th, 21st and 22nd battalions of the Manchester Regiment)
which enlisted local men – friends and neighbours – with the promise that they
would serve together rather than be dispersed to regular army regiments. In this
way it was hoped that more men would volunteer. There were pals battalions
from cities like Liverpool and Leeds and from smaller towns like Grimsby ('the
Chums') and Accrington in a 'phenomenon particular to northern industrial
towns'. From Salford, adjoining Manchester, came four battalions of Salford Pals,
the 15th, 16th, 19th and 20th Lancashire Fusiliers. Northern working-class men
in the ranks of these battalions were commanded by southern officers, many
from the public schools. Almost 10,000 enlisted in the Manchester Pals, many
of them clerks from the city's cotton-broking businesses.[19] Of these, 4,776 were
killed in the course of the war.[20]

Why did he enlist? He was very nearly 34 years of age, making him an old
soldier from the outset. Many men from his background or of his age declined

to serve, or found more sedentary ways of helping their country in official capacities within government. Many liberal intellectuals and socialists opposed the war outright. Tawney never set down a clear statement of his reasons – or if he did it has not survived – but an aspect of his thinking was caught in a letter he received a few days later from J. L. Hammond, the great pioneer of social history in Britain, who had become an admirer and confidant of Tawney's. Lawrence Hammond disapproved of his decision to fight, though he thought it improper to intervene in a matter of individual conscience of such magnitude. Given Tawney's promise as a scholar and reformer, he was simply 'anxious that you should come back unhurt'. Hammond, who supported Britain's participation in the war, expressed the motive that he believed explained Tawney's decision: 'If we think that this brutal and barbarous duty is a duty to others, why not for us?'[21] Tawney did think that there was a duty to resist German aggression which was the manifestation of the malformation of German values and society. On 22 September 1914 he had added his name to a letter in *The Times*, 'Authors and the War', which endorsed an earlier letter, 'Britain's Destiny and Decision', signed by a wide variety of writers. Both sets of signatories supported Britain's involvement in the conflict, citing the violation of treaties and international norms by Germany, the brutality of German behaviour and Britain's responsibility to uphold her obligations to Belgium. Tawney's letter was signed by writers 'who have interested themselves more especially in the history and progress of democratic ideas' and included G. D. H. Cole, R. C. K. Ensor, Barbara and J. L. Hammond, and George Unwin, Tawney's mentor and professor of economic history in the University of Manchester.[22] Later, Hammond himself would join up.

In his later pamphlet of 1917, *Some Thoughts on Education and the War*, Tawney characterized the German spirit as 'the antithesis of individuality, of spontaneous personal aspiration and endeavour and sacrifice'. It was a spirit 'which organises men but does not inspire them, which cultivates them but does not love them, which makes a mighty state but neither a democracy nor a church'.[23] It followed that if this spirit had to be opposed, and if ordinary workers were to do the fighting, the same solidarity which had led Tawney into workers' education must lead him also into war. For some years he had identified himself with the cultural and political aspirations of workers; to leave to them alone what was a common duty would have been a kind of betrayal. This was not a conventional kind of patriotism, though Tawney evidently felt that the best of British values were worth defending and upholding. But it was patriotism of a sort, an identification if not with a reified nation and country, then with its ordinary people. As the secretary of the Longton Tutorial Class, Harry Jenkins, wrote to him at the time:

'I know you are doing this for the highest motive of all, devotion to one's country quite apart from personal and material considerations, and for that reason I feel that whatever in my power lies to carry on your interrupted work here, I will do it for your sake.'[24] The claim that Tawney took up arms because Germany was 'a metaphor for political evil' and that he was moved by his Christianity to take his place in the ranks are not supported by the evidence.[25] There is no reference at all to a specifically religious obligation in any of his public or private writings. To Tawney Germany was not a metaphor for political evil but the thing itself, which he opposed in order to uphold civility and democracy. His last entry in his *Commonplace Book* at the very end of December 1914 certainly contends that the war was a continuation of the conflict of forces, classes and wills in capitalist society – that it was 'the natural outcome of the ideals and standards which govern Western Europe, especially Germany and England, in its ordinary every day social and economic life'. Thus 'if we are to end the horrors of war we must first end the horrors of peace'. But if he was fighting *against* the brutalization and exploitation of everyday life in advanced industrial societies, he was also fighting *with and for* his fellow men.[26]

As is well known, Sergeant Tawney (as he became) did not take a commission but remained with the lower ranks in what has generally been taken as another example of solidarity. In reality Tawney was unclear about his best course of action and dithered about becoming an officer. As he wrote to Jeanette in late 1914,

> I have been in some perplexity about this Comm-n. Everyone here, Chapman, Unwin, an OTC man I saw, urge me to take it on the grounds that there is a shortage of officers. On the other hand I shouldn't myself much like it, and I should feel nervy & out of place pretending to teach what I don't know myself. So I have virtually decided to refuse, at any rate for the present. I don't think you would get any more money if I took it, owing to the expense involved, though people I asked told me I could save a little.[27]

These were the terms of Tawney's internal debate for the next few months as, from several sources, it was suggested that he take a commission. The money was no secondary issue and his letters to Jeanette are filled with calculations on whether the cost of joining the officers' mess would offset any increase in his army pay. Tawney's selflessness in enlisting was costing them dear: as a mere research fellow at the University of London on a short-term contract, there was no obligation to pay him after he joined up.[28] Until 1917 the couple were under acute financial pressure which was briefly alleviated when Jeanette took a job as a Temporary Factory Inspector in the Home Office. When, at the end of 1915 the battalion's Commanding Officer was 'asking questions as to "public school" men who were NCOs or privates' the Adjutant tried again to persuade him to take a commission, but Tawney still declined. 'What do you think?' he asked Jeanette.

> As to the money I find it almost impossible to decide whether there is anything in it one way or the other, & if so, how much. As to myself:- I think on the whole I am probably not more useless as an NCO than I should be as a subaltern and my natural inertia disposes me to stick to the job to which I am more or less accustomed now. I shall always detest the army and all its ways in whatever capacity I were employed; and now I know the unpleasantnesses of a private's and an NCO's life, I am disposed not to probe further into those of an officer's – mere cowardice I dare say. Really I am what you call "indifferent"[29]

Tawney stayed in the ranks, therefore, but it was not the product of an unambiguous desire to serve with the men, though it would be a fair speculation that he probably felt more comfortable with them than with products of his own background. He was made a corporal in the 5th platoon, B Company, 22nd Service Battalion of the Manchester Regiment in April 1915, and a sergeant 5 months later. But as a non-commissioned officer Tawney was subject to what the sociologists call 'status incongruity': it was difficult for him to fraternize with officers, even if they were his personal friends, and they had to treat him as their inferior. As one of those friends, J. W. Ramsbotham, who also became a lecturer at the LSE, wrote to Tawney many years later,

> I wonder if you remember those Sunday afternoon teas [in early 1915] where you and I and your friend and collaborator A. E. Bland were all serving in the army? As you had refused to apply for a commission, whereas Bland and I held one – in fact, he had become your company commander – and as Army regulations prohibited social association in public of officers and other ranks – and I remember *you* were a bit of a stickler for Army discipline in those days – we had tea served in my hotel bedroom.[30]

By a trick of fate one of Tawney's friends and close academic associates, Alfred Edward ('Bill') Bland who *had* accepted a commission was attached to the 22nd Manchesters from early in 1915 and promoted to Captain in the following year. Educated at Christ's Hospital and Queen's College, Oxford, he had worked in the Public Record Office since graduation in 1904 and lectured for the WEA in London. In 1914 Bland had turned down a chair at Melbourne University, choosing to enlist instead. Captain Bland and Sergeant Tawney would have had much to discuss, for sure.

Tawney's first weeks as a soldier were spent drilling in the streets of Manchester. Early in the new year his battalion was sent to a base in Morecambe.[31] In April 1915 they transferred to Belton Park, Grantham as part of the 91st Brigade, 30th Division, and in September to Larkhill, near Salisbury.[32] On 11 November 1915 they landed at Boulogne in France, becoming part of the 91st Brigade, 7th Division in which formation they were to fight.[33] Tawney wanted to be a good soldier and he took the training seriously. He knew that as an older man used to sedentary work he had to get fit – 'for a month or two, till I get into condition, I shall find it rather exhausting'[34] – and he was pleasantly surprised and satisfied that on first practising trench-digging, 'I found I could do it as well as most of the others and am only a little stiff today'.[35] When target practice began in April 1915 he was pleased: 'I did quite well, and made a good "group", ie got all my shots close'.[36] Later he explained that they had 'practised bomb-throwing, getting into trenches and throwing small bags filled with sand as imitation bombs. It is more difficult than it sounds for the trenches are very narrow and deep and if we knock the side we'd probably be blown up'.[37] Like many a soldier, and as someone whose untidiness was legendary, he found the routines painful: 'polishing brass buttons & buckles' for an inspection was 'an occupation which I detest'.[38] Nor did he relish the prospect in March 1915 of travelling back to Manchester to be reviewed by Lord Kitchener.[39] Tawney also used to tell the following story as evidence both of his ineptitude for command and of the British army's hidebound regulations. Apparently

> he was marching some men towards a cliff. He ordered them to turn right, which would have landed them in the sea. Just in time he said "Sorry men! I mean left. I never could tell the difference". He was reprimanded by his officer and he tried to explain how he often got confused about left and right. Said the officer, "I'm not reprimanding you for not knowing the difference between left and right. But NEVER apologise to the men".[40]

As a Tommy's wife Jeanette received a weekly allowance of a meagre 12/6 a week, though first she had to find their marriage certificate to prove they were married. To receive the allowance she had to report to a distant post office where the postmistress treated her as if a supplicant for outdoor relief rather than the wife of a soldier on active service. Part of the problem was another form of 'status incongruity' – that she, a middle-class woman should be married to a common Tommy and in need of public support. In the early stages of the war no institution was capable of adapting to the disruptions and unprecedented personal situations of wartime. Thus, as Jeanette described in her autobiography, women left behind were often treated badly by officialdom.[41] Her comical dealings with the regimental paymaster came to an honourable draw; he agreed to pay her an extra weekly allowance of 3/6 because she lived in London (unlike most of the wives of soldiers in a regiment raised in Manchester) but he docked her separation allowance for the period at the end of 1914 when her husband was billeted in Manchester and 'in receipt of lodging, light & fuel allowance'.[42] For a time she took in a refugee Belgian couple but their demands became too much for her and they moved on. By the end of 1914 the Tawneys' lack of money propelled Jeanette to look for a job, therefore. But she found that she either lacked experience or, with an Oxford degree, was considered overqualified. Her brother's intervention secured her an interview at the Home Office, however.[43] She was engaged for a month's trial 'on a special inquiry oddly enough one in which Will is also engaged concerning the ways in which it may be possible to get more recruits by replacing men's labour with women . . . I find the work interesting but very difficult at first until one has got the ropes firmly in hand . . . It is good to have got some work of such an interesting and important nature'.[44] She was then made a Temporary Factory Inspector at a salary of £200, apparently the first married female inspector to be taken on by the Home Office. For more than a year she travelled the country inspecting works, mills and shops, enjoying more than domestic responsibility for almost the first time in her life, though always battling against illness and lack of strength. When her health broke down in the spring of 1916 her parents wanted her to return to the family home and live with them, but Tawney intervened to prevent this.[45] Subjected to a stream of abuse in a laundry in Godalming, Surrey, she persevered with a prosecution. For 'obstructing a lady factory inspector' the foul-mouthed proprietor was convicted and fined, and the laundry shut down some months later.[46]

Tawney wrote to his wife frequently – two or three times a week at least – and to friends and relations like Will Beveridge and his sister Mil. Much of Tawney's correspondence with Jeanette during this time was about periods of leave: when they could expect it; how they would enjoy it; and why it had not been granted. He wrote occasionally to request warm clothing from family members. He didn't complain very much, though the poor quality of the food when the regiment was based in Grantham had led to complaints: apparently 'one soldier sent his breakfast (which consisted of a piece of bacon small enough to go into a match box) to the Lord Mayor of Manchester & now there is considerable improvement'.[47] There was a good deal of speculation about when and where his battalion would be sent after they were trained and for a few days in October

1915 the rumour was that they were being sent to Serbia.[48] As he then wrote to Lawrence Hammond,

> There are constant rumours of our moving at short notice, whether for France or Serbia, I don't know: at the present moment the latter seems to be the favourite, though I hope it may be the former for I can't get up much enthusiasm for shooting Bulgarians.[49]

But by early November Tawney knew otherwise and broke into Latin to tell Jeanette: 'Our destination is, I feel pretty sure, not the remoter one suggested. According to the present rumour – Latine scripto Censoris causa – ibimus Southampton vendredi et inde in Galliam.'[50]

Tawney had always expected that they would be to be sent to France and he began perfecting his French early in 1915. He took lessons with a Belgian refugee when based in Morecambe, which involved translating *War and Peace* from English into French.[51] He packed his French dictionary before crossing the Channel and while in France he read the *Chanson de Roland* and Saint Simon's memoirs among other French works sent out by Jeanette.[52] Unsurprisingly, his fluency in the language was put to use by his superiors and Tawney found himself constantly on call to organize all aspects of the billeting of British troops on war-weary French communities. Soon after landing in France he wrote that he had 'interview[ed] the mayor on his way to market, an old gentleman driving a loaded cart very slowly with the puzzled expression of one who wondered what les Anglais could be up to here.'[53] Later he reported that 'I have had long stories of stolen fowls, and borrowed furniture poured into my ears, and a sympathetic listener comes to be regarded as a friend of the family.'[54] His own first billet in France, about fifteen miles behind the front line, was an unconventional affair: as he wrote to his sister, 'I and another sergeant sleep in a little hut one half of which is occupied by a pig – a very clean and quiet one, and the other half by us.'[55]

A consistent theme running through Tawney's letters from France was his admiration and affection for the French: 'They are very decent people and my minute attainments in French are an enormous advantage ... I admire the women very much. They work all day, as there are no men to do anything, and though obviously depressed, are courageous.'[56] He confessed that he 'rather like[d] loafing about French villages: the people are pleasant and I enjoy gossiping with them & seeing how they live. Such French peasants as I have met seem to me a courteous and civilised set of people, with whom one can converse without awkwardness.'[57] The warmth of his welcome in many French homes heartened him. In one letter he related that he had returned to a restaurant he had patronized 3 months before and the lady of the house had greeted him with genuine warmth and affection. He also returned to the home where he had been billeted and the French occupants recognized him immediately and were overjoyed to see him returned – and alive.[58]

Tawney, like so many British soldiers, was irritated and often appalled by the ignorance of the British public, who could not visualize the nature of the warfare across the Channel, and by the crude jingoism of the British press which encouraged civilians to demonize Germans. As he recalled in a lecture given during the Second World War, 'in the last war there was little hatred of Germany among men at the front. It was only when one returned home on leave that one encountered among old ladies of both sexes sentiments of an atrocity that made innocent soldiers feel quite ill.'[59] In comparison he believed he saw a different attitude in France:

> What is truly elevating in the French, what inspires one in conversation of quite humble people . . . is that they feel France is fighting for an ideal which is not purely French, that she represents a wider patriotism than that of any one nation, that she is, in a sense, the trustee of the future of humanity . . . And so they do not commit the schoolboyish folly of The Times, Daily Mail etc., in identifying the whole German nation with the crimes of the military caste & general staff . . . No, the French perhaps because they are suffering more than us, have kept their heads better.[60]

Tawney first went into the line in December 1915; thereafter it was an alternating pattern of between 4 and 7 days spent in the trenches followed by a similar length of time recuperating behind the lines. In letters home he played down the dangers all the time:

> The fact that my company had no casualties at all last time it was in shows that there is not much risk of being hurt . . . I rely on you not to let yourself be worried. I know that when one is at home one thinks of the trenches as the scene of constant peril. Really they are nothing of the kind. It must take at least 1000 shells to hurt one man, and of course shelling goes on only for a very small portion of the time. What one thinks most about is the weather.[61]

To Beveridge he was rather more honest:

> The Boches make a good deal of sniping, but they seem to drop into a settled routine – so many shots at certain points at certain times – and when one picks up the idea one keeps away from the dangerous points & is fairly safe.[62]

He lamented the deadening effects on the emotions and the intellect of periods spent in the trenches:

> The artificiality of war lies rather heavily over one's spirits, and the world of permanent and spontaneous human interests seems to be behind a kind of drop curtain which won't lift till one marches back out of the range of the guns and out of sight of villages given over to soldiers and a countryside rearranged for the purposes of destruction.[63]

He complained of the lice and the vermin, and the mud that clung to everything when it rained – as it did persistently in February and March 1916. The problem of the mud was exacerbated by the standard uniform: 'What one requires is fishermen's oilskins. What they give one is greatcoats of a spongy material which sucks up all mud and water within reach.' Instead of decent rucksacks 'we are given a thing like a lady's hatbox – an evil thing at all times but an instrument of torture on one's back'.[64] By April conditions had improved and Tawney then sent Jeanette a poem for publication: 'Would you care to send it to *The Nation* if you think it good enough. If so sign it "infantryman" or something non-committal and keep my name out of it – and make them pay you'.[65]

> To G
> At noon he chatted frank & gay
> At one I saw him borne away
> One hideous formless wound.
> A sandbag held his shattered face
> Feet, hands & chest at every pace
> Slipped crimson on the ground
> He has left this world of beautiful things
> The hawk that hovers, the lark that sings
> In the smoke of the bursting shell.
> When he fell its sweet song did not cease.
> He has left all these; he has left me peace
> Once more – Pass friend, all's well
> (*Infantry man*) or *From the Trenches, April 1916*

A week later he added a little commentary on what he'd written in another letter:

> I'm afraid my verses were rather gruesome (- perhaps in more senses than one! -). The description is worse than reality. It is not a poetic fancy about the hawk and lark. I have watched the former hover for rats and mice even when shells must have been passing within 50 yards of them and larks sing continually when it is fine.[66]

If hardly among the best of First World War poetry, the very familiarity of the themes in Tawney's poem, so like so many other poems from the trenches, confirms its authenticity: the fine line between living and dying, the contrasts between men's conflicts and the natural world; between the song of a bird and the roar of a shell; between the battle and the peace of death are common to so much of the writing that distinguished and in a certain way redeemed the First World War.

Tawney had time for personal and political reflection while in France. There are no reasons to doubt that his private religious faith had ever wavered, but there was evidently a long period in his life when he had not felt able to express his religious commitment by taking holy communion. However, as he wrote to Jeanette on 26 December 1915,

> Today I did two things which I have not done for a great many years. I played a game of football in the afternoon. And I attended a communion service in the morning. I am glad I did the latter. I have always had qualms as to whether a person like myself had any business to take part in the Central Office of the Church. But I think one must follow one's intuition or instinct in these matters . . . and I feel I did right. It was a pleasant service attended by one officer (the Major who looks a decent sort of chap) and a few men and NCOs & held in a little French school . . . The atmosphere of bareness & simplicity & absence of all except the essentials was elevating & pacifying to one's spirits.[67]

He was also moved to reflect on the relationship between life in the army and the wider health of British democracy. In a remarkable episode he was summoned to British headquarters at St Omer, along with three other members of the Fabian Society – Frederic [Ben] Keeling who was later killed on the Somme, R. D. Gillespie and C. M. Lloyd – and also Jimmie Mallon who had come over from London, 'to discuss what action the government might take in view of the labour troubles on the Clyde' with the head of recruitment at the War Office, General Geddes. They composed together an 'appeal from the Trade Unionists at the front to the Trade Unionists at home' asking that the troops be supported by their worker-comrades, but the document was never published.[68] In an equally remarkable letter to Will Beveridge, who had recently moved to the Ministry of Munitions, written on Christmas Eve 1915 when the rest of his company were drunk on the alcohol that Tawney, as the French speaker, had procured for them, he set out his wider concerns. He began with the sheer incompetence of the military: 'Oh these soldiers! Perhaps they are really good at astronomy or poetry or something! But as to war! If only they would clear out and leave it to be settled by a committee of civilians!' Military discipline was in reality 'a code of rules for preventing any sort of new idea struggling into the august presence of the authorities', and the staff officers – Tawney absolved the regimental officers below colonel – were characterized by 'stupidity and conceit, conceit and stupidity, with, of course, a good deal of violence thrown in'. The 'higher command is not up to the game'; nevertheless in the absence of a means of disclosing their incompetence, 'they escape scot free, or with nothing worse than a Peerage'. A month later he wrote in similar terms to Jeanette: 'The difficult and important thing to do is to get brains in command & to scrap ruthlessly the social traditions which make it easy for gentlemanly fools (not always so very gentlemanly, though!) to be officers.' Staff officers are appointed by 'patronage and jobbery'. When they failed, causing the deaths of thousands, they were not removed from command but given 'more men to throw away in their next bungle. The state of things must be even worse for the Regt. Officers than it is for the NCOs and men. We suspect there is muddling; they see it at first hand, and are, I suppose, as helpless as we are to put things straight'. Two years later he wrote of commanders whose 'blank gentlemanly ineptitude flings away golden opportunities and countless lives'.[69]

Tawney was expressing a common complaint during and after the Great War, that British lions were led by donkeys. It is the complaint of front-line soldiers throughout History, and, in opposition to it, various attempts have been made more recently to rehabilitate the British high command after 1914. In Tawney's case however, his experience of the army fed, confirmed and sharpened his criticisms of the British class system which, despite all need and evidence, resolutely set its face against the promotion of talent to the detriment of the national interest in peace as well as in war. What was needed to win the war was the full democratization of British life. In a letter to A. L. Smith, now Master of Balliol, in late 1917, he argued that the inability to harness the energies and commitment of the people was the cause of military failure:

> This war seems to have caught us halfway in transition to democracy. We have not the kind of strength we should have if the mass of the working people felt that this war was their war, not an enterprise for which their rulers want their arms, but not their minds and hearts.

Tawney criticized the 'intellectual direction and leadership' of the war, noting that 'one cannot expect a respect for intelligence in an emergency, if one has not cultivated it before the emergency arose'.[70] The conduct of the war exemplified the wasted potential of the nation and demonstrated how an inadequate and exclusive social and political system limited national power. In highlighting the worst features it made the case for reform more urgent and credible, however. As Tawney was to show by his actions once he was discharged, there was an opportunity to harness popular energy through democratization and education.

This critique of British society and the war effort was important in Tawney's political development, though hardly unexpected. His earlier campaign against the ancient universities had been animated by similar concerns. The generals were an easy and predictable target, perhaps, and Tawney was only giving voice to the complaints of thousands of British soldiers in the lines. But, reflecting on Beveridge's challenges in organizing manpower and production on the home front, Tawney moved on to another and more surprising target in his letter from late 1915:

> The further problem of making the B[ritish] Workman and Employers decently public-spirited and less totally selfish can't, I fancy, be handled in under a generation or two. A year with the former has taught me a good deal – among other things that his philosophy, as much as that of his masters, is "get as much and give as little as you can". He has been brought up to that creed – though of course very many rise above it – and one can't change the habits of four or five generations in a year or two. (It is the old game of decasualising the man who has been carefully taught to be a casual).

In the movement for workers' education Tawney had met only those who had 'risen above it', largely products of the respectable upper reaches of the working class and petit-bourgeoisie, all of them animated by the desire for self-improvement and many of them equally committed to using their education in forms of public service. The majority of the working class was quite different, however, and if Tawney did not fully realize this before the war, he was under no illusions now. Army life showed him the limitations of all men, the officer class and the workers. Alienated from his situation and from all those around him (most of whom, he wrote, were, that Christmas Eve, 'now in different stages of intoxication'), Tawney ended his letter remarking again on the virtues of the French as compared with the English:

> I don't mean to be killed if I can help it, but if I am it will be a small consolation to be killed here, & on the whole I prefer to think of myself as fighting for this country than for England. If I survive and can scrape together enough cash, I should like to settle down in France a bit.[71]

Perhaps this preference for France and the French should be taken as a temporary index of his general alienation in the trenches. At other times during the war

Tawney conjured up heartening images of Merrie England to encourage him and others: 'I have always wanted to see Somersetshire and Gloucestershire properly. Taunton, where they make gloves, looks charming from the train and then there are Wells & Glastonbury and Tewkesbury. I love these old towns, that were the great towns of England before modern industry made life hideous and cosmopolitan.'[72] But these letters and other comments of a similar type running through his correspondence demonstrate how Tawney interpreted the war as a challenge to the emerging democracy from a society still clinging on to vestiges of a suffocating *ancien regime*. Indeed, he frequently compared Britain in 1916 to France in 1793 to the former's disadvantage. When revolutionary France 'was really fighting for her life . . . about 6000 officers were sacked in a year, and privates promoted wholesale.'[73] Tawney was no supporter of Terror; but the opening of British society to merit and talent became, through these military experiences, his leading post-war concern.

Meanwhile there was a war to fight and Tawney and his comrades knew they were being readied for an attack. The 22nd Manchesters had arrived at the Somme, opposite the German-held village of Mametz, 5 miles east of Albert, on 1 February 1916.[74] They faced a formidable system of German trenches and strong points. In May 1916 the soldiers around him – 'dear innocents' he called them – hoped and believed that 'peace will be declared in three months'. But the historian 'being cursed with the power to look before & after', gave it 'till Xmas 1917 or 1918'.[75] As preparations were made for a summer offensive, in late May 1916 he was granted a week of leave in England which evidently went well:

> We had a glorious time and I shall live on memories of it. I have never seen England look so beautiful, and with you in the middle of it, it was unforgettable. I feel enormously more cheerful. Nothing can take away that time with its perfect setting of golden weather & May & dazzling grass and trees.[76]

This lyricism was not uncommon in his wartime correspondence. Indeed, his descriptions of some of his experiences and of the landscape and countryside in France were actually collected together, shorn of all personal and militarily-sensitive references, and then published as a long article in the *Manchester Guardian* under the title 'First Impressions of Active Service'.[77] Tawney's descriptive powers became more evident the closer he came to a major event or action in his military career. On 9 June 1916 the battalion withdrew to a camp in the nearby Bois des Pailles where they sheltered in bivouacs.[78] Tawney described his as 'a little green cage of bent bushes with a tarpaulin on the top, & myself & two other sergeants inside'. His letters from there were full of vivid and poignant observations.

> Yesterday evening I walked up onto the ridge behind the last village to watch the bombardment . . . One looked down onto a plain that was the very image of peace . . . In so large a landscape the wrath of man seems extraordinarily ineffective, & life infinitely more powerful than death, so that one forgot that one had come to see the bombardment & looked instead at the sunset & poplars & light on the distant towns. One thing caught my eye, a church tower a few miles off. I was puzzled by it as I could not see what made the architecture seem so unfamiliar. Then I realized with the aid of glasses that its awkward unnatural clumsy look was due to shells, the tower shaken & transept smashed. It gave me the creeps; it looked against nature, like a face distorted by disease. I fancy it was Albert Cathedral, where there is the famous hanging virgin.[79]

He warned Jeanette not to 'be anxious if you see in the papers reports of military movements etc'.[80] He described 'the country behind the line here' as 'crammed with troops, English and French, and vast guns pass through dragged by caterpillars'.[81] There was time for one final letter home on 29 June, a day after their wedding anniversary:

> You can't I know help feeling anxiety, with all your courage. What must help you is the knowledge that we are together always in spirit, & that no changes can separate us. For myself I feel that you & I & all men are, what our forefathers called "in the hands on the Lord" & I am not troubled, even about you, for I trust you to rise above any temporary evils. The only thing that occasionally worries me is anxiety lest I should fail in my small duties. But I know you think of me & your thoughts will help me. I should have liked to leave you my small Imitatio in case anything does happen to me, but it has always been in my pocket, & I want to keep it there, as a bit of yourself . . . How more than fortunate we have been! When I think of you I really feel the overflowing happiness of which the scriptures speak . . . Much love, Ever your lover, Harry.[82]

On the evening before the battle, 30 June, a Special Order was read out to the 22nd Battalion, the 7th Manchester Pals, which included the warning: 'The use of the word retire is absolutely forbidden, and if heard can only be a ruse of the enemy and must be ignored.'[83] At 9.30 p.m. the battalion moved to the specially prepared assembly trenches, some 250 yards behind the front line. At 6.25 a.m. on the following morning, 1 July 1916, the intensive bombardment began.

With 8 minutes to go Stokes mortars started up. In the final moments mines were detonated around targets ahead of the battalion and smoke laid down to obscure a view of the British assault.[84] At 7.30 a.m. Tawney led his platoon over the top in their small part of the Somme offensive. 'B' Company – Tawney's – and 'D' Company led the assault at first: later 'C' and 'A' Companies took the brunt.[85] Each company was divided into four platoons, with two platoons side by side in front and two behind.[86] As part of the 7th Division, the 22nd Battalion was tasked to attack Mametz as an element within a pincer movement. Three battalions from 20th Brigade would advance on the left and two from 91st Brigade on the right, the 22nd alongside the 1st Battalion South Staffordshire Regiment. The 21st Manchesters were to remain in reserve until Fricourt was ready to be taken.

Tawney wrote an account of the attack that was published some months later in which he recounted what happened. It was described years later by Tawney's publisher as 'one of the most moving accounts of the ordinary infantryman's war, which can be read anywhere,' though Tawney's father found it 'almost too realistic for my nerves . . . The old battles of Cannae etc etc may have been horrible but there was no continual rattle, I suppose. The lines before Sebastopol were bad enough but not as bad as what goes on now'.[87] The 22nd Manchester lost more than 350 of the regiment out of the 60,000 British casualties on that day, 'and after being up in action a few days later the number who survived out of the original lot was only 54'.[88] Tawney was hit in the first wave of attack by bullets which went clean through his chest and abdomen and took away part of one of his kidneys. He lay in no-man's land for hours and was extremely fortunate to have survived. Many of his comrades thought he was dead, or, if they knew that he was still alive, that he was going to die soon from his wounds. J. W. Ramsbotham, only a few miles away at Fricourt, believed he had perished and only learnt that Tawney had survived from a letter he received from Unwin later in July in the midst of the continuing battle.[89]

Tawney told his story in 'The Attack' which was written and published in the *Westminster Gazette* just a few weeks later in August 1916. Nearly 90 years later this essay formed one of several sources for a 'docudrama' entitled *The Somme* in which Tawney's experiences, and those of other infantrymen, were dramatized for a television audience.[90] Tawney's account begins on the evening of 30 June among the bivouacs and tarpaulins in the wood and Tawney leads us with him on the march to the trenches. There the men take up their positions and Tawney finds time for a snooze. He describes the overwhelming sound of the artillery bombardment at its climax, 'a symphony' like nothing they had heard or experienced thus far. Then, at 7.30 in the morning

> we went up the ladders, doubled through the gaps in the wire, and lay down, waiting for the line to form up on each side of us. When it was ready we went forward, not doubling, but at a walk. For we had nine hundred yards of rough ground to the trench which was our first objective and about fifteen hundred to a further trench where we were to wait for orders.

Fearful that he might simply buckle and collapse with fright, he was at first elated that he 'felt a load fall' and that he could walk forward with purpose. He was sure that he would come through unscathed. They crossed three lines of trenches and took cover in the fourth. They encountered the first of the wounded but had orders not to stop the advance. As they rose to go forward their line was hit by machine gun fire. They fired back and Tawney took aim:

> It seemed one couldn't miss them. Every man I fired at dropped, except one . . . Not that I wanted to hurt him or anyone else. It was missing I hated. That's the beastliest thing in war, the damnable frivolity. One's like a merry, mischievous ape tearing up the image of God.

All around him his comrades were dead, dying, wounded. Tawney crawled along the line and rallied those still alive. He threatened to shoot one man who had buried his head in the ground and was crying, though admitted that he could not have done such a thing. Still, it worked and the boy 'came up like a lamb'. He sent another soldier to make contact with any unit to their right, but he was hit and 'it was as if I'd condemned him to death'. So Tawney decided to reconnoitre to the left himself, looking for the remnants of 'A' Company. Crawling back he saw a 'knot of men lying down to the right' and waved to them to form up with the other survivors. He did not realize that they were either dead or wounded. Tawney 'knelt up and waved again'. He was shot.

> What I felt was that I had been hit by a tremendous iron hammer, swung by a giant of inconceivable strength, and then twisted with a sickening sort of wrench so that my head and back banged on the ground, and my feet struggled as though they didn't belong to me. For a second or too my breath wouldn't come. I thought – if that's the right word – "This is death", and I hoped it wouldn't take long.

But later he comes to a different conclusion: when a lad wriggles up to him and asks 'What's up, sergeant?', he replies 'Not dying, I think, but pretty bad'. He needs to raise his knees to ease the pain in his stomach, but each time he does so, the snipers can see him and start shooting. Then the German artillery starts to lob shells in his direction and he is hit again, but only by a sod thrown up in one of the explosions. He cannot move. He drinks his water. He sucks an acid drop issued in the rations the night before. He watches the sun and waits for the evening. He calls for help but no one can hear him – and if they could it would be suicide to come to his assistance. In the evening he is found by a corporal in the Royal Army Medical Corps and then a young doctor comes to him. Tawney is confused and doesn't know what hit him, literally. The doctor tells him that he 'had been shot with a rifle bullet through the chest and abdomen'. He bandaged him and gave him morphine, but apparently believed Tawney was 'done for'. Despite the sniping, the saintly doctor with a face that shined 'with love and comprehension' refused to take cover. But there was no chance of moving Tawney that night and he spent more than a day in no-man's land. He ends with the calculations:

> We attacked, I think, about 820 strong. I've no official figures of casualties. A friend, an officer in "C" Company, which was in support and shelled to pieces before it could start, told me in hospital that we lost 450 men that day, and that, after being put in again a day or two later, we had 54 left.[91]

In the event, the number of casualties among the 22nd Manchesters, who numbered 20 officers and 754 men at the end of June 1916, was nearer 500 that day.[92] Ten officers were killed and eight were wounded. There were 472 casualties among the men: 241 wounded, 120 killed and 111 missing. 'The 7th Manchester City battalion had ceased to exist in any recognizable form.'[93] A total of 20,000 British soldiers died on that day on the Somme, and a further 40,000 were wounded. The battalion achieved its first objective, Black Trench, after 15 minutes of the advance, and the second, Bucket Trench, to the east of Mametz, at 7.55 a.m. (by which time Tawney was already wounded). But the German machine guns had not been taken out and the 'severity of the fire . . . was intense and accurate', especially from one machine gun placed in a house in the southwest corner of the village.[94] The next phase of the advance was to Danzig Alley Trench, a main German communication trench running from Mametz to Montauban, and the Manchesters took it at 8.15 am but were driven back in bitter fighting as German soldiers emerged from their bunkers in Fritz Trench, unscathed by the artillery barrage. Reinforced by D Company of the 21st Manchesters and elements of the South Staffords, a second assault at 1.30 p.m. that afternoon took Danzig Alley in hand-to-hand combat, and then

Mametz fell later that afternoon.[95] It was a notable success on the first day of the Battle of the Somme, but the various units in the Fricourt-Mametz sector were then instructed to make defensive preparations for counter-attacks, when further German positions might have been taken at relatively small cost if the offensive had continued.[96]

The 22nd Manchesters were relieved on 5 July and moved to Buire where more than 400 reinforcements were absorbed.[97] They were thrown back into the attack on 15 July at Mametz Wood but withdrew the next day after taking heavy casualties once again.[98] The battalion, whose personnel by the end of July 1916 had ceased to bear any relation to the original 'pals' who volunteered in November 1914, remained in France until November 1917 when it was moved to Italy as part of the 7th Division, finishing the war west of Udine. There is a memorial to the 20th, 21st, 22nd and 24th Manchester Regiments in Mametz erected by the Lancashire and Cheshire branch of the Western Front Association and dedicated on 1 July 1994.[99] Many of Tawney's comrades – some 220 men of the Manchester regiments – are buried in Dantzig Alley Cemetery (note the different spelling) to the east of the village on the road leading to Montauban on the crest of a ridge. Mametz Wood can be seen from it.[100] The cemetery contains the graves and memorials of more than 2,000 allied servicemen, including that of Tawney's friend and academic colleague, Alfred Bland, the father of two sons, who was killed by machine gun fire on 1 July in front of Danzig Alley Trench.[101] Tawney later wrote of Bland just before zero hour: 'My Captain, a brave man and a good officer, came along and borrowed a spare watch from me. It was the last time I saw him.'[102] Tawney's other collaborator on *English Economic History – Select Documents*, P. A. Brown, was a lieutenant with 13 Durham Light Infantry and was killed in action on 4 November 1915 aged 29.

Jeanette received a telegram dated 2 July which read: 'Harry wounded sunday sent base please try ascertain particulars. Tawney.'[103] It was written for him. Will then used his 'position in the Ministry of Munitions to send a "priority A" telegram and find out about him – long before the official War Office enquiry centre for NCOs & privates could get particulars'.[104] As late as 6 July they were reporting that he did not appear on their casualty lists. Informed that he had survived but might be close to death, Jeanette then went over to France to be with him.[105] She sent her brother a card on the 13th: 'Harry really better today & is to go to England next batch. He is still very weak & will be ill some months but he is out of danger at present.'[106] By the 17th a postcard to her mother reported that 'We are back in England as our permits only allow for a week. Harry better but it will be a very long matter. H attributes his recovery to his wonderful constitution . . . He lay out 24 hours & then got back to a trench on his own feet . . . H comes to England in next batch but I don't know where he will be yet.'[107] A day later Tawney sent her a note in pencil in his own hand: 'My address is Cowley Section, 3rd Southern General Hospital, Oxford. It's what used to be the Cowley Workhouse. I'm all right.'[108] On the 22nd Tawney's father could take 'comfort to think that Harry is doing so well'.[109] By 1 August he had moved into Wingfield Court Hospital, also in Oxford, and was evidently able to move around and go for expeditions into the city: 'I am going on very well, too well I fear, as I don't want to get fit for duty quickly . . . You will be angry with me! I've bought 2 vols of Treitschke's *History of Germany*, but I haven't bought any books for nearly 2 years & won't do so again and the proximity of Blackwell [bookshop] is like a public house to a drunkard.'[110] Tawney may have taken German bullets, but it did not blunt his curiosity to understand the enemy that had nearly killed him. By October he was recuperating at Cuddeson, the seat of the Bishop of Oxford. Indeed there is a famous story that the bishop, Charles Gore, had visited Tawney in one of the makeshift military hospitals in Oxford and said to the matron as he left, 'You have in your care one of the most valuable lives in England.' She went straight to his bedside to reprimand the invalid: 'Why ever didn't you tell us you were a gentleman?'

Letters came to express relief at his survival and to wish him well. Jimmy Mallon explained that 'in acting as a Tawney Enquiry Bureau I acquired a considerable popularity & as happily the tidings I had to send out were progressively better I still enjoy this renown'.[111] F. M. Powicke the historian was 'so glad to know that you have come through & have the second half of your life in front of you, a joy & encouragement to so many people who love you'.[112] For Alfie Wadsworth it was 'splendid to hear of your progress, but you must have had an awful time'.[113]

The most moving tributes and support came from Tawney's comrades in arms, like Private A. Townend, who was in Tawney's battalion and wrote to his 'Dear Pal Dick' to wish him well,[114] and a soldier called Jack who wrote as follows:

Dear Sergeant, I was very pleased to learn that you are mending nicely. I have been enquiring about you since i landed in England on the 19 of July. I got wounded in the head and right arm July 15th. I have been in hospital in Nottingham until the 5 of October. I am getting to the end of my furlow (sic). I report at the Depot tomorrow Saturday . . . I went in front of the board and passed for home service only. I will now conclude hoping that your cure will be successful. I remain your sincere friend, Jack.[115]

The sheer enormity of the events of early July was encapsulated in a letter from one of Tawney's friends and an officer in the 22nd Manchesters, R. G. Garside, probably written towards the end of the month:

My dear Dick,

Many thanks for your letter. It was indeed good news to hear that you were still living. I must say, however, that your query brought a sad smile to my face. Do you know Dick, Hinsley and I are the only ones left of the old school. All the others save Capt. Marnay got hit on the 1st and Capt. Marnay got it on the 14th so you see we *have* had a time. Briggs, Whiteleg are dead. McCoy, Bradley, Renmer, Elsworth are wounded whilst Whitehead "got" shell shock . . . As to the "boys" Wooley is still living but Brandwood & Penny have joined the great majority. I am afraid you would not recognise the Coy. now. We have drafts of all regiments; the last being territorials. A more cosmopolitan crowd you never saw. One relieving feature is the clash of dialects. A question is asked in perfect Mile End Road and answered in broad Scotch. One man is reproved in East Anglian and then cursed in "Zomerzet". Ye Gods! Bid me discourse and I will enchant thine ear. Dick, you were right and I was wrong regarding the end of this imbecilic campaign. Like Tennyson's brook it will grow forever. Not a sign not a vestige of peace is there on the horizon . . . Should you by any chance here from Mac and Bradley please apologise for my not replying to their letters. Unfortunately we were on the move at the time and I lost them.[116]

Much later Tawney received a letter of good cheer from one of his former students in the Longton class, George Horwill, who explained that he 'would have written before but for the fact that I have been in gaol all the time. I wish you a speedy recovery'. Horwill was among the first conscientious objectors to be arrested and had been in detention and gaol ever since. Admitting that their 'views of the war are just as opposite as is possible' Horwill hoped Tawney would return to work for 'the educational movement; it is more vital now than before the war'.[117] Indeed, many of Tawney's well-wishers hoped that he would involve himself in social reconstruction. Michael Sadler, now vice-chancellor of Leeds University, wrote to explain that 'hardly anything has touched me more deeply than the part you have taken in the war. You have indeed won your spurs. And your example has been a help, even to old fogeys like me'. Later, foreseeing Tawney's next role, he wrote to advise 'that you will be wanted at another kind of national service'.[118] Mallon told him 'get better soon for the tasks of peace are being resumed & your services are badly needed'.[119] And one of his former WEA students, Harry Barker, also on active service, picked up the common theme emerging out of this correspondence in the autumn of 1916:

> Don't worry about being out of it. You surely have done your bit. Besides, I always argued that after the time and trouble some of us had taken in completing your education, it was a great work for you to come to France to be shot at. You are one of the few that really understand things & you will be very useful when the time for reconstruction comes.[120]

While recuperating Tawney wrote a second article, 'Some Reflections of a Soldier', published in October 1916 in *The Nation*, which explored two themes made famous by much of the poetry of the Great War, the emotional and psychological distance between the men at the front and everyone else they encountered in Britain and the Tommies' solidarity with their supposed foe. As Tawney explained the first point, 'You make us feel that the country to which we've returned is not the country for which we went out to fight' or in biblical terms, 'the fact is we've drifted apart. We have slaved for Rachel, but it looks as if we'd got to live with Leah'. He notes the gulf between the realities of battle and trench life and the reporting of the war in the newspapers – 'your Press', as he calls it. War was 'a game played by monkeys and organised by lunatics', a state of 'endless and loathsome physical exhaustion', but none of this is reported, let alone understood at home. The theory of 'attrition', then in vogue, evokes derision for '*The Times* military expert's hundredth variation on the theme that the abstruse science of war consists in killing more of the enemy than kills you, so that whatever its losses – agreeable doctrine – the numerically preponderant side can always win, as it were, by one wicket'. But this was not like playing cricket for Whitelaw's house during his last golden summer at Rugby. He felt fellowship for the men 'who have sat opposite us in mud . . . victims of the same catastrophe as ourselves . . . comrades in misery . . . Hatred of the enemy is not common, I think, among those who have encountered him'. And this is where the two themes combine, because, in their ignorance and impotence, people at home 'seem to discover in hatred the sensation of activity which they have missed elsewhere . . . You do not help yourselves, or your country, or your soldiers, by hating . . .'[121] He returned to the theme of the camaraderie of all combatants in another essay of this season, 'Democracy and Defeat':

> What the facts of war impress upon soldiers is not their national distinctiveness, but their common humanity with men who, fifty yards away, freeze and starve

and sweat in the same mud and rain and heat themselves, who look out on the same shattered villages and unploughed fields, and hunger with the same passion for the return of peace.[122]

The general expectation was that Tawney would be discharged and set free for work of social reconstruction. His father hoped 'that he will never, never, return to the front'.[123] And as Tawney told Will Beveridge, 'I feel pledged to educ. work, if such work is forthcoming & if I can be got out for it.' But 'quite unexpectedly' at the end of October Tawney found that he had been returned to 'light duty and home service'.[124] He was ordered to rejoin the 71st T R Battalion at its camp in Ripon. It was composed 'of men belonging to the 22nd, 23rd and 24th Manchesters, mostly men who've not yet been out, but some who have & have been sent here like myself'. Tawney was frustrated again by the rigidities of the army: 'Surely they can see that I can be of more use to the country than loafing here [?]', he asked.[125] He saw a doctor on November 7th, commenting *inter alia*, that 'I shd never have got here at all unless two kind men had seen I was in difficulty & insisted on carrying my kit bag for me'.[126] A week later he was summoned to a Medical Board and was given 'C3.X – (C3 meaning "employment only" and X meaning "not subject to revision" – at least that's what one's told) . . . That ought to facilitate getting out but I've not heard anything yet'.[127] Two weeks later he was formally discharged from the army as no longer fit for military service. Jeanette wrote a postcard to her brother telling him of the release and added 'He's described as a steady and well conducted NCO'.[128]

Tawney's condition may have spoken for itself and the decision been arrived at on purely medical grounds. But there is a hint of external intervention in the decision to discharge him. Jimmy Mallon told one of his associates, the businessman George Booth (who was a son of the famous social investigator Charles Booth), that the then President of the Board of Education, the Marquess of Crewe, had sent a 'special letter' to secure Tawney's release. The truth of this is difficult to pin down. There are no references to it in the Tawney or Beveridge papers, though it is possible that Tawney was never told about it for fear that he might have jibbed at aristocratic patronage and soldiered on at base camp in Yorkshire.[129] Crewe was a plausible supporter of Tawney, for sure: 'the last of the whigs', he combined wealth, liberalism and a strong interest in educational reconstruction and would have seen the value in setting Tawney free to further this work.

What was the impact of the Great War on Tawney? First and foremost, he lived with pain for the rest of his life and only part of one kidney.[130] It took months to recover his strength, he was still having difficulty walking any distance in the spring of 1917, his health broke down seriously in 1922 when he required an operation to one of his internal wounds, and periodically after that, and illness affected at least two of his parliamentary campaigns in the early 1920s. He never forgot his old comrades and they never forgot him. When the journalist Colin Welch mentioned Tawney in the 'Peter Simple' column of the *Daily Telegraph* as late as 1958 he received a letter (which he passed on to Tawney) from another old soldier, G. J. Benson of Leigh in Lancashire: 'Sir, Your remarks in today's issue of the Daily Telegraph on Professor Tawney bring back memories of the Somme battlefield of 1916. Sgt Tawney and myself shared the same dug out on that front. I was sergeant of the other platoon at the time.'[131] Tawney attended the reunion dinners of the Old Comrades Association of the 22nd Manchesters when he could; he subscribed to the Balliol College War Memorial Fund. According to his nephew, 'the sergeant's rank was certainly the proudest achievement of his life'. For many years after, when at home in Mecklenburgh Square, he padded around or worked at his desk in 'an increasingly tattered sergeant's tunic with the stripes still hanging on'. Many of the officers had been fools: to Tawney 'the heroes and saviours of the British army were the NCOs'.[132] He had learnt much about the instincts and behaviour of the British working class while in the army, but he remained confident of their fundamental decency. As he told a reunion of the students from his first class in Rochdale in 1939, 'Whenever I have to make decisions, I instinctively refer to the standards of conduct of two groups of people – the men of the platoon in which I served in the war, and yourselves'.[133]

For that reason, a generation later, Tawney found it difficult to accept the views on war published by his protégé Evan Durbin. Durbin was then a young economics lecturer at the LSE; he became a Labour MP in 1945 but drowned 3 years later in saving the lives of 2 children. In 1938 he co-edited a selection of essays entitled *War and Democracy*. Durbin's own contribution in the collection was a psychological exploration of the connection between personal aggression and war. When Tawney read it, however, he questioned the association from his own experience. He admitted that he knew of atrocities where men had lost control, but argued that they were rare. 'To the majority war slips quickly into the routine of wearisome, exhausting & unemotional business. Their predominant mood is one of boredom & apathy . . . the main effort of the actual combatants is to keep going somehow.'[134]

Michal Vyvyan remarked that 'the First World War made a bigger mark on his life than on that of almost any other of his academic contemporaries'.[135] Insofar as Tawney wrote and spoke about his experiences, rather than sublimating them, and they came to inform his mature reflections on social and political issues, this may well be correct. Other very notable academic figures like the English scholars J. R. R. Tolkien and Frank Leavis came through the trenches but the experience was not used by them in their professional or public work, though its effects are evident in their writing. Tawney took pride in having served in a war that he believed had to be fought, though till the very end of his life he could 'never think of British generals with anything but hatred and contempt'.[136] Yet it cannot be said that the war changed him. Rather it confirmed what he believed already: that Britain was insufficiently democratized and this held her back not only from military victory but social progress as well. For this reason he threw himself into social and educational reconstruction on his discharge, and this was to dominate his life for the next 5 years or more. But the war did confer upon him a new authority which endured. Many of his peers and patrons, and perhaps even some of his political enemies, recognized his talents; but to those abilities Tawney now added a rare experience of life and death under duress that gave an added confidence and authority to all he did and wrote and helped make him into a public figure. Tawney did not exploit this, but his experience with the men in the trenches was widely known and respected. When he wrote of fellowship and talked of comradeship whether in the labour movement or in society more generally, those who knew something of his life paid all the more attention because here was a philosopher and polemicist who knew of what he spoke.

Reconstruction after the
First World War: Coal

In April 1917 Tawney received a letter from a friend, Gunner E. Hobson of No. 1 Reserve Brigade RFA, from the Ripon camp where Tawney had been based before his discharge. Hobson wrote to congratulate him on his anonymous pamphlet, 'Democracy or Defeat' and to encourage him to persevere: 'Do keep on with your work . . . of democratic reorganisation of England . . . if England can be bent in the right direction, your hellish experiences may not have been all in vain.'[1] Tawney had emerged from the fight dedicated to the wholesale reconstruction of Britain. Indeed, he sincerely believed that only through a democratic revitalization of Britain's institutions and culture could the war itself be won. Over the next several years Tawney stuck to this task. In many different fields – the church, adult education, the reform of the universities and the establishment of a new international order – Tawney made his mark. Then, in 1919, his service on the Royal Commission on the Coal Industry under the chairmanship of Mr Justice Sankey, not only gave him the opportunity for industrial reconstruction specifically but also confirmed him as a public figure. His involvement led him towards a confluence with the Labour Party and to a change in the focus and language of his political writing which swapped ethical opposition to capitalism for the discussion of practical aspects of a socialist programme.

For one who had come so close to death, and who continued to suffer pain and discomfort from his wounds, Tawney's energy was remarkable. Beyond resources of physical strength, he was enabled to live the life of a campaigner (with a little tutoring of adults and undergraduates thrown in) by virtue of patronage. Part of his salary in this period was paid by the WEA and the rest by George Macaulay Booth, a son of the shipowner and social investigator, Charles Booth, and a businessman himself who had been brought into government by Lloyd George to spread business methods through Whitehall. Booth knew

Jimmy Mallon through their joint service on the Tailoring Trade Board, and at the end of 1916 Mallon 'asked Booth if he would contribute two-fifths of R. H. Tawney's salary for five years while Tawney organised and implemented the WEA's campaign. Booth agreed, and in 1919 he increased his contribution to three-fifths'.[2] Tawney was a licensed and salaried advocate for the WEA and democracy itself in these years. He was also elected a Fellow of Balliol in April 1918 under a statute enabling the college to make special elections 'of persons to perform definite literary, scientific, or educational work', and as a college lecturer there he taught economics.[3]

Soon after he had recovered, Tawney was one of those, including Tom Jones, Mallon and Zimmern, who breakfasted on 28 November 1916 with Lloyd George, then still the Minister for Munitions. At the minister's request they drafted a memorandum that same day on 'the need for a new spirit in government and the conduct of the war'. It called for a renewed national commitment to democracy and freedom in 'a form of national concentration at once consistent with our highest traditions and compatible with the ideals which led us into this struggle'. They called for energy and commitment to win the war and moral and spiritual regeneration while doing so.[4] Though the group did not know it at the time, they were thus on the fringe of decisive events that would, within 10 days, see Asquith replaced by Lloyd George as prime minister and renewed vigour imparted to the war effort.

Bishop Gore, echoing William Temple, once said that 'unknown people come to me wanting something new and important started. They always say "Get someone like Harry Tawney", as if there was anybody like Harry Tawney'.[5] But Gore himself secured Tawney's help in preparing, with other leading churchmen, the report *Christianity and Industrial Problems* (1918) which called for the application of Christian values in the wholesale reappraisal of conditions of work and of the economic relationships between labour and capital in post-war Britain. In this he was joined by a contingent from the WEA, including Mansbridge and A. L. Smith, who also sat on the steering committee of 28.[6] Tawney joined with Temple in the movement the latter had begun for 'Life and Liberty', which was designed to win a measure of autonomy from the state for the Church of England to enable it to take a more overt and campaigning stance on social and economic questions. Tawney's famous essay from early 1917, 'Some Thoughts on Education and the War', which was republished as 'A National College of All Souls', was an almost romantic appeal for an educational crusade as a fit memorial for all the suffering endured through the war.[7] Beatrice Webb presented him in her diaries in 1918 as among 'the circle of rebellious spirits and idealist intellectuals' who had gathered around the Webbs, including also Jimmy Mallon, Arthur Greenwood and Arnold Toynbee.[8]

Parochial as it may have been in the aftermath of a world war, Tawney could not stand aside over the issue of the reform of Oxford and Cambridge, which was unfinished business from the Edwardian era campaigns he had led, and he helped form a group in Balliol in 1919 to discuss the issues involved. It was known as the 'TT Club' because it met weekly at teatime on Tuesdays during term.[9] Displaying his customary tenacity over this issue, when the Royal Commission on Oxford and Cambridge was established under the former prime minister Asquith in 1919, he gave evidence to it and also prepared briefing papers for the Labour Party. Tawney pointed to 'three main defects' in the ancient universities: they were 'too exclusive because too expensive'; their resources were not used 'in the most economical manner' owing to the financial independence of the colleges; and their government was both inefficient and out of touch, requiring external representatives from the public. He advocated the pooling of all endowments and resources within the universities, the management of college estates by central commissions in each case, an end to waste and duplication, the reservation of free places specifically for students from secondary schools funded from public sources and the award of scholarships on the basis of need alone. Significantly, Tawney said or wrote nothing about the educational needs of women.[10] Little of this was endorsed by the Asquith Commission or enacted under subsequent legislation, the Oxford and Cambridge Act 1922. Much of it has a distinctly contemporary ring, however, and is still heard in both universities nearly a century later.

Of greater immediate impact was Tawney's work in the cause of adult education under the short-lived Ministry of Reconstruction. The different civic projects sponsored by the Ministry of Reconstruction at the end of the war generally came to little, but in the case of adult education something of lasting value emerged.[11] Chaired by the then Master of Balliol, the historian A. L. Smith, and meeting through 1917 and 1918 in that college, the Ministry of Reconstruction's committee on adult education included many of the leading figures in the movement, but it was Tawney who drove things and who ultimately wrote the report, just as he had written the 1908 Report on *Oxford and Working-Class Education*. It is said that the paths which criss-cross the main Balliol quadrangle were laid down by Smith and Tawney as they walked and talked about workers' education at this time. Much broader than the *1908 Report* in that it surveyed adult education of every type, the '1919 Report' so-called, led to no immediate institutional initiatives or innovations, but provided a type of template for the development of the movement through the interwar years.[12] It was prefaced by a long and remarkable document, an interim report that only Tawney could have written, for it amounted to a wholesale assault on the damage done to men and women – their bodies, minds and souls – by the industrial system, and presented education and self-improvement as a kind of spiritual antidote to long hours, low wages and economic exploitation.[13] The final report surveyed the history of adult and workers' education and made the case for them as general responsibilities of the whole educational system: local and central government, universities and voluntary organizations should view them as integral aspects of their provision, necessary for the creation and maintenance of a participative democracy, and an invaluable school of citizenship in themselves.

But Tawney's horizons were wider than these longstanding commitments. He was outraged by the behaviour of the irregular police force, the so-called 'Black and Tans', during the Irish Civil War, and considered the policy pursued by the British government in continuing to physically resist the demand for Home Rule a 'moral catastrophe', displaying 'abominable wickedness'. He wrote in fury to his friend George Bell, another great twentieth-century churchman, to ask that the church speak out.[14] He was dismayed by the intimidation of the police in furtherance of official wartime censorship, still in place in the spring of 1919. This had prevented the periodical, the *International Review*, from publishing four of Lenin's speeches delivered in the previous year. He joined with a notable group – Noel Buxton, Arthur Henderson, J. A. Hobson, H. W. Massingham, Gilbert Murray, J. A. Spender, Sidney Webb and Leonard Woolf – in a letter of protest to *The Times*.[15] The immediate post-war problem of hunger and want in central and eastern Europe, and the wider issue of establishing a more just economic order than was emerging from the peace treaty negotiations at Versailles, led Tawney to assist Gilbert Murray, Leonard Woolf, J. M. Keynes, Olive Schreiner, Noel Buxton, Norman Angell and others – unfamiliar allies for Tawney from a liberal and cosmopolitan background – in the establishment of the 'Fight the Famine Council', an offshoot of which became the Save the Children Fund. Indeed, these may appear to be unfamiliar issues for Tawney whose interests and concerns had hitherto been almost wholly domestic in their focus and whose very 'Englishness' has often been used as a criticism of him. In fact, Tawney published a remarkable and little-known article in 1917 that demonstrates his capacity to think broadly and address international issues. Entitled 'The Sword of the Spirit' and published at the end of 1917, just before Woodrow Wilson's 'Fourteen Points Address' set out allied war and peace aims, Tawney's essay was a meditation on the point of the conflict with a strong spiritual-religious inflection. In essence, he argued for a peace consistent with the highest principles with which Britain entered the war, one embodying the commitment to 'national freedom, and for a growth of international solidarity based upon law'. This would be a fitting memorial for all those who had died: 'it would be treason to the dead' to 'continue the War for motives of economic advantage or nationalist ambition'.

Tawney sensed a loss of purpose: 'we fight', he wrote 'in an obscurity'.

> Men feel that the war which they supported is not the war which they are now asked to support. They are coming to believe in increasing numbers that it is being continued for reasons different from those for which it was begun, and that, if the welfare of the world is delivered from the nationalist ambitions of Germany, it may end by being sacrificed to the nationalist ambitions of the Allies.

Fearing a descent into atavism – what he called 'the Prussian spirit' – he wanted a clear restatement of British war aims and to hold Britain to the negotiation of a just peace, arrived at fairly and consensually. He believed that 'a moral as well as a military strategy' would be to Britain's advantage. It would inspire the British to redouble their own efforts while undermining the will of 'reasonable Germans' to fight on for 'their own militaristic government' in an unjust cause. The broad terms of that peace included 'a League of Nations . . . the freedom of peoples to determine their own political destinies, and . . . a guarantee of equal citizenship and cultural autonomy to all racial groups which do not form independent states.' The 'Sword of the Spirit' was a brilliant and, in its way, a beautiful essay – generous, wise and magnanimous – which could only have been written by someone who had endured the trenches and knew why a liberal peace was required. As he expressed it, 'what encourages soldiers is one thing, and one thing alone – the thought that if they must endure, they endure for the sake of a lasting peace.'[16]

Tawney was everywhere in these years, granted a roving commission to work and agitate for social and also humanitarian reform. He and Jeanette had taken rooms overlooking Parliament Hill Fields in London, but Tawney was also away teaching in his beloved North Staffordshire and in Oxford. He moved, in fact, from one campaign to the next, writing reports and publishing articles as he went. It was not surprising, therefore, that on 1 March 1919 Tawney should have received a telegram: 'The Prime Minister would be glad if you will consent to serve on the coal commission under the chairmanship of Mr Justice Sankey.

Meetings will begin immediately.'[17] It is probable that his name was suggested to Lloyd George by the Webbs, who met the prime minister at a private dinner to discuss the composition of the Commission.[18] Tawney's membership of the Sankey Commission changed his life: he became a public figure, he made direct contact with the leadership of trade unions, he was drawn further into the Labour Party, he worked closely with Sidney Webb, who was another member of the Commission, and he underwent a change in his approach to socialism itself. He was the star of the show whose grasp of the structure and economics of the coal industry allowed him to ask the most pertinent questions and embarrass and bamboozle arguably the most unloved and unattractive group in the history of British capitalism, the mine owners.[19] As Beatrice Webb later observed, 'Sidney has come out of the Commission with a great admiration for Tawney, for his personal charm, his quiet wisdom, his rapier-like intellect. Tawney has, in fact, been the great success of the Commission.'[20]

Sankey was a judge of the High Court, and later a Labour Lord Chancellor. His commission comprised three mine owners, three miners, three business-men not directly related to the coal mining industry and three economists including Tawney and Webb. The commission was established because of the parlous state of the industry at the end of hostilities and the deteriorating state of industrial relations within it; its markets had shrunk, its costs were out of control and the coal owners were intending to redress their loss of profitability by wage cuts and the lay-off of miners. But as Beatrice Webb noted, it rapidly became 'a state trial of the coal-owners and royalty owners conducted on behalf of the producers and consumers of the product, culminating in the question – why not nationalize the industry?'[21]

Tawney wrote about these issues in many different journals and newspapers in 1919 and 1920, and his analysis of the problems was never contested. The controversy concerned only the possible solutions.[22] Before the First World War approximately 4,000 individuals, the 'royalty owners', leased the coal in the ground to roughly 1,500 companies which mined around 270 million tons of coal per annum from some 3,200 pits in 16 coalfields in Britain. The companies sold it on to numerous distributors – perhaps as many as 30,000 – who themselves sold it on, either directly or indirectly, to the consumer. In total the coal mining industry employed over a million workers. From 1915 it was subject to state regulation under a Coal Controller to secure and increase coal production for the war, stabilize prices for the consumer, prevent industrial disputes and the disruption of production, and subsidize the less remunerative collieries. Under this regime the shareholders in coal mines did remarkably well because the price was set at an artificially high level: in order to make even the most geologically challenging pits profitable, the subsidy per ton to the owners was set at a level that guaranteed large windfall profits for those whose coal was cheap and easy to hack out of rich seams. But the market for coal contracted sharply after the war: domestic demand began to fall while the export trade was devastated by a combination of factors – the development in some nations of their own domestic coal industries, the increasing use of alternatives to coal such as gas and hydro-electricity, and also post-war political and economic chaos. British exports to Italy in 1920, for example, were half of their level in 1913. Exports to Germany and Russia had effectively ceased.

If the external factors affecting the industry were adverse after 1918, its internal structure had always been grossly inefficient. As Tawney put it later, 'The British coal industry resembled a pampered youth who refuses to grow up. Its structure had been crystallised in the days before serious competition had become a reality.'[23] There was no overall organization of the industry and no economies of scale in a highly fragmented structure. The pits were worked as independent fiefdoms without cooperation between owners with contiguous mines.[24] Collieries bought their equipment individually; adjoining mines were maintained and pumped clear quite separately; they organized the freightage of the coal and its marketing independently.[25] Coal wagons on the railways, of which there were an estimated 1.4 million, were the property of individual railway companies, mine owners and merchants, and were more often than not empty as they were shunted around the country. The consumer was at the mercy of an inflated number of middlemen who all took their cut. Meanwhile, in a quarter of a century 'some 25,000 persons have been killed in the mines, and some three and a quarter million have been injured.'[26]

In one celebrated series of exchange in the commission's hearings, Tawney questioned the Mining Association's chief spokesman and witness, Joseph Alfred Pease, first Baron Gainford. He was a colliery owner himself with interests in the Northumberland, Durham and Yorkshire coalfields, and a former Liberal minister in the Asquith administrations.[27] Gainford supported profit-sharing schemes as a solution to labour difficulties and Tawney pointed out 'that more than three-fourths of them have been a complete failure'. They clashed over the level of profits that might be taken legitimately by owners from their mines, and over the impact of excessive profits on the remuneration of miners and the prices paid by consumers. When Tawney asked how consumers could remedy the unnaturally high costs they were charged for their coal, Gainford replied that they should go without coal until the price dropped: 'Then the only remedy you propose is that there should be a consumers' strike? – That is it.'[28]

Tawney was both appalled at the evidence of callous inefficiency on such a scale and in every corner of the industry, and fascinated by the potential it offered for a process of rationalization by the state. As he put it in the most understated way in an academic journal, 'it is hardly possible to resist the conclusion that, in spite of the skill and enterprise shown by individual companies and managers, the present organization of the industry does not make the most economical use of the coal resources of the nation.'[29] He was much more outspoken in a pamphlet for the Labour Party:

> Coal, it is no exaggeration to say, was wasted up to 1914 as though it were water. Its production and distribution were carried on, not on any co-ordinated system, but with a single eye to the profit of individuals, colliery companies and merchants. It was only when the nation was confronted with the necessity of economizing its supplies that an attempt was made to reduce to some kind of order the existing chaos.

But wartime regulation under a coal controller was not enough to end the chaos – only public ownership would do:

> The inability of mere "control" to reorganize the industry and the constant struggle with private interests in which the Coal Controller was engaged are a proof that the external regulation of private capitalism by a Government Department cannot by itself succeed in securing justice either for the worker or for the consumer.[30]

The Sankey Commission found it impossible 'to consider the question of wages and hours without at the same time considering the general question of the organization of the industry.'[31] It split three ways in separate reports outlining alternative solutions to the immediate dispute between the miners and mineowners. Sankey's proposals, which increased miners' remuneration and cut their working day, were accepted by the miners after a ballot. Later in the year Sankey issued a further report, supported by the three miners and the three economists, calling for the state purchase of the nation's mineral resources and collieries with fair compensation to the owners. It went on to devise a new administrative structure for the industry including local and district mining councils to coordinate production, each with a designated number of places for miners themselves. There would also be a Minister of Mines and a national mining council to advise the minister. The industry was to be financially autonomous, rather than under Treasury control; the mines department was to be managed 'with the freedom of a private business' and kept clear of civil service practices and methods. The key institution in the structure was intended to be the district council overseeing production on a coalfield: there was to be no question of 'managing the industry from Whitehall'. The three mine owners and two of the businessman would accept the nationalization of minerals but opposed state purchase and control of the mines under any such administrative structure. They merely advocated new mechanisms for wage bargaining based upon the model of the existing Whitley Councils.

Tawney was amazed and delighted by Sankey's conclusions: to have the support of the chairman was an undoubted coup. As Jeanette wrote to her mother, 'Harry is deeply interested in the final Coal Report. It is truly astonishing that a Judge should have been converted by arguments & to such an extent that the miners' representatives have not sent in more than a very brief Report & say that they are in substantial agreement with the Chairman.'[32] Tawney took away many lessons from the 4 months of work on the Commission. They were all contained, however, in the deceptively simple conclusion that 'the first remedy for high prices is to see that the organisation of the coal industry is improved, rather than to reduce the wages of the miners or to lengthen the hours of labour in the mines'.[33] The root of the problem was in the chaos of the industry; reform it, and justice for the miners would become relatively easy. If he became a trusted advisor to the Miners' Federation of Great Britain after 1919, Tawney was more than just an advocate for their interests. He regarded himself as an independent voice calling for sane public administration on the basis of the evidence. Moreover, justice for the miners would be more than merely pecuniary because it would also give them, under these proposals, a shared role in the future governance of their industry. An industrial dispute over wages had, once investigated, become an enquiry into the defective structures of a whole industry and beyond that, of the political economy of the nation. As a member of the first coal commission Tawney had undergone a practical education in the relationship between the state, private enterprise and the public of a rare sort.

The results of that education were evident 6 months after the Sankey report was published in some notes Tawney drafted 'on the state of the coal industry' for the Archbishop of Canterbury, Randall Davidson, which he sent via George Bell.

Coal and its problems were now generalized by him into yet wider economic and social questions regarding the future of the working class and the structure of all industry. Coal was the 'test case' which could be used as a basis for systemic reform.

> Every clear-minded man recognises that in the next few years there must be a real change in the position and status of the working classes, and in the relation of industry to the community. The future – moral as well as economic – of the country depends upon that change being brought about by Constitutional means. Is that possible? The coal industry is a test case (a) because economically it is, like the railways, ripe for reorganisation, which many other industries are not, (b) because of the strength of the miners' organisation (c) because the defects of the existing organisation of the industry have been thoroughly exposed and several schemes have been worked out in detail for its reconstruction. If the burning question of the coal industry can be settled there will be a revival of faith in the possibility of orderly progress. If it cannot – if the "interests" are too strong and the government too timid, there will be a reaction towards "direct action" among all organised workers. The danger of the present situation is that Labour is much stronger in industry than it is in politics. If it becomes evident that political action cannot find a settlement of industrial issues, that danger will be accentuated.[34]

Tawney set out here his own position regarding the intense industrial unrest that stretched from 1919 to 1926. He favoured the constitutional and parliamentary route to socialism, opposed industrial action as a proxy or substitute for political reform and laid an obligation on the constitutional authorities to address workers' grievances and solve them.

Tawney then set out four possible alternative solutions to the question of coal – the same four that he rehearsed later in several journal articles. The industry could return to the pre-1914 status quo ante 'with all its problems and tensions'. It could maintain wartime regulations into peacetime, but control of the industry had pleased no group, whether mineowners, mineworkers or consumers. As he explained elsewhere, this had none of the advantages of either private enterprise or public ownership: the owners were guaranteed their profits and had no incentive to take initiatives, while the Coal Controller had no means of compelling them to adopt improvements.[35] A third option was to reconstruct the industry as a system of regulated monopolies, but history showed that where these had been established 'they control the public more effectively than the public can control them.'[36] The final option was 'public ownership plus a scheme of joint control between the state, consumers, and all grades of mine workers', which Tawney supported. He did so because

> There is a growing demand on the part of workmen in many industries for what is called a share in "control" . . . they do desire to exchange the position of "hands" for that of partners. They desire a share in the government of industry for the same reasons that they desire, and have won, a share in the government of the state.[37]

He emphasized the word 'share': 'there is really no desire for what is called "syndicalism," that is, the management of the industry exclusively by the workers in it', but those who did the work must be represented on the boards controlling the industry.[38] With typical prescience he warned of the consequences of inaction: 'The facts are known, and the issues have been thrashed out in public . . . If we fail here we may have ten or fifteen years of embattled class struggle. If we succeed, we shall have opened a way for the orderly transformation of industrial relations.'[39] He was wrong only in the estimate of the duration of the struggle, which subsided in the late 1920s.

Tawney was aware of all the objections to such a solution, and in all his discussions of the reorganization of the coal industry in this period he presented them fairly and justly, as he did for the Archbishop in these notes. As he explained, it was variously argued nationalization would entail inflexible centralization, administration by civil servants, treasury control, rule by the Miners' Federation of Great Britain and so forth, each of which would destroy enterprise and entrepreneurship, and he tried to answer these objections in turn as best he could. In other essays he was scrupulous in making a distinction between the ownership of an industry and its administration: 'when the question of ownership has been settled, the question of administration still remains for solution. The possible types of organisation, if private ownership is terminated, are various, and the practical merits or demerits of Nationalization depend largely on which is selected.' The supposed advantages of public ownership would not flow automatically and might even be stymied by the wrong administrative structure; in turn, the feared emergence of its vices would depend 'upon whether the administrative system established is such as to encourage or to repress them'. As Tawney understood 'the type of organization to accompany public ownership . . . is precisely the most complex and important of the questions at issue.'[40] The success or otherwise of nationalization would depend upon 'the precise form of administrative machinery under which the industry is managed'.[41] He also recognized that the spirit in which workers embraced any new arrangements would be crucial to their success. They could no longer be treated as 'servants executing orders'. They would have to be given 'a collective responsibility for the character of the service' so as 'to make positive contributions to the administration and development of their industry'.[42] The nation and its labour movement would have to 'draw the public spirit and professional pride of the workmen in to the development of the industry,' for they stood 'in a position of responsible partnership with the community'.[43]

These considerations did not imply insuperable doubts about public ownership but only Tawney's honest recognition that the opposition's arguments had to be answered. With this in mind, he came together with Laski in the aftermath of the Sankey Commission to publish together the minutes of the evidence presented there by Viscount Haldane under the title *The Problem of Nationalization*.[44] Haldane had been Secretary of State for War and Lord Chancellor in the Liberal administrations before 1914: he was known to favour the nationalization of the mines.[45] His testimony had focused on the practicalities of government administration of the mines, and by implication, other industries as well. He had contended that it would be perfectly possible to recruit public servants with the necessary talents and to train them for the management of a business. Using this evidence, Tawney and Laski disputed the prevalent view that 'only considerations of private profit are adequate to the provision of efficient management' and that administration by the state was a recipe for 'inertia and soullessness'. Given the indisputable evidence that the organization of the coal industry 'had broken down . . . we need a spirit willing to experiment with new forms if its defects are to be remedied'. But the elision here between 'management' and 'spirit' is revealing: even when discussing bureaucracy, Tawney could intuit that nothing would be achieved unless undertaken on all sides in a spirit of cooperation and mutual advantage.[46]

This continued to be his position in the years that followed. Lecturing in Chicago in 1948 he emphasized the need 'to rationalise and re-equip' industries that were then coming under state control and 'to enlist the cooperation of workers in increasing output'.[47] In 1953, after the nationalizations of the Attlee administrations were complete, he returned to the conditions and the spirit required to make them a success:

> Nationalization, thus conceived, is a means not an end. It is important less for what it does than for what it enables to be done. Its success depends, not on the mere change of ownership, which, though a necessary first step, is no more, but on the advantage taken of the opportunity offered by it to carry through

measures of reorganization which private enterprise was unwilling or unable to undertake; to create services, not only directed by first-class management, but animated throughout by a strong esprit de corps; and, by enlisting the active co-operation of employees, to make the industries concerned a model on which the workers in them look with pride, those outside them with envy and admiration, and the public with confidence.[48]

It must be recalled that in almost all cases the industries taken into state ownership were old, inefficient, often subject to strong and growing international competition, and had lacked imaginative leadership. The subsequent history of underinvestment, overmanning, low productivity and poor management, coupled with the political temptation not to rationalize industries in sensitive locations where unemployment was already high, is well known and is a chapter in any history of Britain between the 1940s and 1980s. Tawney had made plain the conditions which nationalization required to be a success; those conditions were never met, though clearly some would argue that it was not the execution of British nationalization but its very conception which was at fault.

One of the latter was his older colleague at the London School of Economics (LSE), Graham Wallas, one of the most prominent of the early Fabians of the 1880s but someone whose fealty to liberalism led to a break with the socialism of Shaw and the Webbs.[49] He reviewed Tawney's *Acquisitive Society* on its publication in 1921 with some scepticism. Noting that Tawney's 'social sympathy [was] as authentic as that of William Morris' he nevertheless questioned Tawney's basic assumption in the book 'that associations of producers shall be given greater independence so that they may develop the virtues which result from professional feeling'. He queried Tawney's faith in the control of industry by producers. He had been a member of the London School Board from 1894 to 1907 and suggested in response the example of teachers: it would not do to give teachers control of education because so many other people and groups have a stake in it, and so many social processes and functions depended upon it. The same, Wallas argued, was true of agriculture: it is not just those who labour on the earth who make it possible or who are interested in its outcomes. 'Mr Tawney also seems to me to exaggerate the degree to which the grant of self-government will of itself increase the "public spirit" of the producer.' Wallas simply doubted this, fearful that professional independence (or in another form and by another name, workers' control) might encourage the selfish use of monopoly power against other groups, interests and consumers. He also questioned Tawney's preference for social service over the profit motive: many people, he contended, act in socially beneficial ways while seeking their own economic advantage. In an argument going back to the eighteenth-century political economy of Adam Smith and the Scottish Enlightenment, he suggested that social service and self-service are not necessarily antagonistic. (Interestingly, it was a point also made by William Temple who, in an interview in 1926, 'thought that Tawney's outright condemnation of the "acquisitive instinct" . . . went too far'.)[50] In short, Wallas pointed to an alternative explanation of the weaknesses of British nationalization: not its failure in practice, which was Tawney's concern, but its false assumptions in theory and from the outset.[51]

The clarity of Tawney's social and economic analysis of the coal industry assured him of influence and an audience. His dissection of the coal question was an example of intellectual brilliance all the more striking because much of it was undertaken in public in the cross-examination of hapless witnesses. No doubt he was able to persuade many people of the case for public ownership in this manner and by deploying these powerful arguments. But perhaps of even greater interest and significance is that he persuaded *himself* of the case. Before the First World War, Tawney's socialism was ethical and spiritual, and he was sceptical of the Webbs' approach which conflated socialism with state control and substituted forms of social administration for sheer conviction. Now, with Sidney Webb at his side – and they did indeed sit together at the Royal Commission hearings – Tawney was being converted to a manner of thinking about social and economic questions which he had largely avoided and sometimes rejected.[52] Before the First World War Tawney spoke and wrote relatively little about the state and its role in realizing socialism. Now, in the analysis of the coal industry he became converted to the cause of public ownership, a cause he would champion thereafter. Tawney was right about the coal industry and when faced with the facts a neutral like Justice Sankey came to the same conclusions. But could the solutions to the disorder of such a grossly inefficient industry be generalized and made applicable to the rest of Britain's major enterprises? Moreover, Tawney as a young man had rejected the Webbs' contention that 'socialism equals efficiency' which, as he argued, might be true but was beside the point. To Tawney, the justification for socialism was that it would be morally superior, not technically more effective. The coal commission was a turning point in Tawney's career, the time and place he was noticed widely. But it was also a turning point in his thinking because he adopted a position in 1919 which, though it was entirely plausible in the circumstances and was to become the dominant idea in British socialism for the next half-century, he had previously argued against with passion and eloquence.[53]

The transition in his thinking was complete by the time he delivered six lectures in the United States at the Williamstown Institute of Politics in August 1924, published the following year as *The British Labor Movement*. Essaying all aspects of his subject he showed himself to be a brilliant historian of British labour whose ideas would still find favour today among historians. The book is of most interest, however, in demonstrating his faith in the Labour Party and state socialism at this time. Tawney could see that the war itself had turned the party from 'the political wing of an industrial movement' into a national party appealing to people of all types, in which they could vest their 'hopes of a serious policy of social reform'.[54] This explains the very notable migration to it of intellectuals in the immediate post-war period. He defined himself as one of these: he had been attracted to Labour because 'the particular reforms which appealed to me appeared . . . to have little chance of being realized' without its emergence as a national force – though in saying this he overlooked for purposes of clarity and concision his longstanding commitment to socialist policy since his student days.[55] But now he embraced socialism as the application of state-led utilitarianism rather than Christian morality: the test to be applied was 'how far in fact we succeed in mobilizing our national economy in the most efficient manner and in distributing the products in such a way as to produce the greatest aggregate well-being'.[56] This was the very doctrine and language of efficiency which he spurned before the war in his *Commonplace Book*. There, he had argued with Fabian socialists who had put their faith in civic administration and social mechanisms rather than spirit and soul.[57] Now, he was more appreciative, though evidently not without some measure of doubt, about their efforts 'to turn Socialism from a romantic Utopianism into prosaic schemes of reorganization based on detailed investigation and capable of piece-meal realization through the existing machinery of national and local government'.[58]

In the years that followed the Sankey Commission Tawney was a trusted advisor to the miners. Indeed, gamekeeper turned poacher in 1926: having sat in judgment on the Sankey Commission, 6 years later Tawney was the chief spokesman for the MFGB before the next Royal Commission on the coal industry chaired by Sir Herbert Samuel, the former Liberal minister, which included among its members Will Beveridge.[59] Once more the immediate issue was a crisis in profitability which the owners were seeking to solve by wage cuts and/or increases to the working week. But on this occasion, and under the influence of Tawney, the miners, acting tactically, did not present evidence on the crisis developing in the mines, which would have been superfluous, their case having been made so many times before, but on the future of the industry under nationalization.[60] Tawney presented sophisticated memoranda on behalf of the MFGB and endorsed by the Trades Union Congress and the Labour Party, proposing the integration of the coal and power-generating industries in a new conglomerate 'for mining coal, manufacturing electrical power on a very large scale . . . and producing, in addition, gas, fuel oils, ammonium compounds, chemical base materials for tar, and other by-products'. Instead of being a declining industry on its own, coal should become part of an enlarged and modernized power-generation industry, utilizing the newest technologies.[61] It was a bold gambit to turn the attention of the Commission and nation towards a better future rather than an embattled present, and Tawney's written submission and oral evidence started from the assumption that nationalization was the first requirement for modernization: indeed, it was axiomatic throughout his evidence that the problems of the industry were caused by the inefficiencies of private enterprise rather than the obduracy of the miners. Profitability could be re-established by efficiency rather than by cuts.[62]

Tawney was questioned by Samuel, by his brother-in-law, and then by Mr W. A. Lee, a representative of the Miners' Association on the Commission. He took the stand for hours; he showed great command of the organization and economics of the industry; he was on sparkling form throughout. To reinforce the point that centralized and bureaucratic management can become remote from the workforce and the coalface, Beveridge asked Tawney 'whether you yourself are a working miner?' and Tawney replied that 'I have never had those advantages, Sir William'.[63] When Lee began questioning him over supposed political subversion of the miners by syndicalists and intellectuals like himself, Tawney paraphrased his views thus: 'that about 1913 the Miners' Federation was bitten by a mad dog'.[64] Late in his exchanges with Lee Tawney ventured an appreciation of the coal owners: he did 'not think the owners have no imagination. I think their history of this crisis is highly imaginative'.[65]

All his interlocutors were sceptical about the complex machinery Tawney set out for the management of the new super-industry. Herbert Samuel put to Tawney the conventional objections to nationalization which Tawney had already rebutted in his pamphlets and speeches. With Beveridge he held a public seminar on the reorganization of the mines which began with a discussion of administration but moved on to the psychology of the miners. Tawney emphasized their 'strong desire to be consulted about the development of their industry': 'If you are going to carry on the industry effectively you have to get their confidence and their public opinion on the side of the administration'.[66] Yet Tawney did not have all the best lines. Though Lee's attempts to pin the charge of political extremism on the miners were disrupted by Tawney's ridicule, his later questions on the place of the state in the proposed new arrangements caused Tawney greater difficulty. Lee drew a distinction between the government 'standing in a detached position between private owners of mines and the workers, and the position in which the State is compelled to come in as the owner of the mines and the employer of the miners itself' which Tawney rejected.[67] Lee also had an eye for 'the illimitable resources of the state' which, he believed, would be called upon to prop up ailing industries under nationalization.[68] In this case subsequent history proved Lee correct, and it was to the disadvantage of the miners. The politicization of disputes within an ailing nationalized industry which required public subsidies became routine because, as Lee argued, it was inevitable, and the power of the state was such that it did for the miners in the end. Tawney put his faith in the sympathy of a benign state, but what if it should use its power in ways that were hostile to the miners and to workers in other nationalized industries as well?

The Samuel Commission could do nothing to end the disputes within the coal industry and the country slid towards a General Strike in the weeks after it ended its hearings in early 1926. Tawney kept a 'Diary of Negotiations' from March until May of that year which he described much later in this way:

> I was at the time rather closely in touch with the MFGB, and acting as a kind of informal advisor to the miners. The Mss notes in my writing must, I think, have been put together because I probably saw more of the daily vicissitudes of the crisis than any other outsider, and wished to keep a record. I used to draft a certain amount of stuff for the miners to use in letters to the Press and so on, and may have thought it advisable to set out a statement of the facts for my guidance.[69]

During the General Strike itself Tawney had a place in the TUC's headquarters in Ecclestone Square from where he dealt with the press. There is a good story, emanating from Jimmy Mallon and told much later to the Labour MP Lena Jeger who was Tawney's close friend in his last years, that concerns these frantic days. Apparently 'Tawney wrote a strong letter to *The Times* and, being pushed for a deadline, put J. H. Thomas's signature to it. Next day at Ecclestone Square RHT bumped into JHT who said, "Did you see the prominence *The Times* gave to my letter?" RHT replied: "See it? You bloody fool I wrote it". Mallon added that it was the only time he heard Tawney swear.[70] Tawney's attitude to the General Strike in 1926 appears to have been clear-eyed, realistic and in line with his remarks to the Archbishop on the coal industry: he supported it out of loyalty to the good cause that the miners were fighting for, but he had no wider political ambitions beyond securing justice for them. He was one of several who, in the days before the stoppage, lobbied Randall Davidson to intervene and suggest a plan for conciliation.[71] Immediately the strike was over, Tawney wrote another of his brilliant analyses, in 32 handwritten pages, of its origins, course and likely effects, and sent it to Temple, perhaps for onward transmission to the Archbishop. This, too, is notable for its clarity and cool good sense. Tawney displayed great sympathy and solidarity with the miners but embraced no political cause beyond that.[72] His nephew recalled going with him to visit another of the great socialist intellectuals of this era, G. D. H. Cole, in Oxford during the strike and Cole saying

> "We are living in a revolution". Tawney did not comment. I think he disliked confrontation talk to that pitch and I remember he evaded answering the question "do you hope the General Strike is a success?" His interest was in the limited aim of forcing the government to follow the policy he advocated which would end the Coal Strike or "lock out" as he regarded it . . . Tawney was not interested in what one might call a syndicalist triumph; it was the coal mining stoppage and recourse by the government to the available remedy as he saw it, which concerned him . . . I am sure Tawney considered it his duty without knowing where the strike would lead, to show his sympathy with the leaders of the General Strike: it had become Party and not just Union policy and he was a good party man.[73]

When the General Strike ended and the miners stayed out, still refusing to accept pay cuts or an increase in their working hours, Tawney continued to plead their cause and to offer his services in fashioning a fair settlement in the industry, 'assuming the Government wanted a compromise and were not simply out for a Treaty of Versailles in the coal industry'.[74] As he wrote in a memorandum to his old friend Thomas Jones, now the cabinet secretary, in September 1926, in which he called for magnanimity on the part of Baldwin's government, 'The only hope of bringing things to a close is to start with some form of national agreement as promised by the Chancellor'.[75]

In the years before 1926 Tawney tried three times to be elected as a Labour MP, first in Rochdale, a town where he had many personal contacts dating from his WEA classes there, in the Coupon Election at the end of the First World War; and then in South Tottenham in November 1922, and in Swindon 2 years later in October 1924. In 1918 he was endorsed by the Rochdale Trades and

Labour Council where his election agent, a Mr Frith, was 'confident of (his) return'.[76] In addition to the usual party literature, Tawney put out a poster with commendations from the non-conformist ministers in the town, more than 40 trades unions, the famous Rochdale Equitable Pioneers Society which had founded the consumer cooperative movement in the 1840s, and the United Irish League. William Temple endorsed him on behalf of 'churchmen' adding for good measure 'I should like immensely to help Tawney', though it was all to no avail.[77] A comrade from the Western Front, Bill Louth, recalled of that 1918 campaign that although he was the only one of the candidates to have been a combatant, Tawney was too fastidious and principled to use this to his advantage. There was a notice on the wall of his committee room that 'All references to the candidate's military career are prohibited'.[78]

Tawney was adopted as the Labour candidate for Tottenham before he fell seriously ill in the autumn of 1922. He offered to withdraw but the branch committee decided unanimously that he should carry on, though their endorsement of him was somewhat ambivalent: 'We feel that whenever an election comes, that Mr Tawney has so endeared himself to those who know him, & have heard or met him, and that the revulsion of feeling against the government is so strong, that we could fight the battle – with a good chance of winning – in his absence'.[79] At the end of his life Tawney recalled the 1922 campaign with a matching diffidence: 'I have a fairly vivid recollection of my days as a candidate at Tottenham, when, owing to the efficiency of yourself and other active workers, I more nearly got in than in any other seat in spite of – or because of – the fact that I could not do any canvassing myself as I was in bed in hospital'.[80] To make up for his absence the local party asked Harold Laski to organize a rally in the constituency and coopt the services of students from the LSE: between 30 and 40 of them worked for Tawney in Tottenham. Meanwhile the local party asked Tawney's friends and colleagues to send messages of endorsement for his candidacy which might be made public. Letters poured in extolling his virtues from Mansbridge and Cole, Bertrand Russell and H. G. Wells, Bishops Gore and Temple, Sidney Webb and C. P. Scott, and even Ramsay MacDonald who Tawney would come to loathe in a few years. But even these luminaries could not win enough support and Tawney fell about 2,000 votes short.[81] Tawney was not too crestfallen: as he wrote to Gilbert Murray, 'it was for the best, as I shall not be much use for some months'.[82] When Tawney wrote to ask George Bernard Shaw to open a function in the constituency at this time he received a reply on a picture postcard worth quoting: 'Do you suppose I should still be alive now – at 66 – if I opened bazaars? On your life, make it an iron rule never to open anything, least of all that most loathsome of all bourgeois mendicity institutions, a bazaar. Tell the South Tottenham enthusiasts to go to Bath. G. Bernard Shaw.'[83]

It was ill-health that finally put paid to his parliamentary ambitions. Tawney was also unable to campaign in the 1924 election in Swindon where he had been adopted as candidate. As Jeanette reported to her mother in the following year 'we have reluctantly had to give up all idea of Parliamentary life for Harry. He had recurring attacks of pain in his side this autumn and there seems no alternative. It has come as a great disappointment to me as I like the people at Swindon so much.'[84] Later, in1931, he was invited to become the Labour candidate for Colne Valley, but he turned it down and was, in any case, in China for that catastrophic election.[85] And there is evidence that further invitations came his way later in the 1930s when he was well into his fifties. In late 1935 Beatrice Webb recorded in her diary that Jeanette has asked her 'to dissuade him from sacrificing his health and his livelihood by accepting a seat in the House of Commons from the miners or some other proletarian admirers'. She kindly obliged: when Tawney asked for her advice, expressing his concern that he should be doing more 'to make things better during his lifetime,' she assured him 'that his influence would be hopelessly wasted in the House of Commons – that he would find life in the House of Commons as a private member intolerable, that his gift for thought and expression ought to be used to think out the broad lines of Labour policy during the next decade, in principle and in detail.'[86]

Tawney poked gentle and self-deprecating fun at his 'uniformly unsuccessful habit of parliamentary candidature'.[87] Several of his friends and contemporaries felt that Tawney, in the words of his *Times* obituary, 'was perhaps not really fitted for the work of the House of Commons . . . The loosely built, untidy figure with a heavy brown moustache and a remote and habitually concentrated look was unmistakably that of a scholar rather than a common-room man'.[88] They were probably correct: his talents were not for the oratorical flourish in the House of Commons, or for socializing with constituents, but for the well-reasoned, closely argued and ironic essay, or the WEA class. He could be a good committee man but frequently lost patience. Tawney's nephew thought him too didactic:

> I think Tawney was rejected in parliamentary constituencies partly because they thought he was too much of an intellectual, partly also because he simply was

not personally combative; he was not by nature a debater but a teacher. In a way one might say this was due to his moral self-confidence, his feeling that he was right in spite of his outward humility, a famous trait.[89]

Frank Emery, his admiring student, simply thought him above politics and too good for it:

Unlike Laski I don't think Tawney was ever politically-minded in the Laski sense. Tawney was above political expediency or political parties. Political theories yes, and social doctrines yes ... But the everyday humdrum life of politics I should say no ... I remember going to Rochdale when Tawney was fighting the Rochdale election, and hearing people say, Well this man's a genius, this man's a really great man he's far too good for Westminster, this man will never get in because no one will vote for a God. They'd rather vote, you know, for the orthodox party person, but this man – look at him, he's no politician.[90]

Tawney is sometimes said to have stood for the Independent Labour Party (ILP) in the Rochdale campaign. But if 'a good party man' for the Labour Party he was certainly not orthodox enough for the ILP. His papers include a remarkable letter from the ILP's then chairman, Philip Snowden, later Chancellor of the Exchequer in the first two Labour administrations and briefly in the cabinet of the subsequent National Government, in which he formally and viciously disowned Tawney, suggesting that he seek the nomination of the local Labour Party instead, which he did. The issue was over Tawney's principled resignation from the ILP in 1914 over the First World War. The ILP was against Britain's participation in the war and Tawney thought it right to resign given his opposite views. Snowden explained that within the ILP members had been allowed to hold different opinions, but resignation was unacceptable: 'the fact that you attach so much importance to your differences of opinion with the ILP on the war that you sacrificed your membership, shows that you regarded this disagreement as of far greater weight than your agreement with the party on its social policy.' Snowden added that it would be unconstitutional for the ILP to nominate a person who was not a member of the party: 'We were induced to give our support to your nomination in the first instance because we were under the impression that your membership had lapsed through inadvertence on your joining the army.'[91] This was petty, dogmatic and sectarian behaviour. It was also callous in the extreme when so many hundreds of thousands had given their lives so recently, and many hundreds of thousands more had been wounded for their country, like Tawney himself. Tawney's reactions are unknown: he just pressed on with his campaign to represent the people of Rochdale. But Snowden's behaviour may add a personal element to Tawney's capacious disrespect for Ramsay MacDonald and his leadership of the Labour Party in the 1920s and 1930s: through it all, Snowden was at MacDonald's right hand, and he betrayed his party far more egregiously in 1931 than did Tawney in 1914. Principled resignation is no betrayal at all.

Tawney's growing reputation in the post-war period was welcomed by Jeanette, for one, who revelled in Tawney's celebrity in 1919 and the new social life it led to. As she wrote to her father 'I feel as though Lord Haldane Monday, Bishop of Bombay Tuesday & Crown Prince [of Sweden] Wednesday is rather much for one week.'[92] There was even the ultimate mark of 'social arrival' to be savoured, dinner with Nancy Astor and her guests, who included on this occasion General Pershing and his staff who were about to return to the United States, as well as Rudyard Kipling and Lord Reading.[93] But the establishment's embrace went only so far, and certainly not as far as the offices of the *Saturday Review*, which, at the very same time Jeanette was enjoying her taste of the high life in the summer of 1919, and under the headline 'Bolshevism at Oxford', launched a campaign against Tawney and also against his old college for appointing him to a fellowship. The appointment was 'not merely an academic but a national outrage'.

> Mr R. H. Tawney and Mr Sidney Webb are openly associated with the extreme wing of the Labour Party; they are the "intellectuals" who write their manifestoes and reports . . . The Master and Fellows of Balliol may be communists and socialists to a man, if they choose: but they have no business to teach socialism to the sons of the proprietary classes. Some regard should surely be paid to the views of the parents . . . Some seven or eight years ago All Souls College appointed Mr Tawney to lecture to tutorial classes, which are, we believe, composed of young artisans. And then we are alarmed to discover that so many of the rising generation in all classes are anarchical Socialists! What else can be expected? We protest against a Left Wing Socialist indoctrinating undergraduates at Oxford with confiscatory ideas.

Tawney was accused of 'preaching Fabianism at Oxford' (which should hardly have bothered anyone, even if true, which it wasn't). When the Sankey Report was published the *Saturday Review* dismissed it, adding for good measure: 'This is the kind of political economy which Mr Tawney has been appointed by the Master and Fellows to teach the undergraduates at Balliol' (which probably *was* true). The *Saturday Review* finally ended its tirades welcoming a new student magazine emanating from 'Tory Trinity' College next door to Balliol which they hailed 'as an antidote to Tawneyism'.[94] Tawneyism, however, could not be stopped, and over the course of the interwar years it became enormously popular with both young and old, especially in universities. Tawney's papers include a poem entitled 'Long Vacation' which had been snipped out of an unknown newspaper. Its first stanza is quite enough:

> Elizabeth lies in the hammock with a book they've told her to read –
> A book by Professor Tawney, a very good book indeed;
> There's sun on the distant cornfields; there are cirrus clouds in the sky,
> And Elizabeth lies in the hammock and watches them drift by.

A more substantial and fitting mark of Tawney's new status was the public concern for him when he fell ill in September 1922 while on a trip to Germany and Austria. Subject since the war to recurrent pain from his wounds, he had an especially bad attack while at an educational conference in Schloss Brühl which required hospitalization and rest in Germany and then an operation on his return to England. A few days after the operation he contracted pneumonia.[95] At one point in this period Laski had written sorrowfully to his great American correspondent, Oliver Wendell Holmes, that Tawney was dying.[96] Tawney was forced to miss the Michaelmas and Lent Terms of 1922–3 at the LSE. Letters poured in to Jeanette to wish him well: they ranged from the members of the Tottenham branch of the Amalgamated Engineering Union and WEA students he had taught to Labour MPs and public figures and were an index of growing recognition and also admiration.[97] Indeed there were bulletins on his progress in the press.[98] As one young admirer from these years, the future economic historian William Court later reflected, 'It is difficult at this distance of time to make clear to those who never knew him or who never read his books when they were written the exceptional position held by Richard Henry Tawney in scholarship and politics in the twenties . . . the twenties and thirties marked the peak of his influence as a public man.'[99]

Tawney Between the Wars

In the summer of 1920 the Tawneys made their first trip to the United States. Harry was invited to teach for a term at Amherst College in Massachusetts and the months away were evidently delightful: as Jeanette reported to her mother, 'everything is fresh and so attractive . . . there is no rationing here & a great abundance of food . . . We feel quite tired still but are sure that this will do us both no end of good.'[1] Tawney was invited to speak in several universities, including on the west coast, where they greatly admired the architecture and sheer ease of life in Berkeley.[2] After a trip northwards they returned across the Canadian Rockies by train. At Harvard the Tawneys met another socialist writer and thinker who would be intimately linked to the London School of Economics for the next 30 years, Harold Laski, and Laski wrote immediately to an LSE professor of the preceding generation, Graham Wallas, that he

> easily capitulated to their charm . . . I liked the breadth of his general views, though I was a little inclined to doubt whether he saw the significance of psychology in politics even while he admitted that most of the current economic problems are at bottom psychological. But his ability and charm were singularly impressive.[3]

Tawney formally joined the LSE staff that autumn as lecturer in economic history on a part-time basis at a salary of £600.[4] He had been associated with the School since 1913 in his position at the Ratan Tata Foundation and had been engaged to do some occasional teaching there since 1917. In his first term he taught two courses on 'English Economic Developments between 1485 and 1760' and 'Social Developments Since 1760'. In 1922, though still part-time, the title of Reader was conferred on him when the previous Reader in Economic History at the LSE, Lillian Knowles, was promoted to the chair there. Illness forced him to take two terms of leave in 1922–3, as we have seen, and on Knowles's death in 1926 he took on the role of Head of the Department of

History. While she was still alive, in a characteristically generous manner he had declined to take a mooted second chair in Economic History because of his younger colleague Eileen Power: 'the appointment of two professors now might conceivably be held to make impossible the appointment of Miss Power to a Professorship in the future.'[5] In the event, neither the existing chair nor the mooted chair was filled in the years after Knowles died. Tawney was devoted to Eileen Power, an altogether attractive woman and accomplished scholar of late medieval economy and society who captivated and charmed her colleagues with her conversation and wonderful dress sense. Beginning her career teaching at Girton College, Cambridge in 1913, she moved to the LSE a year after Tawney in 1921 and started work there on the economic position of women in the thirteenth and fourteenth century. She was the first woman to hold a chair in Economic History (from 1931) and the first to give the Ford Lectures in English History at Oxford in 1938–9. Tawney and Power edited a book of *Tudor Economic Documents* together which was published in 1924. Their relationship was wholly platonic – and Power actually married in 1937 Tawney's student and friend Munia Postan, later Professor of Economic History at Cambridge – but she was very important to Tawney whose relationship with her as fellow workers in the same subject was unlike any other he had with a woman, whether colleague, friend or relation.[6]

In 1929 Tawney asked for a year's leave of absence, which was granted, and for a lightening of his teaching and administrative load: 'I have for some time felt an increasing desire to reduce my teaching load, in order to have more time for research and writing, and recently this desire has been reinforced by medical warnings. I want, therefore, to ask whether the School could see its way to arrange the work of the History Department in such a way as to leave me more free than is the case at present.'[7] Tawney's elevation to the revived Chair of Economic History in July 1931 at a salary of £1,000, largely paid for out of a grant to the LSE from the Rockefeller Foundation which made donations to several British universities at this time, solved the problem.[8] For the next decade Tawney enjoyed professional status and stability in this position, though following 'a sort of faint attack' in July 1938 when he was found to be anaemic and 'in a debilitated condition following excessive nervous effort' he took sick leave for a term that autumn.[9] Whether his nervous exhaustion had anything to do with the Munich crisis at that time is unclear, but Tawney was certainly greatly exercised by it. It was understood that Tawney's chair was in effect to be mainly a research post. Nevertheless, he undertook 'little if any less teaching from 1931 to 1940 than other professors' at the LSE, and from 1940 to 1945 he acted again as head of the History Department.[10]

Arnold Plant, later a senior civil servant, who had been Tawney's student in the 1920s and colleague at the LSE in the 1930s, recalled that he 'never took a leading part in the internal School politics, although he was always well-informed'. Plant did 'not think he could bother himself with wrangles over status and salaries'.[11] Tawney was never interested in purely professional matters and was too high-minded and too busy with more important projects to worry over the petty details of his job, or of others' jobs. This subject is entirely lacking from his correspondence. But issues of principle were another matter. When Laski said some foolish things in Moscow in 1934 and was threatened with an enquiry by the University of London on his return, Tawney joined with a small group of colleagues to protest in *The Times*: 'The novel suggestion that a university may properly conduct an inquiry into expressions of opinion by its teachers on matters of public interest appears to us a menace to academic freedom and to national well-being'.[12]

Plant speculated that Tawney's detachment from LSE affairs could have been because the Director of the School from 1919 until 1937 was his brother-in-law, Will Beveridge. If Beveridge enjoyed broad support among the LSE's staff in the 1920s, his authority diminished drastically in the 1930s when he interfered in their freedom of political expression.[13] Tawney was displeased by this, but kept his distance from the controversies as the price worth paying to prevent mutual embarrassment and to preserve domestic peace.[14] The two old friends corresponded very courteously and formally over matters concerning Tawney's appointments at the LSE, though because they were in close contact there on a daily basis, no other private correspondence between them survives. 'Harry' was a frequent subject in Jeanette's letters to her brother, but she never went into details about his work or thoughts. Tawney seems to have received his due from Beveridge and no more; there is no hint at all of special favours being granted to a brother-in-law of the Director, nor of them ever being asked for. Indeed, when Tawney's contract with the LSE was up for review by the LSE's Appointments Committee during the Second World War the prevailing feeling seems to have been that he had not been treated especially generously by the School despite bringing it great esteem – that 'his treatment has not been commensurate with his services'.[15]

Tawney was a devoted teacher, though not a gifted lecturer. Postan remembered that when he read his essays to his tutor in the 1920s, Tawney would procure a notebook and take notes: he took this as evidence of Tawney's respect for his students and humility as a scholar who could learn from his pupils.[16] Plant recalled that

> Tutorials with Tawney were always strictly business: what had I discovered in the dozen or so Tudor pamphlets I had just been through at the B[ritish] M[useum]? He encouraged us, or at any rate me, to think that I was unearthing material that he had missed, that I was going to teach him something. "Good heavens, where did you find that?" "What was the date?" . . . The meanest tyro was made to feel he was a collaborator.

And Tawney took pains: 'His pupils were well aware that he devoted most of his time to public and social work . . . Despite all of this he never missed a tutorial. He always conveyed the impression that he had all the time in the world to devote to our three-weekly sessions.'[17] The clergyman and theologian Ronald Preston had been Tawney's pupil in the 1930s and he recalled how Tawney 'gave a generous welcome to, and took time and trouble over, the most immature student who came his way'.[18] When, as a student, the future economic historian, W. H. B. Court, wrote to Tawney for advice, he was surprised and delighted to receive 'a prompt and friendly reply'.[19] The recollection of Tawney's younger colleague, the sociologist Richard Titmuss, that he 'took as much exquisite care preparing a talk for a group of social workers as he did for a group of distinguished historians. Excellence was for all, it was not for him to discriminate' is borne out by the many lecture drafts which survive among Tawney's papers.[20] His kindness crossed the oceans as well. In 1946 at Melbourne University one of the historians, Kathleen Fitzpatrick, wrote to a friend to explain that some of her students had just 'produced a letter from R. H. Tawney. I don't know whether the name means much to you, but to us it means "The Master".' The students had written to Tawney with an enquiry, he had asked another renowned historian of the early-modern period, J. E. Neale, for the answer, copied it out, and then sent it back to them in Melbourne.[21] In draughty church halls or municipal classrooms where he took so many of his WEA classes, addressing smaller groups of adult students, Tawney was the master of his craft. But sadly, in a large, formal lecture theatre he was not an outstanding lecturer: 'His prose was characteristically Miltonic or Churchillian, and his lectures echoed the perorations of his style of writing, each passage working up to a climax at which he would drop his voice, gabble his words and lose the richness of his concluding judgment in diffident inaudibility.'[22] Tawney's voice was higher than one might expect and without a wide register, his spoken manner slightly clipped like an NCO giving an order or reading out a list of names. He had a slight difficulty with his r's which he sometimes rolled or sometimes pronounced as a w.

In the 1920s and 1930s, assured of his position in the academic and political worlds and with a salary, which, if not generous, gave him security for the first time in his career, Tawney was quite literally at the height of his powers. What kind of man was he? Frank Emery, his old student, spoke eloquently of the power of his personality and his example:

> Something seemed to emanate from the man, which you absorbed unconsciously ... And I think that ran through the whole of the man's life. Whatever he did seemed to result in this kind of a transference from himself to other people, a part of his amazing personality, part of his genius, part of the whole nobility and character of the man himself.[23]

Postan, who knew him more intimately, recalled the 'flow of spontaneous eloquence and wit ... I've never heard anybody converse in that way. It was a grandiloquence that came so naturally to him, that he didn't sound ... grandiloquent'. To deal with that wit one had to be 'disrespectful ... candid and jocular and somewhat outrageously rude sometimes'.[24] Richard Rees agreed that he was 'both amusing and witty' but could also be 'pretty severe when he wanted to be'.[25] The Indian writer Ved Mehta, who was an undergraduate at Oxford in the 1950s, met him once there in his old age and was reminded 'of Socrates at his most ironical ... like Socrates he would either be absolutely silent, or deliver an endless monologue'.[26] Ernest Green, his close colleague in the WEA, recalled his impatience (and his talent for forgiveness as well) and his outrageous demands on WEA administrators when he wanted information quickly: 'he had very little knowledge of business procedure. He was a profoundly academic person, a man removed from the sordid affairs of this world and a man who hardly realised the practical difficulties which faced the administrator'.[27] Rees agreed, recalling 'his professorial vagueness and absent-mindedness carried really to almost inconceivable lengths'.[28] According to Mehta, 'he gave the impression of being a Platonic Ideal of the absent-minded scholar'.[29]

His tastes were simple ones. Arnold Plant used to visit him each summer on trips from Cape Town where he was based for part of the 1920s: 'A loaf of bread and some cheese would arrive on a tray, to be dumped on the flattest pile of books on the table, and we would talk for a couple of hours ... He was a scholar who had a good appetite ... After the last war, bread-rationing was an irritation which he enjoyed circumventing.'[30] At Oxford his favourite novelist was apparently George Eliot.[31] As he wrote to Denman, she 'sees through you all at once with a look.'[32] Later he read a lot of Joseph Conrad, describing him as 'the best of contemporary English novelists' in 1914 when his mother-in-law sent him *Under Western Eyes*.[33] A few weeks before the Somme, Tawney re-read Conrad's *Victory*, a novel about redemption.[34] It is not hard to see why Conrad appealed: manly stories of great and noble deeds, of men who defied the elements or social conventions or their fate, chimed with Tawney's radical and independent sensibility. Michal Vyvyan recalled that his uncle quoted most from Belloc and Chesterton: 'his sympathy with them was complex.'[35] Late in his life Tawney enjoyed less elevated literature: 'I always remember his interest in what people call thrillers and bloods and detective stories, because I supplied a good many of them on loan ... he wasn't interested in the ones that [were] supposed to be subtle and complex and complicated. The simpler the plot the better he liked it.'[36] It is a matter of some curiosity that G. D. H. Cole wrote thrillers and his friend Tawney read them. Thus did the two greatest British socialist thinkers of the century spend their time.

Tawney's physiognomy was a subject for discussion throughout his life. People referred again and again to his 'noble' features. One of his neighbours in the 1950s, a Miss Allen, drew him on several occasions and saw him through artists' eyes. To her, 'his face was that of a countryman, his head was noble, the chin of a fighter. His shoulders were square, and his body thickset.' She described his head as 'a contradiction, and yet a complete whole. A very extended high brow – the very strong steel-like jaw, the aristocratic features in between, and the purposeful shoulders ... made a whole'. She admired the way he wore his hats – usually a Homburg – 'with bravado'.[37] But as Emery explained: 'he was completely oblivious as to what clothes implied. I think Tawney would have walked about naked if that had been so to speak, sufficient to walk about in. But he was just that kind of man, as you know clothes meant nothing to Tawney, appearance meant nothing to Tawney.'[38] This was always a cause of friction with Jeanette, of course, especially before their marriage. But Tawney's friends (who did not have a mother-in-law to impress and placate) found the whole ensemble very amusing: as one of them apparently said of him, 'though he spoke with the accent of the University and carried his head like the Monarch of the Glen, he looked like a manual worker who hadn't bothered to tidy himself up for a collar and tie job.'[39] Lena Jeger recalled after his death that the only arguments she observed between Harry and Jeanette 'occurred when I was collecting jumble for the local Labour Party and he would tear back from her his sergeant's jacket from the First World War, the moth eaten old homburg, a perforated pullover'.[40] In that homburg he looked nothing so much as 'a street musician caught by gunfire'.[41] Another neighbour recalled sharing a taxi with Tawney who emerged from his house with a distinctly 'Napoleonic look': one coat sleeve turned inside out and his hat sideways on his head. But he also ventured that there may have been an element of cultivation to Tawney's haphazard style.[42] Arnold Plant disagreed, however:

> He seemed the genuine original, robust Old Bill character straight out of Bruce Bairnsfather's war cartoons. His dress and appearance were notorious: always the same old tweeds throughout the year, with the seasons distinguished by the number of waistcoats, buttoned up or open, worn over a foundation cardigan. There was apparently never time to get his split old boots mended. I don't think it was actually a pose. The day's programme might include meetings with local chapels of a craft union at a pub, some lecturing, sessions with Cabinet Ministers, city luncheons and WEA committees, and the dress that suited the workers' meeting served to "declare his interest" wherever else he had to be.[43]

Meanwhile Titmuss mused that his untidiness was neither natural to him nor cultivated by him but unconscious: 'it was almost as if, unconsciously I believe, he was inviting people to adopt attitudes of superiority in order to show how little he cared'.[44] The sight of a 'huge untidy old man in ill-fitting clothes' padding about Bloomsbury in size 11 boots was a fixture in the neighbourhood. He was 'an improbable urban squire' whose brown tweed suit 'always looked as if it had been slept in'.[45]

The level of disorganization around him was comical and legendary: Jack Wray, former head of the TUC's education department, knew of an occasion when he had entertained William Temple to supper 'and removed three musty volumes from his bookshelf to reveal two cold chops on a plate'.[46] After Jeanette died, their housekeeper, Mrs Rice, would prepare his weekend meals in advance, itemizing what he should eat and when. But when she returned on Monday morning she discovered that his breakfast had become lunch and his dinner had turned into breakfast.[47] The historian Brian Rodgers recalled sitting in Tawney's study when there was a 'kerfuffle': 'Tawney very nearly missed an important lunch – he had lost his tie. It was found, in a vase on the mantelpiece'.[48] His desk was simply notorious, awash with paper, books, the paraphernalia of pipe-smoking and the remains of lunch. According to Ronald Preston, 'Books and papers lay everywhere. One deduced there was a table in the centre under piles of them.'[49] According to a portrait of him published in *The Observer* in 1953,

> Tawney inhabits a world beyond mere professional untidiness. His room . . . bears most resemblance to a small though generously-stocked second-hand bookshop. A large table may be assumed to lie beneath a central pile of miscellaneous debris. To one side of this compost heap sits Professor Tawney, furry and benign, filling his pipe with herb tobacco and lighting it with innumerable boxes of matches.

His colleague, T. S. Ashton, recalled that

> At the School of Economics during his absence in Australia, the opportunity was taken to tidy his room, plane the floor, colour the walls and turn it into a proper habitation. When I took him to see it on his return he showed anxiety, sorry, he showed anxiety and dismay: "I should feel like a worm on a billiard table in there" he said. But in a week or two he'd restored it to the type of disorder he enjoyed.[50]

Ascetic in so many ways, his one indulgence was his pipe, in which he smoked not tobacco but a herbal mixture made in the Vale of Evesham not far from where he lived in Gloucestershire. This concoction

> had the merit or defect of continuing to burn when the pipe was put aside and on two occasions at least I saw him while lecturing suddenly burst into flames. Tawney leaned down, gently patted his pocket [and] said "I see I burn prematurely" and continued his discourse, the smoke still emerging from the burnt pocket.[51]

The secretary of the local ward of the Holborn and St Pancras Labour Party, Cliff Tucker, used to give the aged Tawney a lift to ward meetings: 'as the discussions warmed up he would place the pipe in the pocket of his old tweed jacket. I knew his box of matches was therein and used to be on tenterhooks awaiting the conflagration.'[52]

One other characteristic worthy of note was Tawney's love of domestic animals and their love for him. 'When you went for a walk with him in the country one dog after another came trotting up to him, ignoring you to be patted and talked to.'[53] As a student, he described one family holiday in Dawlish where a 'young, brown, unmannerly interloper' had taken to him and 'persists in trying what my trousers are really made of'.[54] He had two dogs called Bob. The first delighted the young Michal Vyvyan, but was lost in London.[55] As Tawney wrote to Jeanette from the trenches, 'I often think of how we used to walk around with poor Bob. Dear fellow, we will never see such another dog. But I shall get another after la guerre & try to pretend he is as nice, though I'm sure he will never smack his tail on the floor & jump on my knee in the same way as Bob did.'[56] He wrote to his sister Mil soon after landing in France that he had attracted the attentions of a brown puppy that had followed him one day and now lived with him in his billet.[57] The second Bob, acquired by Tawney in the 1930s, was a notably intelligent creature, a sheep dog 'whose adoration of his master was only matched by his master's of him' (sic).[58] Bob accompanied Tawney to church in the Cotswolds and when his master went forward to take the sacrament

> his dog went too and squatted by his heels as he knelt before the altar. The vicar was compliant, he said that the dog adopted a very reverent attitude, but when the vicar left the parish his successor objected to the presence of the animal and it was all Tawney could do [from] telling the new incumbent that the dog was a better Christian than he. To the pecadilloes of dogs he was more than complacent.[59]

Nor did Tawney ration his affections or discriminate. He admired cats as well. Ashton recalled him in old age nearly missing his train because he wanted to say goodbye to the Ashton family cat and feared, wrongly as it turned out, that he might have packed the poor creature in his overnight bag.[60] Richard Rees recalled seeing a cat outside the house in Mecklenburgh Square and remarking that it looked as if it was coming to make a call. 'Tawney said – you know on the judgement day, if one has to make out a case for us, I think the fact that these little creatures lived amongst us, and always, wherever they went, felt sure of a welcome, probably is one of the best things about the human race.'[61] Michal Vyvyan remembered Tawney saying once 'that puppies were the best proof of the existence of God'.[62]

Harry and Jeanette found a *modus vivendi* during these years. Harry was often away at conferences, on research trips, or meeting colleagues. On these occasions his letters home were always affectionate but never intimate, and were written as if in a state of emotional semi-detachment. However, all their experiences together, most notably during the First World War, had led to the making of a bond between them which they knew to be enduring and unbreakable. As he wrote to her in April 1928, 'Whatever misfortunes overtake us, we can console ourselves with the thought that we have what many people, poor things, miss.'[63] This wasn't an intense love, nor yet the ties that come from having a family together, but it was devotion nevertheless. In this period Tawney came to recognize that

Jeanette's interest in people and her sociability were assets he lacked on his own and skills of great value in life. 'You would have got to know everybody & made friends with them, which I can't do,' he wrote on one occasion: 'It's wonderful how many people's hearts you captured,' he wrote on another.[64] His temper was still a problem though there is evidence that his explosions were brought on by what might be termed 'external provocations', such as Ramsay MacDonald's offer to him of a peerage in 1933, and then, more seriously, the first weeks of the Second World War. 'It grieves me to think of it: I get at times so depressed, and then I take it out on you,' he wrote early in December 1939.[65] Jeanette learnt to tolerate the shambles around him. Not that she was a paragon of household virtue: she was described as 'a devoted housewife, but her ideas of domestic order were almost as elementary as those of Tawney himself', and visitors remarked on the tins and boxes she left on the kitchen floor.[66] Occasionally Jeanette helped him with his work, for example, copying out details of Lord Berkeley's estates in 1608 from papers held in the Gloucester Library, which she evidently enjoyed.[67] Her parents both died in the course of 1929, Annette having lost her formidable faculties some time before this.[68]

Harry and Jeanette's lives were much enhanced by the purchase – with the financial assistance of brother Will – of a country home, Rose Cottage, Elcombe, near Stroud in the Cotswolds. It was primitive in many respects and by no means comfortable, but it had 'one of the most magnificent views down to the Severn that can be seen anywhere' and Tawney was to describe it much later as 'the most delightful place in which I have ever lived'.[69] They spent increasing amounts of time here. Tawney liked to fish and meet the locals in the pub. Indeed, his non-academic lectures began to feature the locals, whose hostility to the Munich agreement and patriotic support for the war itself were relayed to American audiences to give a flavour of authentic English opinion.[70] Clara Rackham who had been a factory inspector with Jeanette during the First World War recalled Tawney's love of walking, picturing him striding 'across the country, disregarding obstacles, the rougher and wetter the way, the more he seemed to enjoy it'. Often he would make his way to the home of an old man, almost a hermit, where they would discuss the habits of the local badgers.[71] According to his obituary in the *Manchester Guardian*, 'Tawney liked to think of himself as a peasant who had strayed, or been driven, from the soil. He was, indeed, by nature a countryman.'[72]

Jeanette's health remained a constant handicap and concern. She was sent to a nursing home in the summer of 1918: 'when Harry ran for Rochdale and

I was ill with thrombosis they tried to persuade me to go up and be wheeled around if only that I should be seen.'[73] There was a serious operation of an undisclosed nature in 1928 which immobilized her for 'a good many months'.[74] She was hospitalized in 1931 with a recurrence of thrombosis while Tawney was in China. This developed into double pneumonia and required months in hospital.[75] A report from her physician survives, dated 1937, and he recorded at that stage that she had had '12 operations in her life beginning with tuberculous osteomyelitis. She has had injection for varicose veins, appendicectomy, cholecystectomy, and operations on both antra. In 1931 she had a large thrombosis of the leg with double pneumonia and pericarditis'.[76] He confirmed a weak heart. Phlebitis returned in the autumn of 1944, coupled with heart disease, and she was in Westminster Hospital for 2 months then.[77] By this stage she was no longer able to cope at Rose Cottage without help, and when the help was no longer available they had to temporarily suspend their visits. As Tawney wrote to Jimmy Palmer at the very end of 1944, 'we have personal, as well as public, reasons for hoping that the war may end this year and enable the School of Economics to return to London.'[78] The evidence is unambiguous that Jeanette was genuinely and seriously ill at many stages of her life rather than being a hypochondriac, or suffering from any psychosomatic conditions brought on by her mental and emotional states. As many another wife, she blamed her husband for some of her problems: 'I do get a great deal of sense of pressure at the back of my head when I get heated, try to find a retort worthy of Harry, or sit in the sun, or lose my temper. It has not a long duration, but it is disagreeable and turns me giddy if I stoop at all.'[79] Harry's health also deteriorated as he aged: he had to take a period of unscheduled leave in 1938 as a consequence of nervous exhaustion and he was prone to chest infections in his 'fifties and 'sixties.

In this period of his life Tawney undertook some major journeys and research trips, sometimes with Jeanette and sometimes without her, most notably to China in 1930 and again in 1931. It has sometimes been argued that Tawney was an essentially 'English' thinker, with the implication that his ideas, grounded in domestic historical and political experience only, did not travel well and limited his influence outside Britain. Whether or not that is the case – and we shall return to it at the end – it cannot be said that his focus on English history and institutions was a consequence of ignorance of the world outside. Tawney travelled a very great deal for an academic figure of this period, in fact, and while this in itself does not negate criticism of him for being intellectually insular, it at least demonstrates that he was not ignorant of, or inexperienced in life abroad and, indeed, outside the developed world.

He went to Germany at least four times in his life: on graduating in 1903, then in 1906 on a holiday with William Temple (though it is possible that this trip occurred a year earlier and that Tawney went again in 1906),[80] then on his honeymoon for an extended period in 1909 and finally in the late summer of 1922 for an educational conference in Berlin where he saw the hyper-inflation at first hand.

> The effect of the perpetual fall of the mark is that anyone who has any money spends it immediately because in 24 hours its value may be halved. The ordinary German cannot eat meat more than once a week, can't eat butter – to buy a pound costs more than a day's wages – and cannot get enough milk for his children. How they live is a puzzle ... In fact at present the most ordinary business of life is a gamble because prices move not only from week to week but from hour to hour.[81]

These German visits were important to him: as his nephew recalled, 'Tawney must have attached some importance to his German researches or impressions at the time, for I remember my mother speaking with respect many years later of Tawney's travels and contacts before the war with German life and thought.'[82]

Tawney was twice in the Soviet Union. On the first occasion in the spring of 1931 he and Jeanette took the Trans-Siberian express westwards across Siberia ('The extensive plains that stretch uninterrupted to the Arctic Circle are impressive. It was wonderful to see the frozen rivers & the sledges') and stopped in Moscow on the way home. Here, they spent a month at the Marx-Engels Institute under the auspices of a Russian historian of seventeenth-century England, a Professor Riasonov.[83] On the second occasion, at the very end of the Second World War in the summer of 1945, he was part of the British delegation attending the 220th anniversary celebrations of the Soviet (Russian) Academy of Sciences along with the historians G. M. Trevelyan and G. P. Gooch.[84] Through Tawney's life there were several trips to Paris and to the French countryside, quite apart from his months there during the Great War. He gave lectures in Copenhagen and in Lundt in Sweden in 1951, and he went in person to receive an honorary degree from the University of Melbourne in 1955.[85] His trips to Mandate Palestine at the end of the 1920s and to China in 1930 and 1931 respectively, will be dealt with below.

There were also five trips to the United States, each of which Jeanette made with him. In 1920 he taught at Amherst College and they made a leisurely tour through the United States and Canada on their way home. He went again in 1924 to give the lectures at Williamsburg which became the book *The British Labor Movement*. In the spring of 1939 he gave lectures on seventeenth-century economic history at Columbia University in New York and on 'democracy and the current political situation' at Chicago University. They spent 11 months in the British embassy (and Tawney travelled around the United States giving lectures) in 1941–2. They returned for a final visit in 1948 when Tawney lectured at Chicago again, this time on the subject of the post-war Labour government and the creation of a welfare state. (Hearing of the shortages and rationing in Britain, on this trip they were given clothes by many Americans, including a professional dry cleaner who gave them all his 'unclaimed items'. They organized their shipment in eight large trunks and distributed them across London and the Cotswolds.)[86] The lecture tours were lucrative and as he told Beatrice Webb the high fees were 'useful at paying off debts'.[87] He came to know the United States well and he saw most parts of it, but he did not understand America or have deep feelings for the people. As he wrote to Beatrice Webb after his wartime sojourn in the United States,

> While there are many individual Americans whom I like, and while I admire certain features of their society, eg their social equality and freedom from a caste system, I cannot say that I think the tone of American life – or at any rate, of the life which a visitor sees most – is wholesome. There is so much self-righteousness, so much criticism of other countries and so little criticism of America, so much advertising and publicity . . . so much pretence that fourth-rate work is first rate. The most hopeful feature is the extraordinary advance made by organised labour in the last ten years, not only in numerical strength, but in public standing and influence . . . Big Business no longer reigns alone, as it did when I first went to America.[88]

To one American correspondent who wrote to him on his 80th birthday he observed that

> When I was in North Carolina for a time, I felt the people there were more of human beings than the inhabitants of the Middle West, of which Chicago represented the latter. I have several good friends in Chicago, but public opinion there seemed so dominated by money making that I felt they made their own lives less happy than they might have been if they had been less prosperous and more contented.[89]

When Dorothy Emmet also conveyed the birthday congratulations of her seminar at Columbia University to Tawney, he replied rather less than charitably,

> I am very fond of individual Americans, some of whom are real friends, but my sentiments about them collectively is that of Tennyson's Lincolnshire farmer on the subject of the poor (except that I would substitute the rich for the poor) namely, that "in the lump they are bad". However, don't tell them that, or they will have a fit.[90]

Not only is this a remarkably extensive list of international engagements and experience: Tawney also had the luck, or perhaps the knack for being in places at crucial moments in history. France in 1916 and Washington at the time of Pearl Harbor are only the most obvious such examples. He was in the United States at the time of the great debate over the ratification of the Versailles Treaty, in Berlin at the time of the inflation, in Moscow within weeks of victory over Nazism and in China when the Japanese invaded Manchuria. There is a sense that Tawney not only wrote about history but also saw it close up. If he chose to write about what he knew best, we cannot say it was writing undertaken in ignorance of others' historical experience. It was rather the opposite: his experiences in different countries, often at periods of national and international stress, sharpened his abilities as a historian and as an analyst of Britain.

His trips to Palestine and China are intrinsically interesting and also present another side to his politics. In the spring of 1928 he went to Jerusalem for a meeting of the International Missionary Council. He was far more interested in his environs than in the conference, where he felt 'distrust[ed] as a socialist'. The son of the High Commissioner, Herbert Samuel, took him on a tour of the Dome of the Rock; the Jewish Labour Confederation, the Histadrut, took him to see settlements in the fertile Vale of Ashkelon. He saw Nazareth, Galilee and Tiberius. From Haifa he took a boat to Alexandria and from there he sailed home. At the conference itself Tawney's responsibility was to draft a report from its 'Industrial Committee' but he found himself drawn towards delegations representing the younger Christian churches in colonized areas like India, China, Africa and the Philippines whose theology, politics and language interested him greatly.[91] He wrote a report on the conference for the *Manchester Guardian*, subtitled 'Arguing with Western Christianity', drawing attention to this new Christian spirit. Tawney described the spokesmen for these emerging nations

> who have found a distinctive conception of Christianity and who desire to make it clear that there are elements in European civilisation which they find somewhat

difficult to reconcile with it . . . If even a small number of men in Africa and Asia feel as they feel, and can speak as they can speak, then the old relations between Europe and non-European countries are contrary to the nature of things and are no longer tenable. In the West Christianity is sometimes thought of as soporific. In Africa and the East, as in the Roman Empire, it appears to have some of the qualities of an explosive.[92]

Tawney sided with the coming world in its moral condemnation of imperialism and greed, and in its request that the church support this new movement. He wrote as if he had not heard this kind of language and message before, but it interested him greatly as an antidote to political complacency and conventional piety.

Two years later Harry and Jeanette went together to China during a year of leave from the LSE. Tawney had been commissioned by the Institute of Pacific Relations to prepare a report on agricultural reform in a region notorious for famine, and this became his 1932 book *Land and Labour in China*. Pulling the strings to procure the invitation and to encourage the Tawneys to accept, was Eileen Power. She had spent a year in China in the early 1920s and was captivated by the people, their history and culture. Harry and Jeanette sailed from Rotterdam to Shanghai on a cargo vessel carrying only six passengers. They spent several weeks in Nanking, the capital of the then Republic of China, making the close acquaintance there of Prof John Lossing Buck, an agricultural economist at Nanking University, and his wife, the writer Pearl Buck, later the first American woman Nobel Laureate in Literature and the author in 1931 of an enormously popular novel about Chinese peasant life, *The Good Earth*. They saw Peking, the Great Wall, the Ming Tombs and were fascinated by it all, though also frustrated by the backwardness, especially the absence of roads and the failure of the Chinese to provide facilities for tourists. Tawney was especially frustrated by the absence of any statistics on China but, wrote Jeanette to Will, 'as experts disagree to the extent of a few millions about the population even [,] there is no use getting too much flustered.'[93]

Tawney's second trip in the next year followed a request to him from the League of Nations 'to accompany an educational mission to China, which it is sending at the request of the Chinese government.' He refused at first, but he put their subsequent request to him to Beveridge: 'I recognise that one ought, if one is able, to do what one can to forward the League's work in a matter of this kind. The present mission is the beginning of cooperation between

China and the League and is important.'[94] He was rather more honest with Bishop Bell:

> Thank you also for your good advice about the League. I have begged them several times, a la Jonah, to get someone else. But I don't suppose they will lift a finger to do so. I suppose I shall have to go, though I rather hate the idea . . . I like the Chinese – or the few I know personally – but I see no chance of anything much being made of China for a few hundred years.[95]

He was granted unpaid leave of absence from the LSE for one term in 1931–2. He met his three colleagues in the delegation in New York in early September 1931: Dr C. H. Becker from Germany, Prof P. Langevin from France and Dr M. Falski from Poland with whom he struck up a friendship. Together they travelled across America and then sailed across the Pacific, to Yokahama in Japan. Tawney also saw Kobe and Kyoto before travelling on to China. Tawney reported that 'everyone seems pretty vague as to what we are to do when we arrive: it seems clear now that an attempt to cover any large part of the subject is hopeless, but we must wait till we reach Nanking before coming to any decisions (sic) what exactly to do[96] . . . We are all complete novices and I'm afraid we're likely to spend several weeks in beating about the bush.'[97] They arrived in China on 30 September 1931 and stayed for about 3 months during which time they visited Shanghai, Nanking, Chinkiang, Tientsin, Peking, Hangchow and Wusih.[98]

Their situation was made worse by the Japanese invasion of Manchuria at exactly this moment. Not only did this consume all energies and attention in China – 'it is difficult for the Chinese to think much of other things' – but it led the Chinese authorities to appeal for assistance to the League, which, infamously, failed to provide any after weeks of prevarication.[99] As Tawney put it with delicacy, 'to talk of the League here is not very popular'.[100] A further, though more minor, complication was that Tawney was in China during the sterling crisis which famously forced the pound off the gold standard – 'I was told that sterling was actually being refused in Tokyo yesterday,' he reported.[101] But as he was being paid for his services in Swiss francs, against which the pound was dropping in value all the time, the value of his remuneration was going up.[102] He also missed the subsequent general election in which he had been asked to stand for Colne Valley and in which the Labour Party was routed, an outcome he did not lament over much.[103]

There were interesting diversions, of course; on the voyage across he attended an impromptu dinner for all the passengers who had been at Oxford, hosted by the brother of the King of Siam who had been at Balliol when Jowett was Master. Then, when in Nanking, where the mission was based and where he was able to renew his friendship with the Bucks, he reported that 'we dined with Chang Hsu-Liang, the so-called "Young Marshall", the ruler of the north, and the son of Chang Tso-Zen, the old bandit war-lord who was blown up, it is alleged by the Japanese, some years ago ... [Chang Hsu-Liang is] a dapper fragile little fellow, with a lively bird-like air.' Tawney's room in Nanking overlooked a canal where he could see Chinese families at work and play: 'The life is vivid and interesting, especially the children ... except when they kill fowls very slowly so that there is a dreadful crying for several minutes, I enjoy being near the real people instead of the seeming endless intellectuals.'[104] Serious research into Chinese education proved very difficult, however, and Tawney complained of the corruption, pretences and disorganization of the officials and 'intellectuals' they met: 'the Chinese, though amiable and polite, as always, are, with few exceptions, extremely difficult to work with: they don't understand their own system, rarely answer questions correctly, and supply useless statistics.'[105] The lack of preparation in advance for the educational mission, the absence of secretarial help and the short time available to them also contributed to their difficulties.[106] From Nanking they travelled to Peking, Shanghai and Hangchow before returning to the capital. Tawney wrote of the difficulty of bringing 'the mission into contact with the life of the peasant ... when we return to Nanking ... I shall try to get Buck to take us into some of the neighbouring villages'. He did indeed accompany the Bucks on a day's expedition to Cowhead Mountain but it seems likely that this was for recreation rather than research.[107] Nevertheless, the group completed their task and their report was published by the League in 1932 as *The Reorganisation of Education in China*. Tawney's last full letter home included a remarkable passage on the sheer scale of the problem that was China in the early twentieth century:

> If I lived long in China I should cease to struggle; the weight to be lifted is too heavy, the power of the past & of nature is too overwhelming for the individual to resist. Most Chinese make the best of a bad job, hope little and expect nothing, and take what they can get in their personal lives without troubling about principles, causes & movements. The walls to be torn down before one gets to any reality are so infinite, the formless, opaque matter to be struggled through is so vast and dense that one is tempted to give up in despair. Even now after inquiring and reading for 2 months I cannot understand certain obvious aspects of the educational system. And everything else seems to be of the same kind.[108]

Tawney reflected deeply while in China and peppered his long letters to Jeanette, who was in hospital at the time, with thoughts on the country's prospects and on the international situation in general. He could see that it was a crucial test of the League itself:

> If it does nothing, *c'en est feint de la Ligue*, at least as far as this part of the world is concerned, and probably all up with the government also, which has taken grave risks in staking everything on the League's intervention, and, if nothing effective results, will have to pay the price.[109]

He was right about both these predictions and also about a third: 'If the League proves impotent its credit in China will have gone, and, sooner or later, she will turn to Russia. I hope for the best, but am not sanguine.'[110] If for 'turn to Russia' we substitute what Tawney perhaps meant in a vague sense as 'turn to communism' the prediction was realized years later. Indeed, Tawney was remarkably prescient in his wider understanding of the international economic and diplomatic crisis emerging in 1931.

> There will be plenty still to come, for we're in for a troubled ten years, and it may be for fifty. Everything has come to a head recently – the necessity of a resettlement of European crimes – the Franco-German question and disarmament – the breakdown in the East, the gravity of which stares one in the face here, but is probably not realised except by a few people in Europe, and the social crisis with the intensification of the class struggle which it involves. It is difficult to remain hopeful, but one endeavours to do so, and peg away at getting some new ideas, or some old ones restated, into people's heads.[111]

Through the chance of being in China, he was enabled to appreciate international affairs from a novel perspective in the east, and he could see not only the elements of a coming crisis, but also the gravity of that crisis. In only two aspects was he proved wrong: watching trenches being dug around Nanking in late 1931 he dismissed the idea of a Japanese attack: 'the last thing the Japs will do, whatever happened, would be to get across the powers by bombarding Nanking.'[112] Not in 1931, perhaps; but in December 1937 with the League a proven failure and the western powers impotent, there were no restraints at all on infamous Japanese behaviour. Tawney's prediction that it would take centuries to get China moving was also wrong: it took only decades.

Tawney's letters home in these months were pessimistic in tone: Jeanette was ill and in hospital; China was in turmoil; the Labour Party in Britain had lost power. But that should not deflect from a remarkable and highly creative passage in his life when he applied what he knew best – the history of agrarian society and the reform of education – to the improvement of a backward and alien civilization. As Michal Vyvyan commented, 'his lasting powers of assimilating what was entirely new to him in the way of social and economic facts and his enthusiasm in doing so is demonstrated to my mind amazingly in his book about agrarian China.'[113]

Land and Labour in China is a minor classic. It was presented first to the Institute of Pacific Relations at its conference in Shanghai in November 1931 under the title 'A Memorandum on Agriculture and Industry in China' and then republished as a book in its own right in the following year. Neither title is helpful as a description of the work because in barely 200 pages it is much more than a study of China's rural and urban economies. As an analysis of China's overall situation – economic, social, political, cultural – midway between its liberal and communist revolutions of 1911 and 1949, and based not only on English-language sources but also on Chinese data translated for Tawney by his Chinese associates there, it ranks as one of the most informative and insightful studies of that nation in its twentieth-century transitions. By design, Tawney never strayed very far from a verifiable fact or statistic when one was available. It is all the more authoritative and definitive because it is written with academic rigour by someone who had spent his professional life studying economic and social transitions from feudalism to capitalism. This, of course, was why Tawney was invited to China: his experience in the analysis of rural societies undergoing stress and change in the early-modern West was, it was hoped, transferable to the question of Chinese relative backwardness in the 1930s. While Tawney himself questioned that assumption throughout the book, and was characteristically modest at the book's opening about the originality and ambition of the work, it was not a mistake to have sent him.[114]

There was never any danger that Tawney would adopt a posture of western intellectual superiority in his approach to China, and the book's first chapter is a lyrical and deeply respectful introduction to China's history and traditions. Tawney at once scotches the then common comparison between contemporary China and medieval Europe – 'the hackneyed reference to the Middle Ages is sadly overworked'.[115] But throughout the book, as much to get his own bearings as to provide guidance to his readers, he makes comparisons with aspects and periods of European history. Thus if modern China was in no sense 'medieval', a comparison with fifteenth-century Europe 'outside the great commercial centres of Italy, Germany and the Low Countries' was not altogether far-fetched. Indeed,

China appeared to have 'stepped, without an intervening period of preparation, from the fifteenth century to the twentieth'.[116] The predicament of the Kuo Min Dang (KMT) government in Nanking, which was unable to control any but the nearest provinces in 1931, was compared with the situation of twelfth-century Paris.[117] When making the argument that China would in future rely on one or more provinces taking the lead in economic and social modernization Tawney commented that 'some region must play the part of Prussia and Piedmont' as in nineteenth-century Europe in spreading the spirit of reform.[118] When considering 'the possibilities of rural progress' in the book's fourth chapter he began by analysing how European societies had escaped rural poverty and insecurity in the period after 1800.[119] But the book's approach and ultimate message is never derivative of western experience and example. Indeed, writing in the midst of a great western economic depression and only too aware of all the social evils that had attended the West's transition to industrial capitalism, Tawney's argument throughout and at the end was that China's path had to be her own: 'It is in herself alone, in her own historical culture, rediscovered and reinterpreted in the light of her modern requirements, that China will find the dynamic which she needs.'[120]

Tawney worked upwards from the rural economy, through Chinese economic institutions and the first stirrings of industrialization, to Chinese political and educational organization, anatomizing Chinese society and emphasizing the interrelationship of all its elements. 'A stable state is equally difficult of creation until the social conditions of rural China have been substantially improved. Political organisation rests on economic foundations. When the latter crumble, it crumbles with them.'[121] In a country where the amount of farm land per head of the population was 'just over half an acre',[122] where agricultural productivity was low,[123] and where natural disasters – drought, flood and famine – were routine, the foundations were extremely weak. Tawney took the analysis through sections on agricultural methods, problems of marketing rural produce, the availability of rural credit and the insecurity of land tenure among the peasantry. He dwelt on the further insecurities caused by endemic banditry and outright war to present a picture of 'a large proportion of Chinese peasants . . . constantly on the brink of actual destitution'.[124] The remedies were unsurprising: the improvement of road and rail communications; agricultural reorganization including the introduction of rural cooperatives; the development of modern industries.[125] Intriguingly, when discussing rural reform Tawney recognized the need to increase the basic size of landholdings to make them large and productive enough to feed the peasant families dependent on them, and also 'to find alternative employment for part of the population seeking a living from the land'.[126] If not quite the commercially motivated enclosures of sixteenth-century England, the logic and expediency of improving agricultural efficiency by moving people from the land into new industries was not lost on him. Indeed, as Tawney recognized, it was the development of manufacturing and extractive industries in Europe since 1800 which had enabled the continent to support a population of half a billion at a higher standard of living than ever before.[127] The lesson for China was clear.

Tawney did not discuss politics directly, merely in relation to its effects on economic and social improvement. He was no advocate for Chiang Kai-Shek's regime though he did suggest ways in which administration from Nanking might be made more effective and honest, and help bring order to the countryside, for this was a prerequisite for progress.[128] He mentioned the Chinese Communist Party in passing only.[129] But he was very interested in Chinese institutions – the legal and educational systems and the bureaucracy – and their failings. Tawney described the impact of the political anarchy and bureaucratic sclerosis he had observed and experienced. He had argued earlier in the book that modern industry depended not on 'the machine, but the brains which use it, and the institutional framework which enables it to be used. It is a social product, which owes as much to the jurist as to the inventor'.[130] Later economic historians of the Industrial Revolution who have placed their emphasis on the cultural, legal, political and religious contexts in which eighteenth-century British technology and enterprise flourished, rather than focusing on the new technologies themselves, have agreed with him. It followed that institutional reform was required to give China a more open, trustworthy and efficient public administration as a foundation for economic confidence and investment. It also followed that resources and effort would have to be applied to the educational system, and Tawney dwelt here, in his final pages, on the defects of Chinese universities in particular. They required, among other reforms, higher standards and the closer engagement of tutors with their students to establish a 'spiritual society' in which curiosity and originality might flourish.[131] It was a theme taken further in Tawney's second encounter with China inscribed in *The Reorganisation of Education in China*.

This was the work of all four educationists who travelled to China in 1931 but was drafted by Becker in Berlin and then translated into English by officials at the League of Nations. It includes a charming photo of the delegation at a 'Primary School in Nanking' in which everyone else in the frame is posing for the camera but Tawney, in his three-piece suit and holding his trilby, is playing with a little boy.[132] At the report's heart was the conviction that amidst the chaos of war, famine, civil discord, national fragmentation and international conflict since the Chinese revolution of 1911, education was crucial to the coherence and progress of any future Chinese nation. The report's recommendations can be imagined given the situation in China in the early 1930s: the development of an efficient and rational schools administration, the construction of a well-trained teaching profession whose members were 'masters of their subjects', a system of free and compulsory elementary education from the age of six to be followed by a decent system of secondary education and the consolidation of tertiary colleges to provide fewer but better universities. The Chinese authorities were also enjoined to send investigative delegations to Europe to study best practice there.[133] Tawney and his colleagues drew attention to the social and national divisions created by the education of an elite of the Chinese in an ocean of illiteracy.[134] They advocated a new focus on the teaching of the sciences though not simply for utilitarian or materialistic reasons, for science might engender a change of mental attitude, favouring an inquisitive, experimental and original approach to learning, instead of a fealty to traditional authorities.[135] The chapter in the report on adult education advocated education for modernization above all other considerations. The basic focus of adult education in a country where 80 per cent were illiterate had to be reading and writing: if parents could be taught the advantages of literacy they would be more likely to educate their children.[136]

This report, most of which was not Tawney's work, showed none of the earlier tenderness in *Land and Labour* for a once-thriving civilization, no reverence for the customary ways and culture of a traditional society, but embraced the paramount tasks of reform, rationalization and modernization. 'If China is to be rapidly modernised, men must look forward rather than back,' it contended.[137] Tawney liked especially his fellow commissioner from Poland, Falski, but complained that he was blind to the historical and cultural situation of China: 'criteria applicable to a centralised western state are irrelevant in an oriental civilisation falling to pieces.'[138] Tawney was very displeased that the final draft of the report was not shown to all members of the investigative commission for their comments and corrections and he complained long and rather bitterly to Gilbert Murray about this in the latter's capacity as the chairman of the League's committee of intellectual cooperation.[139] The final report made disparaging references to American influence over Chinese education which Tawney thought unjust to the United States, likely to deepen hostility towards the League among Americans, and likely to weaken American efforts to help China. The criticism afforded to one particular experimental institution, the Mass Education Movement at Ting Hsien, also seemed wrong. Tawney battled to get corrections to the published report and a public retraction of these incorrect aspects by the League's secretariat. He placed a letter in *The Times* under the title 'The New China' in which he made his amends to both Americans and Chinese for these mistakes.[140]

He came to care for China. In March 1932 he joined with others to write to *The Times* to request more urgent flood relief for the Chinese, for example.[141] Later he was a member of the China Campaign Committee which called for an end to the Japanese occupation of the country and western humanitarian aid for Chinese victims of the Japanese military actions.[142] Subsequently he was deferred to as *the* expert on China in the British Labour movement. He used to enjoy talking about his experiences there: the young John Saville, a labour historian of the future, was an undergraduate at the LSE in the mid-1930s and recalled a supper party with Tawney at which he told the story of Feng Yu-Hsian, the so-called 'Christian General' who baptized his converts, mostly men from his own army, with a hosepipe.[143]

When Tawney returned home at the end of 1931 it was to a changed domestic political context: he had left with a minority Labour government in office and he came back to a coalition, the National Government, headed by the former Labour prime minister, MacDonald, but dominated by the Conservative Party. Writing from China, Tawney had no illusions: he knew that in the October 1931 election the National Government candidates would succeed but he was not prepared for the scale of the 'catastrophe'. He expected defeat but not 'anything so crushing as had occurred'.[144] Yet he welcomed the result as an opportunity to begin again: 'the whole outlook of the Movement requires to be changed to something much more drastic & more set on fundamentals.'[145] It was also a purgative that removed party leaders he profoundly distrusted, even if their influence would endure. 'I still feel glad that MacDonald and Co. cleared out, but I fear that a good deal of the mentality which they represented will be with the party for a good many years.'[146] His complaints went beyond the personal to a wholesale critique of the tactics of the second Labour government, and its 'pusillanimity'.[147] It should have pursued a socialist policy and dared the other parties to defeat it; instead, craving respectability and acceptance, it tried to remain in power while policy drifted. Tawney would certainly not have agreed with more recent interpretations which have largely absolved the MacDonald administration for the political and economic debacles in 1931.[148] Thus, in Tawney's view

> the Labour Party has deserved what it has got . . . for its half-heartedness, its lack of definite convictions, its refusal to stand by its principles and risk defeat for them. I feel personally to blame, for I knew all along in my heart that that was what it ought to do and was not doing, and went on pretending out of a kind of dishonest loyalty that it was certainly for the best and would some day live up to its ostensible beliefs. But it never did, and till it has a change of heart, it never will.[149]

Written from Nanking in November 1931, this analysis and also self-criticism formed the starting point for Tawney's endeavours – in which he was certainly not alone – to rebuild the Labour Party on a more durable and more intelligent basis in the 1930s. Meanwhile he resigned from the Economic Advisory Council, a body set up in 1930 to provide regular, expert economic guidance to government in troubled times. It contained representatives from all the major sections of the economy, including four economists (Keynes, Cole, Tawney and Sir Josiah Stamp), but was not judged to have been a success, not least because consensus eluded it. As Tawney wrote home, 'if I could ever have done any useful work there I don't see how it's possible for me to do it now.'[150]

Tawney's argument in 1931 and subsequently was that the party was intellectually unprepared to govern. Lacking intellectual resources and ideas it had no answer to the crisis it faced. 'The truth is that what a Social-Democratic government can do largely depends on the pains it has taken to mature its plans before its advent to office gives it an opportunity of acting on them,' he wrote in 1948.[151] In a long article for the *Times Literary Supplement* 2 years later to celebrate the half-century of the party, he defined its capital sin in the 1920s as 'one of omission . . . its neglect to plan or preach a programme sufficiently bold and distinctive to rally it supporters'. Instead of a programme the 1929 administration served up 'a collection of oratorical generalities' and 'its intellectual staff work [was] beneath contempt'. Instead of governing and then appealing to the country if baulked in parliament, it chose a timid course of compromise, thereby 'seal[ing] its fate before it had entered office'. Tawney argued that the Labour Party had been efficient at winning power but had no conception of how to use it: 'The first two Labour governments had carried into office the propagandist's mentality, which is eloquent on all reforms and specific on none.' The 1931 defeat 'drove home the lesson that . . . however good the cause, it requires knowledge, the careful preparation and criticism of alternative plans, the "intolerable toil of thought", in order to prevail.'[152] His reference to the 1929 programme, 'Labour's Appeal to the Nation', is especially interesting because he wrote it. He had written the 1928 document, *Labour and the Nation,* and he was coopted in 1929 to the committee preparing the election manifesto.[153] His story of its proceedings is instructive: 'at the end of the morning everybody present realised what he [Tawney] had known at the beginning – that committees can't draft. "I told them" he said, "that I would go home and write the whole damn thing myself in the afternoon and bring it back this evening"'[154] Neither the process nor the policies he included in the document, which were a miscellany of pious wishes for home and abroad, pleased Tawney in any manner. In 1934 he was certain that 'the business of making programmes by including in them an assortment of measures appealing to different sections of the movement must stop.' Socialism was about priorities and coherence, not the offering of so many carrots to so many donkeys.[155] Interestingly, and as further evidence of Tawney's argument that the Labour Party lacked resolve and intellectual acumen, Ramsay MacDonald was reported in 1930 as 'very angry with Tawney for having put such advanced ideas into *Labour and the Nation*.'[156]

Tawney continued this critique of Labour and of British socialists in general in *Equality.* They conducted themselves, he observed, as if the best way to give the public confidence in their cause was 'to convince it that they feel no confidence in each other'. This did not go down well in 'Little-Puddlington-on-the-Wolds', known and beloved of Tawney from his frequent sojourns in the west country, where the competing clamour of Labour voices and confusing tactical advice led the inhabitants to conclude 'that allotments are more useful than meetings'. They were not about to vote 'for a parrot-house' and had no time for extreme views. The movement had to be 'both sensible and trenchant'; it had to 'persuade its fellow-countrymen that . . . its idealism is not lunacy, nor its realism mere torpor'.[157]

In 1932 Tawney joined with Stafford Cripps, Aneurin Bevan and Clement Attlee to form the Socialist League and agitate for a different approach. This may have been 'the small informal group' which Tawney reported to Beatrice Webb in late 1933 as including himself, the Coles, Laski, Horrabin, Postgate, Cripps and Attlee. Tawney had intended to ask specialists with expertise in different areas of the Labour Party's policies to join the group from time to time but found this aim frustrated by sectionalism: 'the different sections simply do not, and sometimes will not, swap and pool ideas.'[158] The intensity of Tawney's feelings over the Labour Party's multiple failings since the mid-1920s can be read in the article which was republished as a pamphlet for the Socialist League 2 years later, *The Choice Before the Labour Party*. This encapsulated his contempt for MacDonald's party which 'crawled slowly to its doom, deflated by inches, partly by its opponents, partly by circumstances beyond its control, and partly also by itself'. The defeat in 1931 was not the result of 2 years of crisis in government 'but a decade of Labour politics' during which the party had lost a clear sense of its meaning and purpose and could not present itself effectively 'to plain men'. The failings in office, when the party was characterized by 'intellectual timidity, conservatism, conventionality,' came from that loss of purpose and direction. In response, Tawney asked that all party members and its MPs commit themselves to socialist policies, work to explain those policies in the country at large, eschew 'the policy of office at all costs' and avoid also the establishment's embrace.[159] Tawney was in no doubt that the temptation to take the establishment's honours and decorations had played a role, however deeply buried in the collective psyche of Labour ministers, in the manner in which Labour had governed after 1929 and the way in which the National Government had been formed in August 1931. He used to say that 'livery and an independent mind go ill together'. As one of his obituaries put it, he 'chastised with scorpions the social climbers of his party in 1931'.[160]

Tawney recognized only one exception to this last point: 'While the House of Lords lasts, the party must have spokesmen in it,' which required that they take hereditary peerages. He added, tongue in cheek, that perhaps the party's annual conference might vote resolutions of sympathy for those so chosen.[161] A rumour in 1929 that Tawney was going to the Lords made him 'furious'. 'The party,' he said, 'has a right to ask for your services but not to humiliate and insult.'[162] When a peerage was formally offered to him in 1933 by Ramsay MacDonald, he turned it down in a manner that has passed into political legend – or perhaps that should be legends, for there are several variants of the story. Jeanette used to say that Tawney's temper was at its most ferocious ever on the day he received MacDonald's invitation. In the simplest version, that told by Jimmy Mallon, Tawney replied to MacDonald on a postcard as follows: 'Not even dogs tie tin cans to their own tails.'[163] An alternative to that has the added sentence 'What harm did I ever do to the Labour Party?' And there is a third version that has Tawney penning in reply 'one of the most mordant and rudest of essays since Swift about the vanity of titles', though if he did it has not survived.[164] Whichever we choose, the point is clear: though historians tend to ignore or dismiss the prevalent view in the 1930s that MacDonald and his cronies had been seduced by the lifestyle, baubles and vanities of high office and social acceptance and were psychologically prepared to undermine and betray their party in August 1931, Tawney believed in that interpretation of their behaviour. No socialist worthy of the name should fall prey to such blandishments, therefore. But he continued to think that peerages were an exception. Ernest Green, General Secretary of the WEA, recalled many conversations with Tawney on ethics and politics. Green, too, was offered a peerage by Clement Attlee, but like Tawney he declined it. When he told this to Tawney, his mentor chided him and said that he'd been foolish. In response, Green 'told him that I had simply followed his example, and his reply was that "you were offered it by an honest man, and I wasn't."'[165] As Tawney's nephew commented later, 'I do not think he ever trusted MacDonald for a moment whereas he did continuously trust Attlee for whom he had immense respect as a man and politician.' Vyvyan, indeed, placed the origins of distrust much earlier than the 1920s: 'I doubt whether he ever forgave MacDonald for his attitude over the war of 1914' which MacDonald had opposed.[166]

It is hardly surprising, therefore, that Tawney kept his distance from the Labour Party in the 1930s, preferring to meet with trusted political and academic friends in a variety of groups and societies designed to intellectually invigorate socialist politics and plan for a future when Labour would again take power but this time know what to do with it. One of these was a very local affair organized by Postan and Eileen Power, now married and also living in Mecklenburgh Square, who formed a group 'to discuss the sociological and historical implications of economic problems' and heard papers from young academics, including the historian and political scientist, Denis Brogan, and the sociologist, T. H. Marshall.[167] Tawney took on the role of mentor to younger men who might guide the party intelligently in the future. He had met Hugh Gaitskell during the General Strike when the latter, then a student at Oxford, had served as a driver for the Oxford strike committee and made several forays to London. Tawney, who always distrusted the internal combustion engine, apparently remarked 'how dangerous it is to let young men take charge of projectiles'.[168] Evan Durbin became a colleague of Tawney's at the LSE. Both men had experience of teaching for the WEA, Gaitskell for a year in locations around the Nottinghamshire mining district after graduating, and Durbin in regular classes through the 1930s. Both men were also at the centre of a network of formal and informal groups in which the politics and economics of a future Labour government were thrashed out, and in which Tawney took his place. One of these, including also figures like the economist Barbara Wootton, Postan and Power, Leonard Woolf and the young Arthur Creech Jones who was then a research officer for the Transport and General Workers Union and later a junior Labour minister, met 'to discuss the problems which face the English Labour Party in any attempt it may make to set up a Socialist Community by democratic methods'. Tawney was its father figure. This group, never to adopt a formal name, set out a detailed economic plan for an incoming socialist government based upon nationalization of key industries and the banks and the central planning of macro-economic policy, the test of all measures to be economic and social efficiency as well as justice.[169] The fruits of these meetings and discussions, linking together intellectuals and some younger politicians, can be found in collections of essays, *New Trends in Socialism* (1935) and *War and Democracy* (1938), edited by George Catlin, an Oxford-educated political scientist teaching at Cornell University and the husband of the writer Vera Brittain, and in Durbin's own book, *The Politics of Democratic Socialism* (1940), which was dedicated to Tawney and five other members of these seminars.[170]

At the end of the 1930s, in a lecture given in Chicago, Tawney made some interesting and critical remarks about the Labour Party. He recognized the strengths that came from it being a trade union party, which was thereby 'in close touch with the working-class movement'. Nevertheless

> trade unionism is, in some way, not a good school for politics. Its preponderance results too often in the selection as parliamentary candidates of elderly officials, who have served their organisations well, but lack political sense, to the neglect of abler men. It causes too much attention to be concentrated on small gains and immediate reforms, and too little to be devoted to larger and more fundamental issues. It makes the Labour Party appear too much a party of the industrial workers, and fails to rally the great mass of discontent which approaches politics by other roads. The professional man, journalists, University teachers, who come[s] to the Movement as members of societies or constituency parties, have often broader views, a direct knowledge of subjects which the trade unionists know only at second hand, an experience of the ways of their opponents which enable them to see through their bluff and poses. But they also have their characteristic failings. They are apt to be doctrinaire to excess.

Tawney went on to qualify this point, indeed almost to contradict himself, contending that the alliance of trade unionists and intellectuals 'has worked well in practice' and was nothing like as fractious as sometimes presented by journalists.[171] But this expression of frustration with well-meaning representatives of the labour movement, expressed far from any British audience, is interesting and instructive. It suggests that he was never entirely comfortable in a party that was slow to adopt new thinking, and that was suspicious of intellectual leadership. As early as 1914 he had committed this to his *Commonplace Book*: 'The rise of the capitalist = the poodle in Faust turning into the devil. The Parliamentary Labour Movement = the devil turning into the poodle'.[172]

Many of his contemporaries marvelled at his adaptability which allowed him to play so many different roles simultaneously as teacher, scholar, soldier, public figure, advisor and political activist. But Tawney may not have found it quite so easy to blend into different social and political movements and organizations as this variety suggests. His relationship with the Labour Party for more than 50 years was not an easy one, though he would hardly be the first intellectual or university teacher to have had his differences with it. With the advent of the Attlee administration in 1945, though there might be constructive criticism, there could be no quarrel at all. But before that there was always a sense that Tawney considered himself (and perhaps was made to feel) something of an outsider who had come up by a different and singular route – university, social work, adult education, democratic agitation – to a confluence with a party of trade unionists. As a young man from this background he had clashed with George Lansbury who distrusted intellectuals in general and the WEA in particular.[173] Now, in succession to MacDonald, Lansbury was leader of the Labour Party between 1931 and 1935. True to his analysis of Labour's failings, Tawney put his admittedly diminishing energies in late middle-age in the 1930s into the cultivation of the next generation of Labour's intellectual leaders. But his remarks in Chicago suggest some doubts that the alliance he was hoping to remake between 'workers by hand and by brain' inside the party would ever be an easy or comfortable one.

The main purpose of Tawney's trip to Chicago in March and April 1939 was to lecture on the crisis in European diplomacy. Hitler had by various means taken the Rhineland, Austria, the Sudetenland and now the rest of Czechoslovakia, and Tawney attempted to explain to an American audience how and why this had occurred. He had no influence over British diplomacy in the 1930s whatsoever, nor over the policies of the Labour Party on foreign affairs, except perhaps on China. But Tawney was very quick to see the elements of a crisis emerging and converging when in Nanking in 1931, and he remained both prescient in his predictions and accurate in his analysis of the flaws in

British diplomacy over the coming decade. Like many Britons, it cannot be said that Tawney appreciated the distinctive pathological character of Nazism: he seems always to have understood it as a continuation of the German militarism and expansionism of the First World War. Hence, in association with others, including Lloyd George, Hugh Dalton, A. D. Lindsay, Stafford Cripps and Michael Sadler, he was quick to oppose German requests and threats to rearm as early as 1932, some months before Hitler came to power.[174] Precisely because he had fought German militarism once before, he wasn't about to give in to it now. As his nephew explained his view with a flavour of Tawney's authentic and distinctive irony,

> he saw a unity in the economic, cultural and military potency of Germany ever since he had learned in 1914 that the 20th century function of the "Huns" as he generally called them, was not to be that of exemplars in municipal socialism and national insurance policy . . . any representative of German culture could be for him a "Hun". [175]

While he gave some credence to the conventional British account of the rise of Nazi Germany in the 1930s which focused on the iniquities of the Versailles Treaty, its war-guilt clause and the understandable desire to repossess 'German' territory, he nevertheless saw the regime as reflecting something permanent in the German psyche. As he told his Chicago audience, 'that National Socialism draws part of its strength from its appeal to certain permanent elements in the national tradition must, I think, be accepted', and he included in the list the desire for mastery, the sense of racial superiority and the propensity to discriminate and persecute.[176]

Harry, Jeanette and Will made references to the international situation in their correspondence through the 1930s: as Jeanette wrote to her brother early in May 1933, 'The German business is awful and makes one despair of the world.'[177] The Tawneys helped a range of academic figures still in Germany in the 1930s, and also those among them who found their way to London. Max Beer, who had written a very important history of British socialism, published in 1919, and who had lived in London for many years until he was deported during the First World War, was an old friend of Tawney. As Tawney wrote to Will requesting a donation,

> He is now in Berlin and writes to me that his means of livelihood has, more or less, stopped as his books do not sell under the present situation, and of course he cannot publish articles. I have sent him a little money to go on with

and have asked Webb, Hammond, Hobson and other people to send me small sums . . . Beer is about 69 and it is hard luck that he should more or less starve at the end of his life.[178]

In fact, within months they had helped Beer reach London, and Jeanette was engaged trying to find him somewhere to live.[179] At the end of his life Tawney corresponded with Dorothea Oshinsky, a medieval historian at the University of Liverpool, another refugee from Nazism, whom they also helped in the 1930s and 1940s.[180] There were others as well, probably resulting from Tawney's position on the Advisory Council of the London Society of Jews and Christians (afterwards the Council of Christians and Jews) to which he was appointed soon after that organization was founded in 1927.[181] The Society promoted 'good will and mutual understanding between Jew and Christian'.[182] After Krystallnacht on 9 November 1938 Tawney added his name to a famous letter to *The Times* in which its many non-Jewish signatories simply recorded their 'solemn protest, before the conscience of civilization, against the persecution of the Jews in Germany'.[183]

Tawney had joined with a wide and politically diverse group, including Norman Angell, Eleanor Rathbone, Harold Macmillan and his old friends Zimmern and Mallon, in setting out a plan to strengthen international order and deter aggression under the League of Nations on 1 August 1936.[184] Within days of its publication Spain was pitched into civil war and this time he joined with, among others, Ernest Barker, F. M. Cornford, C. Day Lewis, E. M. Forster, Julian Huxley, H. G. Wells, Ralph Vaughan Williams and Virginia Woolf, to protest against Franco's invasion and military campaign against a legitimate, democratic Spanish government.[185] When the Austrian government, before the Anschluss, brought charges of high treason against 27 socialists and threatened them with the death penalty, Tawney protested again in similar company.[186] Later, at the time of the Anschluss, he wanted a much firmer line with the dictators. Acknowledging that this entailed risks, he was clear that 'the risk of war will be greater in the future if we let things go on sliding.' But he had no wish to subject the next generation to the experience of his: 'at moments like this I feel a horror at appearing to contemplate even the possibility of a war in which they will be slaughtered.'[187] Unsurprisingly, Harry and Jeanette were profoundly hostile to the Munich agreement in the autumn of 1938. 'If the news on the wireless this morning is correct, I fear we have presented Hitler with another diplomatic victory at the expense of the unhappy Czechs.'[188] As Jeanette then wrote to her brother,

The international situation looks so grim now that one wonders how much longer Chamberlain's so-called peace will hold . . . It really seems unbelievable that Chamberlain should have surrendered as he did. We regard it as almost a revolution in a democratic country for the PM to have gone off on his own like that without the experienced diplomats and to have given away whatever he was asked for.[189]

Tawney, meanwhile, placed a long letter on Munich in the *Manchester Guardian*, which, following the initial chorus of praise for Chamberlain, examined closely what Tawney referred to as 'the hymns to the Prime Minister'. While he did not rule out some concessions over the Sudetenland, Tawney would not have submitted to German threats: the correct course of action was 'to inform the German Chancellor that Great Britain, France, and Russia stood together on the points at issue, and while prepared to take part in peaceful negotiations, would act as one in resisting violence and threats of violence'. Tawney did not assess the substance of the German case; rather, he opposed German conduct because of its resort to duress: 'It is hardly possible . . . to resist the conclusion that force remained the major premise throughout the negotiations'. He was critical of British unwillingness to make common cause with the Soviet Union, which was a 'deliberate act of policy' that he put down to the old hysteria over 'Bolshevism'. He complained that Chamberlain had ignored the House of Commons 'until the essentials of it had been settled between himself and Herr Hitler'. His own strategy for foreign policy was clear, and clearly different:

> Joint action with France, Russia, and other states which accept as a basis of their policy united resistance to aggression and the peaceful settlement of all disputes; a clear statement of British aims, so that foreign powers, friendly and unfriendly, can understand them, which at present they too often do not; a willingness to address such genuine grievances as may exist, especially when that course involves some sacrifice by ourselves; a refusal to be frightened when gangsters brandish revolvers.

Tawney ended the letter with a touch of characteristic irony: 'It is possible that prayers of gratitude prompted by relief at having saved our skins by the sacrifice of a brave and enlightened nation may be acceptable to God; but it is not so certain as it is now the fashion to suppose'.[190]

A month later, after Krystallnacht, Jeanette wrote again to Will:

> I confess that I never believed it possible that Hitler could devise the sort of persecution of Jews that is now in progress. It makes Chamberlain look a bit ridiculous. We listened to his Guildhall speech and were amazed at its mediocrity. I remember Canon Barnett saying that it was triviality more even than sin that hides God.[191]

Their contempt for Chamberlain was compounded by admiration for Churchill. When her brother made her a present of Churchill's recently published biography of his ancestor Marlborough – an interesting choice in January 1940 – Jeanette replied in a letter revealing much about their politics. 'Your Marlborough is *quite* delightful & we are so grateful for it. Churchill has a fascination for us both & he writes so well & makes everything so interesting.' She went on to vindicate Churchill in another way by criticizing in the same letter Edward Carr's notorious recent book: 'Have you read E. H. Carr's 20 years Crisis (sic)? It has had a very good press but annoys me by its pro-Chamberlain bias & sneers at Churchill all in footnotes! It would be fairer to be in the text.' And for good measure she added this at the end about the Nazi-Soviet Pact of August 1939: 'Have you news of the Webbs? I should like to know how they feel today about Russia.'[192]

Take each of these remarks and scraps of information about their views and actions in the 1930s on their own and they may not amount to much. Take them together and the pattern is clear and important for an appreciation of Tawney, and also of Jeanette. In the 1930s many were swayed by the possibility of appeasing Hitler, while others had put their hopes in the Soviet Union, but Tawney was never deflected from a clear view formed early that a crisis was coming in international affairs in which tyranny and aggression would once again have to be faced and fought, and that there was no salvation to be had in Moscow, at least not at first and until the Soviet Union was itself attacked. He was right, of course, and his capacity to judge politics and diplomacy so accurately adds not only stature to the man but also authority to everything he wrote. It lays to rest the idea that Tawney 'gave little attention to international relations'.[193]

Socialism and Christianity

Tawney is often considered to be the leading theorist in the history of British socialism on the strength of two books published in maturity, *The Acquisitive Society* (1921) and *Equality* (1931). It has been argued that these works develop ideas which he first formulated before the Great War, and so brought to fruition the continuous and coherent development of his thought, capping the construction of a single corpus which gave logic and purpose to British socialism.[1] In fact, the two books are different in style and form; whereas *The Acquisitive Society* is allusive and aphoristic, *Equality* is a series of discussions about outstanding issues in state and society, from the ownership and management of industry to the abolition of the public schools. Perhaps of greater importance is the difference in their focus: *The Acquisitive Society* is concerned with personal behaviour, above all our ravening search for wealth and our propensity to consume, whereas *Equality* is about the practical reordering of society. The contention of this book is that this difference is crucial to appreciating the dualism in Tawney's thought – the contradiction between his earliest ideas about socialism which are premised on the individual and concern matters of personal behaviour and belief pre-eminently, and his later ideas which are far more conventionally focused on the actions of a reforming state to socialize capital, redistribute income and wealth, and create, by a process of management and direction, the infrastructure for a socialist society.

This change in focus occurred, it is argued, in the years after the First World War, and was caused by Tawney's involvement with the problems of the coal industry from the (Sankey) Royal Commission of Inquiry of 1919 until the General Strike of 1926. The coal industry was an egregious example of competitive and unregulated capitalism, displaying the worst aspects of economic individualism, including the greed of the coal owners, the gross inefficiency of the pits they owned and the exploitation of their workforces. The industry had been subject to state intervention during the war on a temporary basis; it now required formal nationalization as Tawney quickly came to see. But the assumption that followed – that nationalization of all the major British industries under a benign state – would necessarily be to society's benefit was much more contentious as an economic and social proposition, and ran counter to Tawney's earlier attachment to socialism as an amalgam of public morality, personal conduct and voluntarism. This was also the period when he stood as a parliamentary candidate for the Labour Party and was drawn into its affairs, writing indeed its 1929 election manifesto: this, too, brought him into the mainstream and pulled him away from his earlier conception of socialism. Of course, Tawney did not jettison these earlier views and his powerful instinctual commitment to individual reformation. He continued to talk and write about personal duties and behaviour throughout his maturity and into old age even when also conceiving socialism in the more conventional state-socialist form that came to dominate British public life. He himself recognized the dualism in his approach, and in the traditions of British socialism more widely. That is why examining Tawney's developing ideas of socialism is both interesting and representative: interesting, because the positions from which he started are now very unfamiliar, though they were much more common among socialist pioneers at the start of the twentieth century than is recognized, and representative, because Tawney's inner divergence or contradiction – call it what we will – tells us much about the problem of finding a workable form for socialism in Britain during and also after Tawney's lifetime. The discontinuities in Tawney's thought lead us, in other words, to the dilemmas in British socialism.

Tawney left no account of how he became a socialist in the manner of one of his heroes, William Morris.[2] Arguably, however, it is not hard to understand the process and the influences on him in his early manhood. Indeed, of greater significance is not why and how he became a socialist, but what kind of socialist he became. Taking from Rugby and Balliol their strong ethos of public service, assimilating with this the philosophical idealism in Oxford derived from the teaching and example of T. H. Green, combining this with a growing awareness of social deprivation and inequality, which was such a powerful theme in the 1890s and Edwardian period, and adding to it a certain amount of personal cussedness and the desire to be different, gets us some way to understanding why a highly intelligent young man from a relatively privileged background should become committed to social change and align himself with socialism. Many young men of his class felt the pull, though some, like Will Beveridge, went into Edwardian progressivism – a type of indigenous social liberalism –

instead. But the two positions were separated by a permeable membrane and liberals and social democrats traded positions, views and identities throughout this period.[3] Indeed, progressive liberalism was usually a far more radical creed than the labourism of the trade unions and early Labour Party which were committed to the advance of the working class long before they were committed to the ideas of socialism.

Tawney was not a systematic thinker and by instinct thought it inadvisable to try to define socialism. It was 'a word the connotation of which varies, not only from generation to generation, but from decade to decade' and was notable for 'the different and sometimes contradictory currents of thought which intermingle in their natural complexity and exuberance and crudity'.[4] His own beliefs as a socialist can be pieced together from many different sources after about 1903, but by far the best of them, and the best known of his early confessions, is his *Commonplace Book*, compiled between 1912 and December 1914 – the last entry was written a month after he joined up and just before he went for basic training to the Morecambe base – which was published in 1971. The *Commonplace Book* contains different entries across this period, including observations of social and industrial conditions, arresting things that friends and students said, and ideas that Tawney had which he wanted to formalize by writing down. In this period Tawney's ideas were very much his own: though he was associated with many notable social institutions and initiatives, he was not yet closely involved with the Labour Party, nor with any other socialist grouping. As such, the *Commonplace Book*, which discusses socialism as a type of private, personal conduct, is written by a man who was yet to link himself to more formal and public political structures, and is a more radical and unorthodox text because of it. As one discerning commentator put it in 1960 towards the end of his life, 'Where Fabians and Marxists attacked the defective working of the social machine, Tawney attacked the machine itself.'[5] Precisely because it contains ideas and positions which Tawney was 'trying out' and experimenting with, and which remained unpublished in his lifetime, the book must be treated with care. On the other hand, the very intimacy of the *Commonplace Book*, containing Tawney's private reflections, makes it a rich and revealing source, comprising several recurrent themes, and a very good place from which to begin an analysis of his socialism. The argument recently advanced that historians should discount the *Commonplace Book* as unreliable because it contains unpublished and unpolished material, as if it is only ideas expressed in public that can be authenticated and accounted relevant, runs counter to the practice of all biographical analysis.[6] On the contrary, Tawney's jottings, pithy comments and occasional short essays provide a vivid insight into his interior world and deepest convictions, and have rightly been prized as a valuable source.

If there is one essential idea in the *Commonplace Book* it is that society must be 'moralised' – that its essential processes must be brought in line with moral thinking largely derived from Christianity, for 'modern society is sick through the absence of a moral ideal'.[7] For Tawney, 'the industrial problem is a moral problem, a problem of learning as a community to reprobate certain courses of conduct and to approve others'.[8] He compared the industrial problem to the cause of anti-slavery and mused that the challenge faced in his own day in reforming industry was 'analogous to, though different from, that which confronted the Abolitionists'.[9] 'The social problem', likewise, could not be solved by simply increasing the living standards and income of the poor because it was about 'the moral justice of your social system' rather than merely the distribution of income and wealth within it.[10] And in a challenge to academic orthodoxy, then and now, Tawney advocated what might be termed a 'moral sociology'. Around him practitioners of this new discipline were seeking to build a value-free social science on the basis of 'profound information', the better to achieve academic credibility. Tawney, however, was impatient of 'writers who pile up statistics and facts, but never get to the heart of the problem'. Indeed, his strict moralism queried their new explanations for poverty and deprivation: 'sociologists . . . substitute inexpediency for sin and social welfare for conscience . . . the first step towards an improvement in social life is to judge our social conduct by strict moral standards'.[11]

This may have been a veiled criticism of the methodology of the Webbs, fact-gatherers extraordinary, whom Tawney admired greatly but from whom he differed, especially at this early stage in his thinking. As he jotted down in July 1913,

> It will be said: "abolish economic privileges, and there will be enough wealth for all to live, and for all to lead a spiritual life". This, I take it, is the Webbs' view. Now economic privileges must be abolished, not primarily because they hinder the production of wealth, but because they produce wickedness.[12]

Tawney is sometimes, but wrongly, associated with the Fabian Society, the grouping of socialist intellectuals around the Webbs which had been formed in the 1880s, and which in this and subsequent periods provided much of the creative thinking for the labour movement.[13] He was a member from 1906, but a passive one – though sympathetic to individual Fabians – because he rejected their state-centric view of socialism: indeed, a second theme in the *Commonplace Book* is his critical engagement with a tradition of thought then emerging as dominant in British socialism. Part of the distance was one of style and culture. 'Believe me', he wrote to Jeanette, 'I do understand what you say about the Fabians. A good many of them, like most clever people are prigs (I am a prig without being clever)'.[14] Both he and Jeanette were alienated by their cosmopolitan style. He disliked 'their talk and their posing' and she found them 'too intellectual' and 'destructive of too much that spells England', though she admitted that her judgments as a young woman were immature.[15] But far more important than their style was the fundamental Fabian idea that society could be reformed by controlling the state – that socialism was a matter of gaining access to existing structures directly or by influence in order to impose new administrative solutions, and that through these solutions and new mechanisms a fairer and more equitable society could be constructed from the top down. Fabianism was synonymous with efficiency: the British state and British capitalism were profoundly inefficient, in the Webbian view, whereas socialism, which was more rational in itself than classical liberalism, and which could draw on the strengths intrinsic to social consensus, would be much more effective in its use and distribution of resources. In the Fabian view, economic privilege should be abolished because it was inefficient; in the opinion of the young Tawney it should be abolished because it was morally wrong. The classic statement of their difference is caught in the following entry for December 1912:

> The attitude of governments to social questions is wrong, profoundly wrong. But it is wrong because the attitude of individuals to each other is wrong, because we in our present society are living on certain false and universal assumptions . . . What we have got to do first of all is to change those assumptions or principles. This is where I think the Fabians are inclined to go wrong. They seem to think that you can trick statesmen into a good course of action, without changing their principles, and that by taking sufficient thought society can add several cubits to its stature. It can't, as long as it lives on the same spiritual diet. No amount of cleverness will get figs off thistles. What I want to do is to get clear in my mind what those moral assumptions or principles are, and then put others in their place.[16]

Put another way, the Fabians 'tidy the room, but they open no windows on the soul'.[17] Fabianism was about efficiency and mechanism; socialism, to Tawney, was about morality and individual regeneration. 'People often argue that the industrial system is justified by its "efficiency". But this [is] the shallowest of claptrap. For what is at issue is not whether it is efficient, but whether it is just.'[18] Indeed, with a surer grasp of popular attitudes and prejudices than many another Fabian, by 1912 Tawney doubted if Fabian solutions could work: 'All experience seems to me to prove that people, or at any rate English people, will not accept efficiency as a substitute for liberty.'[19] The difference is caught also in the practical application of Fabian ideas to the reordering of social institutions like the poor law system, whereas, at the same time, Tawney was dedicating himself to the improvement and liberation of individuals and their communities through education. Indeed, his lifelong commitment to educational improvement must be understood as the corollary of his early socialist views and their focus on individuals. Unlike the Fabians, Tawney worked from the bottom up.

Another distinguishing feature of his thought, therefore, was voluntarism (as opposed to statism) and the political and social pluralism which went with it. The best example of this in his life and thought was his commitment to the WEA which he joined soon after it was founded in 1903, and shaped while still a young man. Tawney's commitment to self-governance at all the levels within it, and his defence of its independence, were not just corollaries of his commitment to education, but to a model of the good society based on voluntary endeavour. This was what attracted him to workers' education in the first place and explains why he could not accept the alternative tradition of the Labour Colleges in which the curriculum and the intellectual outcome were determined for the students in advance. Tawney's enthusiasm for this way of organizing education was enduring. His last extended contact with William Temple before the latter's untimely death in 1944 was, rather sadly, a disagreement between them over the latter's plans for a reorganization of adult education following a conference Temple had convened in Oxford in January of that year.[20] Temple proposed the establishment of a department within the Board of Education to organize adult education and draw on public funds, and a unitary Adult Education Council as well to spread interest in it.[21] Tawney demurred, for 'the Adult Education Movement is, in reality, a number of different movements, each with a character and outlook of its own, on the preservation of which its vitality depends . . . What is needed is to develop many different kinds of work from the most informal to the most intensive.'[22] He also opposed the establishment of an intermediary Council as a bureaucratic obstacle: 'Such a body cannot do the work itself, and I do not want a buffer between the Board and the bodies which can do it.'[23]

To Tawney, there was a spiritual and organizational aspect to democracy, which had to be more than the mere casting of votes. In an address to the

WEA during the Second World War entitled 'Adult Education for the New Community' he argued that the state had an obligation to 'secure[s] for the individual other and diverse loyalties': 'the individual must be a citizen of his industry, his political group, of a variety of other organisations within society which claim his interest, of his nation, and of the wider civilisation of which he is a member, and a citizen of the kingdom of the spirit.' As he went on to explain, 'the essence of the true spirit of democracy' was a nation composed of 'a host of voluntary associations of all sorts and kinds.'[24] Or as he put it in the preface to the 1938 edition of *Equality*, 'democracy is unstable as a political system as long as it remains a political system and little more, instead of being, as it should be, not only a form of Government, but a type of society and manner of life in harmony with that type.'[25] Hence, for Tawney, socialism was best understood as the resultant of a true democracy, which comprised not just the political system and the institutions of civil society, but also the economy. As he defined British socialism for an American audience in 1941,

> It means the extension of democracy from the sphere of government and law to that of economic life. Arbitrary economic power, exercised for purposes of personal profit is as incompatible with democracy as arbitrary political power. We mean to make the management of industry responsible.[26]

After teaching at the WEA's summer school in Balliol in 1910, one of his students wrote to him with his reflections. 'Yours is a great job' he wrote. 'That of quickening the Soul of Democracy. I wish you luck in it.'[27] According to Tawney's last research student, the historian of the seventeenth-century British state, Gerald Aylmer, his supervisor had been a Christian, a democrat and a socialist in that descending order.[28]

Tawney's disagreement with Fabianism was, in reality, an aspect of a more profound interrogation of the dominant social philosophy of the modern age, utilitarianism. In their focus on efficiency and expediency, and exclusion of morality, the Fabians were an exemplification of Bentham's enduring principle of 'the greatest happiness of the greatest number'.

> As far as the English socialists, in particular, are concerned, they have taken the criterion of public well-being straight from Bentham almost without question, and their criticism of the radical individualists has taken place within the limits of this formula ... They have, as it were, said "True[,] that economic system which promotes the well being of the majority most is best. Only you do not really understand the methods to be used. When you are as clever as us, you will not change your ends: you will adopt our means."[29]

Tawney, on the contrary, was challenging the ends themselves – the material enrichment of the majority. And he also challenged the tolerance in the utilitarian approach of antisocial or exploitative practices imposed on the few in the interests of achieving the happiness of the majority: 'Suppose cheap goods could only be obtained by tolerating brutalizing conditions among those who produce them, are those conditions justified?' Of course not.[30] Tawney wanted absolute standards to apply absolutely: if a thing is morally wrong, whatever the outcome, we must desist: 'no amount of convenience . . . can justify any injustice'. Indeed, bringing his faith to bear, he argued that 'there is a higher law than the well-being of the majority, and that law is the supreme value of every human personality as such.'[31]

Utilitarianism was pernicious in practice because it understood happiness in only material terms, and another theme in Tawney's early thought was his opposition to materialism. This had both intellectual and practical implications. In practice it meant that Tawney was critical not only of the owners of capital, but of the workers as well: 'The working classes and the English Labour Movement have made one tragic mistake. They have aimed at comfort, instead of aiming at getting their rights.'[32] Written just before he joined up, Tawney would have the truth of his statement confirmed by his experiences alongside working men in the army. Workers could be 'bought off by instalments of "social reform"'. Equality, he wrote on several occasions, is not about quantities but about principles: it will not be achieved by ensuring that everyone has equal amounts, or at the very least, that the poor are no longer so poor as compared with the rich. 'Peace comes not when everyone has £3 a week, but when everyone recognises that the material, objective external arrangements of society are based on principles which they feel to correspond with their subjective ideas of justice.'[33] What Tawney described as 'faulty economic relationships' could not be remedied merely by increasing 'the share of wealth received by the poorer or worse paid of the two parties'.[34] In any case, despite the claims of various false messiahs – 'modern prophets, utopists, sociologists' – there was no 'certainty that when we have cured poverty we shall be better pleased with ourselves'.[35] The argument was well made and experience gives it credence, but at points Tawney verges on the utopian, or at least the unreal himself. Materialism may not be good for the soul, and its pursuit may corrupt, and people may prefer at some abstract level economic justice to higher wages, but it is surely difficult to condemn an Edwardian working man for wanting more and for understanding comfort in traditional terms.

The immediate political implications of this anti-materialism can be seen in the *Commonplace Book* where Tawney took issue with all the variants of English socialism then on offer: 'state management deadens spiritual life' he contended, and 'syndicalist management fosters corporate selfishness' – workers' control of their industries will only substitute one self-interested class for another. So-called 'gas and water socialism', or the municipalization of local utilities which had been underway since the 1880s in many British cities to provide vital services at a fair price, came in for special criticism:

> Some writers point to the striking development of municipal services in the last thirty years as an indication of the triumph of "socialism". This is an awful example of the worship of the letter and the neglect of the spirit. The motive of nearly all these developments has been a purely utilitarian consideration for the consumer. They have not been inspired by any desire to introduce juster social arrangements, nor, in particular, by any consideration of the wage-earner. They have been inspired simply by the desire for cheap services akin to the free trade agitation. In fact the two movements appealed to much the same classes. Manchester manufacturers want cheap gas and electricity for exactly the same reason that they want cheap cotton and machinery. Clearly there are no germs of revolution here.[36]

As these comments suggest, Tawney's opinions were singular and largely isolated him from the range of socialist and labour movements in the Edwardian period. They must also be borne in mind when we consider Tawney's later support for the nationalization of industries.

In intellectual terms, meanwhile, Tawney's anti-materialism may seem an odd position for an economic historian to adopt. Most practitioners of this academic discipline have started from the assumption that economic factors take primacy in historical explanation – that materialism is fundamental to human behaviour. As an economic historian Tawney did not disagree with this – indeed many of his early tutorial classes on the history of the Industrial Revolution were designed to help workers understand how their lives, occupations and communities had been shaped (though Tawney might have said 'deformed') by material factors. But the fascination of economic history for him was to probe the limits of a materialist explanation and to vindicate the influence of other immaterial factors – notably religion, of course – in historical analysis. As he wrote in 1912 in his first great book,

> To the economic historian the ideas are as important as the events. For though conceptions of social expediency are largely the product of economic conditions,

they acquire a momentum which persists long after the circumstances which gave them birth have disappeared, and act as over-ruling forces to which, in the interval between one great change and another, events themselves tend to conform.[37]

The purpose of *Religion and the Rise of Capitalism* is to show the materialist outcome of a change over time in man's spiritual and transcendental beliefs and practices. In this sense Tawney is far removed from Marxism both politically and intellectually. Much of Tawney's work inverts the fundamental model of historical materialism and instead of the economic base determining the superstructure of institutions, cultures and values, the values themselves help shape the base in a constant process of action and reaction.[38]

In the *Commonplace Book* Tawney describes 'Marxian socialists' as 'not revolutionary enough'. By this he meant that they, too, accepted the conventional materialist ends of life and merely argued over the distribution of the spoils.

> They say that capitalist society is condemned because the worker does not get the equivalent of what he produces. He does not. But why should he? The real condemnation of the capitalist spirit is contained in the suggestion that men should get only what they produced. As though we were shareholders in a gold mine to be paid according to our holding of stock! A barbarous, inhuman, sordid doctrine that wld weigh immortal souls and scale them down because they are not economically useful. God forbid that they shld be! This doctrine means that wealth should go to those who care for nothing *but* wealth, and are therefore the least fit to have it.[39]

Despite this, Tawney was interested in Marxism throughout his career and was never dismissive. He wrote various unpublished papers almost as a form of self-education that he might better understand the fundamental doctrines and ideas of an approach to history and a philosophy of life with which he fundamentally disagreed. One of these papers entitled 'Some General Remarks on the Historical Theory of Karl Marx' was given as a lecture at the LSE, probably in the interwar period, and amounts to a very sensitive and well-informed account of the development of Marx's ideas. Indeed, at a stage when the distinctiveness of Marx's writing in the 1840s and his debts to his contemporaries at that time were not generally appreciated, Tawney took trouble to explain the genesis of Marx's ideas before discussing the better-known texts and concepts in the body of the lecture. As if to demonstrate the validity of a Marxian approach, the lecture ended with Tawney's attempt at a long-term social and economic explanation of the Glorious Revolution of 1688 in England in a self-conscious critique of the prevailing political and constitutional approach handed down by Macaulay in the mid-nineteenth century – and perhaps also as a foretaste of the kind of analysis that Tawney himself would attempt in his work on the rise of the Elizabethan gentry.[40]

Later 'position papers' on Marxism, which, from internal evidence, were probably written in the late 1940s or early 1950s and thus during the Cold War are more sceptical than this. Indeed, Tawney had told an audience in 1949 that he was 'not an admirer of Communist doctrine, much of which, as expounded by the faithful, appears to me not only morally repulsive but of an intellectual naivete almost passing belief'.[41] These papers contain many of the now familiar academic criticisms of Marxism. Tawney questioned Marx's generalizations based on 'his knowledge of a few European countries between about 1840 and 1880'. That narrow empirical base had contributed to the inaccuracy of Marx's prophecies of the future. Marx 'took an unduly mechanical view of the operation of economic factors and greatly underestimated the importance of factors which are not economic', and as Tawney asserted in response, 'economic forces act, not directly but through human minds and wills.' Thus, 'the effect of explaining institutions solely in terms of the economic factors is to empty [them] of their distinctively human content, and to think of them solely in terms of forces.' The 'Materialist Conception of History' as Tawney called it, was too broad in its approach to give fine-tuned answers to questions of individual behaviour and causation. Marx underestimated many other non-economic factors in history, among which Tawney enumerated nationalism, patriotism, public opinion and traditional morality. Marxism could also be crudely reductive: Tawney objected to the Marxist rationalization of all statements into expressions of class interest which was essentially self-contradictory, for Marxism condemns itself in this way as just another expression of a class: 'If truth is merely what a group finds it convenient to declare to be truth then that statement is itself an example of that fact, and the attack on bourgeois morality possesses no more validity than that morality.' He also made the point that political and cultural institutions are not just the product of an environment of historical-materialist forces but develop an intrinsic spirit of their own and become capable themselves of making their history irrespective of context and externalities. 'They acquire, once born, a vitality & a body of values, of their own. They become a legend. Those values and that legend are themselves a causal force.'[42]

Although these comments date from the end of Tawney's career as a historian, they essentially codify a set of positions he had held from the very first. No area of modern history has received as much attention in Marxist historiography as the French Revolution, a subject Tawney was teaching in tutorial classes in 1912–13. But he explicitly rejected a materialist interpretation in favour of an idealist one at that time:

> The revolution had behind it, it is true, vast economic and material grievances, horrible wickedness, cruelty, and mis-government. Nevertheless it was in essence the uprising of a new system of ideas, was based on new standards, without which material injustices would not have been revealed as so intolerable, and was dominated by a new conception of human possibilities.[43]

Also at this early stage Tawney emphasized the place of human agency in history and hence the importance of chance and contingency rather than any form of determinism.

> If we must talk of social evolution, we ought to remember that it takes place through the action of human beings, that such action is constantly violent, or merely short-sighted, or deliberately selfish, and that a form of social organisation which appears to us now to be inevitable, once hung in the balance as one of several competing possibilities.[44]

Tawney's critique of Marxism was an aspect, in fact, of his wider critique of all materialist explanations in politics and history. He did not take special aim at it; rather, he found it to be another of several modes of thought that were intrinsically dehumanizing. Its neglect of personality and of potent historical forces like religion and spirituality inevitably conflicted with Tawney's deeply held belief in the autonomy of the individual and in his or her capacity – indeed their duty – to make moral choices. And Tawney's strongly held opinion that Marxism had failed to provide accurate and sensitive historical explanations – as he asks at one point in these writings 'It is said that the English Revolution of the seventeenth century was a classical "bourgeois" revolution. But what classes in 17 England were the "bourgeois"'? – has important implications when we consider the objections of those, pre-eminently Hugh Trevor-Roper, who took issue with Tawney's ideas on social change in the early modern period. If they thought at the time they were vanquishing Marxist historiography, as may well have been their aim, they were fundamentally mistaken in Tawney's case. Tawney's scepticism about Marxism likewise distances him from some of those on the left who would adopt him: Christopher Hill's claim that 'it is impossible to conceive . . . of Tawney without Marx' was about as wrong as it gets, though on other aspects of Tawney's work he was a perceptive commentator.[45]

A final but hardly subsidiary theme in an analysis of Tawney's thought is the place that his Christianity holds within it. The importance of Tawney's personal faith is accepted by all authorities, above all those who knew him. But the character of that faith defies precision or agreement. Perhaps because of his close associations with Bishop Gore and his wider historical condemnation of the social and economic effects of the Reformation, Tawney has been described as 'a convinced and unquestioning Anglo-Catholic all his life'.[46] 'Tawney belonged to the radical, world-renouncing Anglo-Catholic tradition of Charles Gore and J. N. Figgis.'[47] Others have queried this, however, in a man who was literally schooled in the broad church Anglicanism of Dr Thomas Arnold at Rugby: 'He was no Anglo-Catholic and appears to have been unmoved by ritual and the power of religious experience.'[48] Others again have emphasized the undogmatic and unstructured nature of his belief: his obituary in *The Times*, probably written by his close friend and fellow economic historian T. S. Ashton, describes him drawing upon 'Christian doctrine of a not very theological kind for his devoutly egalitarian philosophy'.[49] Indeed, when interviewed by the BBC in 1963 Ashton said that Tawney's ideas were based on 'not on any settled philosophical system but primitive Christianity'.[50] Meanwhile Tawney's nephew seems to have started with Ashton's view, but was later persuaded 'that there was quite a strong clerical element in Tawney's religiousness'.[51] At the end of his life he went regularly to church but this was exceptional. There were periods earlier when he did not, and also when he did not take the sacrament: when he celebrated holy communion as a soldier in France at the very end of 1915 it was evidently the first time for a period of years.[52] In 1938 Jeanette told Beatrice Webb that Harry was not a regular attender and only took the sacrament at Christmas.[53] Indeed in an entry in the *Commonplace Book* for July 1914 Tawney only added to the uncertainty himself, suggesting that he was then following the line of natural religion towards a confluence with deists and all those who would discard 'the crudities which were inseparable from the "historical conditions" in which Christianity arose' – though in the same entry he went on to endorse the specificity and validity of a Christianity which has at its core Christ as a living embodiment of God, and in which he believed.[54] Perhaps it is not surprising that Beatrice Webb also noted in her diary that 'In his religious opinions, [Tawney] remains a mystery to his free-thinking friends', a mystery probably shared by his Christian friends as well. Indeed, at another time she even wondered if Tawney was 'a convinced Christian or a religious-minded agnostic.'[55]

If the core of Tawney's beliefs is hard to penetrate, and if his observance and attendance ebbed and flowed over his lifetime, it is difficult to uphold the argument that over time there was a linear decline and dilution in his attachment to Christianity.[56] Given Tawney's critical relationship with the Labour Party, the argument that has been advanced that it replaced the church as his chosen vehicle for social advance at some stage in the mid-1920s – as if religion was something to be cast off at will when anything better came along – is implausible and betrays a misunderstanding of the nature of his religious inspiration.[57] Religion was a constant and complex presence in his inner life, though it varied in its character and intensity at different times. His 1937 lecture on Christian Politics (see below) or his 1949 address to the William Temple Society in Cambridge suggests, on the contrary, that he remained deeply attached to a Christian world view and to the social mission of the Church, and that some of his earliest religious ideas in the *Commonplace Book* retained their importance to him a generation later.[58]

Jeanette was also 'shaped by religious conviction, even though it was only relatively late in life that she made formal submission to the Church of England.'[59] But in his faith Tawney was relatively isolated: as Ashton remarked, 'few of those who shared his political beliefs shared what they called his religiosity . . . The failure of many of his fellow socialists to live up to Christian ideals was one of his continuing disappointments.'[60] Referring to rather more than those who lived with him in Mecklenburgh Square, Lena Jeger recalled that 'he never preached to his neighbours', probably because he knew they would not be receptive.[61] Nor was he necessarily close to fellow Christians: 'He was never at home with members of some of the smaller sects, not only because of their pacifism, but because, as he put it, he did not [respect] spiritual any more than social or political aristocracy.' Munia Postan recalled that when Tawney was 'reproached for being a "tart" Christian his reply was that our Lord's injunction was to love our fellow human beings and not necessarily to like them.'[62]

Tawney was personally close to four great churchmen during his life: Temple, Barnett, Bell and Gore. With William Temple there was the easy intercourse of lifelong friends who shared a common background and who were both closely involved with the WEA: Tawney followed Temple as the Association's president. At a formative period in his life Tawney encountered Samuel Barnett at Toynbee Hall who became a mentor to him through their joint campaigns to reform both London's East End and the University of Oxford. Tawney's relationship with George Bell in the 1920s was less intimate and more political in nature: to Bell, and also through him, Tawney interpreted the turbulent industrial relations of the decade, providing the church with insights into the immediate course of disputes and their wider implications. The fourth of these Christian leaders, Charles Gore, a generation older than Tawney and from an aristocratic Anglo-Irish background, had genuine spiritual influence over him. That is unsurprising since Gore has been described as 'the most fascinating and influential bishop of the Church of England in the twentieth century'.[63]

An Oxford don, the first Principal of the High Church foundation in the university, Pusey House, and successively Bishop of Worcester, Birmingham and Oxford, Gore liberalized Anglo-Catholicism both in a doctrinal sense and by associating it with social reform.[64] At Oxford he 'drew undergraduates to both a supernatural faith and a commitment to social action'.[65] In his role as editor and contributor to the controversial late-Victorian collection of essays, *Lux Mundi*, he helped to reformulate and modernize Anglo-Catholicism, bringing it into communication with the development of natural science, ethics and society.[66] The book was subtitled 'A series of studies in the religion of the Incarnation' and Gore, who contributed an essay on 'The Holy Spirit and Inspiration,' became the leading exponent of the incarnationist theology of the age. This emphasized Christ's humanity rather than his distant divinity, and it encouraged Christians to walk with him and live like him – to live full and active lives dedicated to their fellow men and women in the true spirit of Jesus who became a man so that he could save mankind. According to Gore, 'the Incarnation was a self-emptying of God, to reveal Himself under conditions of human nature and from the human point of view.'[67] As God became human so Christianity became humane, an ethical rather than a judgmental creed.

Tawney would have encountered Gore's theology as a student member in Oxford of the Christian Social Union which Gore had helped to found in 1889. 'Its motive' according to Gore 'was the sense that Christianity, and especially the Church of England, had lamentably failed to bear its social witness.'[68] The two men collaborated in the Edwardian campaigns to reform the university; Gore took a great interest in the affairs of the WEA; he was also a public supporter of the campaign to end sweating and in favour of the 1909 Trades' Board legislation. They met and collaborated in several different contexts for three decades and Tawney dedicated *Religion and the Rise of Capitalism* to Gore in 1926, 'a recognition of Gore's leading role in promoting a left-of-centre Christian social ethic.'[69] The intricacies of theology did not detain Tawney – or at least he said and wrote next to nothing about doctrine through his life. Yet the spirit of a social Christianity, whether defined as Anglo-Catholic or not, which he derived from Gore, was perhaps the most powerful of all the external influences on Tawney. Gore taught him his Christian duty, and underscored that being a Christian was a constant calling and a 'hard thing'.[70]

Almost the first thing Tawney ever published was a review of the religious census of London undertaken by the *Daily News* in 1903–4 which he wrote while at Toynbee Hall. Here he reflected on the decline of Christian life in the capital, and, as it declined, on its increasing concentration among the middle classes. There was 'food for reflection in figures which appear to show that one of the great social forces of history is gradually and reluctantly drifting out of the lives of no inconsiderable part of society'.[71] From the outset he was aware that his own religiosity made him part of a declining minority – 'a curiously solitary figure' in the judgment of one historian – and this may help explain his reticence on the subject of faith and its relationship to politics.[72] Tawney drew careful lines between what he believed himself, what he would say on public platforms to Christian groups to whom he spoke occasionally, usually about the social obligations of the Church, and what he would say about Christianity in the rest of his public life, which was, in fact, little indeed. His political speeches, essays and journalism were all secular in content and type from first to last: he did not publicly defend policy or commend socialism on other than empirical, objective and secular grounds.[73] This brings into question the appellation frequently applied to Tawney, 'Christian Socialist'. He was certainly both a Christian and a socialist, but he derived his socialism, as we have seen, from secular and philosophical sources as well as from Christian ones. He joined the radical Society of Socialist Christians when it was founded in 1923, the merger of which with the Socialist Christian Crusade in 1931 led ultimately to the foundation of the Socialist Christian League (SCL) from which the modern Christian Socialist Movement was formed.[74] Tawney was president of the SCL later in his life. Yet he called himself a socialist, never a specifically Christian Socialist, and though the descriptor is not inaccurate, in using it we are likely to break down certain distinctions which he wanted to maintain, with faith on one side and politics on the other. He knew that to talk religion in modern British politics was to limit one's audience and reach.

That said, if we return to the *Commonplace Book*, and to his private reflections, faith plays a fundamental role in his social thought. The presence of the divine in human affairs guaranteed 'the supreme value of every human personality as such'. To Tawney, men and women were 'of infinite importance' and 'each individual soul is related to a power above other men'. Belief in God and a belief in the fundamental equality of all people went together: 'It is only when one contemplates the infinitely great that human differences appear so infinitely small as to be negligeable (sic)." In Tawney's view, inequality was magnified by loss of faith: 'What is wrong with the modern world is that having ceased to believe in the greatness of God, and therefore the infinite smallness (or greatness – the same thing!) of man, it has to invent or emphasize distinctions between *men*.'[75] Above all, in Tawney's theology the divine and transcendent provided a standard by which to judge right and wrong – what Tawney called a 'supernatural reference'[76] – and one that, because it was not man-made, was not open to dispute. As he later explained,

> the unstated assumption of the existing order of institutions & ideas is that society belongs to a purely human or "natural" order & that there are no divine or absolute principles or laws laying down the lines upon which man is to seek well-being. Human arrangements are, therefore, regarded as a matter of convenience, more or less expediency, more or less happiness, th[is] arrangement will do as well as another . . .

In such a moral free-for-all, inequality was inevitable. But

> if men accepted the teaching of the Christian Church, they would have a body of principles not only resting on authority (not the most important point) but setting out the main lines of a moral scheme of the universe & deducing man's duties & rights, freedom, responsibility, justice etc. from a separate chapter of the nature of man & his relation to God.[77]

The meaning of these statements, the way Tawney derives them and his confidence in the moral teachings of Christianity are not the issues: whatever the strengths or weaknesses of his reasoning and his opinions, it is the religious foundation of his social thought which counts.

Tawney's lectures on Christianity tended to follow a pattern and theme: he was interested above all in whether it was a religion of private devotion or of social activism, and while recognizing that it was both, his emphasis and his conclusions were always in favour of the latter. When he came to explain the social theology of his mentor Charles Gore he implicitly endorsed it himself: Christianity was practical rather than theoretical, 'a way of life, not a body of doctrine,' and the church must apply itself to 'the relations of economic life and the conduct of States'.[78] Asked to speak to the William Temple Society in Cambridge in 1949, for example, he began with the observation that to Temple himself all elements of life were the subject for both Christian reflection and also action, including the economy and social relations. Tawney pointed to the potential conflict between a conception of personal religion centred on faith and the wider conception of Christian duty. He had spoken of this before in the 1930s and we are still speaking of it.[79] In one view 'the Christian life is an end not a means. The Church is not a social reform association . . .' But to Tawney 'to dismiss interests, duties, and activities composing so large a part of man's existence . . . seems to me to do violence both to the realities of the human situation and to the social character of the Christian faith'. In any case, if Christianity fails to play a social role, something else will: 'The alternative to religion is not irreligion, it is counter-religion: and the house which is vacated by Christianity does not long remain empty. It is occupied by some form of "idolatory" such as "the worship of riches and the worship of power"'. Thus the churches 'should think out their own social philosophy . . . and [that] they should criticise by reference to them policies, practices and institutions which appear to conflict with them'.[80] As he put it in another lecture, the church

> ought to formulate the Christian doctrine as to questions of property, contract, work, idleness, luxury and economic gain. There is nothing novel in such a proposal. It is all in the Christian tradition. It was done by the Fathers. It was done by the schoolmen. It was done by the divines of the Reformation.[81]

Indeed, the main theme of *Religion and the Rise of Capitalism* was the supersession of the teachings of the medieval church about economic behaviour by those of a radical individualist variety during the Reformation and seventeenth-century revolutions in England. As Tawney wrote in the conclusion to that book,

> The criticism which dismisses the concern of the Churches with economic relations and social organization as a modern innovation finds little support in past history. What requires explanation is not the view that these matters are part of the province of religion, but the view that they are not.[82]

Tawney never ceased to demand that the Church of England set out a clear, moral position on social and economic questions. He recognized that doing so would have two corollaries: a smaller church, which would have lost the support of those who disagreed with this type of religion and its associated political partisanship, and a disestablished church, free to speak its mind and criticize the powers of the day and the state itself. He was untroubled by both these implications.[83]

One commentator described Tawney at the end of his life as an 'anguished romantic' in the tradition of Thomas Carlyle.[84] This is certainly correct, but a better comparison in the same tradition is with John Ruskin, who had remarkable influence over the first generation of Labour leaders in Britain.[85] Through

Tawney's early socialist thought there runs a Ruskinian theme, the repudiation of the pursuit of wealth if wealth is understood only in material terms. Ruskin had famously taught that 'there is no wealth but life' in his essays of the early 1860s, *Unto this Last*. Ruskin's attempt to redefine all the central concepts of Victorian political economy and to replace them with categories and ends with an intrinsically moral component and purpose echoes in Tawney's thinking at this time. Writing in July 1913, he found himself at odds with all the economists, just as Ruskin had been in the 1860s and 1870s:

> We have one group of economists who have attacked certain reforms on the ground that they diminished wealth, and another school who answered them not by saying "let wealth be diminished, *fiat justitia*", but by arguing that they really would not diminish wealth after all. The answer is I believe correct. But it is, nevertheless, devilish; for it suggests that human life, justice, etc. should be measured as items on a balance sheet.[86]

For Ruskin economic questions were resolvable into moral issues; there could be no special, discrete and technical discipline called economics divorced from wider questions of conduct and purpose, for all issues in the relations between people were essentially ethical – or they should be in a reformed society. Tawney said the same: 'what are now called economic questions are questions of moral conduct.'[87] As he foresaw,

> When three or four hundred years hence mankind looks back on the absurd preoccupation of our age with economic issues ... the names which they will reverence will be those of men who stood out against the prevalent fallacy that the most important problems were economic problems, and who taught men to conquer poverty by despising riches.[88]

He provided a more precise indication of the identity of these economic rebels later on in *Religion and the Rise of Capitalism*:

> The distinction made by the philosophers of classical antiquity between liberal and servile occupations, the medieval insistence that riches exist for man, not man for riches, Ruskin's famous outburst, "there is no wealth but life", the argument of the Socialist who urges that production be organized for service, not for profit, are but different attempts to emphasize the instrumental character of economic activities, by reference to an ideal which is held to express the true nature of man.[89]

Tawney was less committed to the redistribution of the goods of the earth to the workers and the poor, than, like Ruskin, to the redefinition of wealth itself and to the teaching of men and women to value other and higher things. Hence he threw himself into a socialism of self-improvement through education rather than into the socialism of redistribution. His goal, like Ruskin's, was to make men and women self-fulfilled, not richer. Thus another theme running through the *Commonplace Book* is the distinction Tawney makes between riches and liberty, or in this case their reverse, poverty and the absence of freedom. As he explained, 'The supreme evil of modern industrial society is not poverty. It is the absence of liberty, that is, of the opportunity for self-direction: and for controlling the material conditions of a man's life. This produces poverty, because it produces hopelessness, irresponsibility, recklessness.'[90] Material progress could never be a substitute for freedom – 'the greatest happiness' could not be bought at the expense of this self-direction. To Tawney, 'the two things are, in fact, incommensurable, necessaries of a different order, and to offer the former instead of the latter is imply irrelevant.'[91] As he wrote in the conclusion to *Religion and the Rise of Capitalism*,

> Both the existing economic order, and too many of the projects advanced for reconstructing it, break down through neglect of the truism that, since even quite common men have souls, no increase in material wealth will compensate them for arrangements which insult their self-respect and impair their freedom.[92]

Later, in a piece entitled 'Christianity and Social Order', which was probably an early draft of Tawney's 1937 essay 'A Note on Christianity and the Social Order' which was published in 1953, he gave voice to a widespread scepticism of industrial capitalism in the context of 'human life and social well-being'. Like Ruskin he argued that

> Economic considerations instead of being the servant of social life become its master, and [that] the commercial interests which in a sane society are subordinate interests like the maintenance of police and the cleaning of sewers are erected into a Juggernaut to which all other interests, education, art and culture, are sacrificed.[93]

Tawney more frequently acknowledged his debts to William Morris than to John Ruskin. In 1908 he wrote in a letter to Jeanette that 'we know that what is best in life is cooperation, service, love, call it what you will: what William Morris meant when he made John Ball say "Fellowship is Life; lack of fellowship is death".'[94] Forty-five years later he used the same quotation to preface his collection of essays, *The Attack and Other Papers*. But Tawney also contributed an essay on Ruskin to the collection published in 1919 to mark the centenary of

Ruskin's birth. He was very aware of the cultural and intellectual context from which the organized labour movement emerged in Britain, a context shaped pre-eminently by Ruskin's social and intellectual legacy, and either unappreciated or forgotten today, more than a century later.[95] Recalling the socialist revival at the end of the Victorian period in his memorial lecture on the Webbs, delivered in 1952, Tawney characterized this context as 'a combination of idealism, good fellowship and an apocalyptic fervour rejoicing that the axe was laid to the root of the capitalist tree and that the day of the Lord was at hand'. He could now see that 'the popular socialism of the day was more head than heart. The faithful demanded from their mentors not political and economic expertise, but fire, conviction and ethical unction in the exposition of the fundamentals of the creed'.[96] In this vein, Jeanette Tawney recalled being strongly influenced as a young woman when she met Keir Hardie, so much a product of this milieu, who was officiating at the baptism of a friend's child.[97]

If this all seemed very distant by the 1950s, and especially alien in a tribute to the Webbs, who partook of none of this and almost certainly disapproved of an ethical and emotional socialism, Tawney recovered it so well and so accurately because he was himself touched by it at the time and after. In later life, this 'ethical unction' declined in ferocity and significance in Tawney and other socialists as they turned from moral denunciation, which was easy, to the more difficult and less-rewarding business of administering capitalism in the interests of all. Tawney could see that for himself, even in his political youth. For he did not lack a certain realism and there were limits to his moralizing. The first piece of work he set his tutorial class at Longton encouraged his students to write broadly about the nature of economics: 'If you were going to devote six months to the study of Economics, what branch should you select, and why; and how should you set about it?' One of the students, E. S. Cartwright, who was to become his lifelong friend, and who later organized Oxford's programme of tutorial classes for more than 30 years, presented an essay in response extolling Ruskin's approach to economics. He would, he wrote, 'choose for study that branch of Economics which deals with Social Conditions and at the same time should look forward to the realization of Ruskin's noble ideal when other ideas of wealth than mere possessive ones may hold sway in economic thought'. Tawney's comment at the end was prescient: 'Our problem at the present day is to put economic activity in proper relation to the other elements of human life. But if we forget the economic motive altogether and overlook the material conditions on which the production of wealth depends, we become mere sentimentalists and dreamers'.[98]

Tawney's early political thinking takes us back to a milieu which has been obscured for decades by historians' focus on the organized Labour movement and Labour Party, and by Labour politicians' focus on the state. Yet this was an age when the founding MPs of the Labour Party admitted, when asked in 1906, to the overwhelming influence of Ruskin and the Bible above all other authorities in the formation of their beliefs.[99] Tawney was in many ways reminiscent of the early socialists in Britain of the 1880s and 1890s who manifested a quasi-religious dedication to their political creed and eschewed electoral politics because it would routinize and deaden the spirit. Like missionaries, they believed in 'making socialists' by speaking, debating and educating, the better to build a socialist society with the sincere convictions of the people at its base. Stephen Yeo has argued that this approach was lost after 1900 as socialism became synonymous with the Labour Party and was subordinated to building a political machine, winning elections and, in the case of the Fabians, permeating the structures of the state.[100] In Tawney it seems to have lived on. His opposition to Fabianism had no personal side to it, certainly: he dedicated *Equality* to the Webbs. But Beatrice Webb could see the differences between them and appreciated the special character of Tawney's prescriptions for a better world. As she wrote in her diary in the 1930s, 'His task is that of a discoverer and an expounder of the new faith (economics based on service of man rather than the exploitation of man by man) not that of a manoeuvrer or politician or even an administrator.'[101]

Tawney at this stage reminds us of the plural traditions of British socialism which may have been managerial to some within it, but was ethical to many others. He could appreciate the limitations of a purely ethical commitment, but it was a crucial element in his early outlook and one that he never ignored or expunged in maturity, even when he found himself having to advise on the reorganization of industries, schools and economic policy in the 1920s and 1930s. He even acknowledged the duality in a famous essay in which he castigated the Labour Party in 1934 for its failings in office and its unpreparedness for power. In 'The Choice Before the Labour Party' he explained that 'socialism has two aspects. It implies a personal attitude and a collective effort. The quality of the latter depends on the sincerity of the former'. Winning power and pulling the levers of government – the outlook which had been dominant in the party since the Edwardian period – would not be sufficient.

> The Labour Party deceives itself, if it supposes that the mere achievement of a majority will enable it to carry out fundamental measures, unless it has previously created in the country the temper to stand behind it when the real

struggle begins . . . What is needed . . . is the creation of a body of men and women who, whether trade unionists or intellectuals, put Socialism first, and whose creed carries conviction because they live in accordance with it.[102]

As Christopher Hill commented later, 'Tawney's Socialism wasn't the state variety – the state ownership of industries and so on – but a very individual sort of Socialism.'[103]

Amidst all the tributes and obituaries when Tawney died, that published in the *New Statesman* stands out as more accurately capturing the essence of his political thought, which is bound up with this tension, than all the others. It explained that

> Tawney understood the nature of capitalism as well as any Marxist and knew that a change in economic power was the condition of his political objectives. In all his books and pamphlets he drove that point home brilliantly. Yet, in an age when socialism of a kind had become a respectable means of regulating economic behaviour, he continued to insist that socialism was fundamentally about human behaviour. He rejected the fallacy – shared by the Webbs and the communists – that a change in the machinery of government was itself enough to change men.[104]

As the *New Statesman* continued, this was 'not a comfortable doctrine' because it placed a moral responsibility on individuals: the change desired in society was not the business of a remote power in government but of the individual desiring that change. And mere political engagement – membership, meetings and campaigning – was not enough: socialism was about how people lived and dealt with others. But if this was a problem for individual socialists, it was a problem for Tawney as well. Making individual socialists was one thing, but how exactly was that translatable into the changes required for the better, meaning the more moral, organization of society? Tawney did not say, believing simply, or so it would seem, that as more people came to reflect on socialism and embrace it, right conduct across the state and society would be achieved. Meanwhile, Tawney was himself drawn into national affairs and administration which led to a change of focus and emphasis in the 1920s embodied in the schemes of institutional and industrial reform set out in *The Acquisitive Society* and *Equality*, books that lack the commitment to, and the passion of, the ethical socialism of his early work.

The Acquisitive Society, published in 1921, is a work of transition.[105] Clearly linked to the moralism of the *Commonplace Book*, it also reflects Tawney's growing social experience, economic knowledge and desire to make general rather than personal arguments. The focus is less on individual conduct than on the right ordering of society. Tawney's assault on the acquisitive society owed much to his confrontation with the coal owners on the Sankey commission: the book is full of references and examples taken from the coal industry which gives it immediacy and authenticity, but which is also a weakness because the sheer disorganization of the coal industry made it *sui generis* and a difficult example from which to generalize. At this stage Tawney did not know enough about other industries to balance and qualify his remarks about coal.[106]

Tawney begins and ends the book with reference, as before, to conduct and principles: 'social institutions', he argues, 'are the visible expression of the scale of moral values which rules the mind of individuals, and it is impossible to alter institutions without altering that moral valuation'.[107] As in his earlier writings, it was necessary that society 'rearrange its scale of values. It must regard economic interests as one element in life, not as the whole of life'.[108] Two ideas, economic function and economic purpose, dominate the work. Tawney argues that any and every economic enterprise should function for the benefit of the community and fulfil a socially useful purpose. The key criterion should not be 'what dividends does it pay' but 'what service does it perform?'[109] Thus the idea of function was 'incompatible with the doctrine that every person and organisation has an unlimited right to exploit their economic opportunities as fully as they please'.[110] Function and purpose were evidently not devoid of moral freight: as Tawney put it, they offered 'not merely a standard for determining the relations of different classes and groups of producers, but a scale of moral values'.[111] But if his thinking before the First World War was focused on personal conduct, and was therefore difficult to apply to society in general and was open to the charge of subjectivity, the concept of 'function' offered a clearer, less contentious and arguably more objective standard for discriminating between the socially beneficial and the malign.

By the tests of function and purpose, contemporary capitalist society was failing: too many of its enterprises were designed for the acquisition of wealth for its own sake or for the sake of an owning class at the expense of the majority. Tawney pitched 'the discharge of social obligations' against 'the exercise of the right to pursue . . . self-interest'.[112] He drew attention to the potential conflict between an individual's unfettered rights and the concept of a social function where economic activity must make a positive contribution to society. Hence he argued that rights were conditional, to be exercised according to context and in relation to public purposes. Industrial life would in this manner be converted to emphasize 'the service of the public, not . . . the gain of those who own capital'.[113] He called for a reform of the economy to meet collective needs and for a reordering of human values that would make economic activity a means to life rather than an end in itself. 'Functionless property', in which category he placed the useless products of a consumer society – 'futilities' as he called them, or all accoutrements of conspicuous consumption – would not be produced. In an interesting glance backwards to a much earlier radical tradition in Britain, Tawney discriminated between all those who work and all the rest who live off rents, dividends and other forms of unearned income:

> The real economic cleavage is not, as is often said, between employers and employed, but between all who do constructive work, from scientist to labourer, on the one hand, and all whose main interest is the preservation of existing proprietary rights upon the other, irrespective of whether they contribute to constructive work or not.[114]

This was the sociology of the Chartists in the 1830s. He also called for a resurrection of 'the peculiar and distinctive Christian standard of social conduct'.[115] The book's conclusion, criticizing the reluctance of the church to engage in discussion of the morality of economic and social behaviour, thus pointed forward to Tawney's subsequent historical study of the church's abdication 'of one whole department of life' in *Religion and the Rise of Capitalism*.

There is a beguiling clarity and cogency to *The Acquisitive Society* which makes it among the most satisfying of Tawney's political works. There are almost no references to the writings of other economists and social theorists: it is an uninterrupted argument from a single source. What it lacks in detail it compensates for in its moral certainty.[116] But a reader may still ask how those economic functions and purposes declared to be legitimate are to be determined, by what criteria, and by whom? Tawney gives no sense of the institutional structures that his reforms would require. Anyone aware of his thoughts in the *Commonplace Book* will find surprising his new focus on efficiency as the rationale of economic reform. A whole chapter in the *Acquisitive Society* is entitled 'The Condition of Efficiency' and there Tawney presents his central concepts of function and purpose as conducive to more efficient production and the better provision of services to the public. Tawney wrote the book in mid-stream, in other words. He hadn't jettisoned the moral imperatives of his youth, and he never would; but wider experience, the desire to ground his ideas on something more substantial than his own ethical presuppositions, the hope of academic recognition and the attempt to reach a wider audience impelled a compromise with more conventional and systematic socialist economic thought. Tawney was still interested in the ends of economic life, and still defined them in relation to a moral standard, but the means by which they were to be achieved were also important to him now, and the satisfaction of social need was a much higher priority than in his earliest encounters with capitalism.

Equality, published a decade later, and based on his Halley Stewart Lectures of 1929, was a more contextualized study in which details of the social conditions and arrangements of interwar Britain were deployed by Tawney in making a case for wholesale social reform. An unequal society misapplied resources to the comfort and privileges of the few when the many required better homes, schools and hospitals. It failed to develop the talents and skills of the population: thus inequality limited the productive capacity of society. It protected powerful vested interests, whose perpetuation was an affront to a true democracy; and it encouraged social and class divisions, limiting what might be achieved in a society and economy organized on the principle of cooperative effort. Tawney was less interested in achieving an equality of income than in ending the advantages and privileges of a social élite: 'We may not succeed in establishing a parity of pecuniary incomes, nor is it important to do so. We can certainly, if we please, wind up for good and all the whole odious business of class advantages and class disabilities, which are the characteristic and ruinous vices of our existing social system.'[117] His aim was an 'equality of environment, of access to education and the means of civilisation, of security and independence', and his primary concern was to make a case for institutional reform.[118] A civilized society was marked by its determination to eliminate inequalities arising from its own organization. 'The important thing is not that it should be completely attained, but that it should be sincerely sought. What matters to the health of society is the objective towards which its face is set.'[119]

As desirable in itself, and as the means to the elimination of privilege, Tawney called for progressive taxation to fund communal services in health, education and welfare. Private schools should be opened up to all children irrespective of means; a standing industrial commission or 'Planning Department' with powers to intervene and remodel each industry would direct the British economy; among those industries, the most important would be transferred to public ownership; and in the new nationalized enterprises the workers themselves would play a managerial role. Tawney even discussed the form of cumbersome bureaucracy required for directing a centralized and socialized state: 'The sanction in the background, if obstruction were encountered, would be the transference to public ownership of the industry concerned.'[120] Overall, *Equality* burns with indignation. Tawney writes with barely controlled rage at the many deficiencies of British society. There is much information – historical, sociological, economic, medical – on poor conditions, insanitary cities and the disparities between the elite and the rest. When he writes about the goal of 'equality of opportunity' it is with irony because so few then enjoyed even the basic opportunities required for full civic participation.[121]

Equality was an important milestone in the development of socialist thinking in Britain and a prescient guide to the intentions and achievements of the Labour governments after 1945.[122] But Tawney's focus on the particular weakened the book as a more general, philosophical discussion of equality, and as a lasting contribution in the history of political thought. There is relatively little discussion of equality itself as a philosophical concept or historical objective. Tawney largely ignored the categories of civil, legal and religious equality which had been so central to the history of the preceding liberal age. He never mentioned the special disabilities affecting women, though there had been a women's movement fighting gender inequality in Britain since the 1850s and his own wife had been an active feminist in the early years of their marriage. Of the subject of racial inequality there is not a trace. The work of precursors like Tocqueville and Mill who had diagnosed the strengths and weaknesses of egalitarian societies in the nineteenth century was mentioned rather than engaged. How equality was to be defined and why it should be the essential goal of an industrial society was never argued through but taken for granted. Tawney wrote for an audience in agreement with his programme for *social* equality specifically, and did not attempt to present counter-arguments to this as fully and fairly as might be expected if *Equality* was to have been something more than the presentation of a single case related to a specific society at a particular moment.

Tawney's passionate moralism and his emphasis on selfless fellowship cannot fail to move and inspire readers. But much of the work was an angry attack on a relatively small and privileged elite and Tawney often seemed more insistent on bringing this group down than on lifting up the rest of society. His aim, he declared was 'to destroy plutocracy and to set in its place an equalitarian society'.[123] Plutocrats might be fair game in any age, but he did not sufficiently differentiate between those with vast wealth, a legitimate object of his scorn perhaps, and the hundreds of thousands of property holders and businessmen whose fortunes were modest and whose living standards not notably plutocratic, even if above the average. Businessmen in *Equality* are always coal owners and rentiers, rather than small employers or creative entrepreneurs. Tawney's model of economic life is equally narrow. Throughout the book there is a focus on the virtues of investment and purposeful production. Consumption is ignored or depicted as the frivolous pastime of the idle rich rather than the motor of a modern economy. In this regard Tawney had not read his Ruskin (or the work of J. A. Hobson) well enough, for there was a notable tradition of radical political economy in Britain which had placed consumption at the centre of its economic model. Industries are lumped together by Tawney without any discussion of the conditions under which they operate, specifically their markets and the level of international competition they face in them. In the context of the stagnant or declining markets faced by many staple British industries in the 1920s, low wages might be explicable at least, if not defensible.

Some of his prescriptions, including, for example, his opposition to 'the social poison of inheritance' whether of small or large fortunes, betrayed a blindness to unchanging and ubiquitous aspects of human psychology whether in the rich or the humble.[124] However strong he believed the case against inheritance to be, in arguing for its strict limitation by taxation and law Tawney owed it to readers to set out and answer the case in its favour. The great political thinkers – Hobbes, Locke, Hume, Bentham, Mill – have generally started from a theory of human behaviour and an appreciation of human motives, needs and frailties, and have built their models on this basis. As the later critic Raymond Williams, who came from the same educational and political traditions as Tawney, pointed out, Tawney assumed that men and women could be persuaded to see the world through his eyes and would comply with his principles for moral reformation. The assumption, as Williams noted, was an indication of Tawney's limitations as a political thinker.[125]

Equality, famous though largely unread, is not Tawney's best political work, which was reserved for his essays or articles rather than any full-length treatise. His style of writing and his intellectual approach were better suited to indicating the direction to be travelled than mapping the terrain of any newfoundland. But *Equality* reads like the work of a dedicated state socialist, who, if he might refrain from the wholesale socialization of economic and public life, would nevertheless use legal and fiscal means to reform British institutions. The focus on the state and on institutions is quite different from the focus on individuals, their spiritual needs and their God, which so strongly marks the character of his thought before the First World War. The insistence on achieving economic and material equality is likewise strikingly different from the overt anti-materialism of the *Commonplace Book* in which Tawney repeatedly disavows as unworthy the objective of putting more money in the pockets of the workers. To struggle for the improvement of the living standards and opportunities of the poor was hardly at odds with his early ethical socialism; but Tawney originally conceived that campaign as one to be achieved through argument and persuasion and focused on individuals. Twenty years on, it had become a series of manoeuvres requiring the powers of the state and the threat of coercion, and was focused on industries, shareholders and property owners. It could easily be contended that the older Tawney was a realist who had come to understand the ways of the world and who now appreciated that offering men and women a moral path would not be sufficient. But the younger Tawney was the more original and radical thinker, a socialist of the heart if not of the head, a natural democrat who rejected political imposition via the machinery of the state. *To make socialists* rather than *to impose socialism* was always going to be a more difficult strategy, and perhaps that is why Tawney diverged from the positions of his youth. But its fruits might have been more enduring. Tawney himself used often to quote Cromwell on his 'plain, russet-coated Captain that knows what he fights for and loves what he knows': that was the way to make a real revolution.

Whether Tawney was himself convinced by the state socialism he laid out in *Equality* is an open question. He espoused it in the 1930s and 1940s but if one looks carefully through his writings it is clear that Tawney never really forsook his earlier positions. His paper for a 1937 conference on 'the Church and Social Order', subsequently republished in *The Attack* in 1953 and as a pamphlet entitled *Christian Politics* in the following year, recalls the youthful thinker who derived human equality from the divine. It has been described as 'the best statement of his innermost personal beliefs in relation to society'.[126] Here he returned to the argument of the *Commonplace Book* that man's humanity is God-given and shared with the deity, and that compared with this, all social, national and racial differences are simply trivial and by their nature 'anti-Christian' because they are a denial of God's intent and purpose.

> The necessary corollary, therefore, of the Christian conception of man is a strong sense of equality. Equality does not mean that all men are equally clever or equally virtuous, any more than they are equally tall or equally fat. It means that all men, merely because they are men, are of equal value.[127]

Tawney recognized the diversity of human attributes and needs in this lecture and recommended that 'forms of provision should be equally diverse' to accommodate these differences. 'The essential point – the essence of equality – is that such diversities must be based, not on the accidents of class, income, sex, colour or nationality, but on the real requirements of the different members of the human family.' In this lecture 'equality' denoted neither equality of opportunity nor equality of outcome but an equality of status and respect. Since we are all equal in the sight of God, argued Tawney, we should be equal in each other's valuations and behaviour. All should be treated justly, all respected equally and all have their needs met; but because we differ, our needs must be met in different ways. That difference is not inequality if equality of esteem is assured.[128] *Equality* had set out a programme of public policy designed to equalize conditions in society; in this lecture Tawney returned to the interactions of men and women and to their divine inspiration. The scale of the argument was entirely different and the divine derivation of equality itself would not have been to all tastes, but arguably this is the authentic Tawney, the Christian egalitarian rather than the secular state socialist.

Tawney appreciated the tension between these two approaches and traditions because he was himself subject to the duality. But he could not harmonize them: state socialism and personal socialism always remained different and contradictory aspects in his thought as they had been in the Edwardian period. During the crisis in the coal industry after the Great War Tawney was not only a member of the Sankey Commission and an advocate for the miners, but also wrote extensively in the press and journals to explain the problems of the coal industry and to justify the nationalization of all the pits. Sometimes, as in a lecture he delivered in the United States in 1920, he recognized that merely reorganizing coal mining would not be enough – that nationalization would fail unless it could 'draw the public spirit and the professional pride and the solidarity of the workmen into the development of industry'. To do this, the industry itself would have to be reconfigured as a 'public service' rather than a business, and the men themselves would have to see that they 'are in a responsible partnership with the community'.[129] As it turned out, nationalization, let alone the engendering of a new public spirit in the industry, was a political impossibility at this juncture, but it is arguable if a new spirit was ever realized after the mines were nationalized in 1946. In an address in 1952, ironically to the University of London Fabian Society, he commented that 'we have not yet taken with sufficient seriousness the problem of creating conditions which cause the rank and file of industry to feel that they are responsible partners'.[130]

Nationalization, now long gone, might have stood a better chance if all employees, managers, as well as workers, had sympathized with the spirit Tawney wished to bring to industrial reorganization. But by the time of his death Tawney was aware that instrumentalism – the determination to advance socialism by using the instruments of the state to refashion society to accord with socialist ideals in the absence of moral and spiritual change – had become the dominant and unassailable position in the labour movement as a whole, with consequences that point towards present dilemmas on the left in British politics. In 1949 Tawney had warned 'that the peril of the future will not be the grosser forms of exploitation which were the scandal of the past, but an equable level of complacent materialism'.[131] Much earlier he had written much the same thing in respect of 'all decent people': 'No political creed will ever capture their hearts which begins by saying simply "we will give you a little more money. We will still measure success by the old standards. But we will let you have more of it."'[132]

Education

Tawney is most famous for his historical and political writings. If his role as an educationist is remembered, it is as a pioneer of the WEA and adult education more generally. Yet in maturity he probably gave more of his time to the cause of educational reform – and the reform of English secondary schooling most notably – than to anything else, and he probably did more than anyone else to achieve this in the 1920s and 1930s. The campaign he led was entirely straightforward for it was the cause, quite simply, of a good education for all children. Achieving this laudable and hardly revolutionary end proved to be enormously difficult, however, and robbed Tawney of time and strength that might have been applied to other issues, and perhaps to unwritten books. It was an essential element of his political outlook, nonetheless: the ethical transformation he looked for could only come about by changing values and assumptions, and education was the key to this. As he wrote in 1924, 'The society based on the free cooperation of individuals, which is the ideal of the Socialist, depends, in short, on the widest possible diffusion of education.'[1]

Tawney took an interest in all aspects of education at nursery, elementary and university levels as well. His concern for the welfare of younger children, for example, including his support for fresh air, school journeys and camps, playgrounds, physical education and sport, is summarized in a chapter on 'Health and the School' in one of his earliest and most important pamphlets, *Education: the Socialist Policy*, published by the Independent Labour Party (ILP) in 1924. As he wrote there, '"Body" and "mind" are not two separate entities . . . They are different aspects of a single personality. What nature has joined it is not for the Educational Authorities to put asunder.'[2] A decade later he joined with a group of educationists, including Susan Isaacs, to promote the building of new nursery schools as an integral aspect of slum clearance and urban regeneration.[3] Attention to the health of children was 'not an addition to their education, but part of their education, and at certain ages the most important part of it'.[4]

As a young graduate he had pursued the reform of Oxford and Cambridge; later in his career he served for one 5-year term on the University Grants Committee (1943–8), which distributed public funds to higher education.[5] His most notable service on this body was to co-write a paper in 1945 with Sir Henry Tizard,[6] the chemist, university administrator and pioneer of British air defences using radar, urging the expansion of the university system, partly through the foundation of new universities, to accommodate the increasing number of qualified school-leavers from a reformed secondary education system and to meet the nation's increased need for skilled, professional workers.[7] His aim was always a version of what has become known as the 'Robbins Principle', though articulated by him more than a generation before the Robbins Report of 1963 into university provision and access: 'to ensure that the Universities are accessible to men and women in all sections of the community, irrespective of their income, provided solely that they have the inclination and capacity for a University education.'[8] Although not directly involved in the establishment of Keele University in a district, North Staffordshire, which he knew so well from his tutorial classes there before the First World War, the idea of Keele was intimately bound up with the educational revival he had led locally, and he gave the project his blessing and support.[9]

Then there was his national position in adult education as president of the WEA (1928–44), an advisory member of the British Institute of Adult Education, an academic advisor from 1919 of Ruskin College, Oxford, and through his continuous service on the Central Joint Advisory Council on Tutorial Classes from 1917 to 1945. This broad experience, combined with his political commitment to education, made him a formidable advocate with unrivalled knowledge of the different elements of education. As Ernest Green, the General Secretary of the WEA, explained soon after his death,

> I have been with him on many occasions on deputations to Ministers of Education, to Archbishops on questions regarding the solution to the religious difficulty in our schools and I've always found that on those occasions he was able to be convincing, he was able very often to be educative, and to place under some position of awe those who recognised that his knowledge of education was almost supreme.[10]

His greatest contributions were undoubtedly to the education of adolescents and he deserves recognition as one of those whose commitment led to the 1944 (Butler) Education Act, flawed though this was in Tawney's opinion. It did not take long for him to understand that many of his students in the classes he taught for Oxford and the WEA before the First World War were handicapped by defective, or in some cases, non-existent secondary educations. Whereas elementary education had been compulsory in England since the early 1880s, many children before and after the First World War ceased to attend school at 12 or 13 years of age, leaving without either the skills required for economic life or the knowledge and culture required for personal life.[11] Only 7 per cent of boys and 5.4 per cent of girls born before 1910 went on to secondary school, for example. That these proportions approximately doubled in each case for children born in the next two decades can hardly be accounted a national triumph.[12] Many of the worker scholars taught by Tawney resented their ignorance and the absence of contact with intellectual life which marked their experience up to the point they attended a tutorial class; their travails led their tutor to see that the reform of secondary education was the prerequisite for their personal liberation and for any and every social reform. In making this discovery and this connection Tawney was merely following in the path of those who had begun university extension lectures in the late-Victorian generation. Michael Sadler as the Secretary of Oxford's Extension Delegacy from 1885 had organized and promoted a famous conference in Oxford in October 1893 to assess the future of secondary education. This had stimulated the appointment 2 years later of the Royal Commission on Secondary Education chaired by James Bryce, the Liberal minister, diplomat and intellectual. Sadler himself served on the commission, and its recommendations provided, in Tawney's phrase, 'the intellectual foundations' of the subsequent 1902 Education Act which empowered new local educational authorities, at their discretion, to establish academically selective grammar schools for secondary education.[13] Tawney was to put heart and soul in the interwar period into furthering this initiative and turning what he called 'the skeleton of a public system of secondary education' into the real thing, 'a system of free and universal Secondary Education.'[14]

Educational Reconstruction was one of the many issues Tawney took up as he recovered from his wounds at the Somme. As he later explained,

> Reconstruction and a better world have been promised to the nation as a reward for the losses and tireless labours of the Great War. There is one supreme way of reconstruction: the creation of such a system of education as will secure the physical, the mental, and the spiritual uplifting of the present generation of children.[15]

He set out his own views in an article in *The Times Educational Supplement*, subsequently republished as a pamphlet by the WEA as *Some Thoughts on*

Education and the War, and later anthologized as *A College for All Souls* in the collection of his essays, *The Attack* (1953). Here, at the start of his engagement with national educational policy, as a continuation of his pre-war ethical socialism, and while the war continued and the casualties mounted, the case for education was made on spiritual and emotional grounds. The failings of English education had undermined the war effort, but educational reform at its close would give a higher purpose to national life, redeem the nation and its sacrifices, and prove Britain's commitment to the higher values for which it professed to be fighting. 'A reconstruction of education in a generous and liberal spirit would be the noblest memorial to those who have fallen . . . It would show that the nation was prepared to submit its life to the kind of principles for which it thought itself justified in asking them to die.'[16]

He made contributions of a more practical and pragmatic type to the preparation of a pamphlet under the title of 'Educational Reconstruction' which the WEA published in November 1916 and which Tawney welcomed and promoted in one of his leaders for the *Manchester Guardian* in early 1917.[17] The WEA called for a range of progressive measures: sufficient free nursery schools from ages 2 to 6; compulsory elementary schooling to follow; universal full-time education to the age of 14; the school-leaving age to be raised to 15 within 5 years without exemptions, with maintenance allowances for pupils over 14 as required. The hours worked by juveniles who had left school were to be limited while their education was topped-up in compulsory continuation classes for young people in work. Public scholarships would then allow the cleverest to proceed to university. In truth, though the details changed somewhat over time, this programme was the basis for most of Tawney's educational activism thereafter.

The WEA, of which he was president from 1928 to 1944, was one locus for his campaigns; it formed his base and headquarters, providing him with a position from which he could intervene in educational debates. But there were others as well, notably the Labour Party's Advisory Committee on Education (LPACE) on which he served for many years, one of a series of advisory committees on policy which Tawney helped establish within the Labour Party in 1918 at the time of its adoption of its constitution. He used his leaders in the *Manchester Guardian* to spread his ideas and critique those of recalcitrant interwar governments. There was also his place on the Board of Education's Consultative Committee on Education from which to lobby and influence officials and politicians. He held a position on the Board for the whole of the 1920s, benefiting from 'periods of extension by special consideration' of his original term of service. Thus in the early 1920s he fought against cuts in educational expenditure under the so-called 'Geddes Axe' of public expenditure by publishing articles in *The Highway*, the WEA's journal – 'Make the Children pay for the War' and 'Economy and the Education Act 1918' for example – and the *Manchester Guardian*; by drafting a memorandum for the LPACE; and by serving on a joint committee of the WEA and National Union of Teachers to coordinate opposition to government policy.[18] Later there were smaller and ad hoc organizations to which he gave his time and name, such as the School Age Council, based at Toynbee Hall, committed to raising the school-leaving age.[19]

It was during this campaign against reductions in educational expenditure that Tawney drafted most of the most famous and accessible of all his statements of educational policy, *Secondary Education for All*. This short book began as an attempt by him in 1921 to address a narrow question for the LPACE concerning scholarships and so-called 'free places' for secondary education. It was decided to expand it into a full-scale statement of Labour's education policy in advance of expected elections and was reviewed by the Advisory Committee itself and by the Labour Party's Executive Committee before it was published in the spring of 1922.[20] It was to serve as a guide to the local initiatives on which educational advance would likely depend in the 1920s, and it set out the 'instalments of reform' which the Labour Party should support in this incremental process.[21] It defined the most urgent educational task before the nation as 'a large increase in the secondary school population'.[22] Its basic argument was that all children over the age of 11 should receive an academically distinct period of secondary education until the age of 16, clearly differentiated from primary education before that. Tawney argued that education was not a series of unconnected events but a progression through three demarcated though linked stages, elementary, secondary and tertiary. Within this structure, secondary education should be 'free and universal'. The charging of fees by secondary schools should cease, especially in view of the practice in some educational authorities of admitting fee-paying children 'on easier intellectual terms than the children of poor parents who can enter them only with free places'.[23] Continuation education from the age of 14 should cease, as well; if provided, it should cover the years from 16 to 18. Much of the pamphlet was taken up with strictly practical suggestions for educational improvement, such as the upgrading and building of more accommodation for secondary schools.[24] The case being made depended on both the economic benefits to society and the enrichment of individuals that would flow from more and better education: 'What society requires for the sake both of economic efficiency and of social amenity, is educated intelligence.'[25] Interestingly, Tawney opposed educational uniformity: he recommended an equality of provision in schools of different types but of equal esteem, rather than an identity of provision in one type of school providing one type of education only.[26] Nor was he opposed to academic selection in a context in which every child, of whatever ability, was sure of a good education:

> If the majority of boys and girls receive a full time education up to 16 then, what is even more important, quite apart from the selection of special talent for special cultivation, the rank and file of the community will carry into their working lives the idealism, the corporate loyalty, the intellectual alertness which are fostered during the impressionable years of adolescence by the life of a good school and their outlook will gradually permeate and transform the whole structure of society.[27]

The case was made with Tawney's characteristic pungency and sarcasm. Complaining that the nation spent so much more on defence and on the consumption of alcohol than it did on education, he compared Britain to an individual 'who turned his house into a fortress armed to the teeth in which he swilled alcohol in the drawing-room and kept his children on short rations in the coal hole'. He wondered 'whether the policy of "making the children pay for the war" is quite the most appropriate tribute to the fathers who fell in it', and 'whether, if the ship is really sinking, "women and children last" is the motto by which the British Empire desires to be remembered'.[28]

There was nothing very radical about these ideas and Tawney never claimed any originality or personal authority when pressing the case.[29] He worked with the grain of existing practices and institutions and essentially focused on the expansion of provision rather than thinking afresh about the purposes and structures of education.[30] He accepted many of the educational assumptions of the age concerning academic selection and diversity of provision, for these were not considered by him to be problematic and did not stand in the way of basic educational provision which was always his aim. His intention was not to revolutionize education itself, but to provide it in the first place. Thus his major concern was always the school-leaving age – ensuring that every child was schooled until the age of 16 in an appropriate, though not in the same, manner. Such problems as this bequeathed to a future generation were not his concern, which is not to say that he did not care, but that he did not recognize them as problems at that stage and probably considered them second-order issues in any case.[31] Occasionally, elsewhere, Tawney made the argument for a later school-leaving age in more impassioned and elevated ways than he had done in 1922. When writing to the educationist Fred Clarke in 1940 and complaining about the type of unskilled labour that most 14-year-old school-leavers were forced into, Tawney was unrestrained: 'What really matters to young people is not so many hours school instruction per week. It is that they should grow up a little longer in the atmosphere of a spiritual society, such as a good school is, and very few factories can be.'[32]

Secondary Education for All, although uncontroversial, was nevertheless the policy of a political party. The case being made gained authority and wider purchase when it was developed and publicized by the Consultative Committee of the Board of Education in what became known as the Hadow Report of 1927. Sir (William) Henry Hadow, historian of music and the vice-chancellor of Sheffield University, was the chairman of the Consultative Committee through the 1920s. Receiving a reference from the Board in 1924 to consider the future of secondary education, the Committee questioned dozens of witnesses and representatives of different educational associations, and produced its report, *The Education of the Adolescent*, in 1926. It, too, essentially accepted the consensus that secondary schooling should be clearly differentiated from the elementary level and extended for all children up to the age of 16 eventually, though the target was to reach a universal leaving age of 15 by 1932 as a first step. It, too, did not recognize a difficulty with educational selection at age 11, and different types of schools providing different sorts of education for a range of different aptitudes. Among a group of distinguished educationists which included the political scientist Ernest Barker, who was chairman of the drafting committee, Cyril Burt, the educational psychologist, and Percy Nunn, the principal of the London Day Training College, which under his guidance soon became the University of London Institute of Education, Tawney could not assume a dominating role. In truth, his influence was not required: the way forward was clear and attracted the support of most educationists, not just the committed progressives.[33]

Persuading government and vested interests was quite a different matter, however, and Tawney found himself engaged in conflict with administrations of every type in the interwar period, whether ministries of the left, the right or coalitions. In 1918, at the time of the so-called Fisher Education Act, his support for compulsory continuation education after children left school until they reached the age of 18 brought him into conflict with the Master Cotton Spinners and Federation of British Industries which opposed all restrictions on their freedom to employ teenage labour on their own terms. It provoked

Tawney's famous article, 'Keep the Worker's Children in their Place', in which he was scathing about the 'pitiful' argument that British industry depended for its continuance on juvenile labour, and outraged by the assumption that only a very few children were worthy of education beyond 14.[34] As he repeated 4 years later, 'In England, it is not ungentlemanly to steal halfpennies from children, and industrial interests, it may be assumed, will oppose any reform which interferes with the supply of cheap juvenile labour.'[35] After the struggle against the post-war coalition's 'Geddes Axe' there was an argument later in the 1920s over *The Possible Cost of Raising the School Leaving Age*, the title of a pamphlet Tawney composed, which was based upon a speech he gave to a conference at the Kingsway Hall in London in October 1927. His case was that increased expenditure on education could be offset by savings made in the unemployment fund by keeping children in school for longer; indeed, jobs usually done by youths might then be taken by older workers, reducing unemployment itself in the process. But within government this latter point was disputed for there was no evidence to support the contention that older people would naturally take the sort of jobs vacated by the young. Tawney found himself in dispute with Sir Arthur Steel-Maitland, a slightly older and almost equally brilliant product of Rugby and Balliol, who was the Minister for Labour, and also the President of the Board of Trade, Lord Eustace Percy, both Conservatives.

He expected that the 1929 MacDonald administration would be more sympathetic to educational advance, especially when one of his former collaborators in educational policy, Charles Trevelyan, who had written the preface to his 1924 pamphlet, *Education: The Socialist Policy*, was made President of the Board of Education for the second time. But despite Tawney's private encouragement and also public pressure to raise the school-leaving age, the leadership of the Labour Party and notably MacDonald himself, were unenthusiastic, especially when educational reforms affecting the funding of voluntary (i.e. religious) schools threatened opposition from the Catholic Church, to the possible electoral detriment of the party. The measure was omitted from the King's Speech in July 1929 and Tawney wrote in fury to his old friend Dick Denman, now a Labour MP:

> People are now waiting to see if it is like any other Government and if, having been returned to power it intends to jettison its undertakings with regard to children on the ground that they do not count in elections. If that is its attitude I imagine the response of many people will be that of myself, namely, that they will not lift a finger to return a Labour government again.[36]

Desperate and disillusioned, he wrote again declaring it 'a question of sincerity & honesty – a moral issue . . . Our loyalty is due, not merely to the Party, but to those causes for which it stands. The welfare and happiness of children is surely the most sacred of them.'[37] The measure was reinstated, but twice in 1930 bills to raise the school-leaving age to 15 were withdrawn for lack of time in the legislative schedule. When the bill was defeated in the House of Lords in early 1931 it precipitated Trevelyan's resignation.[38] Nothing was done by Labour, therefore, only adding to Tawney's growing exasperation with a party whose MPs seemed so supine, and to his contempt for MacDonald, an attitude he shared with Trevelyan. The party's division in 1931 was to be lamented but could be blamed on MacDonald alone; in the matter of the school-leaving age the whole party seemed culpable. Tawney and Trevelyan subsequently teamed up to compose a policy document for the Labour Party's Local Government and Social Services Committee in February 1934, cajoling Labour towards the full implementation of the Hadow Committee's proposals to create a 'unified secondary system' based on the abolition of all fees in grant-aided secondary schools and the raising of the school-leaving age.[39]

This was to be a long march, and Tawney's commitment did not flag. A further pamphlet, *The School Leaving Age and Juvenile Unemployment* followed in early 1934, for example, making again the case for an extension of the leaving age in an age of mass unemployment. There was both satisfaction and frustration to be had in the 1936 Education Act passed by the Baldwin administration. For while this did allow for the raising of the school-leaving age to 15, it also permitted exemption for those adolescents of 14 who could find 'beneficial employment', a suitably vague and undefined term, but one that could potentially have exempted the majority of children at age 14. Tawney picked up his pen once more and produced another pamphlet in February 1936, *The School Age and Exemptions*, protesting against the failure to introduce a universal leaving age and demonstrating, *inter alia*, his mastery of all the arcane details of English educational administration. The School Age Council wrote to *The Times* as well, but the bill still passed with the exemptions in place, to be operative from 1 September 1939.[40] Its provisions were suspended by the Education (Emergency) Act 1939 because of the outbreak of war, though by the 1940s, and assisted by growing public interest in social reconstruction after the conflict, the raising of the school-leaving age became one of the objects of social policy that was accepted almost universally and it was included in the 1944 Education Act, though set at 15 rather than 16.

Tawney lost his patience at many stages of this long campaign; he and many others were exasperated that such relatively minor and inexpensive changes to the most vital of public services should create such opposition (and sometimes apathy) and take so long. Reflecting in 1940 on this endless history of political obstruction Tawney was understandably uncharitable about 'our rulers' who had fought so obdurately against raising the school-leaving age: 'Heaven, doubtless, will forgive them, though I can't.'[41] But he never lost faith in the objective itself. Through a generation and more of advocacy and almost interminable committee work, he also showed himself loyal to what is now a controversial principle, that of diversity in secondary education, a theme that deserves careful and lengthy discussion. It is often said, usually in surprise if not in condemnation, that Tawney supported grammar schools. He did indeed, but in the context of a diverse system of provision where resources and opportunities were not rationed according to the type of education and school, but were offered to all on an equal basis. He saw different types of secondary education as entirely natural and uncontroversial, but emphasized that all children should be given opportunities wherever they were being educated and in whatever manner.

In *Secondary Education for All* he was clear that 'the greater the variety among secondary schools the better for education . . . The demand of Labour for the democratising of secondary education implies no wish to sacrifice the peculiar excellence of particular institutions to a pedantic State-imposed uniformity'.[42] The position was reiterated by Tawney 2 years later in 1924 in his pamphlet, *Education: the Socialist Policy*: 'The greater the variety of type among schools, the better, for the need of education is experiment, individuality and the enthusiasm of the pioneer . . . But variety of type does not imply difference of quality; it should correspond to differences in the needs and capacity of the children, not in the income of the parents.'[43] As he explained further, 'The question of the precise type of curriculum most suitable for [secondary schools] is one to which, as we have said, the only right answer is half-a-dozen different answers.'[44] A decade later in a lecture given to the New Education Fellowship he returned to the theme, emphasizing that his aim was 'the establishment of the completest possible education equality'. He went on to explain what this meant:

> Equality of provision is not identity of provision. Educational equality no more implies that all children should be offered the same kind of education than equal consideration for the sick implies that all patients should be offered the same

kind of treatment . . . It is to be achieved not by meeting different requirements in the same way, but by taking equal care to ensure that varying requirements are met in the ways most appropriate to each. What it does involve is that varieties of educational provision shall be based on educational grounds alone, and that the existence of differences of educational treatment or opportunity which have their source merely in differences of economic circumstance shall be recognised as an evil which, though it has an historical explanation, is none the less gross, and for the removal of which no effort is too great.[45]

Educational diversity was to be encouraged at secondary level, and only educational criteria should ever play a role in determining the type of education offered to children. He made plain that the challenge was to establish a free system of different types of provision of equal status and then to send children to the schools which best suited their needs.

> Children who would be better fitted for the more practical curriculum of a central, or "modern" school are sent to "grammar" schools, because the latter are supposed to carry a higher prestige. Children better suited for the latter are sent to the former because the former are free and the latter charge fees. Such an arrangement is difficult to justify on educational grounds.[46]

In the same year, in the Sidney Ball Lecture at St John's College, Oxford (founded in memory of the socialist don who had played a role in workers' education in the Edwardian period), Tawney repeated the formula required: 'to treat all institutions giving full-time education after 11 – senior, central, junior technical, and what today is called secondary – as different species of one genus varying in curricula and method but equal in quality and status'.[47] In the course of delivering three lectures on education in the following year in Cambridge he went into greater detail and expressed opposition to what became known as the 'Eleven-Plus' as the means used to select children for secondary education, though not to selection itself:

> We need, in short, to get out of the barbarity of determining a child's future by an examination held at 11. Selection is necessary; and provided the penalties of not being selected are not excessive, is innocuous. But it should be selection between alternative educational paths, not, as in the past, between educational opportunity and the absence of it. It should proceed by differentiation, not elimination.[48]

He again returned to his consistent argument: 'Equality of provision is not, of course, identity of provision. It is to be achieved, not by meeting different requirements in the same way, but by taking equal care that they are met in the way most appropriate to each.'[49]

In the 1938 edition of *Equality* Tawney went further still, arguing that it would be a distinguishing feature of a society organized on the basis of true social equality that it met the diverse needs of different individuals. The greater the equality, the greater the diversity, in fact:

> Human beings have, except as regards certain elementary, though still sadly neglected, matters of health and development, different requirements, and (that) these different requirements can be met satisfactorily only by varying forms of provision. But equality of provision is not identity of provision. It is to be achieved, not by treating different needs in the same way, but by devoting equal care to ensuring that they are met in the different ways most appropriate to them, as is done by a doctor who prescribes different regimens for different constitutions, or a teacher who develops different types of intelligence by different curricula. The more anxiously, indeed, a society endeavours to secure equality of consideration for all its members, the greater will be the differentiation of treatment which, when once their common human needs have been met, it accords to the special needs of different groups and individuals among them.[50]

Tawney acknowledged different 'intellectual endowments' between individuals and also possibly between classes, though he added the important rider with regard to the latter that 'the truth of the possibility has not yet been satisfactorily established'. However, it did not follow 'that such individuals or classes should receive less consideration than others, or should be treated as inferior in respect of such matters as legal status, or health, or economic arrangements, which are within the control of the community'. There was an irreducible minimum of rights and standards which all deserved, but beyond that was a realm of difference and specialization from which each would benefit.[51] As he expressed it later in the book,

> To criticise inequality and to desire equality is not, as is sometimes suggested, to cherish the romantic illusion that men are equal in character and intelligence. It is to hold that, while their natural endowments differ profoundly, it is the mark of a civilized society to aim at eliminating such inequalities as have their source, not in individual differences, but in its own organization, and that individual differences, which are a source of social energy, are more likely to ripen and find expression if social inequalities are, as far as practicable, diminished.[52]

Thus educational equality was to be

> achieved in school, as it is achieved in the home, by recognizing that there are
> diversities of gifts, which require for their development diversities of treatment.
> Its aim will be to do justice to all, by providing facilities which are at once various
> in type and equal in quality.[53]

He continued to make the same point two decades later, after the 1944 Education Act, in the first version of his lecture 'British Socialism Today' as delivered in 1952: 'As a socialist I have no objection to the existence of a diversity of different types of schools [with] different forms of management – on the contrary I welcome it – but the diversity should be based on educational, not social considerations.'[54] The journalist and Labour MP Lena Jeger, who knew him best in his later years and who did most to keep his name and influence alive in British public life after his death, interviewed him for *Tribune* in 1960 and wrote this: 'Tawney is rightly considered the great apostle of equality. But this does not mean egalitarianism. Equality of opportunity to develop the inequalities which are the glory of the human character is his aim.'[55] Two years later when she wrote about his death for the *New Statesman* she commented that 'he combined with his concern for equality a patrician contempt for the slipshod, the idle and the cliché'.[56]

Given this, it is not difficult to understand Tawney's ambivalence towards comprehensive education or the schooling of children of all abilities in a single institution. As J. R. Brooks has demonstrated, he never really knew what he thought about the ancestor of the comprehensive school, known as a 'multilateral school' or 'common school', when it was first introduced by a small number of local education authorities in the 1930s, and gave conflicting assessments of its promise dictated by the nature of his audience. His uncertainty was the result of genuine doubt but it is notable that he generally supported common schooling when addressing the Labour Party or its committees.[57] Certainly by the early 1940s the LPACE included many who favoured taking further the experiment in common schooling: in 1939 it had urged multilateral schools as 'an immediate practical policy'.[58] Tawney's long campaign for secondary education had taken so long, in fact, that in the interim educational thinking had moved on and a new generation had emerged to question his assumptions founded on educational differentiation and diversity. Tawney accepted the conclusions of the committee set up in 1941 under the conservative educationist, Cyril Norwood, to review the secondary school curriculum and examinations.[59] The Norwood Report, published 2 years later, endorsed and reinforced the tripartite division of secondary schools into grammar, technical and modern, and was immediately controversial. When Tawney argued in the *Manchester Guardian* in March 1945 that secondary modern schools 'are likely to provide the education best calculated to give the majority of boys and girls a hopeful start in life' and that there was no reason to suppose that they 'will necessarily be regarded as inferior to the more specialised grammar and technical secondary schools,' he demonstrated his growing isolation from new trends among progressives and the left more generally, though the leadership of the Labour Party and Labour local authorities remained resistant to the multilateral idea.[60] Even had he been able to prove that in terms of esteem the different types of schools were equal in the public eye and provided in their own manner a good education for their pupils, the debate had moved on to question whether it was just to individuals or beneficial to society that differences of any sort should be imposed on the nation's children, especially by means of a sudden-death examination at age 10 or 11.

When the Spens Report, published by the Board of Education in late 1938, failed to endorse grammar schools with the strength some believed to be warranted, one supporter of them, the suffragist and political campaigner Clara Rackham wrote to Tawney to protest, evidently expecting his agreement:

> I wonder what you think of the Spens Report [?] It has some excellent things in it: I am only a little nervous lest the standard of work in the "Grammar Schools" should seriously decline so that their products can no longer compete with the children of the Governing Classes who are educated in "public schools".[61]

Here was another reason for their retention. It was probably his admiration for the highest academic standards that led Tawney to support one grammar school in particular – the 1792 St Marylebone Grammar School – threatened with abolition by the London County Council (LCC) in 1951. The LCC had led in the creation of multilateral schools in the late 1940s and early 1950s by the amalgamation of different institutions, but the very size of many of the resulting comprehensives alienated some supporters and certainly bothered Tawney.[62] C. H. Rolph, the biographer of Kingsley Martin, wrote an article in the *New Statesman* in defence of Marylebone Grammar and its achievements. He received literally 'hundreds of blistering denunciations' and Martin remarked that in his 21 years of editing the *New Statesman* no staff writer had ever received such a hostile correspondence from readers. But Martin also received three letters in defence of Rolph: 'Of these the most unexpected, welcome, and marvellous was a personal one to Kingsley from Professor R. H. Tawney . . . Tawney's support for the preservation of that grammar school was, I remember, unequivocal.'[63]

There is evidence that Tawney was reflecting on his commitment to educational diversity at the end of his life and coming to appreciate both the problems inherent in selection at 11 under any system and by any means, and also the virtues of comprehensive schools, though it is certainly not conclusive of any change in his basic position. In the 1960 version of 'British Socialism Today' he observed that

> the secondary education of the majority of children is now given in the Secondary Modern School. Some brilliant examples of such schools exist; but many of them still remain, it is to be feared, the old elementary schools called by another name. Because of the traditional superiority of the traditional kind of school known as a Grammar School, the struggle to win a place in it is intense, with the result of disillusionment for those who fail and over-pressure on all. No amount of scholarship provision can take the place of a drastic improvement in the quality of primary education accompanied by the prolongation of the secondary school life of all to sixteen.[64]

The solution was not the destruction of the grammar schools but improvement of education in the early years, the extension of the school-leaving age, and perhaps by implication, the improvement of Secondary Modern schools. In a letter to an old colleague who had played a role in much earlier educational struggles and who had written to him on his 80th birthday, Tawney replied that

> it is kind of you to remember *Secondary Education for All*. It has, of course, been long out of date, and I am very glad to see that your conception of the comprehensive school appears to be winning its way. At one time during the last war I thought that the English governing classes were a little repentant of their traditional educational snobbery, but I fear that the change, if there is one, is still only skin deep. It is a great pity that the Germans, instead of bombing cathedrals and so on, did not devote themselves to the public schools.[65]

Perhaps it is significant and characteristic that Tawney turned quickly from the subject of comprehensive schools to re-emphasize his lifelong opposition to private schooling, saying nothing about grammar schools.

Notwithstanding these last comments in 1960–1, Tawney remained remarkably consistent all his life in his support for educational selection at secondary level, for the concept of educational differentiation to meet the different needs of different groups of children, and for grammar schools. At the very end, he began to appreciate possible difficulties with this approach but he did not see the solution to them in the abolition of grammar schools. We cannot guess what he might have thought later under the influence of new educational thinking in the 1960s had he lived longer. Similarly, it would be anachronistic to apply educational ideas developed at that time to a much earlier period and convict Tawney of supporting social and educational inequality. We have to understand Tawney's views on secondary education in his terms and in the context of interwar Britain. In his years teaching in adult education he encountered so many students of both sexes who had the ability and interest to sustain an academic education at secondary level and beyond but whose circumstances precluded it. It was the waste of educational talent among people he met who were so obviously academic in their abilities and outlook which most upset and influenced Tawney. The challenge he faced in the 1920s and 1930s was to construct a clear and separate concept of 'secondary education' to follow elementary instruction; to extend it in length beyond the age of 13 or 14; and to ensure that educational decisions were in no way taken on financial grounds and that no child was deprived of the education he or she required and deserved on the basis of his or her background or circumstances. This was not the same debate as that which began in the 1950s on the back of Tawney's achievement. He had helped to establish a *system* of secondary education that applied to all children, whereas those who followed him asked whether the differentiations within that system were fair to individuals and good for society overall.

If we borrow a phrase from another debate on opportunity, though one that was about race rather than class, and which took place in the United States rather than Britain, Tawney believed sincerely that a secondary school system could be founded for the good of all children on the principle of 'separate but equal'. The problem, however, was that different types of schooling in mid-twentieth-century Britain attracted different levels of funding and different levels of esteem, and resulted in different levels of opportunity. Separate was inherently unequal in practice. Does that make Tawney's conception of educational differentiation at 11 invalid? He believed axiomatically that adolescents had different needs and capacities and that one type of schooling would not be suitable for different types of temperament and differing types of skills. It is a view widely held, both then and now. But he welcomed diversity in a context in which resources were divided evenly and fairly and society in general appreciated different types of ability and talent as of equal worth. In the eyes of some proponents of comprehensive secondary education Tawney's thinking contained a fundamental flaw, because educational diversity must always and inevitably lead to a type of educational apartheid (as the American Supreme Court argued in Brown versus Board of Education of Topeka, Kansas in 1954). To others, the problem was not in the conception but in the execution – the manner in which the secondary system developed after 1944. Dragging Tawney into this debate now is certainly unfair to someone who wrote and thought about education most intensively between the world wars, and, given that lapse in time, is also unproductive. But we can conclude that in his own time and for very good reasons, sincerely held, Tawney supported diversity, selection and the attainment of the highest academic standards – and looked askance at the abolition of grammar schools.

Arguably his attitude to the public schools can be explained in similar ways. Tawney was always quite clear that schools accepting public funds had to be accessible to all and open to merit alone: it would be unconscionable to subsidize educational and social exclusivity. For this reason he was probably more hostile to the Direct Grant schools, generally highly academic institutions which were funded directly by central government rather than by local educational authorities, but which also levied fees, than he was to the public schools which took no funds at all from the public purse. Under the Butler reforms as set out in 1943–4, Direct Grant Schools were to be allowed to continue levying fees, and this narrow question worried Tawney far more than the intractable issue of private education in general. Of course, he deprecated the public schools as destructive of social solidarity; where education should have been the solvent of social divisions the public schools only reinforced them. The unity of social classes and their place within a common culture were themes he returned to throughout his life and were especially relevant in this context.[66] Fees charged by public schools made them socially exclusive and made it impossible for children of ability from humble backgrounds to attend them. His soul rebelled. But Tawney could not bring himself to demand their abolition. His respect for their educational standards was one reason for this; another was that same respect for diversity and experimentation which he also valued and which private schools were, by their very nature, better able to preserve. Hence in 1934, on the occasion of the retirement of J. H. Bradley, the founder of Bedales School, the first co-educational boarding school, Tawney added his signature to a letter of tribute to 'one of the great educationists of his generation', also signed by Cyril Norwood, Percy Nunn, Michael Sadler and the then prime minister, Ramsay

MacDonald.[67] But he was also held back, we may suspect, by his recognition that abolition would be an assault on personal and institutional freedom. Tawney wrote his article, *The Problem of the Public Schools*, which was published first in the *Political Quarterly* and then as a WEA pamphlet, during the Second World War at a time when many private schools were in financial difficulty and some were close to accepting state support. In that eventuality Tawney had lots of ideas to increase the proportion of children who should attend them on the basis of merit alone, paid for by the state on scholarships. He suggested also the sort of public-private partnerships between schools which have become common in recent years. His hope was that in this way fee-paying schools could be incorporated into the system of secondary education which was the goal for which he had always worked. His aim was the replacement of social elitism with, to Tawney at least, a far more acceptable academic elitism. But his article failed to set out a clear and convincing strategy for dealing with fee-paying schools which remained beyond the reach of the state, and by their very nature these included the wealthiest and most prestigious foundations responsible for the education of the traditional governing class. The article ended with a call for them to voluntarily serve genuine educational needs, but stopped well short of coercion or abolition.[68]

In more than half a century the terms of these debates have hardly altered, making Tawney in this respect at least, our contemporary. His capacity to recognize merit in arguments for educational uniformity as well as in arguments for educational selectivity, makes him almost an exemplar of *both* sides of one of the great fault lines in modern British life. His early and long commitment to differentiation in secondary schooling fell out of fashion, especially on the left in the two decades after his death. But since then governments of all stripes, in response to evidence of declining standards in state education and of a failure to stimulate the brightest pupils in comprehensive schools, have tried to create more diversity among secondary schools. Their good faith in doing this has often been questioned and challenged. That Tawney of all people held similar views from the 1920s to the 1950s could be dismissed as irrelevant or anachronistic, but may more appropriately give pause for careful and sustained reflection.

History

Six years after Tawney's death, in his inaugural lecture as Professor of English Constitutional History in the University of Cambridge entitled 'The Future of the Past', another historian of the sixteenth century, Geoffrey Elton, took remarkable aim at R. H. Tawney. Elton recognized Tawney's personal qualities and the reverence in which he was held among historians. Nevertheless,

> With great regret I am coming to think increasingly that there is not a single work which that very good man Richard Tawney wrote which can be trusted. I think that in all his work he was so dominated by his preconceptions unconsciously (well, partly unconsciously) that everything he wrote was written to a propaganda purpose. And the result has been very drastic.

Tawney, continued Elton, was 'proving a point', and in consequence his history, and that of 'his school', was 'in great parts mistaken'. It 'was not good, not sound, not right, not true'. In a footnote in the published lecture Elton provided more detail:

> *Religion and the Rise of Capitalism*, for instance, demonstrates Tawney's fatal propensity to fit a great mass of material into a predetermined framework. The picture of puritan or protestant thinking on social problems is so one-sided and so readily destroyed by admitting overlooked evidence to the analysis that the effect which the book has had must give one pause . . . Because Tawney, a great man, had a real concern about his own world, he wrote very effective history, but it was also history in blinkers, confirming present-based prejudices and attitudes from an investigation of the past which came up with the answers required by the faith that inspired the search. But behind this possibly commonplace trouble lay the remediable failure to consider all the evidence and to understand the manner in which it came into existence.[1]

A decade later in a letter to the *Times Literary Supplement* Elton continued the campaign:

> At least one generation, and that a crucial one, was given grounds for believing that everything that contributed to the greatness and success of their country derived from sinful selfishness and money-grubbing wickedness. But this was not a truth demonstrated by Tawney's scholarship; it was a revelation from which he started and which directed the whole tenor of his argument. Tawney's example persuaded a powerfully influential school of historians that they may employ a method which involves selective study designed to document a previous conviction and neglectful of the changed setting in time, and that they are justified in doing so if their purpose is to serve a progressive cause.[2]

Another historian, Eric Kerridge, the author of an encyclopaedic history of the Agricultural Revolution, mentioned by Elton in passing in the assault on Tawney, and actually one of Tawney's pupils, was even more outspoken at this time:

> Tawney the politician barred the way to Tawney the scholar. Time which he might have given to studying history was devoted instead to the Fabian Society and the Labour Party, and he tended to see the world, past and present, in terms of socialist dogma. Hence his wholly untrue picture of early capitalism as cruel and greedy, destructive alike of social welfare and true spiritual values. No one would wish to deny that Tawney was a great man, but his greatness caused him to lead whole generations of History students into grievous error.[3]

Elton laced his quasi-academic judgements on Tawney with more overtly political sentiments which will be examined later in the conclusion to this book.[4] It is Tawney's scholarship that is of interest at this stage. Later elevated to the Regius Chair of History in Cambridge and a knighthood, Elton was a very public conservative who might be expected to take issue with Tawney. He was also by temperament and conviction a historian of politics, bureaucracy and power whose most important if not enduring idea was of a 'Tudor revolution in government' which created the administrative structures and ethos of the modern English state in the sixteenth century. This made him suspicious if not critical of those who studied other historical subjects in other ways, approaching his period through social and cultural history, as Tawney did. It was a theme Elton developed elsewhere in his infamous inaugural lecture.

The life of a stimulating and controversial historical idea whether concerning the origins of modern capitalism or modern bureaucracy is never very long, and the incentive to overturn previous orthodoxies is built into the very concept of professional success among academic historians. We should not be that surprised that Tawney's historical interpretations were challenged so quickly after his death, therefore. But these were more than matters of interpretation: Tawney was accused of gross error, and what is worse, politically-inspired bias. This chapter will try to answer these accusations by recreating Tawney's intellectual development and intentions as a historian. The focus will be as much on recreating his view of the past and his sense of the purpose of historical writing as on the historical research and arguments he presented in his books and articles, and the response to them by contemporaries and those who came later. Tawney may have been empirically wrong in aspects of his analysis of early modern English social and economic history, though few historians would be as certain about this as Elton. But it is questionable whether that would have dismayed Tawney whose aim was always to set out bold and arresting theses that would help his readers make moral as well as factual sense of the past. In this wider task he did not fail. Indeed, he left a remarkably coherent and stimulating picture of English society between about 1500 and 1700 – the period from 1540 to 1640 was often referred to as 'Tawney's century' – which is a fixed point of reference to this day in historical discussion. These discussions may have moved on and Tawney's ideas may have been superseded but they provided, as Tawney always hoped they would, a starting point for debate and a stimulus to further research.

Why and how did Tawney become a historian of early modern England? The question is not easily answered from the scanty sources which survive. Any man who read Greats in Oxford at the start of the twentieth century would have studied ancient history seriously and in a scholarly manner, but as part of a liberal education rather than as a prelude to or training for historical research. At some stage between about 1903, when Tawney graduated, and 1906, when he was appointed to a very junior and temporary position teaching political economy and also history at the University of Glasgow he must have conceived of himself as a historian. But as late as 1905 he told Beveridge that he wanted ultimately to teach *economics* in a provincial city.[5] And at Toynbee Hall in 1904–5 he lectured on politics and social institutions. He left very few clues to his intellectual development in his personal correspondence in this period, and such notes and manuscripts as survive from his various books and articles don't yield answers to his motivation, making a purely intellectual biography of Tawney as a historian more difficult than might be expected. He seems to have intuited at this time that through the study of History he could approach the issues that interested him and which, in his view, required attention. As a seventeenth-century historian of the next generation, Christopher Hill, was to comment, 'Tawney's great contribution was asking the right questions.'[6] He seems also to have understood that it would be through History that a much broader audience could be brought to an understanding of their own place in economy and society, and arm themselves with the intellectual tools to change that position. Beyond this, Tawney's cast of mind approached all social questions historically: his instinct throughout his life was to ask first how a particular institution, or situation or social practice had arisen as the necessary prelude to dealing with whatever problem it threw up. To Tawney, an understanding of the past was indispensable for an understanding of the present. Thus after 2 years in Glasgow he reported for duty as the pioneer teacher of the new Oxford tutorial classes who offered his students in Longton and Rochdale a course on the economic history of the eighteenth century and beyond – on the economic and social processes which had created their industries and communities.

This in itself adds a further mystery to the story because Tawney's first major work, *The Agrarian Problem in the Sixteenth Century*, published in 1912, was actually the study of a period he does not seem to have taught extensively at this time. In the preface he famously thanked 'the members of the Tutorial Classes conducted by Oxford University, with whom for the last four years it has been my privilege to be a fellow-worker. The friendly smitings of weavers, potters, miners, and engineers, have taught me much about problems of political and economic science which cannot easily be learned from books.'[7] The WEA had encouraged him to write a textbook for his classes and the terms of his employment under the Oxford University Tutorial Classes Committee included the writing of a book on the economic history of the early modern period: 'Mr Tawney should take four classes and, as an equivalent to the fifth class should be commissioned to prepare a book on the Industrial History of the late fifteenth and early sixteenth centuries.'[8] Yet most of the courses he taught between 1908 and 1913 were on the Industrial and French Revolutions, or about economics (a course on 'economic theories'), and when he ventured back to the seventeenth century it had been to teach conventional courses on the political and constitutional history of 'the Puritan Revolution' rather than a study of the transition to capitalism on the land during the Tudor period, the subject of the *Agrarian Problem*.

The origins of capitalism was the subject that fascinated him through his career and he intuited that the place to start was an investigation of those changes to rural life that led to the dispossession of the peasantry through the enclosure of common lands into large, privately-owned farms, the commercialization of agriculture and the movement of people from the countryside to the towns. Referred to subsequently as 'the transition from feudalism to capitalism', this process, extending over more than two centuries, by increasing agricultural productivity with which to feed growing urban populations, and by creating a workforce for the industrial enterprises of the eighteenth century, marked a fundamental break with the past and the crucial starting point for the study of economic modernity. That Tawney chose the subject of the origins of capitalism is the easiest part of the equation to solve: it drew a young man of imagination and brilliance who wanted to understand the reasons for the social problems he saw around him in the alleys of London's East End, the tenements of Glasgow and the terraces of Rochdale. How else to do that but by explaining the historical origins of a mode of production and a type of social organization that had created the conditions for urbanization and industrialization in Britain first, and then across Europe and North America? When Tawney wrote to congratulate Lawrence and Barbara Hammond on the publication of their foundational study of the social history of industrialization, *The Town Labourer*, he saluted their 'really great work in destroying the historical assumptions on which our modern slavery is based'.[9] This was not far from his purpose in investigating the rise of capitalism.

Tawney was at work on this subject from 1909 if not before. As All Souls Lecturer in History, he came to Oxford each Trinity (summer) Term between 1909 and 1912 to give lectures in the university once his tutorial classes had ended in April. He stayed on into the vacations and from 1910 he taught on the WEA Summer Schools in Balliol. He seems to have used the Bodleian Library and local archives as the basis for the *Agrarian Problem*, which contains illustrative material drawn from the records of estates owned by All Souls especially, and other Oxford colleges also. He also used collections in the Public Record Office.[10] He was able to draw on a pre-existing literature concerning English rural history, including works by F. W. Maitland; the Russian legal and historical scholar, Paul Vinogradoff, who held a chair in Oxford from 1903; and his pupil Alexander Savine, as well as a number of studies already published in Germany on land, trade and prices in England in the Tudor period.[11] Alongside Tawney other British scholars were working on the history of enclosure, though concentrating on the process in the eighteenth century. The most famous of these were the Hammonds, who together published, also in 1911, *The Village*

Labourer 1760–1832. Tawney's book was read in draft by two fellow WEA lecturers, Henry Clay, the economist, and Reginald Lennard, who would later specialize in agrarian history as a member of Oxford's History Faculty.[12] What emerged from Tawney's research was a study that not only set out a provocative account of economic transformation in the sixteenth century but also included within it the research questions that would inform the rest of his academic career: the relation of religious ideas to economic change, and the study of the social changes which were the consequence of Tudor economic transformation, the so-called 'rise of the gentry'.

This was a bold and ambitious set of issues to be essayed by a young man with no training in the discipline he now professed. In the generation before the First World War the subject of History began to be professionalized and to find a place in the expanding system of British universities, and some of those who taught and researched as professional historians were the beneficiaries of a genuine apprenticeship, writing postgraduate theses or learning their craft on enterprises like the *Dictionary of National Biography* which was compiled between 1882 and 1901. Tawney, however, was among those who came to the subject by less conventional routes; he took no university training at all in British history, nor could he point to early involvement in any major historical project. He was teaching his subject before he can be said to have formally studied it. But being self-taught may have had advantages, allowing him to ask the type of large and open-ended question which a professional training, almost by its very nature, tends to cramp and limit. It may also explain why he wrote History in a literary style and with a powerful moral purpose behind it, for Tawney, though he took formal university employment, was always an 'amateur'. This does not mean that he neglected the requirement to work from sources and substantiate his arguments – that he was cavalier about his scholarship in any way. Rather, it implies the absence of the restraints that often stunt scholarly work, and the willingness to develop grand ideas and to link them together in unfamiliar ways. Tawney's work crossed the disciplinary boundaries of history, theology and literature; it also eschewed a strictly political narrative, then very much in vogue, for economic and social analysis. In these ways he was innovative, and also essentially 'unprofessional' in the best sense. When he went to the London School of Economics in the 1920s he found himself in an atmosphere of 'appealing amateurishness . . . when practically no one was teaching a subject in which he or she had taken a first degree', which suited him very well.[13]

Had we greater extant material from his 2 years in Glasgow, 1906–8, it might be easier to explain his invention of himself as a historian. Unfortunately, little has survived from this period among his papers. But in the next phase, between 1908 and 1912, as he taught tutorial classes and set about the research that would lead to the *Agrarian Problem*, we can point to the example of one figure at least as a major influence on Tawney, the professor of economic history at the University of Manchester, indeed the first holder of a chair in economic history in Britain, George Unwin. Tawney went to live in Manchester early in 1909 and Unwin came to the university there a year later. For 3 years they were often in each other's presence. Tawney signalled his debts to Unwin when, at the height of his powers in the mid-1920s, he stopped his own work to edit a volume of Unwin's essays for the Royal Economic Society following the latter's death in 1925.[14] Unwin's social and religious ideas also influenced William Temple, especially his book *Christianity and the State* (1928) which followed soon after the publication of Tawney's edition of Unwin's works.[15]

Unwin was born 10 years before Tawney and came from a humble background in Stockport, Cheshire. He was the son of a railway clerk and left school at 13. He won a scholarship to the University College of South Wales at Cardiff, and from there he went on to study Greats at Oxford.[16] He had this in common with Tawney, as well as travels in Germany after graduating, which took him to Berlin where he attended lectures by the influential German economic historians Gustav Schmoller and Adolph Wagner, and his residency, like Tawney, in a settlement: in Unwin's case it was Mansfield House in Canning Town, London.[17] They also had the early modern period in common: in 1904 Unwin had published a major study of *Industrial Organization in the Sixteenth and Seventeenth Centuries* which embodied 'his belief that the mainspring of social progress was to be found in the voluntary association of individuals for common ends', whether those groups were trade unions, friendly societies, businesses, guilds, chapels, schools or city corporations.[18] Unwin thought political history and the history of states to be of secondary importance; 'societies based on kinship, on economic needs, on culture and religion, are primary.'[19] He was, in fact, a radical individualist in his politics with a strong scepticism about the role that the state should play in social and economic organization. Unwin thought that History showed the power of mutual self-help and individual character to remake and improve the world.[20] Unsurprisingly, he went on to write a study of pioneering entrepreneurship and industrial collaboration in his book on *Samuel Oldknow and the Arkwrights* (1924). To Tawney, on a very different ideological trajectory,

these ideas were a challenge and in that challenge was formed a close friendship
in which Unwin shared his unrivalled knowledge about social and economic
life in the Tudor and Stuart ages in sparkling exchanges: 'conversation with
him', recalled Tawney, 'meant glissading among precipices, and one never knew
where next the spirit would carry him.'[21] They agreed in one thing, for sure:
that history was a branch of moral philosophy.[22] If Tawney ever had a historical
mentor, it was Unwin.

The Agrarian Problem, which emerged from this milieu (and which Unwin
read for Tawney, describing it as 'so excellent a piece of work'), was a book
about the changing balance of classes on the land in the Tudor period.[23] The
consolidation of estates under the control of large landholders and the eviction
of customary tenants is explained in the context of wider economic changes
and illustrated by the laments of sixteenth-century pamphleteers who wrote
about the results of enclosure and rural depopulation but couldn't understand
the forces causing them. Tawney carefully differentiated between different types
and phases of enclosure. He depicted a rural economy which was not stagnant
before the sixteenth century and which allowed for small-scale enclosures by
more fortunate or industrious peasants as part of the developing natural order
of rural life. But in the Tudor era there were large-scale enclosures by single
proprietors as pasture for sheep became more lucrative than traditional tillage.
The growth of a textile industry provided incentives for wool production and
hence for pasture. Meanwhile inflation forced landholders to aggressively
exploit the economic potential of their estates, and the rents they charged their
tenants followed the upward trend of prices. Smallholdings were gradually
amalgamated into large leasehold farms for pasture. This period in turn was
superseded from the end of the seventeenth century by the enclosure of
common land and its conversion into large arable fields. More fundamental
than the changes in land-use and ownership in this sequence was the change in
the very conception of land itself: it marks 'the transition from the mediaeval
conception of land as the basis of political functions and obligations to the
modern view of it as an income-yielding investment'.[24] Tawney noted that in
the sixteenth and seventeenth centuries the process of consolidation was led
by landed magnates but resisted by the Crown which favoured social stasis
for political reasons: economic disruption brought with it threats of political
disorder. Hence the periods when consolidation was most notable coincided
with periods of monarchical weakness such as the mid-Tudor crisis and the
Civil War, 1640–60. Tawney thus subverted the traditional whig interpretation

of the seventeenth century as one of increasing corporate and personal liberty at the expense of a corrupt crown: the real threat to the rural society came from a rapacious aristocracy who undermined the traditional rural economy even as they challenged the royal prerogative.

This was a radical thesis which carefully intertwined economy, society and politics in a new manner: it was methodologically as well as conceptually innovative. But Tawney went several stages further in tantalizing glimpses of more ambitious arguments in which he linked changes on the land to the origins of modernity itself. Was this crisis really the triumph of 'more progressive methods' in agriculture required to support a future urban population? Was it 'a new and decided movement in the direction of economic individualism'? What was its place in 'that transition from medieval to modern conditions of agriculture which, starting in England, has spread eastwards through almost every European country . . .?'[25] If Tawney left these questions hanging quite deliberately 'as riddles for the reader', the book embodied two less well-trailed ideas by which he would continue to probe these issues in the rest of his career. First, Tawney recognized an important change in the rise of those middling freeholders able to capitalize on Tudor economic conditions and expand their landholdings: 'The upward movement which went on among this class in many parts of England meant a change in the distribution of material wealth which necessarily involved a corresponding change in the balance of social forces and in the control of political power . . . Certainly the yeomanry were growing in political power, and were strong in that spirit of self-respect and pride in their order.'[26] Here was the origin of Tawney's argument that the age saw a 'rise of the gentry'. Second, he recognized that changes of this type and on this scale involving not just new economic behaviour and practices, but also an altered understanding of the purpose of economic enterprise and of the relations between social groups, required something else and something more if they were to be explained adequately. He argued that 'the occurrence of rapid changes in the structure of an old and stable society implies either some radical revolution in the basis of economic life, or some great change in men's conception of social expediency, or, what is most likely, an economic and a spiritual change occurring together.'[27] He recognized that in the sixteenth century 'economic issues [were] not yet separated from questions of personal and political morality', but his implication was that they would be in time.[28] The relationship between economics, morality and religion, merely glimpsed in 1912, would be the subject of his most influential history book *Religion and the Rise of Capitalism* more than a decade later.

In the interim Tawney survived the Great War and alongside his many public duties and appointments after 1916, took a position in economic history at the LSE in 1920. The discipline of economic history was in its infancy – Tawney recalled later on that at this stage it was 'something of a parvenu'.[29] His desire to spread an interest in his subject found expression in a number of ways. He co-edited two major collections of documents on either side of the war, for example. The first, *English Economic History: Select Documents*, published in 1914, was co-edited with two other WEA tutors, A. E. Bland from the Public Record Office and P. A. Brown, a lecturer at Durham University, both of whom, as we have seen already, were killed in the Great War. It was designed to complement existing collections of historical documents concerning political and constitutional history.[30] The second, a much more specialized work edited with his colleague at the LSE, Eileen Power, and published in 1924, was a three-volume collection of *Tudor Economic Documents* which had begun life as a selection of material used by undergraduates in the University of London who were studying Tudor economic history as their final year special subject.[31] If projects like these made economic history more accessible to students, Tawney also took a role, though not a central one, in the attempt to bind together practitioners of the new discipline in the Economic History Society, the publisher of the *Economic History Review*. Munia Postan recalled that as a student taking tutorials with Tawney in 1923–4 his tutor had complained bitterly that one of his essays had been published in the German periodical the *Vierteljahrschrift für Soziale und Wirtsschaftgeschichte* because no English periodical existed 'which would be willing or able to publish an essay on that subject at that length'.[32] Tawney took the chair at the inaugural meeting of the Economic History Society held at the LSE on 14 July 1926 and helped direct its new *Review*, the first issue of which was published the following January, by suggesting authors for articles and reviews. But if enthusiastic, supportive and always loyal to the *EcHR*, as it became known, he was not intimately involved in its editorial functions or in the organization of the wider society.

His own very singular auto-didact background as a historian and very broad conception of the province of economic history led him to question and sometimes oppose 'professionalized' historical studies and the delimitation of the subject into separate sub-disciplines. Much later in the 1950s when the Economic History Society was invited to join a section of the pan-European International Committee of Historical Sciences dedicated to economic history alone, Tawney's soul rebelled. He had spent the best part of his career trying to win academic recognition in the mainstream for economic history and, as he wrote to Postan, he was against

> voluntarily surrendering the claim of Economic History to be regarded, not as a merely peripheral interest, but as one, though only one, of the keys which all historians must use. The right course, therefore, for economic historians is, in my opinion, not to seek to be recognized as a distinct body representing within the International Congress a special department of History. It is to endeavour to permeate all departments of historical work.[33]

To be sure, Tawney published specialized essays in learned journals. But his best work and efforts went into publications which straddled the public and professional domains. This instinctive suspicion of specialization married to a humane approach to scholarship which decried turning people and their history into deductive abstractions led him to underrate the importance of economic theory. Late in his life he told one former pupil not to treat economic history 'in too exclusively an economic matter'.[34] As another of his pupils, and later his colleague, Arnold Plant recalled,

> The history of political ideas was encouraged, but he had nothing but derision for my growing concentration on abstract economic theory. Generalisation based on empirical historical research was respectable, but mathematical models of the kind fashionable today were of no use. Adam Smith's *Wealth of Nations* was good stuff, but the neo-Ricardians were lost in a cul-de-sac. This debate went on for decades . . .[35]

The Acquisitive Society was a work of social commentary and political thought which established Tawney in the public eye as a moralist pre-eminently rather more than a historian. Yet its second chapter was an essay on English History which laid out his still developing ideas on a grand scale and for a broad audience.[36] Tawney's starting point was the Reformation which, he argued, began a slow revolution in morals and outlook which led by stages to modern capitalism. Religion, once at the heart of all public culture, entered the private domain, 'remote from the daily life of mankind'. Individualism then supplanted 'the idea that social institutions and economic activities were related to common ends' and that they were 'amenable, like personal conduct, to moral criteria'.

> The conception of men as united to each other, and of all mankind as united to God, by mutual obligations arising from their relation to a common end, which

vaguely conceived and imperfectly realized, had been the keystone holding together the social fabric, ceased to be impressed upon men's minds, when Church and State withdrew from the centre of social life to its circumference. What remained when the keystone of the arch was removed, was private rights and private interests, the materials of a society rather than a society itself.

Church and state abdicated their responsibilities and the function of authority by the eighteenth century was to protect individual rights, above all in property. Eighteenth-century society, following John Locke's exposition of the indefeasibility of private rights, 'recognized no moral limitation on the pursuit by individuals of their economic self-interest'. If society had once been conceived in terms of its moral purpose, it was now merely an amoral 'self-adjusting mechanism'. The result was a regime of 'private property and unfettered economic freedom' which provided the context and foundation for industrialization. The nineteenth century then realized as a deformation the individualist doctrines of the eighteenth century; those doctrines were the delayed product of the Reformation and its destruction of a holistic social philosophy where private desires were accommodated and confined within a structure of public behaviour and sanctioned social ends.

Quite what readers made of this panorama in a dozen pages is unclear. In style and type it was an argument familiar in the history of English radicalism since the seventeenth century: a prelapsarian myth of harmony and unity that was followed by rupture, dissociation and exploitation. Read as an archetype, this was a version of the Fall of Man, of the Norman Yoke imposed on free and prosperous Anglo-Saxons, of Merrie England subordinated by dark, satanic mills. At one point in *The Acquisitive Society* Tawney wrote that

> Whatever the future may contain, the past has shown no more excellent social order than that in which the mass of the people were the masters of the holdings which they ploughed and of the tools with which they worked, and could boast, with the English freeholder, that "it is the quietness to a man's mind to live upon his own and to know his heir certain".[37]

This supposed golden age was undermined by the rise of capitalism, starting with those processes on the land in the sixteenth century that Tawney had already documented and explained in the *Agrarian Problem*.

What could only be sketched in a work of social criticism was developed more carefully in *Religion and the Rise of Capitalism* published in 1926. The book began as the first set of memorial lectures in honour of Henry Scott Holland, the theologian and social reformer who had died in 1918, which Tawney gave at King's College, London in 1922, not long after *The Acquisitive Society* was published. The book was dedicated to, and prefaced by, Charles Gore. Tawney's book has often been set beside Weber's classic essay *The Protestant Ethic and the Spirit of Capitalism* (1904) in something known as the 'Weber-Tawney Thesis' on the origins of capitalism, prompting also speculation on Tawney's debt to Weber. There is no evidence that Tawney read Weber's study at any stage before publication of *Religion and the Rise of Capitalism*, and Weber is not mentioned in any of Tawney's writings before the First World War, though he does refer in the *Commonplace Book* to the work of the German scholar Gerhart von Schulze-Gäevernitz through whom British scholars were introduced to Weber. 'I wonder', he jotted, 'if Puritanism produced any special attitude toward economic matters [?]'[38] Tawney's musings in the *Commonplace Book* add evidence to that contained in *The Agrarian Problem* that he was trying out ideas linking capitalism and Protestantism at this time, but suggest thereby that these were ideas that came naturally from his own research and writing rather than being borrowed.[39] In trying to explain changes in Tudor economic behaviour Tawney had hypothesized a link with the Reformation and its doctrines that owed little or nothing to the work of others. Indeed, *Religion and the Rise of Capitalism* is to be linked closely to Tawney's edition, published in 1925, of the *Discourse on Usury* (1572) by the Elizabethan diplomat, courtier, judge and eventually Dean of Durham, Thomas Wilson (1523/4–81). Wilson, a man of wide affairs, here denounced the growing practices of large-scale money lending for new capitalist enterprises and enclosures on the land as immoral breaches of the Christian code.[40] Wilson was an intriguing example of Tawney's wider thesis of the fundamental change in economic behaviour that occurred in the sixteenth century.

We need to recognize in addition, as Tawney did himself, that Weber and he were investigating different things. Weber had wanted to understand the effect of reformed religion on the inner life, motives and economic behaviour of individuals specifically, and to explain the role of religious ideas in the formation of a capitalistic personality. Tawney, on the other hand, focused on a broad transformation in social ethics, the slow retreat over centuries of a Christian social tradition. Tawney wrote an introduction to the first English edition of Weber's essay to be published in Britain (translated by the American sociologist Talcott Parsons) in 1930 in which he pinpointed their essential difference on the first page: 'The question which Weber attempts to answer is simple and fundamental. It is that of the psychological conditions which made possible the development of capitalist civilization.'[41] He made several criticisms of Weber's thesis: that Weber neglected the importance of changes in economic organization and social structure during the period; that he underestimated the importance of Renaissance political thought; that he overlooked similar ethical transformations in Catholic authors; that he presented Calvinism as uniform when it took different forms in different places and periods.[42] He ended the introduction with another important difference between them: Weber had traced 'the influence of religious ideas on economic development' but it was no less important to 'grasp the effect of the economic arrangements accepted by the age on the opinion which it holds of the province of religion.'[43] In Tawney's argument the 'spirit of capitalism' filled the ethical void caused not only by the emergence of Protestantism but also by the wholesale retreat of all Christian religion from the public sphere which had followed this.

Religion and the Rise of Capitalism was largely based on Tawney's close reading of English pamphlet literature of the sixteenth and seventeenth centuries. In this sense it is a properly historical study, albeit one that essentially fills out the second chapter of *The Acquisitive Society*. On the other hand it begins with reflections on the present – on contemporary efforts to revive a moralistic Christianity and on the relations of the church to the state – as if Tawney were setting out to use History to throw light on contemporary questions. If Christian social ethics had changed for the worse at the Reformation, it is Tawney's hope in writing the book that they might be reinvigorated and applied effectively in the twentieth century.[44] This historical study of crucial attitudinal changes in the early modern period was designed to show that things were not always thus, that there was no reason why the modern church should not take a stand on economic morality and social organization, one that took its inspiration from the version of the past which Tawney was providing. It is this blending of past and present, and of history and morality, that academic critics have decried, but which was the essence of his whole approach, and which general readers found so refreshing.

In Tawney's argument medieval Christianity never doubted its obligation to define appropriate economic morality. To thinkers of this period – though Tawney is vague indeed in his definition of the period he means – 'society is a spiritual organism, not an economic machine' and economic activity 'is one subordinate element within a vast and complex unity' which requires regulation 'by reference to the moral ends for which it supplies the material means.'[45] Why, then, did modern Christianity ignore the question entirely, as Tawney saw it?

According to Tawney, 'the capitalist spirit' was 'as old as history' and was not the product of the Reformation.[46] Earlier Christian civilizations had contended with it and confined it to its proper place. But Protestantism, and Calvinism in particular, replaced social solidarity with individualism, and encouraged the separation of economic from ethical interests. In England at least this was not an instantaneous outcome of the Reformation and traditional doctrines 'lingered, venerable ghosts, on the lips of churchmen down to the Civil War'.[47] But by the late seventeenth century the quest for material gain became the central and sanctioned mission of life, rather than one aspect of wider obligations and responsibilities.[48] According to Tawney by the time of the Restoration in 1660, 'religion has been converted from the keystone which holds together the social edifice into one department within it, and the idea of a rule of right is replaced by economic expediency as the arbiter of policy and the criterion of conduct'.[49]

Puritanism in England had vanquished not only the 'surviving elements of feudalism' but also the monarchical state 'with its ideal of an ordered and graded society'. In this way, battling on these two fronts, it had prepared the way 'for the commercial civilization which finally triumphed at the Revolution'.[50] It had also turned religion from the rule of all conduct in society into a purely personal and private affair: by the eighteenth century 'it is in the heart of the individual that religion has its throne, and to externalise it in rules and institutions is to tarnish its purity and to degrade its appeal'.[51] As this reveals, Tawney had strongly ambivalent feelings about Puritanism, admiring it for the challenge it had mounted to monarchy and hierarchy and for the 'virtues of enterprise, diligence and thrift' which were 'the indispensable foundation of any complex and vigorous civilization', but condemning it also for its unbridled individualism, both spiritual and economic.[52] Insofar as Tawney spent much of his life advocating a social Christianity which engaged with society and its problems, he was, in his own mind, trying to counter the baleful effects of the narrowing of the Christian compass by 'the Puritan Revolution'.

Tawney never lamented the Reformation in any of his books or articles. It was a fact, a fixed point, unchallengeable. He was interested in its effects on social structure and behaviour rather than its theological rationale; his was not a religious argument about the nature of Christian belief but an intellectual case about its historical outcomes. Nevertheless, his academic position seems to have encouraged the view that he harboured a deep nostalgia for the unreformed church and hence led to the assumption among some who did not know him well that he was an Anglo-Catholic. Historical discussion meanwhile has focused on Tawney's misjudgements and errors. He was remarkably vague in all his references to the middle ages which are depicted almost as if they were a state of mind and an immanent social philosophy rather than a civilization in time and space. He failed to differentiate between different facets and theological schools within the Reformation, largely generalizing on the basis of Calvinism only. As Elton contended, his portrait of Puritanism as a religion of materialism fails to capture its complex spirituality and the agonized search for evidence of election among those who embraced it from the later sixteenth century onwards. To Marxists, an argument in economic history resting on beliefs, values and behaviours which paid little or no attention to material conditions and the factors of production was wrong in theory and from first principles, let alone in other ways.

All of this is fair and true, but set against Tawney's intentions and the book's impact and success, beside the point. *Religion and the Rise of Capitalism* was a heady synthesis tying together many of the crucial elements of modern history, including the waning of the middle ages, the Reformation, the rise of Puritanism, the Civil Wars, the triumph of the landed aristocracy after the Restoration, the growth of the middle class and the origins of industrialization. To read it was to be taken on an entirely unfamiliar journey through centuries of British history that made sense of the past for readers in the present because it explained to them where 'modernity' – commercial society, industry, cities – came from. Early modern English history had hitherto been understood in terms of a conventional political narrative and the celebration of the growth of English commerce and power from the Age of Elizabeth to the Age of Empire. Here was a different version, one resting on different building blocks: ideas, doctrines and social behaviours replaced monarchs, parliaments and the exploits of English sea dogs. Tawney 'helped powerfully to destroy the hold which an interpretation of the seventeenth century, cast mainly in terms of Parliamentary politics and constitutional law . . . still had upon the public mind'.[53] As Christopher Hill commented, Tawney 'directed the gaze of historians away from the narrow stage of politics and action to the then infinitely wider one of society and life'.[54] Published in the year of the General Strike, it took time for the book to become widely known and find its place on reading lists and the shelves of public libraries. By that time, in the early 1930s, this critical study of the *origins* of capitalism seemed the perfect historical complement to the *crisis* of capitalism then being endured. Tawney's book could not explain the Slump and contained nothing at all on modern economic history, but its depiction of early capitalism as destructive of spirituality and deficient in humanity filled a psychic need among many of its readers who believed that capitalism was not only inefficient but also illegitimate. History reinforced the present, obliquely explaining why wheels were not turning and millions were idle. How could it be otherwise if capitalism's rise had required the undermining of social solidarity and of a wider social ethic in the triumph of unrestrained individualism? As the economic historian W. H. B. Court was to write later, *Religion and the Rise of Capitalism*, 'one of the books which everyone read . . . responded brilliantly . . . to the mood of a time of sharp disillusion and changing social values . . . in the quiet of the late twenties it was still possible to read Tawney's book and to be impressed by the power of his argument, especially if one was disposed to be critical of society.'[55]

In exploring the relationship between religion and economic life in the early modern period Tawney had dealt with one of the two intellectual legacies of the *Agrarian Problem* and in the process gained a position as the leading economic historian of his generation. There remained the question of the social changes caused by the economic transformations of the sixteenth century and beyond which his first monograph had raised as an issue in 1912. He returned to the theme in the introduction to his edition of Thomas Wilson's *Discourses on Usury*, published in 1925. He also explored it in his Raleigh Lecture before the British Academy in 1941, 'Harrington's Interpretation of his Age'. He then tried to codify his thinking on early modern social structure in an article published in the *Economic History Review* in 1941 entitled 'The Rise of the Gentry 1558–1640'. We may imagine that he saw it as a significant essay in social history but essentially innocuous. In the event it was to ignite a famous historical/political controversy, one subsequently encountered by successive generations of undergraduates studying History, which still has relevance among professional historians today. As an aspect of Tawney's biography it probably left little residue save for distaste; throughout the controversy he behaved with characteristic generosity of spirit and maintained both academic and personal dignity. The controversy is much more revealing of the psychology of his adversary Hugh Trevor-Roper than of Tawney.

That 'The Rise of the Gentry' was published in early 1941 explains a great deal about the circumstances of its composition and Tawney's reasons for publishing his essay. The disruption of academic life at the start of the Second World War left the leading British journal of economic history short of anything to publish at a stage when universities and colleges had shut their doors and decamped from cities to the provinces, students were being called up, their lecturers were being drafted into a variety of military and intelligence functions and even elderly professors like Tawney himself were offering their services in war work. By 1941 Tawney was lecturing in Cambridge to his students from the LSE, and within months of the article's publication he was in the British embassy in Washington DC. It is more than a fair speculation that Tawney volunteered his article at this stage – when it was still in many ways unfinished – to keep the *EcHR* going rather than see his pride and joy cease publication, perhaps for the duration.

The essay's argument is simply stated: that in consequence of a number of factors, including the availability of land sold off at the time of the dissolution of the monasteries, the impact of inflation, the greater degree of close financial control exercised by smaller landholders and the fact that their composite or consolidated estates were better able to take advantage of the changing economic conditions than the large and differentiated estates of the aristocracy which were usually strung out across several counties, the lesser landholders rose in wealth and status relative to the greater landholders.[56] As Tawney summarized, 'The squirearchy was less exposed to the vicissitudes which ruined some aristocratic families; while, keen farmers and business men as many of them were, they were in a better position to reap the fruits of commercial progress and improved methods of agriculture.'[57] Tawney adduced much impressionistic and literary evidence in support of this argument: he probably put more faith in the accuracy of contemporary comment on economic conditions than did most of his colleagues then and would economic historians today. His most important empirical evidence, which became the focus of dispute, was a calculation of the ownership of multiple manors in seven counties of England at four dates: 1561, 1601, 1640 and 1680.[58] Between 1561 and 1680 the number of landholders owning 4 manors or less in these counties rose in his calculations from 1445 to 1684. However, over the same period the number of landholders owning more than 10 manors fell from 612 to 347. Impressionistically, the number of lesser landholders grew but the wealthiest landholders were losing their grip and declining in numbers and wealth. In Northamptonshire he estimated that 'something between two-thirds and three-quarters of the manors secured [at the Reformation] by private persons had gone originally to the squirearchy. By the early years of the next century, the proportion in their hands was over nine-tenths'. In this county the Dissolution 'did not so much endow an existing nobility, as lay the foundations of a new nobility to arise in the next century'.[59]

Tawney was very careful to discuss problems of definition and interpretation throughout: in subsequent exchanges this academic caution was ignored by his adversaries. His definition of the gentry was multifaceted: the core 'consisted of the landed proprietors, above the yeomanry, and below the peerage, together with a growing body of well-to-do farmers, sometimes tenants of their relatives, who had succeeded the humble peasants of the past as lessees of demesne farms; professional men . . . and the wealthier merchants . . . this upper layer of commoners, heterogeneous, but compact.'[60] He embraced social complexity and rejected simplistic Marxist analysis of social change: 'to speak of the transition from a feudal to a bourgeois society is to decline upon a cliché.'[61] The article eschewed sociological or Marxist jargon, relying on the texts and commentaries of contemporaries to make its points. Tawney knew that it was notoriously difficult to be precise about social categories in this or any other period: he used terms like 'the gentry' and 'the middle class' as identifiers, conscious that they merely differentiated complex groups in dynamic social structures. Anyone who has written social history has encountered this problem. Thus he was properly respectful of exceptions to his generalizations:

> It was primarily a struggle between economies of different types, which corresponded more closely with regional peculiarities than with social divisions. There are plenty of gentry who stagnate or go down hill. It would be easy to find landowners who move with the times, and make the most of their properties; the sheep-farming of Lord Spencer; the enclosures of Lords Brudenell, Huntingdon and Saye and Sele . . .[62]

Given the leisure of peacetime, Tawney might have undertaken detailed research of actual estates to prove or disprove his ideas before publishing. As it was, he recognized and admitted to the pitfalls in merely counting manors:

> Contemporaries commonly thought in terms, not of acreage, but of manors; they spoke of a man owning manors, or selling them, much as today he might be said to hold, or to dispose of, large investments, in order to convey an impression, not to record precise facts. The category, needless to say, is a highly ambiguous one, embracing estates varying widely in magnitude, value and organisation. At best, it covers only one species of real property, and that not the most marketable.[63]

When examining the life and death of the great estates of the age he admitted that 'much is still obscure' though enough was known 'to suggest certain provisional conclusions'.[64] And those conclusions were couched in his characteristically pungent and impressionistic style which many of his readers admired, though which fell quickly out of fashion among professional historians of the 1950s and beyond: 'Political convulsions shook down the estates of one group of absentees; financial embarrassments sapped the staying-power of another. As each over-rigged vessel went on the rocks, the patient watchers on the shore brought home fresh flotsam from the wreck.'[65] Significantly, Tawney left the analysis at this stage and did not draw any political conclusions from it. Other historians may have seen a link between this model of changing social relations over time and a class-based explanation for the origins of the Civil War in 1640 in which the tension between the aristocracy and middle classes led to political conflict. But Tawney did not make that connection. In characteristic fashion he had set out an imaginative and bold thesis, though with many more reservations than were usual in his work. They, at least, should have mandated a balancing caution and respect in those who disagreed with him.

The story of what followed has been very well told elsewhere but never from Tawney's point of view.[66] Space and detail are required to explain the issues and redress the balance. It initially concerned the well-known Oxford tutor, Hugh Trevor-Roper, Student (i.e. fellow) of Christ Church, and author of celebrated studies of Archbishop Laud before the World War II and of Hitler's demise after it, and his former pupil, Lawrence Stone.[67] Stone was a brilliant and ambitious undergraduate at Christ Church whose studies were interrupted by the war. In the late 1940s Stone apparently cultivated Tawney, whose work he deeply admired, though this may simply have meant paying him visits in Mecklenburgh Square where Tawney would see anyone and everyone, and would offer help and encouragement as he could. It did not make him one of Tawney's 'party' or 'school' as Elton would later have it, because there was no school, only a very wide community of admirers.

Staying on to undertake research, Stone became interested in the whole question of social change in England before the Civil War, the theme opened up by Tawney in 1941. Trevor-Roper, also becoming interested in this theme through his work on the Elizabethan entrepreneur, rentier and founder of Charterhouse, Thomas Sutton, shared with Stone some of the material he had found and wanted to work up on this subject in the Public Record Office (PRO), records concerning the Recognizances for Debt. Stone read the material lent to him by Trevor-Roper and then seems to have gone to the PRO to use the material himself and to compose and publish in the *Economic History Review* in 1948 his famous article 'The Anatomy of the Elizabethan Aristocracy'.[68] Initially congratulated by his tutor, on further and deeper reading, and on receiving the complaints of other friends and colleagues, Trevor-Roper realized that not only had Stone 'stolen' this valuable and virgin source from him but he had also misinterpreted the data, and worse, confected some of what he published in pursuit of the thesis that the aristocracy was in decline in the late sixteenth century through profligacy and socio-economic suicide, an argument that owed much to Tawney, as Stone acknowledged.[69]

Trevor-Roper thus set out to confute him, working hard on his riposte to Stone, 'The Elizabethan Aristocracy: An Anatomy Anatomised'.[70] In the process he wrote to Tawney to request elucidation of Tawney's calculations concerning the ownership of manors by peers and gentry in the period 1561–1680 which he had included in his 1941 essay. Trevor-Roper wanted to refer to this in the article and an attached footnote, the text of which he sent Tawney.[71] He felt that Tawney's method of counting had underrepresented the landholdings of the nobility and artificially swelled the relative holdings of the gentry, and Tawney, in explaining his method, granted that the categorization of gentry families subsequently ennobled during this period was a difficulty. Tawney's reply was full and detailed and the exchange was entirely courteous. Tawney ended his letter in characteristic fashion, encouraging the next generation: 'I don't know whether the above information suggests any modification of your note. In any case, please feel quite free to print it as it stands or in any form that seems to you best. I look forward to getting more light on the subject from your article.'[72] In the event Tawney was saddened by the savaging of Stone which he thought unnecessary.[73]

The view of most historians, later shared by the victim himself, was that Trevor-Roper was correct to amend and criticize Stone, who had worked too hard in striving to make his case and cut too many corners, or worse. But why, if he had killed the child, did Trevor-Roper go on to kill the father? Why also attack Tawney whose 1941 article was far more tentative, cautious, exploratory and imaginative, and who was not pursuing any ideological line? To correct an errant pupil is one thing, though to do it in public in such a devastating manner is in itself questionable: tutors teach by example, by restraint, and by quiet words rather than public humiliation. But to train fire on a great scholar, now in his seventies, who had published some creative thoughts a decade before and thereby opened up a new subject, was entirely different. If Trevor-Roper's judgment was debatable with regard to Stone, it was poor indeed with regard to Tawney. Trevor-Roper contended that in vanquishing Stone he had discovered the vulnerability of 'the orthodoxy of Tawney' which allowed him to counter with a different and 'constructive thesis'.[74] At times during this affair Trevor-Roper was respectful and appreciative of Tawney, freely admitting to admiration.[75] Yet in a letter to Bernard Berenson in the summer of 1952 he had also written that he was 'preparing a little aluminised bombshell on the English 17th century and then, when it has been placed on the hieratic throne of the most respected of our professors, I shall retire in haste, to avoid the explosion'.[76]

In an action that might be open to interpretation, Trevor-Roper had written to Tawney early in 1951, perhaps when he began work on the article, to ask him for an offprint of 'The Rise of the Gentry'. In reply, Tawney doubted if any were left in his possession, not least because spare copies of learned articles published during the war were not very numerous.[77] Trevor-Roper's answer to Tawney's article was set out in 'The Gentry 1540–1640' in the first ever supplement to the *Economic History Review* in 1953.[78] It was too long to be published as a conventional article in the journal (Trevor-Roper would not cut it to a manageable length) with the unfortunate result that it has ever since been difficult to locate. 'History', wrote Trevor-Roper on the first page, 'is an empirical science, and the imaginative work of intellectual pioneers must often be modified by the more pedestrian research which they themselves have inspired.'[79] With this laudable statement of intent there could be no argument. But his aim was not respectful modification in a collaborative spirit of enquiry, paying due deference to a pioneer. Instead, what followed was a highly personalized assault on Tawney's modest and thoughtful arguments that in the extremity of its manner and tone betrayed the author's self-regard and ideological intent. Trevor-Roper referred directly to 'Prof. Tawney' on 52 occasions in the text of the article, not including the footnotes. There could be no doubt that he was targeting both the messenger and the message.

Trevor-Roper criticized Tawney's methods and social categories. Counting manors was 'unhelpful' – a point Tawney had recognized explicitly – because a manor was 'not a unit of wealth but a definition of rights'.[80] In particular, Trevor-Roper objected to Tawney's categorization of peers created after 1561, and counted at the subsequent three census dates, as 'gentry' when counting the number of manors owned.

> While his aristocracy consists of a diminishing group of those families who happened to be noble at the beginning and still noble at the end of the period, his gentry consists both of the gentry who remained gentry throughout the period, and of those men who began as gentry and ended as peers, and of those who began as merchants, yeomen, or anything else, and ended as gentry. No wonder the gentry, thus calculated, appear to "rise" at the expense of the peerage.[81]

Tawney, on the other hand, took the view that these new peers were exactly the phenomenon he was investigating, 'risen gentry': the purpose of his article was to suggest a changing balance between an old governing class and rising challengers to it, and they were the prime examples of this. He had explained this to Trevor-Roper in their correspondence in 1950 though Trevor-Roper did not refer to Tawney's explanation of his methods in 'The Gentry'. As Tawney had written then,

> As to the figures in my article:- my recollection is that I counted as gentry at the second and third dates (1601 and 1641) individuals belonging to families which I listed as gentry at the first date (1561), and which had been subsequently ennobled. I remember wondering how to classify them. As I was mainly concerned with changes in the relative position, as regards the ownership of property, of gentry and peers, I thought that it would be a little illusory to credit to the peers individuals or families among the gentry of 1561 who, partly, I imagine, because of their success in increasing their possessions, were ennobled later. Probably, however, it would have been better to give two sets of figures, one as in my article, and another based on the inclusion among the peers of later ennobled gentry in my list of 1561.[82]

Trevor-Roper took issue with Tawney's use of contemporary social commentary and his reliance on individual cases, apparently chosen to fit the theory. He found several legitimate ways to criticize Tawney's 'arbitrary' distinction between aristocracy and gentry, emphasizing that all landholders faced common economic problems in this era, that most tried to improve their estates and all shared similar tastes: extravagance was not the monopoly of the one class, nor thrift that of the other. 'The whole distinction between peerage and gentry, upon which so much has been built, becomes again what it has always been in England, a distinction of nomenclature and legal rights, not a difference of either habits of mind or economic practice.'[83] Trevor-Roper granted, in fact, that there was genuine social mobility within the gentry, but only among some gentry families and, in the most creative part of his article, he went on to argue effectively that those who rose did so largely through the profits of office-holding under the state or through trade (or a combination of the two) rather than through better husbandry and careful estate management. Indeed, he demonstrated that many of Tawney's exemplars of gentry endeavour owed their riches and position to office and trade, riches that were gained at the expense of the crown rather than at the expense of their local peasantry. The major social articulation was between court and country, officeholders versus 'mere gentry', rather than between gentry and aristocracy, in other words.[84] This was a valuable corrective to Tawney's ideas, though one that could have been presented without vituperation and grandiloquence. Ironically, it was an idea that Tawney was grappling with at exactly the time Trevor-Roper went into print against him, for through the 1950s Tawney was at work on his last major book, a biography of Lionel Cranfield, first earl of Middlesex (1575–1645) the Jacobean merchant, entrepreneur and office holder as Lord Treasurer, who was born the son of a London mercer.[85] To remind Tawney of the value of office holding in this era was like teaching him to suck eggs.

Trevor-Roper's article then diverged into what must be considered a byway. Convicting Tawney of making the argument that the social divisions between gentry and aristocracy were a cause of the Civil War, which he had not argued in his 1941 article, in fact, Trevor-Roper offered an alternative explanation in a long digression focused on the role of the Independents in the conflict, men like Cromwell and Ireton, generally poor and declining small landholders with a grudge. Focusing on the 1650s, Trevor-Roper characterized a declining rather than rising gentry by its politics during the Great Rebellion, an intrinsically weak way of arguing in a debate about the relative fortunes of social groups that was oddly tangential to the main discussion.

When he returned to the theme he ended in surprising fashion. Up to that point his article read as if it was a demolition not only of Tawney and the gentry thesis but also of all such social-structural explanations in History which he took to owe greater or lesser debts to Marxism and its general conception of class struggle driving historical change. But Trevor-Roper then volunteered an alternative tripartite model of the gentry in answer to Tawney's unitary model of the class, consisting of the 'lesser gentry' who remained on their impoverished estates and grew angry, the 'improving gentry', and 'greater gentry', the latter focused on London, with interests in trade and in the court. If in the sixteenth century, an elite of county families enjoyed new wealth and preferment, the rise of all the gentry did not occur until the more sanguine conditions of the eighteenth century.[86] This was a more nuanced and subtle picture of the class, and was backed by some persuasive evidence. For this the author deserved credit. But for all the huffing and puffing, Trevor-Roper had merely offered an alternative and admittedly better model of social structures in the sixteenth and seventeenth centuries, and in offering it he had implicitly accepted that this type of class-based social history was legitimate and important. Trevor-Roper had not vanquished Tawney, merely corrected him, but in a style which betrayed inflated notions of the importance of his arguments, if not of the author himself.

The judgment that he had delivered an 'annihilating *opusculum*' to Tawney's article is in need of revision.[87]

Behind the scenes, and as may be imagined, the article had given the editors of the *Economic History Review*, Munia Postan and Hrothgar Habbakuk, later Principal of Jesus College, Oxford, a number of problems. Negotiations over its length – it was originally delivered at 22,000 words, or more than twice the size of the average historical article – ran into the sands when Trevor-Roper would not make cuts, and for a period it looked as if he would place the essay with another publisher. He only relented when the editors suggested separate publication as a supplement to the *EcHR*.[88] Then, at proof stage, he slipped into the first footnote a very unflattering comment on Lawrence Stone and the editors had to demand its retraction. In the event, after protracted correspondence, Trevor-Roper agreed to something more anodyne.[89] In fact, the editors had admired the piece on first reading, recognizing its importance immediately, and were determined to publish it, though Postan felt that it 'appears to oversimplify and to coarsen RHT's case' and specifically to underestimate 'the importance of agricultural profits'.[90] When Habbakuk wrote to Trevor-Roper to ask him to make changes to the essay he also focused on 'the digression into political history', and suggested that he publish his views on the rise of Independency elsewhere: Trevor-Roper appears to have won that particular tussle, however.[91] The editors also agreed that Trevor-Roper must 'mollify' his references to Tawney: 'Above all, let him concentrate on RHT's thesis and remain silent on RHT himself.'[92] Evidently the first version of the essay was even more outspokenly critical of Tawney than the version as published. This prompted Habbakuk to muse on Trevor-Roper's character:

> I find it difficult to decide whether T-R is a fundamentally nice person in the grip of a prose style in which it is impossible to be polite, or a fundamentally unpleasant person exploiting the general habit of attributing the kindest hearts to the rudest people and using rudeness as a disguise for nastiness.[93]

Describing Trevor-Roper's references to Tawney as 'excessively polemical', Habbakuk pointed out to him that his 'criticisms of the substance of Tawney's thesis would lose none of their conviction' if his references to Tawney himself 'were somewhat more mellow'.[94] It would appear from Trevor-Roper's reply to this letter that he agreed to modify his tone and his *ad personam* references.[95]

The editors also discussed between themselves whether Trevor-Roper should show a copy of the article to Tawney.[96] Whether at their prompting, or at the prompting of his conscience, Trevor-Roper did write to Tawney, though he contacted Richard Rees, Tawney's friend and literary executor first to sound him out. Rees replied that Tawney never referred to Trevor-Roper 'without praise' and actually cut his articles out of the *New Statesman*. He suggested that a 'preview of your bomb, accompanied by a cordial letter could not fail to produce an emollient effect.'[97] But in the most courteous manner Tawney declined the opportunity to read the essay because too busy with other things. 'Besides', he wrote to Trevor-Roper, 'I should, in any case, have felt some embarrassment in criticising criticisms of myself, even if I felt tempted to do so.'[98] It was another characteristically modest reply from a scholar who always encouraged others to have their say, and never let pride come between him and another historian. Trevor-Roper's letter to Tawney does not survive so it is impossible to know if Tawney understood how direct and personalized an attack he was about to receive. Trevor-Roper's private commentary on Tawney's actions at this point was neither strictly accurate nor generous: 'the Old Man of the Trees, Tawney himself (who refused even to see the article before publication), being totally invisible, inaudible and even unmentioned, is now being dismissed, by the advanced anthropologists of my expedition, as a myth.'[99]

Tawney, who had indeed achieved a kind of mythic status by this stage in his career, generally adopted an eirenic detachment from scholarly dispute, but did not remain silent and was moved to publish a short riposte in the *EcHR* in the following year.[100] From its tone it is evident that he was not only professionally displeased but was also personally hurt, for this was no ordinary difference of opinion between scholars seeking to 'get more light on the subject'. He defended both his use of quantitative data and the impressionistic testimony of contemporaries. As Trevor-Roper had objected to Tawney's examples, so he objected to Trevor-Roper's: 'one cannot disprove the reality of a trend merely by producing a handful of specimens which do not reflect it.'[101] Trevor-Roper's use of counter examples in his essay was beside the point: 'In order to refute my by no means novel thesis that, in the period concerned, economic and political tides were running in favour of medium-sized estates and social groups based upon them, Mr Trevor-Roper should have produced equally comprehensive figures showing that no discernible trend affecting the size of estates occurred, or that, if one did occur, its direction was contrary to that suggested in my Table.'[102] He expressed a legitimate grievance that he should be convicted of the counting of manors: 'My comments on the ambiguities of the term were more emphatic than his own.'[103] He defended his categorization of gentry ennobled since 1561 as gentry still, the point he had made to Tevor-Roper in 1950. And he displayed rare displeasure with the tone of his accuser in a famous aside: 'An erring colleague is not an Amalakite to be smitten hip and thigh. My correction of some of Mr Trevor-Roper's misconceptions has, I trust, been free from the needless and unpleasant asperity into which criticism, to the injury of its cause, is liable on occasion to lapse.'[104]

Trevor-Roper would not let it lie and sought to reply to Tawney but the editors brought the exchanges to an end at this point.[105] He tried in the next year to place a letter in the *Times Literary Supplement* but again met editorial opposition. In it he contended that Tawney's thesis had 'supplied the orthodoxy – I would say error – of a generation, which has been accepted with cries of ideological delight by Marxists and Roman Catholics alike.'[106] Subsequently one of Trevor-Roper's Oxford colleagues, John Cooper, published another fierce critique of the use of manorial property as an index of social mobility, once more ignoring Tawney's open admission that this could only be a very impressionistic way of measuring relative wealth and social status.[107] An ostensibly even-handed account of the gentry controversy then followed from Jack Hexter, the early modernist at Yale, but he didn't so much explain the controversy as add his own misguided observations. In the process he muddied the water and distorted the arguments of both authors. At one point Hexter compared Tawney's argument to that of Marx in *The Communist Manifesto*.[108] At another, he set out for his readers Tawney's supposed 'picture of a power-hungry rural middle class moving inexorably towards domination over the ruins of a feudalism that the middle class itself destroyed', a literally fantastic version of the careful arguments Tawney had made.[109] Hexter convicted Tawney of explaining the English Civil War in class terms, which he had not, and then of omitting the discussion of religion and politics in an essay about economic history. The author could barely disguise his partisanship.

Why did Trevor-Roper (and for that matter Hexter) lapse in this manner? Setting aside unattractive aspects of Trevor-Roper's personality that this affair betrays – ambition, pleasure in destruction – his biographer suggests that Trevor-Roper's deeper intent was to vanquish academic Marxism which he now found to be 'tired and clichéd' at a time, the early 1950s, when political Marxism was revealed as 'intellectually dishonest'. 'Tawney's thesis fitted neatly into this orthodoxy' and could be used, or so he thought, for a wider purpose.[110] But as this book makes evident, Tawney was no Marxist. He had consistently rejected its political and academic claims in all contexts, and at the time that Trevor-Roper was using him as a proxy target Tawney was openly critical of communism.[111] Had Trevor-Roper reflected more carefully on the totality of Tawney's work as a historian he might have recognized in his writings the stamp of a thoroughgoing historical idealist rather than a historical materialist. In Tawney's books and articles social and economic change are driven by ideas rather than alterations in the forces and relations of production. Moreover, his interest in the relationship of social classes in early modern history dates from his first book, published in 1912, long before Marxism had any notable place in British academic and political life. In trying to explain the history of the lesser landholders, Tawney was following through the academic logic of his own research since the Edwardian period, not writing under the influence of any ideology or historical theory. In any case, the study of social mobility is not intrinsically Marxist as Trevor-Roper, who married into the aristocracy and was elevated to a peerage, might have been expected to know from his own experience. If every historical argument concerning economic and social change were accounted Marxist, little else would exist except Marxist history.

One of the curiosities of Trevor-Roper's assault on Tawney is the absence of any discussion of what must be seen as the companion piece to 'The Rise of the Gentry', Tawney's Raleigh Lecture to the British Academy in May 1941 on 'Harrington and the Interpretation of his Age'. In the published version of this lecture Tawney refers to his forthcoming article in the *EcHR* and to all intents they are part of the same discussion.[112] In the 1650s, in texts including *Oceana* (1656) and *The Prerogative of Popular Government* (1657), James Harrington wrote about England during the Interregnum and about the origins of the Great Rebellion, developing a social theory in which political power and the nature of the state were determined by the distribution of property holding. Thus absolute monarchies to be such had to be preponderant in their ownership of the land, mixed monarchies reflected a situation where the aristocracy and crown held amounts of property that balanced each other, and a commonwealth must represent a broad and even distribution of landholding. In Harrington's view, social and political upheavals, such as the Civil War, occurred when the institutions of state and the distribution of property-holding no longer matched and reinforced each other. Harrington, among other contemporaries, including Bacon, Selden and Raleigh himself, argued that the growth of a property-holding gentry at the expense of both the crown and the greater magnates had unbalanced the state and created the political tensions which led to civil discord in the 1640s. He diagnosed as the social trends of the age the economic decline of the nobility, the rise of a new urban propertied class and the growing power and willingness of the House of Commons to challenge the monarchy.

If Tawney's description of social change in the seventeenth century had an inspiration, in other words, it was from Harrington rather than from Marx, from a contemporary who witnessed and diagnosed the problems of his age in ways that Tawney found interesting and revealing. As Tawney put it, Harrington was 'the first English political thinker to find the cause of political upheaval in antecedent social change'.[113] Notable also was Tawney's caution in this lecture as in the parallel essay on the gentry. When writing about the large sales of land by church and crown in the sixteenth century, for example, he counselled 'reserve' because 'on the precise effects of these grandiose transactions much detailed work still remains to be done'.[114]

If Marxist historians had welcomed Tawney's history of the gentry as evidence of a rising bourgeoisie that precipitated a bourgeois revolution in the 1640s, Tawney was never so direct or indeed, crude. Earlier, in 1925, he had certainly used the language of class struggle and Marxism: 'land was transferred from the dying feudal nobility and old-fashioned squires to the commercial middle class', he had written.[115] In the long introduction to his edition of Thomas Wilson's *Discourse Upon Usury* (1569) Tawney tended to see all landholders as one class – and all of them as indebted – and to see the social challenge to them coming from city merchants and their agents, the moneylenders, rather than from lesser landholders. Elizabethan society was more blatantly divided between town and country, middle class and aristocracy. But his intellectual trajectory was away from this much cruder social history in the 1920s to a more subtle and nuanced account when published in 1941. Far from embracing Marxism, he moved from economic and social reductionism and towards cautious studies of social mobility within landed society, not between it and the urban middle classes. Thus 'The Rise of the Gentry' did not, so far as Tawney was concerned, contain any overt political implications or conclusions. They were supplied and confected by others. Trevor-Roper had picked the wrong man, the wrong texts and in many respects the wrong historical issue over which to have an argument concerning the explanatory power of Marxism. In the process he had behaved badly and it would seem that, in time, he came to recognize this. As Michal Vyvyan wrote to David Joslin, Professor of Economic History in Cambridge, in 1967, 'I hear, though not on particularly good authority, that Trevor-Roper regrets the whole confrontation and his own position in it even on technical grounds.'[116] As this comment suggests, these exchanges were not forgotten and passed quickly into academic legend and also into the undergraduate history curriculum. The first essay set the Indian writer, Ved Mehta, on arrival at Balliol as an undergraduate in the 1950s was on the 'gentry controversy'.[117]

There are worse fates than to be criticized by Regius Professors of History in Oxford and Cambridge. In both cases Tawney's antagonists were motivated – at least in part – by their political hostility to him. That two such openly ideological figures as Trevor-Roper and Elton, who never made their politics secret or practised scholarly detachment where they themselves were concerned, should have criticized another professor of History for his politics and the role it played in his historical writing is ironic to say the least. Rather than focus on Tawney's socialism or reflexive sympathy for the underdog, their case against his historical writing would have been stronger had they stuck to the question of the relationship between present and past in his work. For Tawney's historical research was structured around issues he saw for himself, pre-eminently the callous nature of Edwardian capitalism which he described in the *Commonplace Book* and in his reports on the tutorial classes he taught. He was thereby led backwards to investigate the origins of capitalism, but always with a view to explaining its contemporary nature and failings. This was not necessarily a weakness, of course. According to Tawney's obituary in the *Manchester Guardian*, 'Only a man profoundly concerned at contemporary injustice could have written his "Agrarian Problem". Only one who has pondered deeply on the social structure of Tudor England could have produced his revealing study 'Life and Labour in China' (sic) (1932) or, for that matter, his 'Acquisitive Society' (1921) or 'Equality' (1931).'[118] The interpenetration of present and past in Tawney's thinking gave him greater insight and made his work all the more compelling: it is surely significant that his most influential historical work was written and published in the 1920s when he was at his most engaged in public affairs. As T. S. Ashton, Tawney's younger colleague in economic history at the LSE, noted when interviewed by the BBC, 'To Tawney as Cervantes, history was not only the preserver and eternaliser of great actions, the professional enemy of oblivion, the witness of things past, but also the director of future times. It was because he was an historian that he was a prophet.'[119] Not everyone wishes to mix prophecy with history, however: the teleological nature of Tawney's major works – the attempt to work backwards from the present and then to explain contemporary affairs by means of historical argument – discounted it in the opinion of some of his peers, and requires that he is read with caution as well as wonder.

The criticisms of the accuracy and veracity of Tawney's historical research made by Trevor-Roper and Elton cannot be dismissed, but once registered and accepted are in a sense superfluous. Ashton noted Tawney's singularities as a historian:

> He had little in common with scholars who, as he put it, "make a darkness and call it research, while shrinking from the light of general ideas"; and he used to speak of the academies where such arts were practised as the haunts of bats and owls. Mere narrative made little appeal to him: "the habit of eating facts raw" led only to dyspepsia. But he was equally impatient of "methodology" and denounced the claim that history was a science as a vain and unflattering pretension. . . .[120]

Many of these opinions were probably derived from his extra-mural teaching at a formative period. He wrote of the danger of academic work becoming self-absorbed, 'divorced from the life of the community' and hence missing 'the opportunity of giving the inspiration which springs from the mingling of different types of experience'. The university teacher of history and the social sciences is enriched and challenged, he wrote, 'when he has spent some years discussing [his subject] with those who have approached it along another channel and interpret it in the light of a different type of experience'. It was under their influence – the influence of his extra-mural students – and in order to appeal to their interests that he wrote history in the way that he did: his audience as he conceived it, and as his wide readership demonstrates, was not a conventionally academic group.[121] Tawney's gift was to apply his imagination and intellect to large historical questions rather than work upwards from facts drawn from the archives. The latter is often an easier method, and Tawney was not at all unfamiliar with the inside of county record offices. His nephew paid tribute, indeed, to 'the trouble which Tawney took over statistics and the pains he went to extract them' though he admitted that Tawney's 'native ability did not lie in that direction'.[122]

Tawney is supposed to have said that 'what historians need is not more documents but stronger boots' in which to walk the terrain and see for themselves. He sympathized with those who wilted at the first sight of an extensive manuscript collection.[123] His special talent was for synthesis and argument on a grand scale, for the connection of historical developments rather than their disaggregation into well documented and carefully analysed mutual isolation. According to Postan, his historical work 'was based on much detailed research [but] it was to a remarkable extent dependent on inspired guesses and flashes of insight and was deeply coloured by his likes and dislikes'.[124] As John Kenyon, another historian of the seventeenth century, observed, 'He was a man of bold thinking, which explains his errors. He was one of the few historians who could seize a whole period and squeeze it and shape it in his hands; such treatment tends to distort the evidence, but it also produces illuminating insights and reinterpretations'.[125] Ashton recognized that Tawney's depictions of the gentry, of puritanism and of early modern capitalism were all open to objection – but those objections were of subordinate account in the assessment of a historian who 'brought a wealth of new material and an imaginative interpretation to the economic and social history of the period'.[126]

Some readers and fellow professionals prefer *terra firma* and become impatient, not to say angry, when historians ignore, select or in other ways fashion the evidence. For others, history is about the force and influence of ideas and they thrill to large interpretative structures of the type Tawney specialized in, which seek to convey a clear sense of the architecture of the past. In Tawney's case 'he strode across the fields of scholarship, caring little for the fences erected by smaller men to hedge off theology from ethics, politics and economics, or any of these from history'.[127] In truth, this is a matter of temperament and outlook, a perennial fault line in the writing and reading of History. Tawney's major demerit for some was that he was so obviously from one side of this division, whereas most historians, lacking his imagination and intellectual ambition, opt for empiricism. But in the writing of History there may be worse sins than inaccuracy or inexactitude, including among them the absence of vision and triviality. Building durable analytical structures in any discipline is challenging, and in the very nature of things, those structures will be vulnerable to attack. But it is surely better to have some structuring ideas as the basis for argument and the motive for further research, than to have merely monographic studies, trees without the wood. Tawney may have been wrong in details, even essentials, but his ideas have endured. It cannot be without significance that in the summer of 2011 a large and distinguished group of late-medieval, early-modern and agricultural historians gathered at the University of Exeter for a conference entitled 'Tawney's *Agrarian Problem* 100 Years On'.[128]

10

London and Washington:
The Second World War

Tawney might have thought that his wartime service for his country had ended on the first day of the Somme offensive in 1916, or perhaps at some time after the First World War when the social reconstruction into which he had put his energies from early 1917 ran out of money and steam in the early 1920s. But like all his generation he had to endure another war. In this case, if his services were not literally in the front line they were very valuable nevertheless. His expertise as an economic historian was put to use in planning for the post-war economy. He wrote one of the most moving justifications for Britain's commitment to the Second World War which, crucially, was published in the *New York Times* in the high summer of 1940. He then spent a year in the British embassy in Washington as 'Advisor on Social and Politico-Economic Affairs' and witnessed close-up the change in the nature of the conflict after Pearl Harbor. Finally, he returned to Britain to throw himself into social reconstruction for a second time during which he lobbied and agitated for the 1944 Education Act and the restructuring of secondary education for which he had fought throughout his career. He maintained a simple faith in democracy and the decency of the people throughout a conflict now widely known as 'the people's war'. In the spring of 1939, with the war imminent, Tawney gave lectures at Chicago University on history, and also on recent diplomacy in which he lamented the failure of British policy in the 1930s. He recalled for his audience that on the eve of the Battle of Trafalgar when Nelson signalled 'England expects every man to do his duty' it was said in reply on the lower decks: 'Does the old bitch think we shan't?' In that spirit Tawney ended his lecture thus: 'Democracy is a way of giving the final decision to the men and women who, in the last resort, have got to stand the racket. In spite of the episodes of the last five years, I remain of the opinion that they will stand it better than the unhappy pawns of the dictators.'[1] Tawney was right.

His initial response in September 1939 was cautious: 'Yes, the war is a catastrophe', he wrote to Durbin,

> though in the circumstances we were, I think, right to go in ... we must try
> to resist the mental insanities which will grow as the thing proceeds ... In the
> meantime, I think the only thing – unless & until one is wanted – is to go on as
> steadily as possible with one's ordinary work. Wars are pathological conditions,
> and life is not all pathology.[2]

Jeanette asked her brother what he felt about the war. '*We* are inclined to feel that we must just go ahead with it though the awful casualty lists – awful by their youth – of the Air Force make one ashamed that we [are] too derelict & cannot take the place of these youngsters.'[3] Tawney hoped he would be used in some capacity and chafed in frustration that the call was slow in coming. He joined the Home Guard in London: later, after his return from the United States, he was a Civil Defence Warden around his village in the Cotswolds. As France fell in May 1940 he wrote to Jeanette that he wished he 'were there, or since that is impossible doing something useful. But, clearly, one is not wanted'.[4] He joined a campaign in July 1940 to oppose the imposition of the new purchase tax on books.[5] And when, in the following year, the Plymouth public library was destroyed during an air raid, he joined with others in a national appeal for books for the town, 'a living proof that although Hitler came and saw Plymouth, he could not conquer it.'[6]

   He went on steadily in the summer of 1940, writing to Beveridge to enquire if Will, who had spent his whole career quietly amassing data on the historical prices of commodities in Britain, had information on the price of wheat, malt and other grains from 1558 to 1650, particularly in East Anglia, so Tawney might calculate the rise in corn rents. Tawney admitted that it was 'absurd to think of such things at such a moment. But I may as well finish off what I was doing in such odds and ends of time as I have'.[7] He remained resolutely optimistic, even at the time of Dunkirk:

> The news about our men in Flanders is agonising. They have done a superb job,
> and a very valuable one, for they have given the French time to organise a line,
> but they have done so at a heavy price ... if we hold them, as no doubt we shall,
> for another six months, I shall continue to think that their defeat is only a matter
> of time.[8]

He evidently thought of the Second World War as comparable in strategy to the war he had fought; of Blitzkreig he could not conceive. He learnt more when he dined with his protégés Durbin and Gaitskell and was told that within the British government 'the French collapse was not unexpected'.[9] When Eileen Power was overwrought at the thought that Britain might give in, he did his 'best to console her by my pugnacity'.[10] As she gratefully acknowledged a few days later, 'I have an ingrained conviction – ingrained during 20 years – that anything you say *must* be right'.[11] But it was Tawney who needed consolation when, less than 6 weeks later in early August 1940, Eileen Power dropped dead of a stroke in Tottenham Court Road aged 51. Tawney gave the address at her funeral at the Golders Green crematorium. He spoke about her personal qualities and effect on others rather than her scholarship, the subject for a later tribute, recalling 'the radiant personality, who flashed with a kind of enchanting recklessness – all gaiety and fire – from one activity to another . . . Her work was far from done; but she was her own greatest work'.[12] Tawney's affection and admiration were widely shared, for Power had a magnetic charm that attracted many.

The London School of Economics was evacuated to Cambridge at the start of the war and its male undergraduates were accommodated in Peterhouse where the Master was the historian Herbert Butterfield. Tawney initially declined the offer of a set of rooms in the college in favour of someone who would be based permanently in Cambridge, though he was given membership of the Senior Common Room and dining rights there. Instead, he took a room at 8 King's Parade and travelled up and down to Cambridge from London and Gloucestershire to give his lectures over 2 or 3 days a week.[13] The college welcomed him and Tawney built a warm relationship with it: as he reflected 20 years later, 'that college has been extremely kind, both to the LSE in allowing it to move its headquarters there during the War, and to me personally in putting me up for a night or two every week when I went up to Cambridge to teach, after our return from the embassy in Washington'.[14] Later Tawney was made an honorary fellow of Peterhouse. He spent more time than he had expected in Cambridge because in October 1940 Harry and Jeanette were bombed-out of Mecklenburgh Square. As Jeanette explained to her brother,

> Our house had a time bomb or two in the square which caused an evacuation of all our tenants. The damage seemed slight and we were contemplating trying to live in the basement and ground floor and had it surveyed for that purpose. When we had nearly decided to apply for this from the landlord there came a vast enemy missile at the back of the house which rendered the whole of the north side of the square more or less a casualty. There were several direct hits

around us and there were several houses demolished on the Grays Inn Rd side of
the square, in Mecklenburgh Street coming out of Guilford Street. Anyway our
house is now uninhabitable and we have to rescue such stuff of ours as we can at
the shortest notice . . . I have been dashing up to London by car and retrieving
what I can.[15]

Tawney's study was the only relatively unscathed room, but that left them with
the considerable problem of collecting together his remaining books in a city
with an acute shortage of packing cases which had all been used up in waves of
evacuation. Improvising brilliantly, they procured from the Cotswolds 'pheasant
baskets, sized 3ft by 2ft by one, which the pheasant farm proprietor was not
using'.[16] For the next months, during the first phase of the Blitz, they spent nights
in London where they could: 'I slept one night at Gower Street and was just
saying to Harry how quiet it all was when our shutters were blown open and the
whole house shook . . . That was the night on which University College was hit
and the students' Indian hostel in Gower Street.'[17] When they came back from
Washington in late 1943 they found another place in Bloomsbury. As Tawney
wrote to Beatrice Webb,

> We have contrived to get 2 rooms and a kitchen for 25/ a week, at an address
> called 29, The Colonnade, Russell Square. The address sounds very magnificent;
> one feels as though one were living in the Colosseum or Parthenon. Really it is
> not a Colonnade, but a rather slummy mews, though the rooms are excellent.[18]

Tawney's first service in the war was to write a report, submitted in August
1941, on the abolition of wartime controls of the economy in the period 1918–21
for the government's Reconstruction Committee under Arthur Greenwood.[19]
The aim was to learn from the successes and failures of the process last time
and better manage the transition to a peace-time economy: 'to ascertain what
lights, if any, the experience then obtained throws on the problems which may
be expected to arise at the conclusion of the present war.' It seems likely that
Durbin had secured this commission for his senior colleague: he was then in the
economic section of the War Cabinet secretariat. The history of decontrol after
the November armistice was of a rapid divestment of the regulation and state
organization of industry. Tawney asked if, in light of the history of the postwar
period, the coalition government under Lloyd George had acted wisely. The
essay first examined the dimensions of the control system as it existed at the end
of the war and then considered the process by which these controls had been
put in place. It went on to examine the process of regulation and deregulation

in different industries, of which the coal industry, almost inevitably, was one. Tawney's report ended by pointing to three types of successful and creative wartime intervention that would need to be revisited at the end of this war: first, 'the great international organisations created for the purpose of pooling the purchase and allocation of essential food-stuffs, materials and shipping'; second, the wartime process of prioritizing certain types of production and goods over others, which he advised should continue; third, short of full-scale nationalization, the maintenance of particular controls imposed on particular industries, many of which would continue to be as rational and beneficial in peacetime as they had been during the war.[20] Overall, though advising an empirical rather than an ideological approach, Tawney counselled that government should be prepared to maintain successful controls in peace. The automatic cessation of control after 1918 had dreadful consequences, pitching the economy into downturn and strikes: 'It would be unpardonable if similar errors were made a second time.'[21] The essay was classic Tawney: it based policy for the present and future on lessons of the recent past; it demonstrated his mastery of economics based upon historical example, precedent and the understanding of social processes over time; it displayed his ability to analyse and understand economic institutions.

The report's impact cannot really be charted – but in many areas of economic life controls were only slowly and carefully removed after 1945. At the time of its submission in 1941, however, it was considered a highly radical document and it would appear that some officials took fright. Tawney had been commissioned to write six papers on the economics of warfare and reconstruction, but this was the only one delivered.[22] He continued to battle against officialdom to have the paper published in 1943 in a shortened and considerably amended version, shorn of its policy prescriptions, in the *Economic History Review*.[23] It says something for the British attitude to the war that plans were being laid for economic transition after victory as early as 1941 – when no victory looked remotely in sight – and that academic publishing continued as before. Yet in 1941 the idea of peace-time planning on the scale envisaged by Tawney, and state control of industry, were considered highly unorthodox. The winning of the war seemed to be a triumph of planning and state organization, however, and by 1945 Tawney's prescriptions were plain common sense.

Tawney's second service was another piece of writing, though of an entirely different type: a propagandistic essay entitled 'Why Britain Fights' which was published in the Sunday *New York Times* on 21 July 1940. The genesis of this piece remains obscure but what little evidence survives perhaps suggests that Tawney composed and placed it under his own initiative. As he wrote to Jeanette in June 1940, 'Currently there's a good deal of red tape to be unwound before one can do even so simple things as explain the attitude of people here for the benefit of an American audience, and I doubt whether, after all, the articles will get to the USA. Still, I am glad to have tried.'[24] Given his unusually extensive experience of the United States, he perhaps felt an obligation to act as an interpreter and intermediary between the nations. He may have been encouraged by his network of American contacts and friends. And there was a genuine task to be accomplished because, as is well known, American opinion was divided over the war and over the merits of ending isolation and coming to the assistance of the British, whether that assistance were to take the form of material support (as in the Lend-Lease programme) or full-blown entry into the conflict.

Tawney's essay began with the kind of paradoxes he liked: the British were fighting 'not in spite of our hatred of war, but because of it'. They were 'not fighting in obedience to the orders of [their] Government' like the peoples of the Axis; 'our government is fighting in obedience to our orders' as it should be in a democracy.[25] Tawney carried on in this style, enumerating 'what we are not fighting for': this included territory, economic advantage ('we shall be lucky if we are not ruined'), racial superiority, animosity to the Germans and 'that singularly unimperial institution called the British "Empire"'. But then he turned from negative to positive: the British were fighting for a way of life and that encompassed a host of democratic principles and institutions:

> Good faith; tolerance; respect for opinions which we do not share; loyalty to comrades; mercy to the weak; consideration for the unfortunate; equal justice for all – the ordinary decencies and humanities of intercourse between neighbours – these things are clearly part of it. So is the power to speak freely one's thoughts, to obey one's own conscience, to do one's duty as one sees it.

The fight was not just one for national survival but for the survival of all democratic and civilized values: 'Great Britain . . . may be an unworthy champion of democracy, but she remains its champion none the less.' Tawney then turned to Hitler himself – 'this evil and unhappy man is the dupe of his own wickedness' – and to the torment of the German people and other European nationalities under the Nazis as further evidence of the requirement to take up arms. He could not resist criticism of British foreign policy in the 1930s: he believed it implicitly, of course, but it was part of a technique in which British sins and omissions were modestly accepted, the better to appeal for American support out of honesty and sincerity. But self-criticism was followed by encouragement and hope: Tawney welcomed the new government under Churchill, seeking to convince his American audience that now Britain had a leadership and policy worthy of both our and their support. He also pointed to the crucial role of the Labour Party in engineering the change of government and in taking command of the organization of the home front at War Cabinet and ministerial levels. He then described the new measures amounting to 'war collectivism' which the government had imposed and which the people had accepted with resolution. And he ended with a Churchillian flourish which probably did owe something to the prime minister's sentiments and cadences that summer, for as we have seen, Tawney was an admirer of Churchill: 'We would rather go down than live to despise ourselves. If we fight against tyranny and are defeated, we shall at least leave a memory which will nerve other men in other ages to fight with better fortune. But we shall not be defeated.' In its style, purpose and arguments, 'Why Britain Fights' stands worthy comparison to Orwell's more famous essay from the same season 'The Lion and the Unicorn'. Both deserve to be anthologized in any volume of war literature.

Tawney's article made its mark. The *New York Times* accompanied it with a wholly supportive editorial emphasizing the shared sacrifices in war of 'the Grimsby fishermen, the Birmingham factory hands, the shipbuilders on the Clyde, the clerks and bus drivers of London'. This was indeed a people's war and Tawney was helping to break down American stereotypes of a conflict directed by a traditional, imperial ruling class and imposed on poor British workers. Tawney received several appreciative letters from Americans thanking him for his services to the British cause in America. One professor from Teacher's College in New York caught the point of the exercise: 'Your letter will go a long way to dispel the notion that there is no difference between Britain and the enemy or that British policy is still dominated by appeasers and by Fascist trends, and that the masses are supine or ignorant or both.'[26] Another professor from Williams College, Massachusetts praised Tawney's 'restraint ..[which] gives your statements tremendous force', a remarkable judgement on one of Tawney's most overtly emotional and outspoken published pieces.[27] A New York lawyer praised his 'clear and forceful explanation of the British position'; another correspondent, the secretary of the International Magna Carta Day Association ('For English Speaking Unity'), suggested that the British government 'reproduce it in large quantities' so he could send it to his membership.[28] Indeed, Tawney's correspondents were those who might be expected to favour Britain's position in the war: liberals, anti-fascists, Jews and self-conscious 'Anglos'. The test of the essay was whether it had reached a much wider and less immediately sympathetic audience.

It was in the belief that Tawney could indeed reach that wider audience that his third wartime service was conceived: to spend a period based in the British embassy in Washington DC during which he would lecture, write and propagandize in the British cause, above all taking the nation's case to American workers upon whose labour and production British survival depended. Tawney was also expected to report back on American politics and their bearing on the emerging Atlantic alliance. Tawney feared that he did not have the personality or skills for a position in public relations: in the event the problems he faced in the United States were rooted deep in the culture and politics of the American labour movement.

Tawney first received an invitation from Duff Cooper, the Minister of Information, to take a post as labour advisor to the director general of the British Information Service in New York, Sir Gerald Campbell. Cooper explained that in this role he would 'maintain contact with American Labour and the Labour Press, and with Government Officials in Washington concerned with Labour matters'.[29] Tawney, who was due to go to Chicago to receive an honorary degree, accepted the offer with reluctance, protesting that he was not an ideal choice for a position in public relations and asking for the assistance while in the US of a trade unionist who would be able to make contacts with the American labour movement more effectively.[30] Neither man was aware that Tawney's article in the *New York Times* had come to the attention of a higher authority, the War Cabinet itself, and that the deputy prime minister, Attlee, was simultaneously suggesting that Tawney should be sent to the British embassy in Washington DC to develop 'close and unofficial relations with the New Deal element in the United States'.[31] As Tawney explained to the LSE's Director on 26 July,

> On Thursday I received a telegram requesting me to interview a Foreign Office official, which I did yesterday. He then stated that the Government had decided to send someone to the Embassy at Washington as "Advisor on Social and Politico-Economic Affairs" and asked whether I would take the post . . . He told me that the post had been decided on after consultations between Halifax, Atlee (sic) and Butler and suggested that I should see Atlee (sic) as soon as possible. I have, therefore, arranged to see Atlee (sic) at 2.45 on Monday next, July 28. The proposal was a complete surprise to me . . . I have not yet reached a decision, and in doing so, I shall not forget the School.[32]

Attlee, the leader of the Labour Party and deputy prime minister, took the credit for sending Tawney to Washington: he 'had the idea that a man of Tawney's high moral and intellectual acquirements' could make a useful contribution to the war effort in America.[33] After seeing him and thinking it over, Tawney wrote again to the Director of the LSE, A. M. Carr-Saunders, to explain that he felt duty-bound to accept: 'In view of the way in which the matter has been put to me by those concerned in the creation of the post at Washington, I feel that I have no alternative.'[34] The LSE's governors agreed to his request for leave of absence and Tawney was required to be in Washington no later than the end of October 1941 and to stay for at least 6 months. But Tawney had his doubts: as he wrote to Jeanette, 'While I must not turn down what may be a duty, without careful thought, I don't feel happy about the idea. I am no good at publicity work, and I have no experience of the Press, or flair for handling it. What is wanted is a "good mixer", and I am not that.'[35] The sergeant of his Home Guard platoon also had his doubts: when told that he was losing an experienced soldier to the diplomatic corps he apparently exclaimed 'of course it is your duty to go, but we are all very sorry for you because you may miss the invasion'![36] Tawney went with written testimonials that he could present to American workers from the Amalgamated Weavers' Association, who mentioned his 'loyal and valiant service' to textile workers and miners, and from the General Secretary of the Trades Union Congress, Walter Citrine, who cited his work for the trade union movement and in workers' education.[37] Given subsequent events, within a matter of months Citrine would most certainly have revised his assessment of Tawney. Beatrice Webb, still in thrall to her illusions, wrote to encourage her old friend to promote a more sympathetic view of the Soviet Union among American audiences.[38] As events were to show, nothing would have done more damage to Tawney's mission and the British cause than to have taken his friend's advice.

His first duty in America was to lecture on the war from the British perspective. He related to his sister Mil that

> the job has turned out a sort of public relations one – a good deal of speaking and endless social amenities. Neither are much my line, but both are supposed to promote Anglo-American good will. Jeanette, as you can imagine, is a roaring success at the second. I spend my time evading the enthusiasm which gathers round her.

Tawney's propensity to impersonate an absent-minded professor was only encouraged by social duties of this type. One of his colleagues in the Washington embassy told a story of Tawney in Chicago at this time. He was invited to lunch on a Saturday but he mixed up the days and went instead on the Friday. His wealthy and generous host didn't flinch and gave him lunch without demur. After the meal he showed him what he described to Tawney as 'the finest private collection of old masters in America'. On the following, correct day, Tawney presented himself again for lunch and this time was part of an invited party of guests. After the meal their host showed them what he described as 'the finest private collection of old masters in America'. 'O no,' said Tawney: 'You can't say that. Someone was saying that to me just the other day'![39] Arnold Toynbee met the Tawneys in Washington and recalled later that they spent their generous allowance on parcels of food and clothes which they sent back to family and friends in England. Toynbee related that their luggage had been lost when the ship carrying it from Britain was torpedoed. Tawney was lent clothes several sizes too small. After a well-received speech to the Garment Workers' Union the assembled tailors suggested they make him a new suit of clothes, but Tawney gave them the suit he was wearing to size the new ensemble, with predictable results.[40]

He lectured on the west coast, in Los Angeles, and at an 'awe-inspiring meeting called the Annual Convention of the League of Women Voters' in Chicago. The place he liked best was Boulder, Colorado: 'high up, with Alpine air, and snow mountains in the background. It would have been nice to stay there and fish'. Being on the road had its compensations, therefore, and was preferable to the job inside the embassy which was not at all to his taste: time there was 'demoralising' with 'no steady turns of work, but constant odds and sods, which take time, but leave one without the satisfaction of feeling that one has finished one job and can start another'.[41] To Carr-Saunders he complained that his work was 'so indefinite – mainly interminable talking – that I find it difficult to judge how far it is of any practical utility'.[42] To his old friend Tom Jones he was more candid:

> My own work – if it can be called work – does not come to much. I received no guidance from the F.O. in London as to what I was supposed to do here except that it was hoped that I should establish contact with "New Deal Groups". I imagine I have done that to some extent, but it does not come to much when it's done. The Embassy was even less helpful. Halifax, whom I respect, was agreeable; but I asked in vain Sir Ronald Campbell – personally a nice fellow – for suggestions as to what, if anything, they wanted done. The fact is, I think, that they were in the dark as to why I had been sent out.[43]

Three files of his lectures have survived, though all derive from a common stem and were tweaked and shaped to meet the needs of specific audiences. Lectures before Pearl Harbor tried to bring home the gravity of the situation in Europe and elsewhere; those given after American entry in the war inevitably emphasized shared burdens and ideals. All his orations presented the war as a conflict of high ideals rather than of aggrandizing states, and of ordinary people rather than elites in the manner of 'Why Britain Fights'. All of them generalized the conflict and presented Britain as 'a trustee who carried a responsibility for the future not only of herself but of all men and women who love freedom'. In most of them he moved on to argue that a vital component of modern civilization was economic and social equality, thus making it possible to turn to the discussion of social reconstruction in Britain during and after the war, a theme with the special role of breaking down American views of Britain as imperialistic, aristocratic and unequal. 'It may fairly be said, in short, that a war on which depends the survival of democracy not only in my country but in Europe as a whole, is being fought in a democratic spirit and by democratic methods.' Throughout, Tawney showed he understood the power of specific words to move American audiences: 'freedom' and 'democracy' were frequently repeated and in one lecture he crossed out 'boundary' and replaced it with that most pregnant of American concepts, 'frontier'.

Tawney was not a great lecturer but he understood his task and his audiences in these months. He universalized the war as one between civilization and barbarism; he emphasized the values Americans held dear; so as not to appear to be a mere jingo, in small asides he showed that he recognized the weaknesses of his own country; he emphasized the sacrifices of all British people and the growing British commitment to social justice and equity. Before Pearl Harbor he ended lectures telling his audiences that they must make up their own minds about the conflict, though he had so weighted the argument that only one conclusion was possible. This may appear to have been a simple task, even a crude one, but it took some artifice and thought to pull off, and Tawney did pull it off: he was self-critical at all times over this period, but these lectures were subtle combinations of all the different messages required to win American support, and masterpieces of their type.[44] They are all the more remarkable in the knowledge that Tawney was presenting a patriotic case to his audiences while reflecting in private on the decline of Britain. In March 1942, not long after the fall of Singapore, he wrote to Temple from Washington to thank him for a copy of the latter's famous work, *Christianity and the Social Order*:

> I feel a certain awe in observing the general course of events as a kind of tremendous demonstration that morality, after all, is in the nature of things, that men reap as they sow, and other commonplaces. With Asia at last coming into its own, the British Empire of the past dissolving, and the British governing classes – exceptions apart – pretty badly discredited – one has the sensation of watching the world being turned before our eyes.[45]

It is a mark of his dedication to the patriotic cause that while he wrote thus to his closest friend Tawney spoke very differently when on duty.

Attlee, an old acquaintance who had shared so many of Tawney's experiences, including public school (Haileybury), Oxford (University College), Toynbee Hall and the trenches, had been instrumental in his appointment and kept in touch with him for the 11 months he was there. He asked him for an informal report in March 1942 to which Tawney replied in a long letter.[46] Tawney's first point was the impact of Pearl Harbor: 'Down to December 7 the economic transformation required to put the country on a war footing had hardly begun', but now – May 1942 – the American economy was climbing towards full capacity. Tawney noted that isolationist sentiment persisted, especially in the mid-west, and he enumerated several hostile or indifferent American attitudes that menaced the war effort and the alliance: a permanent distrust of Great Britain which had always existed; the virulent opposition of the privileged to any of FDR's policies; a pervasive fear of Russia which was strong not only among Roman Catholics and businessmen but even among trades unionists; a dislike of organized labour and finally 'a certain amount of straight pacifism'. He commented on the ignorance and inexperience of many Americans who 'know less of the practical realities of war than a European child'. As to himself, he described a somewhat desultory existence in the embassy 'where a few people write to me and ring me up with enquiries', but was notably more enthusiastic 'about speaking, of which we've done a good deal' and which had 'a certain modest usefulness'.

> As far as most audiences are concerned, the long suit of an English speaker is his ability to give them first-hand accounts of the condition of things in England and Europe, the state of mind of English people with regard to the war and post-war problems, the political situation, the latest developments in different departments of economic and social policy, and so on. Curiosity as to such things is insatiable . . .

For this reason Tawney thought that for the role given to him as a kind of advocate for the British people and publicist for the British cause, a succession of short-term appointments of people in close touch with events in Britain would be better than a single long term of duty. He was now getting restless and wrote of wanting to return to Britain, not only because he believed his job done in the United States but also because of the work still to be accomplished at home:

> I feel rather strongly the truth of what you say in your letter as to the need of getting some positive ideals as to the post-war world put in place in England, whose policy will do a great deal to determine both that of other European governments and the line taken by America. Finally, I feel anxious to do what little I can to keep the case for educational reconstruction in particular, to the front, and to say something about it before the plans are irrevocably settled.

Tawney appreciated Attlee's purpose in sending him: 'I think it is a good thing that there should be someone at the Embassy who represents a different attitude to politics and social affairs from that which Americans – rightly or wrongly – are apt to ascribe to the British diplomatic corps.' He suggested some good Labour men who might replace him, including Arthur Creech Jones, then parliamentary private secretary to Ernest Bevin in the Ministry of Labour, and Gaitskell. At the end of the letter to Attlee he related that he was frequently asked this question while in America: 'If you are not a nation of snobs, why do you send so many snobs to represent you in America?' He returned to this theme in a letter to Creech Jones on his return to London. Complaining about 'gentlemanly amateurs' who knew little, had paltry experience of life and came only from the public schools and Oxford and Cambridge, he advised choosing the staff of the Foreign Office on the basis of competitive examination and then training and educating them properly for their jobs overseas.[47]

Tawney sent back to London three lengthy reports on aspects of American politics and opinion during these months. A fourth paper was a more general and historical account entitled 'The American Labour Movement'. It was written in September 1942 at the very end of his American sojourn, and was rich with the insights that his knowledge of British labour history and his recent experiences allowed Tawney to deploy, though it was deemed too controversial for publication during the war.[48] One of the three 'political' reports was on the American labour movement and the mid-term Congressional elections of 1942; the other two were on the fratricidal relations within that labour movement and the impact of these on British attempts – including his own – to build a common front linking British and American workers in a shared commitment to victory. The analysis of the 1942 elections was well informed, based on a deep understanding of American politics and sociology, and was pungent in its judgment of many of the less attractive figures in American affairs. It featured case studies of four areas where the labour vote mattered to the outcome: Ohio, Illinois, Michigan and New York. It was also salutary on American attitudes to Britain. Our motives in fighting the war were widely distrusted; many saw Britain as 'representative of a grasping imperialism'; there was a common repugnance to the British class system and businessmen distrusted British economic policy.[49]

The other reports detail how Tawney was led to the heart of the historic divisions of American labour, which he tried to bridge, but without any success. Indeed, his efforts only led to controversy and odium among British as well as American trades unionists, and to a strange alliance that Tawney forged with the British ambassador, the arch-appeaser Lord Halifax, against, of all people, the leading representative of British workers, Walter Citrine.

On his arrival in the United States Tawney found an American labour movement divided into two hostile organizations, the American Federation of Labour (AFL) and the Congress of Industrial Organisations (CIO). So deep were the disagreements that any approach to one of the two branches of the movement would be sure to incite the other. The AFL had been founded in the 1880s as an alliance of craft unions uniting skilled workers, and often seemed more concerned to differentiate itself from the mass of unskilled workers beneath than to make a common cause. Its leadership, which had longstanding links to the British Trades Union Congress, was highly conservative: it had largely eschewed politics throughout its history in favour of a 'pure and simple' unionism focused on job conditions and pay. Tawney described it as 'ultra-American in temper, little interested in legislative reforms, suspicious of radicalism, uneasy at the disposition of European Labour Movements to look favourably on plans for social reconstruction, and feeling all the horror of the American bourgeoisie at the Russian Mystery of iniquity'.[50] The CIO had been established by the AFL in 1934 to organize industrial unions in the big mass production industries – automobiles, most famously – but the new organization rapidly fell into dispute with the AFL hierarchy because of its different style, which was mandated by the task of organizing workers without trade union experience in new industries, and its desire for autonomy. By the early 1940s it was approximately the same size as the AFL. Tawney, who was more sympathetic to the CIO, described it as 'a Federation of large, modern unions engaged mainly in the extractive and mass production manufacturing industries . . . It is not so exclusively dedicated to the defence of professional vested interests, it has a more social spirit, and somewhat wider intellectual horizons.'[51] Importantly, most of America's unionized munitions workers were in the CIO, so making warm relations between the Congress and Britain all the more important. The divisions between these two organizations made manpower planning and labour management more difficult for the Roosevelt administration; it made it impossible for Tawney to achieve his aim of constructing links between British and American workers and educating American trades unionists about the conflict in Europe so that they understood the purpose of their labour in American factories, mills and mines.

The Trades Union Congress in Britain was already united with Soviet workers in an Anglo-Soviet Trade Union Committee and this had resolved to enlarge itself to encompass representatives of organized labour in the United States. Tawney was critical of the move, contending that the TUC should have understood the likely response to an Anglo-Soviet committee from American public opinion and the AFL itself, and should have tried instead to construct an alliance of labour movements from *all* the allied countries, which would have met with a warmer welcome in the United States.[52] In the spring of 1942, Citrine, as General Secretary of the TUC, planned to go to America to try to coax the AFL into the Anglo-Soviet fold. Halifax, almost certainly acting on Tawney's advice and reading of the situation, cabled the Foreign Secretary, Anthony Eden in London in April 1942 to warn Citrine 'not to expect either the AFL or the CIO to be very enthusiastic over Russia' and to 'take care to treat the AF of L and the CIO with equal consideration . . . Citrine should make it clear that his relations will be with the American movement as a whole'. Halifax added the observation that perhaps the visit should have been discouraged, but now judged that cancelling it would do more harm than good.[53] Evidently in the Washington embassy there were already intimations that the whole enterprise was miscued and likely to go awry either by inciting American hostility to the Soviet Union or by inciting the AFL and the CIO to detest each other even more. Citrine was cabled directly from Washington and warned of these twin dangers.[54] As Tawney reported to Attlee, 'The imminent visit of Citrine, who is to speak next week to the AF of L Executive on the Anglo-Russian Trade Union Committee, may have raised a new problem by launching an anti-Russian stunt in the press, for which some of the Hearst papers have already given the signal.'[55]

Citrine went to the United States in May and was decisively rebuffed by the executive of the AFL which wanted nothing to do with the Soviet Union,

judging that to become involved in such a labour alliance would direct general
and pervasive American hostility to communism onto the AFL itself. Many
in the American labour movement, in both organizations, also challenged the
very idea that Soviet trade unions were *free* trade unions. Tawney described
the panic of the AFL leadership on learning of the Anglo-Russian trade union
alliance in an image drawn from stage farce: 'It resembled the alarm of a sedate
bachelor on discovering that an elderly aunt had fallen in love with him, and
not content with that, insists on his receiving her disreputable acquaintances,
with the obvious intention of inveigling him to make a settlement in their
favour.'[56] The AFL also gave Sir Walter to understand 'that any official approach
by him to the CIO would be regarded as an unfriendly act'.[57] The AFL suggested
instead that together with the TUC they set up a separate 'Anglo-American
Trade Union Committee'; the AFL would, in this plan, have the sole right to
include other bona fide trade union bodies in the new organization. Recognizing
that the AFL intended to exclude the CIO, Citrine tried to change the terms of
this draft agreement in his negotiations with them (Tawney referred to 'the
insolently disingenuous phraseology' of the document on this matter) but the
AFL would not relent and some weeks later it was accepted by the General
Council of the TUC in London.[58] Before he left the United States, Citrine met
with Halifax and Tawney in Washington on 21 May to discuss the problems
and 'it was pointed out to Sir Walter that there were very strong objections to
the British TU movement setting up a joint committee with the AF of L alone,
to the exclusion of the CIO'.[59] Citrine also met with Roosevelt himself who was
apparently in favour of the AFL joining the Anglo-Soviet committee but with
the CIO as well.[60]

When it became clear that the outcome of Citrine's visit was an Anglo-
American Committee only encompassing the AFL, the reaction of the CIO
can be imagined: its leaders were resentful at being excluded from the original
discussions in the United States – Citrine had not even contacted them before
he arrived in New York let alone arranged to meet them – and 'extremely
indignant' at being excluded from the new organization and forced to wait
on the AFL's good graces for membership. This was a bad enough outcome in
the summer of 1942 for Tawney and the British government; but then Citrine
threatened to exacerbate American labour divisions still further by planning
to return to attend a meeting of the new Anglo-American Committee in late
September. As Tawney reported, 'Unless matters can be straightened out in
the interval, we must expect angry denunciations of the British attitude both

on the arrival of the TUC delegation for the meeting on the 23rd September and at the CIO convention in November.'[61] Such an outcome would have undermined all his efforts and those of the British embassy more generally to engender sympathy and support for the British. Tawney's advice to the Foreign Office was to postpone Citrine's second visit, at least until after the forthcoming Congressional elections. The incitement of anti-British feeling during the elections, which his presence would encourage, would only compound the growing public relations debacle.

Tawney's advice was taken and acted upon and the government postponed the visit of the five-strong delegation, including Citrine. As Eden wrote to Attlee on 19 August 1942, 'It seems a pity that when we have a person of Tawney's calibre in Washington to advise on labour matters, that advice is ignored by distinguished representatives of British Labour who visit the United States.'[62] The decision was taken by Halifax and endorsed by Eden on the grounds that 'British association with one section of American labor . . . might only increase internal American labor differences'.[63] Eden even wrote to Churchill about the situation and the decision to prevent Citrine from making further trouble across the Atlantic.[64] In answer to hostile questions to the Foreign Secretary in the House of Commons on 11 September about the affair, including from the Labour MP Manny Shinwell, Eden explained to MPs that 'in labour matters Lord Halifax had the benefit of the advice of Professor Richard Henry Tawney (of the University of London). The government is fully satisfied of the soundness of the advice'.[65] But Citrine himself demurred on this point: in a speech to the TUC annual conference at Blackpool which was then meeting 'he said he had no confidence in British representatives in Washington who were advising the British government in this matter'.[66] (He later wrote to Eden that the government had been 'unduly influenced' by advisors 'in whose competence to give advice on this question [the TUC] have little confidence'.)[67] Tawney may have taken some solace from the reaction from the floor of the TUC conference where Citrine was criticized for failing to make an open approach to the CIO, and more general comment in the press on the clumsy and antediluvian diplomacy of the TUC.[68] Though Citrine made subsequent efforts to bring American trade unions into collaboration with British and Soviet labour, he failed just as Tawney predicted. The AFL would have nothing to do with Russian trade unions, and the CIO would have nothing to do with the AFL while it was being patronized by both it and the TUC.[69]

The Tawneys returned to Britain at the end of the summer of 1942 and the decision may have been hastened by this complex and vaguely comical affair. Never had the TUC carthorses plodded so relentlessly towards odium, though this time on both sides of the Atlantic. Citrine's behaviour – his relentless path towards failure, criticism and diplomatic friction – might well have reminded Tawney of, and confirmed, those strictures on trades' unionists in the Labour Party that he had voiced in his 1939 lecture in Chicago.[70] Tawney's reports on the affair make very good reading and do not disguise his frustration with trade union leaders in both countries whose vanity, inflexibility and traditionalism made sensible cooperation impossible. Only the young and radical CIO, doing good work in the organization of ordinary workers in America, comes out with any dignity intact. At many points his prose seems to shout out loud the famous British cry of this era 'Don't they know there's a war on?' He found it difficult to fathom why at this crucial moment in the conflict, at the 'turning of the tide' when full production was the order of the day, trade union officials could not put sectarianism aside in favour of the national interest. In these circumstances – and he must have reflected on the irony at many moments – he found himself on the side of a former Foreign Secretary of the 1930s whom he had blamed for so many international ills, not least the war itself.

Before he left Washington, to be replaced by an official from the Ministry of Labour, Tawney received a telegram from Eden 'with which Mr Bevin wishes to be associated': 'Viscount Halifax has told me how much he appreciated having you and Mrs Tawney in Washington and having both your advice and contacts with American labour personalities available to him. Your experience of [the] present-day labour situation in America will be most useful to us on your return.'[71] Perhaps the most remarkable aspect of Tawney's sojourn in Washington was the unlikely working relationship he struck up with Halifax, the Conservative arch-appeaser of the 1930s. According to one of the diplomats in the embassy, William Clark, 'They were an odd couple . . . [but] they were fond of each other, they got on well together.' Clark credited Halifax and Tawney with doing more than anyone else, with the exception of Churchill, 'to persuade America . . . that Britain was in the war for fundamentally moral reasons'.[72] As it happens, theirs was a relationship forged in adversity: 5 days before Citrine's arrival in the US, Halifax had written a very uncomplimentary report to Eden on Tawney's work thus far in the embassy, complaining that he had done very little up to that point: 'what would be perhaps more useful and more suitable here than Tawney whose appeal is rather to university intelligentsia type[s] would be an official of the Ministry of Labour or a man of Civil Service type who has been in close and sympathetic touch with Labour and labour questions.'[73] Tawney had thought just the same thing, but he proved his worth in the end when dealing with Citrine. Not for the first time Lord Halifax had to revise his assessment of a man and a diplomatic situation.

By August 1942 Tawney felt he had done what he could for Anglo-American relations, and had no very strong desire to continue advising the British government on the American labour situation whether in London or Washington. Tawney was keen to get back to the debate in Britain on the future, and perform his fourth wartime service for the nation: assisting with the reform of secondary education. As he told one audience in Washington in 1941, 'We must spend, not less, but more on education, health, housing, and the establishment of security against the contingencies of life. We do not intend, therefore, to yield to the clamour for reduced taxation, but to maintain it and to use its proceeds for purposes essential to the general welfare.'[74]

In the darkest days of 1940 Lawrence Hammond had written to Tawney and had looked forward to the achievement of a decent school-leaving age: 'At the end of the war we ought to have as we had at the end of the last war a strong progressive spirit (we wasted a good deal of it then) and if the Labour Party is not quite incompetent we ought to get the age up to 16.'[75] Once returned to Britain, Tawney was soon repeating his familiar criticism of the Labour Party from the 1930s: that 'adequate preparations' for policies for peacetime were not being made and that 'no feelings exists that Labour is the alternative government, which will be able to take over at the end of the war.'[76] Ironically, it was the Beveridge Report on 'Social Insurance and Allied Services', written by his Liberal-supporting brother-in-law and oldest friend and published in December 1942, which caught the new mood of optimism as the war turned in favour of the allies, encouraging debate about the nature of post-war Britain, and invigorating Labour's thinking about the future. Jeanette wrote to her brother to congratulate him and also to explain that 'so many people are asking me to speak on your Report but I say that I am not up in its technical details.'[77] Educational reform was less technical than the provision of social security, and Tawney and many others had reached a view on what needed to be done years ago. Now, with the publication of a White Paper on Education in 1943 with which he broadly agreed, the struggle was about details: the principle of a coherent system of education from the age of 11 appeared to have been accepted. Tawney wrote to Temple in August 1943 with some notes on the white paper that he had written 'to clear up my own ideas', in which he welcomed its 'general conception'. The conversion of powers into duties within Local Education Authorities 'in respect of the provision of Nursery Schools, Medical Treatment and Meals and Milk'; the creation of 'a secondary system to serve all children consisting of schools varying in type, but "broadly equivalent" in respect of staffing, accommodation etc.'; the raising of the school-leaving age to 15 as soon as possible with 'its further extension at a later date to sixteen' and the establishment of 'young people's colleges, between 15 and 18' were 'reforms of genuine importance'.[78]

Tawney advised Temple that they should broadly accept and welcome the plans. But he worried over the timetable for implementation of these changes and the continuation of fees in publicly-funded Direct Grant schools. Fees were to be abolished in all other types of state-funded secondary schools. 'The effect', he wrote, 'will be to perpetuate the social divisions between different classes of secondary schools. Fees should be abolished in all secondary schools receiving public money', to make them truly open to all children on merit alone. Elite schools, subsidized by public funds, but which talented children from humble backgrounds could not attend because they lacked the means, had no place in the new state system. The provision that the school-leaving age be raised to 15 'as soon as possible after the war' and for 'a further extension at 16 at a later date' was all too vague, and he suggested an amendment that would set 16 as the leaving age within 4 years of it being raised to 15. (That it was not raised to 16 in his lifetime apparently 'infuriated him', and he had been dead for more than 13 years before it was extended for the further year in 1975.) Tawney noted that discussion in the white paper of 'compulsory part-time education' (day-release schemes from work), as well as adult education and access to university, was inadequate in each case. Nevertheless, he admitted that it was 'in most other respects, a striking document' and if the Bill to come were to be based on it 'it will give the country a far better educational system than it at present possesses'.

Tawney set about finding facts and canvassing opinions, writing to several Directors of Education in Local Education Authorities for information and ideas.[79] He became President of the Council for Educational Advance (CEA). This had developed from a WEA initiative in 1942 to create a standing committee of progressive educational bodies to lobby for change, and included representatives from the TUC, the Cooperative movement and the National Union of Teachers. Its stated aim was 'immediate legislation to provide equality of educational opportunity for all children, irrespective of their social or economic condition, in order to equip them for a full life and for democratic citizenship'. In its first year the Council for Educational Advance organized more than 200 meetings on educational reform, evidence in itself of the public interest in the subject.[80] Tawney wrote his pamphlet 'The Problem of the Public School' for the CEA, a variant on the larger article he published at this time, and he probably wrote its 'Notes on the Education Bill' in 1944 as well, for it bears his style. Here, in contrast to a letter to the Archbishop of Canterbury, and behind anonymity, Tawney could admit his discomfort, shared by the WEA and all progressive opinion, over the perpetuation of the 'system of Dual Control' which protected denominational schools and the continued role of the established church on governing bodies and in educational administration more generally. He also called for the building of new schools, attention to class sizes, free lunches, biennial medical inspections and equal funds, *pro rata*, for all LEAs. Tawney's letters in 1943 and 1944 expressed an almost febrile concern that an historic opportunity to reform secondary education would be missed or blown off course by special interests. When progressive opinion began to fear that the forthcoming white paper on Educational Reconstruction would not be sufficiently bold and comprehensive, and Tawney described himself as 'perturbed' in letters to Creech Jones for wider circulation among the Labour Party, Attlee wrote to assure him that there was 'no ground for any perturbation'.[81]

Soon after returning to Britain Tawney met with R. A. Butler and he led several delegations to the Board of Education in the succeeding months.[82] He could see that Butler was sincere in his commitment to educational improvement but, in his view, unconscionably slow and timorous. As Tawney wrote to Creech Jones in April 1943,

> I appreciate Butler's difficulties, but I am afraid that, if he goes on postponing his Bill, it & he may miss the psychological moment. He can overcome the strong opposition which he will meet in certain quarters only if he has strong public support. I think that so far he has it. But he cannot count on it indefinitely.

Tawney struck up a cordial and supportive relationship with the minister. Butler sent him a copy of the Norwood Report in August 1943 and, in his reply, Tawney raised with him the two most pressing issues from the White Paper, the continuation of fees in Direct Grant Schools and the absence of a definite timetable for the introduction of a school-leaving age of 16. But he was warmly in favour of the document: 'I greatly admire its comprehensiveness and vision and am glad that it has had a favourable reception.'[83] Butler sent him copies of the Education bill and the accompanying explanatory memorandum on the day they were published in December 1943, adding the comment 'Your influence & support have been outstanding. RAB.'[84]

For Tawney, because it infringed one of his most basic principles that money should play no part in education, the issue of the continuation of fees in Direct Grant Schools was almost as important as the school-leaving age. As he explained in a letter to the High Master of Manchester Grammar School, Douglas Miller, in January 1943, 'all secondary schools should be free in order that the choice between them be made on educational grounds, and not biased by the fact that some schools charge fees, and others do not.'[85] The WEA and some of Tawney's collaborators in educational reform wanted the abolition of the direct grant and the absorption of these schools into LEA control.[86] Tawney had not reached this conclusion but he did believe that 'all schools in a locality should work together with the LEA to improve the general educational system of that locality, and should accept the principle that all schools should be equally accessible to all sections of the population.'[87] In the following month when the debate continued in the columns of the *Manchester Guardian* Tawney contrasted the bad old days when a secondary education was 'an exceptional privilege accorded to a minority' who therefore paid, with the new situation in which it 'becomes one normal stage in the career of all children': what justification now existed 'for requiring them to pay fees?'[88] In the event, fees continued to be levied by Direct Grant Schools after the 1944 Education Act, and Tawney described it as 'a disreputable social ramp.'[89] He was far less willing to raise anything bearing on 'the religious question' in education, however. He feared that Roman Catholic Labour MPs would oppose the bill unless they could secure an increase in the public funds available to denominational schools for rebuilding after the war.[90] But that was a relatively minor matter: any wider opposition to the continued role of the denominations in the provision of secondary education was to be deterred: 'to throw that issue into the arena will give the reactionaries a golden opportunity to destroy the whole policy of the White paper. I think that would be insane.'[91]

Given his long and arduous struggle for secondary education, it was entirely appropriate that at a meeting of over 200 educational and social organizations, and local education authorities held on 12 February 1944 at the Kingsway Hall, London, at which Archbishop Temple also spoke, Tawney was given the honour of delivering the major address and introducing the resolution welcoming the second reading of the bill.[92] With caveats, as before, he called for its implementation:

> the Bill will give a more ample provision of nursery schools, school meals, more adequate care for the health of children, a universal system of secondary education of which the greater part will be free, a longer school life, the rudiments at least of a system of part-time education up to 18 to which must be added, if the promises of the Minister as to administration are fulfilled, better staffing and smaller classes in Primary schools and an end of the gross scandal of unsuitable and sometimes insanitary school buildings.[93]

The Butler Education Act was the culmination of Tawney's struggle since the Edwardian era to improve secondary education in England. In Tawney's view it did not educate children for long enough, nor did it abolish for all time the paying of fees for state-subsidized secondary education. That was not ended until 1975 when the 'direct grant' ceased. But the measure embodied the major requirements for a systematic approach to post-elementary education, always Tawney's major concern. He was only one of many to whom credit attached for this achievement, but he had done more than almost anyone to work through the issues and to persuade both the public and government of the absolute requirement to ensure education for all to a good standard through adolescence. A year later, in the victory of the Labour Party in the general election at the end of the war, Tawney could take pleasure in the election of several friends and former students, including Evan Durbin who was elected for Edmonton in north London.[94] Tawney was away in Moscow for part of the campaign, attending the 220th anniversary celebrations of the Soviet (Russian) Academy of Sciences as part of the British delegation, but he managed to return in time to speak for Durbin and also for the Labour candidate in his own constituency, Dr Santo Jeger. Both men were returned.[95] More than a hundred of the new intake of Labour MPs were connected to the WEA in some fashion, whether as students or tutors.[96] As he told an audience in Chicago in 1948, 'no less than one in three of the Labour members in the present House of Commons has taken part in its classes.'[97] That, also, was a measure of Tawney's success.

Last Things: 1945–62

Harry and Jeanette moved back into Mecklenburgh Square in the spring of 1947, having been offered a ground floor flat by their landlords, the Foundling Estate, at No. 26. It 'had been badly blitzed' and required extensive renovation before they could take possession.[1] Meanwhile Tawney continued at the LSE beyond the usual retirement age. Under the School's regulations, on reaching 60, members of the academic staff required formal permission to continue in post. Tawney was granted that in 1940 and reappointed to the age of 65.[2] During the academic year 1945–6 he was reappointed again at an increased salary – now £1,150 – for a further 3 years until 1949.[3] He undertook a limited amount of teaching, primarily of research students, and the University of London allowed him to hold the title of Professor of Economic History 'year by year'.[4] A final 2-year term followed at the School on a salary of £1,500 when he relinquished the chair and became Professor Emeritus.[5] Overall it must be accounted generous and considerate treatment indeed by the LSE.

Tawney's friends and colleagues hoped he would settle and write the great work he had always promised on seventeenth-century history, drawing together all his insights and existing essays into a new synthesis. In some accounts this was to have been a grand economic history of the age, in others 'a book on the great age of Puritanism and the Levellers in particular'.[6] T. S. Ashton was a younger colleague in economic history who cared for Tawney in numerous ways in his declining years. As he wrote to him in 1948, 'it would be a tragedy of scholarship (and of something more than scholarship in the narrow sense) if it was never finished'.[7] Sadly, it never was: Tawney, just shy of 65 at the end of the Second World War, was still as intellectually sharp as ever, but he was weary and the scale of the task was beyond him. As A. J. P. Taylor was reported to have said some years later, Tawney's unwritten works were among 'the lost masterpieces of the twentieth century'.[8] Instead, his last book, *Business and Politics Under James I*, published in 1958, was a less ambitious study of the financier, public servant and courtier of the early seventeenth century, Lionel Cranfield, Lord High Treasurer under James I. On hearing that his brother-in-law was reading it in early 1961, Tawney described it to him as

> a dull though informative work, which only a dislike of throwing up a job one had started induced me to complete. I began it from a guess that his papers would be instructive – as they are – but with a prejudice against their author as a capitalist on the make. I ended with a respect for a man who, without being over-scrupulous in business, was in courage and public spirit head and shoulders above the awful gang of courtly sharks and toadies with whom, as a minister of the Crown he was condemned to mix, and who sacrificed his career for the service of the state.[9]

Tawney wrote much the same to another correspondent at this time, adding 'I should have done better to have given it up a good many years ago and turned my hand to something more useful and readable.'[10] It remains a valuable and revealing study of the workings of early Stuart government and finance, balancing Tawney's more general and conceptual work on early modern economy and society.

During this period there was another major commission as well, though the fact that this book was never written was not Tawney's responsibility. At the end of 1948 the Passfield Trustees entrusted with the affairs of Sidney and Beatrice Webb asked Tawney to write Sidney's biography.[11] The Trustees included A. M. Carr-Saunders, the then Director of the LSE, Harold Laski and Margaret Cole. They recognized that Tawney was the most obvious and appropriate choice to write about someone he knew well in so many personal and professional capacities, and Tawney was willing, and he felt, able.[12] He engaged an assistant to begin collecting materials together under his direction. But he wrote to the trustees to explain that, given prior commitments, it would be 3 years before he could write the biography.[13] They took this to imply that he would not start work at all in these 3 years and withdrew their invitation, in itself an unsympathetic and disrespectful act towards their own first choice for the task.[14] On their side, with an eye to Tawney's age and health and their moral duty to preserve the Webbs' reputations, they were keen for him to start the project as soon as possible. Tawney had to explain that research had begun even if writing was delayed, and they reinstated him: as he asked, 'If the Trustees are good enough to think of me on other grounds the right person to undertake the Life, is a delay of eighteen months, however regrettable in itself, so insuperable an obstacle as to necessitate the withdrawal of the invitation made to me?'[15] But worse was to follow. A matter of weeks after this series of exchanges, Tawney discovered that one of the trustees, Margaret Cole, was meanwhile editing a series of essays on the Webbs, later published as *The Webbs and Their Work* in the summer of 1949, though she had never disclosed this to Tawney. He was told that it was to contain essays by very notable figures who knew the Webbs well, such as Shaw, E. R. Pease, who had been secretary of the Fabian Society, and Kingsley Martin, the longstanding editor of the *New Statesman*. He naturally felt that his own guns were being spiked and that these essays would detract from anything he published subsequently. As he then wrote to Carr-Saunders,

> It is one thing to be asked to undertake a piece of original work. It is quite another to be asked to work over again a subject already handled by other persons, and persons who, in addition to being celebrities, possess a more intimate knowledge of several aspects of it than I can claim. I am not willing to spend part of my remaining years of work in doing the latter. . . . It seems to me a question . . . whether, when they knew one of their number was already committed to the production of a book on the Webbs of the kind edited by Mrs Cole, they were really in a position to invite someone else to write Webb's *Life*, at any rate until the book in question had appeared and they and he had seen precisely what it contained.[16]

He also corresponded directly with Margaret Cole who defended her conduct on the grounds that her book was 'essentially ephemeral' and had to be rushed out before some of the contributors became too old or had died.[17] (Laski described the book as 'ungenial and fatuous' with the exception of the essay by Shaw, and historians would agree that it is a slight work).[18] Tawney did not back down, however: 'My assumption that a book about *The Webbs and Their Work* would have a bearing on Webb's life seems to cause you surprise. To me it appears to be an inevitable one.'[19] Tawney thus withdrew his services. As he wrote in one of his final letters to Carr-Saunders, 'one ought to undertake an important piece of work of the kind with confidence and zest, or not at all.'[20] He was plainly outraged by Margaret Cole's behaviour and had no confidence in the Trustees. The project died, and unfortunately, was never revived so that no full biography of Sidney Webb has ever appeared. Carr-Saunders, who had an unenviable position between his author, Tawney, and his fellow trustee, Margaret Cole, was sympathetic and encouraging towards Tawney throughout the exchanges of 1949 and, with some rather weak reinforcement from Laski, tried to persuade

Tawney to change his mind on several occasions. Tawney turned to old friends for advice such as Lawrence Hammond:

> I am 68. I am willing to do my best for Webb's memory if I have a clear field. I am not willing to fill up gaps in other people's work. If that is the proposition, as, in view of Mrs. Cole's book, it appears to be, I think that I am likely to be more useful in getting further with my own work. What is your view?

Giving his views of the affair, Tawney added for good measure that he thought that 'Mrs Cole has been sly and self-seeking and that the Trustees have been to blame in not telling me at the start that she had a book on the stocks and exactly what sort of book it was (I except from this statement Carr-Saunders, who has been kindness itself.)'. Hammond wisely told him to let it go: 'The world can have too much Webb . . . You could find some way of giving your view of him to the world which did not demand such labour and such a consumption of your time and energy.'[21] Tawney was too hurt and too battered by the affair to relent, and rightly declined on each occasion that Carr-Saunders asked him to reconsider. Perhaps the younger man would have coped better with such vexations, but Tawney in old age was more easily upset and demoralized and had not the resilience to carry on. There are grounds for wondering if Tawney would have had the strength to write such a biography in any case, as perhaps Hammond wondered, and reading his letters on the business raises the question of whether Tawney himself had confidence that he could see through such an arduous academic task. His withdrawal not only deprived us of a proper biography of Sidney Webb, but also deprived Tawney of the opportunity to reflect at length on the nature and course of British socialism. All his life he had measured his ideas by reference to those of the Webbs. He had the greatest respect for them, but he had once disagreed profoundly with the Fabian strategy. What would the mature Tawney have said in the 1950s, in retrospect, about those early disagreements in his *Commonplace Book*, about the subsequent development of the socialist cause and also about the effects on him of his alliance with Sidney Webb on the Sankey Commission?

Tawney never ceased to be a scholar, therefore, but was unable to complete any more large projects. He never ceased to engage with politics, either, and had trenchant, uncomfortable and revealing things to contribute until his very end. His attitude towards the Cold War reveals more about the man: his instinctual hostility to political dictation and his natural support for free expression and liberty of conscience – the positions adopted by those radical puritans and Levellers he so admired in the mid-seventeenth century – are both in evidence as, once more, he showed good political judgment in exacting times.

In 1948 anti-communism was close to virulent in American culture and politics. Yet when he went to lecture in Chicago in that year he was bold and direct in requiring of his audiences both freedom of speech and also an understanding of the communist position. In his first lecture he explained why the British had elected a Labour government in 1945 and isolated four crucial and enduring elements of Britain's democratic culture.[22] The first was the respect for consensus which took the form of parliamentary government. The second was 'a passion for compromise'. The third was the defence of individual rights 'of freedom of worship, speech and writing, meeting and combination'. He emphasized that in Britain fascists and communists had the right to say what they would: 'The attitude is broadly that nonsense is its own corrective, and that, in any case, the public has breathed the germs of it long enough to have become in this time immunised to them'. The fourth was 'the mentality which regards political opinions and activities as the private affair of the individual concerned'. Thus, in one of his examples, he explained that though the WEA was largely composed of public-minded socialists, it had been funded by governments of all political stripes. As one Conservative minister apparently told the House of Commons, 'the political opinions of teachers and students were no concern of his.'[23] Tawney was choosing his points and examples with care in order to make his audience reflect on current practice in their own society where many of these democratic virtues were in temporary abeyance.

In his third lecture Tawney asked for tolerance towards the Soviet Union and also much finer discrimination when faced with a range of democratic and socialist societies in Europe and elsewhere. After some broad opening points on the course of Russian and Soviet History, he disputed the idea that 'it is impossible for social and political systems based on antithetic conceptions of the nature and needs of man to live in peace in the same world.'[24] He dismissed vulgar and ignorant opposition to anything vaguely socialistic, and in support of his case vindicated the enhanced role of the state in western Europe as the agent responsible for the expansion of personal and social liberties. Though more a series of points than an argument, it was an effort to encourage just and non-hysterical assessments of the Soviet Union and west European socialism, noting that they were very different political entities, but each deserving of intellectual respect and engagement.

Tawney had no admiration for communism nor illusions about the Soviet Union, of course: only once did his scepticism slip towards the end of *Equality* where he counted among the achievements of the Russian Revolution 'the reconciliation of the racial minorities and agricultural reconstruction', neither of which occurred and both of which policies involved, in their failure, the deaths and forcible exile of millions of people.[25] In 1935, in conversation with Beatrice Webb, he had scorned the British Communist Party 'with its drawing room cult of violence'.[26] Its opposition to the Second World War after the Molotov-Ribbentrop Pact of August 1939 only multiplied his contempt. Rita Hinden the journalist and anticolonialist who edited a memorial volume of Tawney's essays under the title *The Radical Tradition* (1964) later attested that 'he had no illusions about the communist states, and would never have dignified them with the name "socialist"'.[27] But he was asking through these lectures that Americans try to understand more, both about the nature of their supposed adversaries and about the real strengths of their own democracy. Employing British examples, Tawney argued that these lay in the ability to absorb and overcome anti-democratic ideas in open and free debate.

Back in Britain he showed no tolerance for the 'despotic government' and 'police collectivism' of the Soviet system and praised the early Labour Party for keeping the communists out.[28] Yet he went further than mere condemnation of 'vituperation and cajolery': in a revealing lecture given in 1952 and entitled 'British Socialism Today', Tawney made plain his support for an Atlantic alliance against communism. The lecture was given to the University of London Fabian Society and subsequently published in the 1952 *Socialist Commentary*. The essay was reissued in 1960 by the Campaign for Democratic Socialism and then republished in the volume of posthumous Tawney essays, *The Radical Tradition*, where it was shorn of its sections on foreign policy.[29] All four versions are different, but in the first of them Tawney was outspoken on international affairs on which, he ventured

> I differ from many of my fellow socialists. I do not believe that capitalism is the sole cause of wars . . . I do not believe that national fears and ambitions are unimportant as compared with economic interests; on the contrary the terrifying power of the former seems to leap to the eye. I do not believe there is a distinctively socialist policy which at all times can be pursued . . . Finally, I do not believe that in the world of today, neutrality is practicable.[30]

Thus he went on to support an alliance with the United States, though without great enthusiasm: 'As a socialist, while I regret the necessity for it, I feel bound in existing circumstances to support it, since, whatever else such [Soviet] domination might involve, it would certainly mean the end of social democracy, both [in] Great Britain and outside it.'[31] And having called for a greater understanding of the Soviet Union when in Chicago, he called now for a greater understanding of the United States in London, pointing out that for the last 20 years Americans had been electing reforming presidents and now had a much stronger labour movement than before with which the British labour movement should develop close links.[32] A year later, in 1953, he declined to sign a public declaration, 'Let's Start Waging Peace', sent to him by Sir Richard Acland of the short-lived Commonwealth Party and signed by some of the most notable pacifists and disarmers of the era including Fenner Brockway, and the Revs Donald Soper (Methodist) and Mervyn Stockwood (Anglican). He could agree with all those elements of the memorandum concerning human rights, decolonization and increased international aid, he replied, but

> On the other hand, I could not . . . support a cut of unspecified amount in armaments expenditure, at least until I knew more about the course and results of the negotiations now, I understand, pending between the USSR and ourselves and other powers. Nor, until there are signs of the disappearance or further mitigation of the conditions which caused the North Atlantic Treaty Organisation, could I support the British withdrawal from it which I understand your Memorandum to recommend. In my view we are in a better position to prevent another war by remaining inside it than by withdrawing.[33]

Tawney found his own path through the Cold War, in other words, retaining his independence of judgment in all circumstances. His own views, as they emerge here, are consistent not only in relation to each other but also with his longstanding opinions. Communism was anti-democratic and worse; it was alien therefore to British traditions; and faced with difficult choices, an alliance with another democratic state, whatever its flaws, was preferable to any other position. As he told the Fabians, 'the association with [America] of Great Britain seems to me to be inevitable.'[34] But this did not obviate the requirement – a moral requirement to Tawney – to engage with the Soviet Union, try to understand it and find ways of coexistence with it. And it did not legitimate anti-democratic behaviour in western societies which feared subversion. False ideas were best met by better ideas in open debate within a free society.

In 1944–5 Tawney had dealings with the young historian Christopher Hill, later to forge a brilliant career working in Tawney's own period and to become Master of Tawney's old college. Hill was then working on Soviet affairs in the Foreign Office and corresponded with Tawney about a small group of Soviet historians of early modern Britain with whom contact had been made recently by the Moscow embassy. Cut off from British publications and the academic world outside since the early 1930s, Hill and Tawney discussed how they might be brought to England when the war was over.[35] Then, as that neared, it was Hill who helped organize Tawney's trip to Moscow for the meeting of the Academy of Sciences in July 1945.[36] Hill wrote to Tawney again in 1950 for another reason:

> The idea has been mooted, originally by a group of historians at London, of starting a new historical journal. The proposal originated in discussions between Marxists & non-Marxists there & the idea would be to have an agreed basis, what we have described as a "post-Tawney attitude" – i.e. accepting an economic approach, though not specifically Marxist, & dealing (unlike [the] *Economic History Review*) with something wider than economic history (history of ideas e.g.) . . . So you are the person we should most of all like to have on the editorial board, if that is not too much of a burden for you.

Hill had erred in his reference to the *Economic History Review*, to which Tawney, as a founder, was deeply committed. Tawney also queried what he took to be a distinction Hill was making between economic and other types of history, preferring, he wrote, 'that articles on economic organisation and . . . on more speculative matters . . . appeared together in the same journal'.[37] But correspondence with Postan raised another objection to the journal which eventually became *Past & Present*: 'The names you mention as members of the editorial board' wrote Postan, 'are nearly all Communists and fellow-travellers . . . It goes without saying that they will try to get as many non-communists to co-operate as they can, and occasionally they may even print a non-Marxist or anti-Marxist article. However I agree with you that it's most likely to become one of the CP's satellite bodies.'[38] Some of the figures named by Hill in his letter as involved in the new venture – he himself, Edward Thompson and Rodney Hilton – were members of the Communist Party History Group. In other cases Postan was probably mistaken.

This may be set beside Tawney's critical review for an unknown publisher at this time of Eric Hobsbawm's manuscript entitled 'Fabianism and the Fabians 1884–1914' based on his Cambridge doctorate.[39] Tawney noted several factual errors and the neglect of important themes such as the development of the Webbs' ideas over their long lifespans, and their study of English local government. But Tawney suspected something else: 'Mr Hobsbawm's criticisms of their interpretation of Socialism would have gained in effectiveness if he had taken more trouble to convince the reader that he had, before making them, made a serious effort to understand what it meant to its authors.' Tawney disliked the attitude adopted towards good and true people: 'He has for some reason, to write in a patronising tone, as of one possessing a priori authoritative knowledge of the truth and correcting lesser mortals in the light of it' – surely a sideswipe at Hobsbawm's Marxist-inspired critique of English Edwardian collectivism. There was a lack of 'respectful reference' to the views of his subjects: 'It is regrettable that a clever writer should also, at times, be slick, superficial and pretentious.' He particularly disliked Hobsbawm's comparison of Beatrice Webb to St Teresa. Hobsbawm's views on the Webbs and Fabianism were eventually published in an essay which was indeed dismissive of these middle-class reformers.[40] No doubt Tawney was moved by personal motives to criticize the work: he had known the Webbs intimately and could not agree with Hobsbawm's portrait of them. But it seems highly likely that Tawney also read his criticisms of the Webbs as a Marxist critique of a type of bourgeois reformism which the Webbs and their ilk – and Tawney himself – represented to this ideological point of view. And Tawney disagreed not only with Hobsbawm's interpretation but also with the application of party norms and party ideology to people who had laboured so intently for the good of fellow citizens.

In short, Tawney was suspicious of Marxists in English academic life and cut himself off from some of those who became the next generation of social and economic historians, distrusting not only their politics but also their intellectual honesty. Many contemporary historians around Tawney, and certainly the wider circle of his colleagues at the LSE in the interwar period, were socialists. But few if any took inspiration from Marxism, let alone from the Communist Party of Great Britain or the communist movement more generally. He strongly suspected not only that some of the next generation could not be included in domestic traditions of historical writing and social reform but also that they were seeking to subvert those traditions. He would have none of it, and may have underestimated their genuine regard for pioneers of social and economic history like himself. One effect of their emergence, however, was to limit the impact of Tawney's historical writing beyond the 1960s. Whatever their debts to Tawney as signalled in 1950 by Christopher Hill, the next generation wrote British History under the influence of different authorities. Tawney's focus on the economic and social history of classes, which he had written without reference to Marxism, may have continued to be influential and attract attention. But *Religion and the*

Rise of Capitalism ceased to be read, its appeal to non-material forces seeming antique and quaint alongside a new wave of books and articles from the late 1950s influenced in varying degrees by historical materialism.

Tawney also found himself at odds with the spirit, some of the policies of, and some of the leaders of the Labour Party in the last decade of his life, though that was hardly new in his case. He complained to Creech Jones in 1954 that he was

> all for a frank statement of differences of opinion; but I have the feeling that malignant back-biting plus the effusion of hot air, have in the last year or two gone too far. There are quarters in which it seems to be thought a proof of socialist virtue to create suspicion of whatever leading socialists say and do.[41]

At the end of 1960 Rita Hinden found him 'in a great state about the party, tremendously critical of the *New Statesman*, and of the way the trade unions are behaving, of all the seekers after place and power'.[42] He frequently criticized the Labour left, though not from any deliberate and systematic positioning against Labour radicals on his part, but because he thought them wrong on specific questions. A man who had chosen to fight for his country and believed in facing down aggression was never going to accept unilateral nuclear disarmament, nor the pacifism which in many cases lay behind it. On the subject of unilateralism he wrote to Creech Jones to decry 'the cataract of nonsense which is being poured forth by the so-called "Left"'.[43] To Rita Hinden he had written that unilateralism 'would not only be the death of British Socialism, but would also greatly *increase* the probability of atomic war'.[44] He broadly took the position of a Gaitskellite, which, in view of his friendship and support for Gaitskell since the 1920s, is unsurprising. When, in 1953, the *New Statesman* joined a campaign against Gaitskell emanating from the Bevanite left of the Labour Party, Tawney wrote in his support, though his letter went unpublished.[45] Two years later Tawney welcomed Gaitskell's election to the leadership of the Labour Party, delighted that 'one whose courage, in addition to other qualities I admire, is to be in command'.[46] He had no time for Gaitskell's major adversary in the party and a defeated candidate for the leadership in 1955, Nye Bevan, with whom he 'was often in disagreement'.[47] Later he allowed the primary Gaitskellite vehicle, the Campaign for Democratic Socialism which was established in 1960, to publish one of the versions of his essay *British Socialism Today*, which had 'been further amended by the author'.[48] But he also differed from Gaitskell, notably over his attempt to remove Clause IV – that committing the Labour Party to public ownership – from the party's constitution after the election defeat in 1959. On the day after Tawney's memorial service Lena Jeger wrote to Creech Jones and recalled that

> what puzzled Tawney was why anybody should want to change the constitution. "Of course you must change your programme", he kept saying, "but why are all these young men wanting to change the constitution? Who are they anyhow? Of course Sidney Webb and the others never meant clause 4 to mean nationalising every little shop on the corner, or the chap I know in the Cotswolds who has a little loom and weaves all my scarves . . ." We discussed this several times and he never wavered.[49]

Tawney did recognize, however, that the form in which major British industries had been nationalized was defective because public ownership since 1945 had failed to enthuse workers and provide them with a sense of their personal responsibility for the success of socialized enterprise: 'The fact remains that we have not yet taken with sufficient seriousness the problem of creating conditions which cause the rank and file of industry to feel they are responsible partners.'[50]

Years later when, in 1983, the two contenders for the leadership of the Labour Party were both freely quoting Tawney as their bible, and *The Guardian* jested that perhaps Tawney should become the next leader of the Labour Party, Lena Jeger, who had been his MP for the last decade of his life, felt it necessary to lay out his later political beliefs in a letter to the newspaper. He was never in favour of nuclear disarmament: 'The patriotic old wounded soldier from the Somme was always contemptuous of those of us who were in CND, and he strongly supported Gaitskell's "Fight, fight and fight again" speech.' He 'never accepted that conference decisions should overrule the judgement of the Parliamentary Labour Party or individual conscience'. He also rejected the use of block votes in the Labour Party conference as a negation of democracy and rejected decisions based on composited resolutions.[51] As Tawney had put it in his own words, 'They sweep together great things and small: nationalise land, mines and banking in one sentence and abolish fox hunting in the next.'[52] In truth he was frustrated by the pettiness of the party when it was out of power in the 1950s and often told his own MP 'that obsessions about who was leader belonged more to the Nazis than to democratic socialists'.[53] When one of his old students from the original Longton Class wrote to him in a letter expressing classic Christian Socialist principles, he replied that he wished 'the Labour Party, of which I shall continue to be a member whatever its momentary imbecilities, were more on the lines you indicate, than at the critical moments it is apt to be. I console myself with the reflection that at bottom, the rank and file are much better than are the orators who profess to represent them.'[54] And there is a point to another story Lena Jeger collected and saved about Tawney being canvassed in Mecklenburgh Square at the 1959 election by a 'keen young socialist' who returned to the ward room somewhat confused:

> Crumby old boy at number 21. I asked him, very politely, if he was Labour. He said he was Socialist. I kept asking if he was Labour and he kept saying he was Socialist. "Then I put it to him straight and I said, 'What I really want to know is are you voting for Mrs Jeger?'" And he said, "Yes, of course". So I said, "Then you are Labour" and he said "I'm a Socialist". So I put him down doubtful. You can't be too careful.[55]

Tawney's socialism was enduring and in a very real sense above party. It was certainly above a bickering and fractious party, as it had become by the end of the 1950s. In truth, though loyal to the very end, for most of his life he had been frustrated by the Labour Party. At the end of his life Tawney saw himself as steadfast and consistent in positions long held in the party, and to historical lessons of the 1930s which could not be ignored and should not be forgotten: it was, in his view, the Labour Party which had changed.

By the 1950s Tawney was only too well aware that his day was done – in the debate over secondary education and in so many other ways he was gradually losing touch. With characteristic wit he replied to one well-wisher in the following terms: 'Thank you for comparing me with the Bible. If I resemble it, the only likeness is that nobody nowadays believes in either.'[56] There were the deaths of friends to cope with – Temple and the Webbs in the 1940s; Wadsworth in the 1950s for whom Tawney gave the memorial address at a service in St Dunstan's, Fleet Street; Jimmy Mallon just a few months before Tawney in 1961. As Jeanette wrote to Will in 1953, 'So many old friends have died lately that I feel soon I shall have outgrown my generation.'[57] There were illnesses to contend with as well, though they put them to good use. Jeanette had an abdominal aneurysm, a relatively rare condition, diagnosed in 1953, and both of them became objects of medical interest, volunteering 'for the students to pass their finals by diagnosing our ailments. What surprises me about it [is] that we are treated with great friendliness and kindness [and] given 7/6 for lying in bed in a ward for two hours.'[58] But Jeanette's condition forced them to give up Rose Cottage, which they could no longer maintain, and to sell it in 1955. Tawney still went there from time to time 'because the young man to whom we sold it, a comparatively well-to-do Fabian – is kind enough to ask me to pass a night, or nights there.'[59] On those trips he became more and more agitated about the degradation of the rural environment caused by intensive farming and the motor car, lamenting 'the destruction which is taking place in my dear county of Gloucestershire . . . If only the Government would let pedestrians arm themselves, we would settle these brutes, the motorists, in a week.'[60] Indeed, his detestation of cars became a theme in his correspondence in his final years. He felt out of place in hitherto familiar surroundings. At a gaudy in Balliol he knew only 'one or two Dons'. For the rest, 'My impression was that they were mostly prosperous business people who were a good deal younger than me and who were pleased to have the chance for showing off their cars for motoring to London and Oxford and back. Perhaps that is spiteful, but then I hate cars as I do most other so-called mechanical improvements.'[61] Sadder still, the great campaigns of his youth had been forgotten or were simply misunderstood. Lena Jeger told the story of Tawney once meeting a young woman doctor who was living in Mecklenburgh Square. He pointed to No. 45 and said, 'That is the house where Jimmy Mallon and I worked for the Anti-Sweating League.' 'What', asked the woman 'is wrong with sweating?' Tawney replied kindly, 'That is the measure of progress between your generation and mine. One generation and you do not even know what the word means.'[62] In a circularity which Tawney would have appreciated only too well, through the 1950s he would spend a day or two at the St Katherine Foundation in the East End, a mission and community centre in Limehouse run by the charismatic churchman and Christian Socialist, Father St John Beverley Groser (1890–1966), to whom Tawney became very close.[63] Groser recalled Tawney sitting and listening to the problems of local residents for hours on end.[64] He had left the East End half a century before to find industrial England; he returned to its problems at the end of his life.

Mecklenburgh Square proved the cause of considerable difficulty and Tawney was drawn into a long campaign there with the then MP, Dr Santo Jeger, husband of Lena Jeger who succeeded him in the seat after his death, to stop their landlords, the Foundling Estate, from turning the whole site, which had been badly bombed, into a grand hostel for overseas students from the Commonwealth and the United States using the National Thanksgiving Fund for the purpose.[65] In the event a compromise was struck and William Goodenough House still left two sides of the square intact for local residents.[66] In the process of negotiations and reorganization the Tawneys were moved in 1951 from no. 26 to no. 21 where they occupied the ground-floor maisonette. Though this was not initially to their liking, they made the best of it and it became Tawney's home – his third in Mecklenburgh Square – until his death. The blue plaque commemorating his residence in the square is outside this, his last home there. He was a well-loved sight in the Square, seen more often now than in the past when his many commitments kept him away from home. Living above the Tawneys at no. 21 were a married couple named Evans. Mr Evans recalled that in the summer Harry and Jeanette would sit in the square and watch the students play tennis. As for Tawney in old age

> He had a very fine head of – er – silvery white hair, a trim moustache, and a fresh complexion. And he carried himself in such a way that the arms were slightly away from his body, and er – this characteristic walk often struck me when I looked out of the window . . . I think perhaps my most vivid memory of the Professor will be always the back view of this great man going off to post letters. His head held erect, his back very straight, and his arms held slightly away from his body like a penguin.[67]

There were celebrations and commemorations throughout his last decade. Tawney took especial pleasure in the honorary D. Litt which Oxford awarded him in 1950, almost certainly oblivious of his determined efforts to reform the university in the first two decades of the century. Even had the corporate memory of the university been that long and accurate, Tawney's subsequent achievements outweighed any ill-feeling on either side. In any case, Tawney had never been blind to Oxford's merits: as he had written much earlier, 'the affection with which its sons regard that great institution is sometimes mingled with exasperation.'[68] The Warden of All Souls and noted historian of Russia, Humphrey Sumner, found the appropriate words with which to inform him:

> You are loaded with so many honorary degrees that you will probably scarcely notice one more. But we do here, and you will know well enough with what very special pleasure your degree is hailed in Oxford – including, I happen to know, particularly by certain people who would not agree with you politically. *It is presumptuous to congratulate you: instead we congratulate ourselves.*[69]

The Tawneys stayed at the Oxford home of the Regius Professor of Modern History, Vivian Galbraith. After the ceremony in the Sheldonian Theatre there was lunch in All Souls, the Encaenia Garden Party, and dinner in Christ Church where Tawney sat next to his former boss in Washington, the earl of Halifax. He was asked to give the address at the dinner and tried to evade the responsibility but as the Dean of Christ Church, John Lowe, told him, 'I am sure we should all prefer to see and listen to one of the most distinguished of living historians rather than anyone else.'[70] Tawney began his speech recalling that the last time he dined in Christ Church, some 30 years before, he had met one of the university's more august personages and explained to him that he lectured at the LSE. 'Oh yes, of course, the London School of Economics – one of those places like Selfridges, isn't it?' Remembering his time in Oxford he described himself as one 'who, when an undergraduate, preferred to the meretricious vulgarity of an ostentatious first in Schools the dignified mediocrity of an unpretentious second . . .' Reflecting on the experience, he judged as most significant 'the influence on character and imagination of the total impression made by Oxford herself . . . When I consider what Oxford meant to me and my friends, it is less the formalities of an academic education than the influence of these priceless imponderables that I first recall.'[71]

Tawney had been elected a fellow of the British Academy in 1934 and a member of the American Philosophical Society in 1942 while working in the United States. He received honorary degrees from Manchester and Paris in 1941 and 1945 respectively. More followed after Oxford in 1950: Sheffield (1953), London (1953), Melbourne (1955), Birmingham (1957) and an honorary fellowship of the LSE in 1958. His 5-month visit to Melbourne was especially memorable for Tawney and for the historical community in Australia. It coincided with state elections in Victoria and an almighty split in the Australian Labor Party, and Tawney 'couldn't get enough of' it. Every evening he attended another political meeting, accompanied by students whose job it was to keep him out of trouble. 'On one occasion, during a particularly exciting gathering in a little church hall in Carlton, a woman threatened Tawney with an umbrella after his mellifluous voice, exclaiming "Splendid, splendid!", echoed through a room otherwise filled with working-class Australian vernacular of the rough-hewn variety.'[72] Chairs flew, missing Tawney but landing on his student-minder, later the historian of nineteenth-century Britain, F. B. Smith, who bears the scar to this day.[73]

At the end of 1951 Tawney attended a reunion of the surviving members of his first Longton class in the place where it had met originally, the Sutherland Institute, Stone Road.[74] On his 80th birthday there was a luncheon in his honour at the LSE, and a dinner for him, largely organized by Arthur Creech Jones and laid on by the Labour Party in the House of Commons, to which 120 came. They included politicians – Attlee, Dalton, Jim Callaghan and George Brown; two General Secretaries of the TUC, Vic Feather and George Woodcock (the business with Citrine in 1942 having been well and truly forgotten); historians, including Maurice Ashley, T. S. Ashton and Lucy Sutherland; WEA colleagues and former students; and also Margaret Cole, with whom relations had been restored. Many people sent their apologies, including R. A. Butler, by now Chancellor of the Exchequer, who recalled referring to Tawney affectionately as 'Mulliga', as in the Anglo-Indian dish from the Raj, mulligatawny soup.[75] Attlee spoke at the dinner and thanked Tawney 'for having kept before us the highest ideals, reminding us that what we are working for is a change in human nature and the building of a real socialist society'. Tawney gave a speech calling on the party to put more effort into the political education of the public and of socialists in particular: 'I should like to see a much more real effort on the part of the Labour Party to give more instruction.'[76] He reverted to the evening long ago when he had first met the Webbs and walked off with John Burns's hat. And in talking about Sidney and Beatrice, he explained that it had always been impossible to quarrel with them. 'They waited until you had finished what you had to say, and then continued as if you had not spoken.'[77] A Tawney testimonial fund was collected for the occasion, running to several hundred pounds, made up of donations from his friends and well-wishers, and of a £100 each from big trade unions like the National Union of Mineworkers, the Iron and Steel Trades Confederation, the Transport and General Workers Union and the General and Municipal Workers. He was not forgotten in Rochdale from where the Rochdale and District Weavers, Winders, Beamers, Reelers and Doublers' Association sent £15.[78] A brief biographical memoir was also composed by several of his friends – his younger colleague at the LSE, Richard Titmuss, his research student F. J. Fisher, and J. R. Williams – for his birthday celebrations, *R. H. Tawney: A Portrait by Several Hands*. Fisher also edited a festschrift in Tawney's honour – *Essays in the Economic and Social History of Tudor and Stuart England* – to which pupils and admirers, including Joan Thirsk, Ralph Davis, Robert Ashton, Gerald Aylmer, Donald Pennington, Lawrence Stone and Christopher Hill, contributed essays on the period Fisher described as 'Tawney's Century'.[79] A portrait in oils was painted of Tawney by Claude Rogers, which hangs in the LSE and which was subscribed to by figures as varied as R. A. Butler, the philosopher Karl Popper, Hugh Gaitskell and G. D. H. Cole.

Tawney had become that rare thing indeed, a national treasure. Islington borough council named a block of flats on Highbury Hill 'Tawney Court' in 1959. In Stoke-on-Trent there was a Tawney Crescent named after him. In 1960 the University College of North Staffordshire, later Keele University, named its first arts teaching building after him.[80] Balliol College founded a Tawney Society in 1958 'devoted to the study of social problems' and a young Steven Lukes, its secretary in Michaelmas 1960, wrote to Tawney to congratulate him on his 80th birthday.[81] Perhaps it reminded Tawney of the similar society he and Beveridge had created in 1902 in Balliol. The most moving of the many tributes he received at the end of 1960 came from WEA students and associates. One student, who admitted that he had never even met Tawney, wrote in gratitude and affection 'regarding you as being in the direct line of the Great Teachers'.[82] Another, Victor Cohen from Chingford, had not seen him for 40 years:

> I was not young myself, in the early twenties, but I was at once moved by your integrity and modesty. I asked you to speak to a combined WEA class I was then running and your remarks were as incisive as they were reasoned and friendly. You were good enough to send me cards from Moscow and Washington and these I still treasure . . . In an age when we have saught (sic) to raise the standard of living you have contributed to raise the quality of life . . . I am very grateful to you and feel honourd (sic) at having the pleasure of knowing you.[83]

Tawney had not been closely involved with the affairs of his own family but after the Second World War he found himself taking on responsibilities for his sisters. Mil, to whom he was closest, had died in 1947, and Margaret in 1948. Tawney then found himself drawn into the affairs of Agnes and Mary. Agnes had been living in a hotel in Frimley, Aldershot, but in the mid-1950s she was running out of money and her unpaid bills were being sent to Tawney. The solution Tawney sought was for her to join their sister, Mary, in a nursing home in Chertsey where the fees were considerably lower. But Agnes would not budge and Tawney had to arrange for new terms at the hotel. Even though the costs overall came down, his contribution to her fees went up to £120 per annum which he could ill-afford.[84] Meanwhile he continued his longstanding support of his institutionalized brother Stephen.[85] Feeble now in body as well as mind, in 1959 Stephen was moved from the asylum to the elderly men's ward in the Holloway Sanatorium.[86] Tawney was fortunate that the long-serving Assistant Secretary and Accountant at the LSE, Mr H. C. Scriven, was a patient and faithful assistant to him as he grappled with the technicalities of annuities and pensions. Rather than simply the effects of old age, it would seem that Tawney was a genuine innocent who needed help with his tax return and advice about investments. Sadly, these did not stretch far enough to give him a comfortable retirement. Though his salary had always been respectable, their outgoings on rent for a sizeable flat in the centre of London, on good causes like the WEA, and on Jeanette's fancies, left little over to be saved for old age. Tawney's pension from the LSE was only about £500 a year. In truth, it doesn't seem as if Tawney paid much attention to his finances which may not be that surprising. In 1951 he attempted a snapshot of their financial situation on his retirement and concluded gloomily that they did not have enough to get by and that 'it is quite out of the question to keep both the cottage and 26 Mecklenburgh Square after July 1951.'[87]

Through the 1950s he was given financial assistance from a number of sources. First, entirely unannounced, came a research grant from the Nuffield Foundation of £500 a year for 3 years from 1951 'to assist you in completing your proposed studies on the social and economic history of England in the seventeenth century.'[88] Then in 1956 came further assistance from two sources: the Simon Research Fund at the University of Manchester made him a similar grant of £500 a year for 3 years to which no conditions applied, and then an offer of a pension of £250 per annum to cease on the second death out of Harry and Jeanette from the newspaper proprietor and supporter of good social causes, David Astor.[89] Astor called it 'a private arrangement.'[90] Then in 1958 came further private support from Ernest Simon, Lord Simon of Wythenshawe, whose wife Sheena Simon had been Tawney's co-worker in the cause of educational reform:

> I am sorry to hear from Ashton that the landlords are putting up your rent and that you may be forced to leave your house in Mecklenburgh Square . . . I understand that you are comfortable in Mecklenburgh Square, with your faithful housekeeper and all your books and belongings round you, and that a move would be an infernal nuisance. If I am rightly informed that your pension etc. is not enough to enable you to carry on at Mecklenburgh Square, I wonder whether you would let me help? The way to do it would obviously be by a covenant for 7 years.[91]

And Simon organized such an arrangement at £500 a year for 7 years 'or for as long as you or I are both alive'. Tawney did not apply for any of these grants or gifts. It is likely, however, that it was known in certain academic and political circles that he was struggling financially, and the possible intermediary linking Tawney to foundations and wealthy liberal individuals was his good friend T. S. Ashton, now himself in retirement in Blockley in the Cotswolds, who oversaw Tawney's affairs and welfare. Those who knew Tawney may well have found it intolerable that someone who had fought his whole life to bring decency to the lives of others should himself struggle at his end. Tawney's friends rallied round.

Jeanette died on 20 January 1958 at their home after a brief illness which had not been thought to be serious. She had been weakened by chronic conditions and the end came more swiftly than Tawney had expected: as he wrote to Lena Jeger, 'Though my wife had been far from well for some time, it was only last week that we realised how ill she was.'[92] Her funeral was at their local church, St Bartholomew's in Gray's Inn Road, and she was buried in Highgate cemetery on 24 January. At Lena Jeger's suggestion, somewhat later a cherry tree was planted in Mecklenburgh Square in her memory.[93] There were warm obituaries of her in *The Times* and *Manchester Guardian*, the latter piece almost certainly written by Jeger. The former recalled her style of 'ample disorder' but added that she 'had a vitality of thought and feeling which gave an unusual quality to everything she did'.[94] Jeger admitted that she had 'suffered the disability of being thought of too often as either Professor Tawney's wife or Lord Beveridge's sister'.[95] The most interesting and informative memoir was written by Ashton for the *LSE Magazine*. He recalled that 'her home was always open to her husband's pupils and colleagues: and she had a special place in a group of brilliant young scholars and social reformers whose exploits have become part of the legend of the School.' She liked hats, parties, gossip and bargains ('not all of which, it must be admitted, stood the test of time'). 'Everything she did was on a lavish scale – whether it was a matter of household supplies, her wardrobe, or her benefactions.' Ashton also noted that 'there was a streak of mischief in her make-up.'[96]

Tawney struggled on after his wife's death but his friends worried about his self-neglect. They bought him gifts – a wireless, a comfortable armchair, brandy and sherry, a fountain pen and stationery – and there was talk of taking him in his last year on a cruise to Greece, to which this classicist had never been, or on holiday to the South of France, using the proceeds of the Tawney testimonial fund for it. His cleaner and help, Mrs Lucy Rice 'does a tremendous lot for him, but it is still not as much as is necessary'.[97] She was devoted to him and Tawney left her a thousand pounds in his will. Richard Rees found it 'both irritating and exasperating, the way Tawney seemed incapable of taking the most elementary precautions or care of himself'.[98] Lena Jeger, who, as a near neighbour in Mecklenburgh Square probably did most to help him, drew attention to his loneliness.[99] As she wrote to Creech Jones in August 1960, 'He came to dinner here last week – I feel he is ageing very fast now.'[100] Creech Jones, still a Labour MP, wrote to ask for the assistance of the LSE in getting him more domestic help or new accommodation:

I see him from time to time at his home in Mecklenburgh Square, and I always leave feeling completely depressed with the very little which is done for him in respect of improving his physical comforts, and in giving him the care and attention he needs in the last years of his life. I feel that something special should be done for him.[101]

But the LSE, which had always done the best by Tawney, had no suitable premises, nor had University College, London to which Sir Sydney Caine, the LSE's Director, also applied.[102]

Tawney remained in Mecklenburgh Square until almost the very end. Over the new year of 1962 he caught a cold and his doctor telephoned to Rees to tell him what he already knew, that Tawney needed to be moved and cared for. 'The doctor says, rightly, I am quite sure, that he is now permanently unable to cope.'[103] As Rees then wrote to his nephew, 'I am hoping, though without much confidence, to persuade him to go to a nursing home for a few weeks. But that won't solve the long term problem . . . he prefers to carry on with his present rather perilous way of life.'[104] Lena Jeger took up the story for the readers of the *New Statesmen*: Rees and others were successful and Tawney was persuaded to go into a nursing home in Fitzroy Square in Bloomsbury on Saturday 13 January. There was no diminution at all in his mental faculties. He took with him *War and Peace* – an appropriate choice for a man sometimes compared to Tolstoy – and also two novels by Stanley Weyman, the author during the late-Victorian and Edwardian period of many cloak-and-dagger historical romances.[105] (Tawney would surely have appreciated Oscar Wilde's recommendation of Weyman's books as first-rate reading for convicts).[106] When Lena Jeger went to visit him he reminded her 'that Shaw had lived just along the road from where he now found himself'. Tawney died 'very quietly in his sleep' on 15 January 1962.[107] His last public act had been to sign a letter to *The Times*, co-signed by some of his former coadjutors from the 1930s, which was published on 2 January, calling for the abolition of the death penalty.[108]

Tawney was buried after a Church of England service in the chapel in Highgate cemetery on 24 January 1962.[109] 'Only a few of those closest to Prof Tawney were at Highgate . . . when he was buried at his wife's side. In spite of the high wind and rain . . . there was a touch of the quiet country churchyard in the Tawneys' corner under the tall poplar trees'. The priest officiating, the Rev Gordon Huelin, who had been in charge of St Bartholomew's, Gray's Inn Road 'reminded friends of the devout, practising Christianity of Tawney, who, until recently, regularly attended 8 o'clock communion in all winds and weathers'.[110]

His memorial service followed soon afterwards on 8 February 1962 at St Martin's-in the-Fields in Trafalgar Square in London. The lesson was from

Ecclesiasticus xliv, verses 1–15: 'Let us now praise famous men and our fathers that begat us.' Psalm 15 was also an appropriate choice:

Lord, who shall rest in Thy tabernacle?
Or who shall rest in Thy holy hill?
Even he that leadeth an uncorrupt life;
And doeth the thing which is right;
And speaketh the truth from his heart.

Tawney's God was thanked for 'his life and work, for his strength of character and courage, his power of mind and imagination, his hunger for truth and justice, his integrity and friendliness'.[111] Hugh Gaitskell was asked to give the Address but felt unqualified and was initially reluctant, suggesting instead Father Groser who was Tawney's 'intimate friend'.[112] But coached by Creech Jones, he spoke simply and well in a speech in which he drew attention to Tawney's combination of passion and learning. He recalled meeting him for the first time in 1926 amidst the detritus of his study in Mecklenburgh Square and paid tribute to his achievements in history, education and socialist philosophy. Paying tribute also to his strength of character and also his occasional ruthlessness, he described Tawney as 'the best man I have ever known.' But perhaps the finest tribute came from one who knew him more intimately than anyone, Lucy Rice, his housekeeper:

I feel a great loss about all this – as besides being a wonderful employer – he was a very great friend. I can only thank God I was able to carry out Mrs. T's wish and always look after him to the end. After 14 years a great chapter in my life has suddenly ended.[113]

Conclusion: Politics, Reputation and Style

After his death there were many tributes and encomiums to Tawney. *The Times* described him as 'a scholar of rare and luminous quality . . . a lover of learning and the humanities, a dreamer of social justice and equality, of generous mind, whose reserve only friendship could penetrate.'[1] To *The Guardian*, 'he had an amplitude of spirit which accounted for the universality of his appeal.'[2] Herbert Butterfield, the historian and Master of Peterhouse in Cambridge, wrote to the Director of the LSE to explain that in his college 'we always felt that no other great man ever gave such a tug at our affections.'[3] To Postan, indeed, his teacher had been 'the most impressive man I've ever met' and 'the greatest living Englishman'.[4] Thomas Ashton celebrated 'his insight, his kindliness, his courage, and most of all his humility'.[5] But there were contrasting images of him in his last years. The obituary in *The Guardian* pictured the happy warrior at the end of his campaign:

> Tawney lived to see the victory of most of the things he had fought for: the minimum wage, the raising of the school leaving age, the extension of workers' education, the Labour party in office or in strong Opposition, the rise of his subject to full academic status. One thought of all this as one saw him recently resting after a conference of scholars, many of them his own pupils. He sat back, humming softly, happy as a cat in the sun. The warrior of many fronts was at peace with himself and, in the end, not too badly at odds with the world.[6]

When Sir Stanley Unwin asked him to rewrite *Equality* in 1949, Tawney had been able to enumerate those aspects of social life in Britain that had changed in the 20-year elapse since the book had been written, including the partial implementation of 'the industrial programme' he had laid out in one chapter of the book, and 'the expansion of the social services urged in Chapter 4 – health, education, insurance and the rest'. 'Even the preface', he wrote, 'sounds like a voice from beyond the deluge.'[7]

Yet according to Postan, in his later years Tawney was 'worried':

> He was disturbed by the world situation, he resented the signs of failing powers, he hated falling asleep over books. And I believe that certain fundamental problems of – of life also began to re-occur to him, occur is perhaps not the right word, but came nearer the surface probably than they had been for a number of years previously.[8]

Both of these contrasting observations of the elderly Tawney were probably correct: there was much to celebrate in terms of public achievement, but much to lament and reflect upon in a life which had encompassed two world wars, struggles against poverty, ignorance and injustice, the controversies which attend any public figure and personal failings as well. He would surely have thought of those he left behind at the Somme – he wrote about the First World War in his letters at the end of his life – and perhaps also about those men he had shot as he had admitted in 'The Attack'.

Interviewed soon after his death, Christopher Hill spoke insightfully of Tawney's 'combination of shrewdness and gentleness. He was a very shrewd man – he could see through people – but he never took issue with anyone on personal matters, always on principles'.[9] Tawney was not without his critics, however, most of whom came in friendship, but not all. In his address at Tawney's memorial service Gaitskell recalled his impatience, occasional irritability and inflexibility. He was 'too uncompromising to be a very good worker in a team'.[10] Tawney's student, Ronald Preston, went further in questioning Tawney's denigration of self-advancement and profit as valuable social forces, a criticism that William Temple had made of *The Acquisitive Society* 40 years earlier.[11] To Preston this was unworldly and unrealistic: people work for gain and not all gain is selfishness. The trick was to harness their efforts for the good. Preston also questioned Tawney's identification of Christianity with socialism, rejecting the simplistic implication 'that non-socialists are in important respects immoral or unchristian'. Indeed, Preston rejected any attempt to tie Christian principles to a particular economic system. He also convicted Tawney of underplaying man's sinfulness: 'they allow for his grandeur but not his misery'. Where human nature was concerned, Tawney was too much the optimist and utopian.[12]

Critics from the right could be expected, of course. The academic objections deployed by Geoffrey Elton in his inaugural lecture in Cambridge have been discussed already. But Elton had also made overtly political criticisms of Tawney. He wrote in the year after Tawney's death that *Religion and the Rise of Capitalism* 'has greatly assisted in the decline of Protestant self-confidence and the consequent revival of Roman Catholicism, in the reaction against capitalism as an economic system, and even perhaps in the West's increasing inclination to relinquish world leadership'.[13] Three years later in his inaugural lecture already cited he opined that no other British historian 'had a worse, more disastrous effect upon what I may call the national self-consciousness'. According to Elton

> the whole collapse of self-confidence which we have encountered in this present generation . . . owes an immense amount to the influence of this one man and his school, percolating through the public press into the minds of the leaders of opinion, the intellectual leaders of society. Not only the academics, but also the men who write and the men who read.

Elton doubted whether 'Tawney's effect' had been 'good for England'. In presenting a distorted version of history, he had 'produced consequences which were quite incommensurate to the cause'.[14]

This surely verges on the hysterical. Whatever view is taken about his merits as a historian, Tawney was not some malign influence over national affairs but a dedicated social reformer whose greatest public contribution was probably the enormous time and effort he devoted – literally years of his life – to improving the British educational system and the opportunities it gave young and old alike for self-improvement and knowledge. We might have expected a professor of history to have welcomed such expenditure of effort, some of it in the cause of raising popular interest in History itself. The references to Tawney's effects on national morale and confidence are curious meanwhile, calling to mind the very opposite import of the observation of Tawney's friend and literary executor, Richard Rees, that he embodied the assurance of the late-Victorian generation.[15] Tawney did not lack self-confidence nor a confidence in England and its destiny, but it was a different England from the conservative and narrowly protestant England that Elton envisaged.

Gaitskell and Preston shared Tawney's socialism and Christianity respectively. Robert Page Arnot shared neither. A founder and loyal member of the British Communist Party, Page Arnot when interviewed soon after Tawney's death convicted him from the left of reformism and half-heartedness. Page Arnot noted 'a certain shrinking from continuous political action and publicity' in Tawney's behaviour: 'he would put his foot in the water, then take it out again'. He also wondered what sort of socialist it was who opposed the Labour Colleges movement and supported the First World War. He took issue with Tawney's written style which was 'fanciful at times' and notable for 'a certain artificiality' and he implied that Tawney cloaked his opposition to genuine left-wing politics in this high style, as if it was a weapon deployed in his betrayal of socialism. In Page Arnot's view, Tawney sold out: 'With all his talents and devotion . . . nevertheless on fundamental issues he took a path that . . . ended in support of the established order.'[16] Anyone listening to these comments in a radio biography of Tawney broadcast in 1963 might have been surprised to learn that Tawney helped organize a public letter of protest in 1925 when official action was attempted to suppress the freedom of speech of British communists.[17] Indeed, after a police raid on the offices of the Communist Party, Page Arnot was imprisoned, and Tawney wrote to him, offering to send him reading material.[18]

Much of this critique can be contested, not least the claim that Tawney opposed the Labour colleges movement, which was patently untrue. He had chosen to work in one tradition of worker's education, but he did not criticize or undermine those who chose another method.[19] He went to war because of his solidarity with other British workers at the front, and out of opposition to German militarism, and not in support of any aspect of nationalism. Whether Tawney shrank from the social struggle is open to objection, as well: all those long committee meetings through the 1920s and 1930s to make a difference in secondary and adult education, all those deputations, pamphlets, letters to the press, articles in the *Manchester Guardian* and speeches of uplift in a hundred draughty church halls hardly amount to half-heartedness. Nor should we forget that Tawney was a professor of economic history with students to teach, journals to edit, books to write and a department to help run. Yet in truth there is no answer to this kind of criticism from the left because it emanates from a rejection of the type of democratic-parliamentary politics to which Tawney was committed. In Page Arnot's view all efforts to reform education and the social services were forms of collaboration, destined to fail because they would make capitalism stronger. To Tawney, on the other hand, and to the British labour movement more generally, such efforts were the very essence of politics and the rationale of public life. We may debate exactly what is meant by 'the established order' and question if many of the things Tawney wanted really did assist 'the establishment', but if Page Arnot was arguing that Tawney was not a revolutionary, that he worked with the grain, that he respected national and social institutions and the national temper, then all he was really saying was that Tawney represented and embodied the indigenous socialist tradition which has always sought to reform and improve institutions, and which has never been revolutionary in inspiration or intent. Richard Crossman, the Labour minister of the 1960s and 1970s, spoke in relation to Tawney of 'a mind of perpetual radical challenge'.[20] He was not a revolutionary but by temperament was committed to the radical restructuring of institutions to make them more open and just.

This was especially true of his attitude towards the University of Oxford. Tawney was hardly the first leading figure in British life to have nursed contradictory feelings about Oxford. As an undergraduate there he enjoyed himself immensely, perhaps too much. Like many young radicals before – stretching back to the university liberals, so-called, of the 1850s – and since, he knew its internal weaknesses and found its social elitism insupportable.[21] That his commitment to the university's reform before and just after the First World War was honest cannot be doubted. That it may also have been affected by his failure to achieve a first-class degree is a legitimate speculation, though impossible to prove. He chafed at the delay and what he perceived to be the university's absence of commitment at the time that Oxford established the tutorial classes movement in 1908. Yet he found many notable and powerful allies for workers' education within its walls, and at that same stage he was seeking a fellowship himself at one of its colleges. After the First World War he accepted a fellowship at his own college, Balliol, albeit briefly. His first book was largely written in Edwardian summers spent in the Bodleian Library. Oxford frustrated him in its inefficiency and in the waste of its potential to do good; it also attracted him powerfully not only as a seat of learning but also as a source of support. Without Oxford there would have been no alliance of higher learning with the working class; yet Tawney never felt it gave enough, or as generously as it could. Many of his criticisms of the structure and administration of the university were accurate and well made; at other times he misread the politics of the university by demanding more than Oxford's friends of adult education thought advisable or could possibly deliver.[22]

Tawney represents the maturity of the British left, not its capitulation, whereas Page Arnot, described as 'a loyal Stalinist', associated himself with an alien tradition which never thrived and which collapsed in Britain when its alien sponsor collapsed.[23] More recently, elements of Page Arnot's criticism of Tawney have recurred in a lucid and thoughtful essay by Anthony Arblaster who has contrasted Tawney's expansive and radical rhetoric with the more limited institutional reforms he advocated in practice, finding him 'disappointingly cautious and conventional'. Tawney made universalized criticisms of capitalism but only supported the nationalization of industries on a case-by-case basis. He objected strongly to the social segregation of children caused by private education but continued to tolerate the existence of private schools, only calling for them to be licensed and regulated.[24] Arblaster would have liked Tawney to have lived up to his moral denunciations, whereas Stefan Collini, in a skilful and detailed analysis of *The Acquisitive Society,* found Tawney's self-righteous indignation to have been the problem rather than the solution. Claiming the high moral ground in 'the comforting assurance of one's own greater moral seriousness' is no way to conduct a rigorous debate on the ills of capitalism and the alternatives to it. Meanwhile the assumption that morality and socialism are indistinguishable and that they presuppose each other which runs through the book is disputable and also shallow. Collini points to the same simplistic and unhelpful 'binary polarity' between self-interest and morality that had troubled Graham Wallas and William Temple when the book was published.[25]

To try to answer arguments like these is not to contest them, for they are valuable and necessary correctives to an uncritical appreciation of Tawney. Yet it should be pointed out that Tawney's focus on what could realistically be achieved in the reform of social institutions, as opposed to what was ultimately desirable but unattainable, was a virtue in the eyes of many contemporaries. The history of his engagement in the reform of secondary education shows just how difficult it was to secure even the smallest of changes and how dedicated he remained nonetheless. In his unwillingness to legally prohibit private education he was honouring principles of personal and civil liberty which, whether we approve of private education or not, must be inviolable in an open society. And in light of the history and the demise of nationalized industries, his caution appears wise and far-sighted rather than timid. Without a good economic case for state ownership and, as Tawney kept arguing, an appropriate administrative and managerial structure for each industry coming under public ownership, nationalized industries would fail – which they did.[26] Collini, meanwhile, is surely correct in his strictures on one of Tawney's most famous books, but as the present study has argued, neither *The Acquisitive Society* nor *Equality* do justice to the range and depth of Tawney's thought, and were intended by him as publications of the moment, closely related to their immediate context rather than timeless statements of the principles of socialism.[27] In his political and historical writing Tawney was often cautious, apologetic, tentative or provisional. He aimed to stimulate, to suggest, sometimes to goad.

Tawney's signal weakness was not half-heartedness, reformism or even moral superiority which is a vice shared by many writers on politics, but a particular type of insensitivity or blindness with regard to women and their place in society. This had its private manifestation in his relationship with Jeanette, who, though offered respect and affection, was never given the emotional and sexually fulfilling relationship she had expected. We must account this Tawney's greatest failure, one that owed something to his upbringing, education, natural shyness and his singular sense of marriage as a kind of civic partnership. In public, Tawney occasionally supported women's causes. He protested in 1933 when the University of Liverpool slipped into women's contracts the stipulation that they must resign from the teaching staff on marriage.[28] He supported the limitation of women's working hours under the proposed factories bill in 1936.[29] He gave support to a campaign to raise funds for Hillcroft, the women's adult education college in Surbiton.[30] But in no sense was he a feminist: these were good causes to be supported as such. Educated and socialized only among men, with the exception of Eileen Power and Beatrice Webb, his friends were almost exclusively men, and he thought largely of men's needs, generalizing them into the interests of all the community. Indeed, the most notable feature of lives like those of Power and Webb was that they had succeeded in traditionally male domains like academia and public policy, and Tawney admired them for that as much as for their intrinsically female qualities. He could hold his own with the hearties at Rugby school, the Tommies in the trenches and male trade unionists in his adult education classes: he was comfortable around men and used his intellect, when he lacked the muscle, to command their respect. It was Sergeant Tawney's French rather than his strength which impressed the 22nd Manchesters. He had no feminine qualities, no instinctive understanding of women and little experience of them to offset these lacunae. His books and articles, speeches and lectures were written with an audience only of men in mind.[31]

Tawney's life spans those years during which Britain achieved a kind of stability as a mature industrial society, roughly from the 1870s to the 1960s.[32] The upheavals and instabilities of early Victorian capitalism were behind it; the affluence, deindustrialization and growing cultural pluralism of the present age unforeseen. Tawney's age was marked by profound social tensions and deep inequality which drew him into public affairs at many points, but the issues of the period – how to integrate the working classes with the rest of British society, how to increase social opportunities for the mass of the British population, how to build a society that was democratic in all senses – were constant and enduring. They were to be solved in a nation that was sure of its economic and political position in the world, and whose subjects interacted in a common cultural context where differences of race, religion and ethnicity (though not of class) were more muted than in many other comparable societies.

This stability was ruptured twice during Tawney's life by world wars, and he was himself ruptured in the first of these conflicts by a bullet which passed through him, leaving him with lifelong pain. In the second conflict he and Jeanette were bombed out of their home during the Blitz on London. In both cases Tawney was in no doubt that the wars had to be fought. Historians have emphasized the role of the wars in accelerating pre-existing trends, from the growth of the state to the social and political enfranchisement of women. Outwardly, Tawney's own experience and reaction to the wars conforms to this pattern. After being invalided out of the army in late 1916 he threw himself into democratic and social reconstruction; on his return from Washington in 1942 he took the lead for a final time in the campaign to secure an adequate secondary education for all children. But in both cases he was returning to issues already joined which had become insistent as a consequence of heightened social consciousness during the conflicts and which now required solution. Inwardly, therefore, it might be argued that for Tawney the wars changed little. He joined up in 1914 in furtherance of the solidarity he had already shown to workers; his deep democratic sympathies were assaulted by German ideology and actions, especially in the 1930s. When able, he pursued the social and educational causes he had always favoured, though now in more propitious circumstances. There were differences between the wars, of course, which Tawney recorded. He admired the stoicism and shared sacrifices of his compatriots in the second war, a theme in all his lectures in the United States in 1941–2. Yet he had earlier lamented the gulf in knowledge and sympathy that separated the western from the home fronts in 1915–16 in his second essay on that war, '*Some Reflections of a Soldier*'. In giving expression to this grievance he was duplicating the sentiments of very many soldiers who were frustrated and sometimes enraged by civilians' incomprehension of their experience in the trenches. In short, though Tawney's experiences of war were singular, his reactions to the conflicts follow well-understood patterns, even down to his recurrent criticisms of the British general staff.

Tawney grew up with the Labour movement. Born at the start of the decade in which 'the social question' was first posed and systematically investigated, he reached his majority just as the Labour Representation Committee was founded (from which the Labour Party was soon to emerge) in 1900. His most active decades were then spent in the often frustrating business of assisting the Labour movement in the achievement of its social objectives and political goals.

He retired in 1945, aged 65, with a majority Labour government in power for the first time and its programme, which he had helped shape over many years, being introduced. He died just as the questions changed: affluence reaching down into the working class, cultural pluralism and diversity, and for a single generation, social mobility, seemed by the 1960s, to have consigned Tawney's world into a long lost and unlamented past. As his own period was drawing to a close his sympathetic and perceptive publisher, Sir Stanley Unwin, wrote to him with a suggestion: 'Is there any hope of persuading you to write a book on the experiences of your generation, i.e. the social changes since about 1880? Few of the younger generation have any notion how much has been accomplished since that time and without any revolutionary upheaval.'[33] There was indeed a 'Tawney generation' and it lived through and defines a distinct epoch in British History composed of political reform, social welfare and two world wars. Tawney contributed to each of these in full measure.

Tawney has been seen as a very 'English' figure. Postan remarked on 'the intense Englishness of most of Tawney's interests and preoccupations';[34] Ashton observed that his 'socialism, like his church, was essentially English'[35] and David Marquand correctly recognized that he belonged 'to a thoroughly English tradition of moral protest which is far older than formal socialism'.[36] Occasionally one senses that his Englishness has been viewed as a weakness, as if his rootedness in his own culture were some sort of handicap. Alasdair MacIntyre convicted him of 'that essentially English quality, insularity'.[37] To Anthony Arblaster, Tawney was a prisoner of 'his national environment' and the distinctively 'British version of social democracy'.[38] There *was* an endearing intellectual parochialism to him: in old age he cheerfully admitted to never having read anything as alien and exotic as Freud: 'while I admire some psychologists some of the books they write tend to make me react in the contrary direction.'[39] His professional world and historical imagination were indeed shaped by England, though it was the England of Cromwell, the Puritans and the Levellers rather than of more comforting and consensual groups and moments in English History. To many of those who read and admired him, especially those who knew something of class conflict and political turmoil in early twentieth-century Europe, this 'Englishness' was not a limitation or failing but a strength and attraction. At the end of his life he received a reflective letter from the notable jurist, comparative lawyer and refugee from Nazism, Otto Kahn-Freund, who explained that

> I am one of those – there must be thousands of them – to whom you have given new perspectives and encouragement through your work. I remember

how, shortly after my arrival in England as a refugee from Germany, I read *The Acquisitive Society* and how my eyes were opened to new foundations and aspects of socialism, and how you gave me insights going beyond the Marxist tradition from which I came. Somehow your book gave me hope and assurance at a very critical moment. Indeed it strengthened my resolve to remain in England, and I think it has had a lasting influence on my thinking.[40]

Tawney did indeed focus on domestic rather than foreign affairs. As his nephew recalled, 'I have no doubt he adhered to his party's doctrine as regards the evolution of Indian self-government [but] I do not think it was ever a preoccupation of his.'[41] But as this book has shown, he travelled very widely and saw history being made at several crucial moments in the twentieth century – in France in 1916; in Germany in 1922 during the hyper-inflation; in China at the time of the Japanese invasion; in the United States when Pearl Harbor was attacked. Tawney also showed himself to be an acute analyst of international situations whose judgment and capacity for accurate prediction add to his authority. He could see that the Japanese invasion of Manchuria was a decisive test of the League of Nations and that it was the beginning of an extended world crisis; he knew that appeasement of the dictators was both morally and prudentially wrong; he understood that his duty in 1940 was to use his pen to help align the United States with Great Britain; he was never deceived as to the nature of the Soviet regime; he knew that American anti-communism was a betrayal of her own democratic values; he also knew that whatever the demerits of an Atlantic alliance and the possession of nuclear weapons, the alternatives were worse. If this was the product of an insular 'Englishness', then Tawney was all the better for it in comparison with many interwar and cold war internationalists whose commitment to peace or to the 'Soviet experiment' so-called, led to gross and morally-compromising misjudgment. There was nothing limited or myopic in Tawney's view of the world or his understanding of the nature and tasks of democratic socialism. That very rootedness in the long history of English radicalism and empiricism, and his attachment to the struggles and also to the pleasures and traditions of English people, gave him a very clear-eyed view of history and politics which informed his thinking rather than limited or shackled his imagination. Tawney once reminded readers that Marx himself was 'well aware' of 'an indigenous English socialism which, except for the inspiration to all creative thought given by France, owed nothing to foreign influences'.[42] It was a tradition of which Tawney was a part and which probably ended with him.

Tawney's historical works were read by sixth-formers and undergraduates throughout the English-speaking world in the 1960s and 1970s. Almost everyone studying for a History degree then encountered the dispute over the rise of the sixteenth- and seventeenth-century gentry at some stage, whether taught as a component of English History or as debate to be studied in courses on historical method and the interpretation of evidence. By the 1980s, however, the range and depth of new research had surpassed Tawney and different questions required answers. Whether one subscribed to Geoffrey Elton's view on Tawney's reliability or not was no longer important; the debate had moved on. In regard to his political writing that was even more the case: as the 'social problem' moved from actual to relative deprivation, and the institutional task became one of sustaining rather than building the welfare state, so Tawney lost his place in reading lists. Nevertheless, Tawney's name was invoked by Labour politicians in a way that differentiates him from other socialist thinkers of his era like the Webbs, Laski and Cole whose reputational burial was swift and complete. His humanity, his authority and his legend seemed to lend him greater traction and durability as an influence and a source, and association with him was more frequent than with other socialist pioneers because it seemed to add lustre to whoever invoked him.

So important was he to socialist and progressive politics in Britain that the formation of the Social Democratic Party (SDP) as a centrist breakaway from the Labour Party in 1981–2 led to a public debate on his political legacy when the new party chose to call its policy forum The Tawney Society. Participants included the former Labour minister Shirley Williams and the author of Labour's election manifesto of 1945, Michael Young, against the socialist historian and polemicist Raphael Samuel and the then leader of the Labour Party, Michael Foot, in a debate largely conducted in the *Times* and *Guardian* newspapers. Lena Jeger wondered aloud what Tawney himself would have made of the SDP taking his name in vain.[43] The philosopher Anthony Flew reminded readers that Tawney was a committed advocate of nationalization and Clause IV of the Labour Party's constitution.[44] Diane Hayter, the then general secretary of the Fabian Society, was outraged over 'an unseemly tug of war for the soul of R. H. Tawney' and was assured of Tawney's view of the matter:

> Tawney would be turning in his grave if he had known that the Social Democrats were using his name in such a fashion. They are betraying his memory. It is dishonest. I do not believe that SDP members support his ideals. If he were alive he would sue. He would still be in the Fabian Society, and he would still be in the Labour Party.[45]

From the University of Kent the economic historian L. S. Pressnell wrote in to complain of all false appropriations of Tawney's aegis, for he was the property of everyone.[46] Michael Foot wrote to the *Times* observing that the leaders of the SDP had in the recent past purged themselves and their works of the word 'socialism' and asked with his customary irony whether the Tawney Society would purge it also from Tawney's works. They 'debase the name of Tawney' he thundered.[47] But Foot could not contain himself, and warming to his theme in a contemporaneous piece, he contended that Tawney 'soaked himself in Marxism' and then promoted a Marxism 'more telling than anything written by the orthodox Marxists themselves . . . Has not Tawney ranged himself on the side of those who damn not merely the Labour practitioners of parliamentarianism but the process itself?'[48] This was exactly the type of overwrought left-wing hysterics that Tawney so disliked in Foot's mentor, Bevan. Sanity was restored in two long pieces for *The Guardian* by the historian and tutor at Ruskin College, Oxford, Raphael Samuel, who, seeking to do 'justice to Tawney's memory', carefully examined his moralism, Christianity and loyalty to working people and compared it with the SDP's conscious dissociation of its new, classless and non-religious radicalism from the traditions and struggles of the labour movement. Tawney's socialism was intellectually rigorous and emotionally intense, the product of his identification with radical causes and struggles in history, and of his 'epic sense of the past'. In contrast, the manifestoes of the SDP which had restored capitalism 'to a place of honour' were simply shallow. The SDP might promote 'egalitarianism' but it had little in common 'beyond the name' with Tawney's *Equality*.[49]

Tawney's defenders in the Labour Party and on the left were answered by Michael Young (Lord Young of Dartington), chairman of the provisional committee of the Tawney Society, who had been one of Tawney's pupils at the LSE. Young protested that the new party sought to honour Tawney by naming it after him. Quoting from Tawney's 1949 essay '*Social Democracy in Britain*', Young claimed to subscribe to it all, and pointed to the Labour Party's failure to achieve Tawney's aims. Elsewhere, Young defended their use of his name because 'Tawney was par excellence a democratic socialist'. Young went on to note Tawney's opposition to the subordination of Labour MPs by the party's conference and to explain that this 'was the issue on which the SDP was formed', though in truth it was only one of various specific and also wider and more ideological reasons from the secession.[50] He could also have made the point that the third version of Tawney's 1952 lecture *British Socialism Today* was published in 1960 at the height of the Gaitskell-Bevan struggle by the Campaign for Democratic Socialism, an organization founded by, among others, Roy Jenkins and Bill Rodgers, to put the case of the Labour right wing, and in many respects the ancestor of the SDP. We must take it that Tawney agreed to this re-publication and understood the use that would be made of his lecture. The SDP's case was shot down by one of its own MPs, John Horam, who had recently defected from the Labour Party and was the vice chairman of the new party's policy committee. He explained that the new Tawney Society had no official status in the emerging party and was merely an informal grouping. He went on to give socialists the argument: 'Where they [the founders of the Tawney Society] have gone wrong is to invoke the name of R. H. Tawney who, great man though he was, was undoubtedly a socialist, and socialists belong in the Labour Party, not the SDP.'[51] Eighteen months later an editorial in *The Guardian* on the forthcoming Labour leadership contest observed that both the leading contenders, Neil Kinnock and Roy Hattersley, were notable quoters of Tawney in their speeches. The paper suggested that perhaps Tawney should become the next leader of the party:

> There must now be a strong case for his installation as Leader at least until the party's present difficulties are resolved. Not only is it difficult to find anyone in the Labour Party who disagrees with his analysis: it is near impossible to find anyone in the SDP who disagrees with it either and a powerful faction in that party continues to claim Tawney as their own spiritual ancestor.[52]

More than 20 years prior to these exchanges and commentaries, a young Shirley Williams, then General Secretary of the Fabian Society, had written to Arthur Creech Jones to associate the Fabians with the celebration of Tawney's 80th birthday. 'I often feel,' she wrote, 'that those who have contributed most to the socialist movement go unrecognised, and we should hate that to happen in his case.'[53]

Shirley Williams knew then what should have been absolutely self-evident in 1982 as well. There can be no doubt where Tawney was located as a socialist and where he should have remained: in the Labour Party. However much it demoralized and dismayed him through his life, as he vouchsafed to a well-wisher in 1960, 'I shall continue to be a member whatever its momentary imbecilities.'[54] In particular, it is difficult to imagine someone who had once been so close to British trade unions joining a new party which explicitly opposed the degree of influence of trade unions in public life and in the Labour Party, and which wanted to create a new progressive politics shorn of the left's reliance on the organized labour movement. Tawney reflexively sided with working people and the trade union movement throughout his life and the attempt to appropriate him by moderate Social Democrats was doomed to fail. Without doubt he was a socialist and Labour man to his core, though one who believed in a party and movement that encouraged democratic participation and open debate. As Michal Vyvyan observed at the very end of 1981,

> I suppose he could be called a social democrat. I mean a social democrat in the modern sense although I think Tawney's tie to the historical English Labour Party would have been far too intense and sentimental for him to be tempted to identify himself in any way with the new Social Democratic Party in this country.[55]

However, as this book has shown, his relations with the Labour Party were often strained. He was very close to two of its leaders: Attlee, who had shared so many of Tawney's experiences, and Gaitskell, his protégé. Yet he argued with Lansbury over his dogmatism and anti-intellectualism, and with MacDonald over almost everything – his pacifism, his lack of preparedness for power, his parliamentary tactics between 1929 and 1931, his embrace of and by the establishment, his offer to Tawney of a peerage. As for Philip Snowden, that his economic as well as his political judgment would fail so badly in 1931 would have come as no surprise to Tawney on the basis of Snowden's mean-spirited treatment of him when he was candidate for Rochdale in the Coupon Election. And to Tawney, Nye Bevan was a loud and self-important romantic who was plain wrong on many important questions. Beyond these leaders, Tawney, like many intellectuals who have been associated with Labour, grew weary of the party's inability to prepare for the use of power by carefully researching issues and prioritizing among them. He was only really in contact with Labour's leadership during the 1920s. In the 1930s he kept his distance, though he played an important role in identifying and training the next generation. If we cast back to the 1908 Report, *Oxford and Working-Class Education*, which Tawney wrote, we can see the continuity in his approach to power. He always believed that Labour politicians required a high-quality and searching education which would provide them with the intellectual resources with which to govern. He had seen how it worked at Balliol at the height of its influence, as it sent men out to run the state, the church, the empire, the schools. The labour movement required and deserved nothing less. Unfortunately, his strategy of educating the movement so that it would use power effectively and would not be easily dislodged, was never appreciated and welcomed by the party, and 1931, in Tawney's view, was the result, the nemesis.

Many socialists in Britain were patriots; many opposed pacifism; many saw through the Soviet Union from an early stage; many opposed the claims of the Communist Party of Great Britain. Later, many understood the need for an Atlantic alliance and were against unilateral nuclear disarmament. Many, before the 1960s, were even in favour of grammar schools. But take all these positions together and a much smaller proportion of those who called themselves socialists in the early and mid-twentieth century would have subscribed to them all. Raphael Samuel contended that when it came to party politics, 'in Labour Party terms he was rather moderate or "centrist", and mistrustful of what he called the "heroics" of some of Labour's more radical middle-class recruits'.[56] This is true, but it is also evident that on every question Tawney used his own judgment and experience and had no fear at all of standing out against a consensus. He was a loyal Labour party man but he saw no reason to agree with the party when he believed it mistaken. It was right and proper that Tawney was claimed back by Labour in 1982. But those who would invoke him should respect his differences from the party in his own lifetime, for only in that way can he be appreciated properly, and his lessons – such as the need to find, use and deploy intellectual resources in politics – be understood and applied.

The argument of this book is that Tawney's confluence with the organized Labour movement after his membership of the Sankey Commission in 1919 led him to adopt a more conventional state-socialist position which was at variance with much of his thinking up to that time. The authentic Tawney is the young Tawney whose socialism was moral and spiritual and who practised it in workers' education, where individuals, and through them, whole communities could be inspired by ideas of fellowship and service. This makes Tawney almost the last of the socialist pioneers in Britain for whom socialism was a type of 'religion' (and for Tawney, with his strong Christian inspiration, it certainly was), rather than a spokesman for the collectivist state which is what he appears to have become by the publication of *Equality* at the start of the 1930s.[57] Ethical socialism was not displaced from his teaching, and Tawney continued to speak and act in ways that made it urgent and relevant. But he also accepted the much more conventional state socialism of the Fabians which he had earlier opposed, root and branch. At the end of the First World War this became the orthodoxy of the Labour Party, enshrined in clause IV of its constitution, and Tawney, though aware of its defects and its differences from his own personal political faith, adopted it and became its advocate. Within a few years of his death the problems with state socialism were evident: nationalized industries were uncompetitive, managed poorly, so politically sensitive that their reform was almost impossible, and under the influence of trade unions that, as was their purpose and function, put their members' interests above the interests of the industry itself and those of consumers and the community more generally. Graham Wallas had foretold this in his review of *The Acquisitive Society* at the very point when Tawney threw in his lot with 'Clause IV socialism'.[58] Tawney himself had always appreciated the dangers, writing in 1925 that

> The most general criticism brought against public services is that they tend to be overcentralized and top-heavy, to paralyze initiative and to conceal responsibility, to play for safety and to avoid risks, to hold their own, not by ability, but by the mere weight of obstructiveness, to offer mediocrity the protection of a system in which torpor is organized, and against the leaden inertia of which both the man of creative talent and consuming public rage in vain.

Since the 1970s British socialism has had to reposition itself and has become identified with high social expenditure in support of state welfare services, and with the public sector in general. Speculation may be dangerous and unwarranted, and a historian enters unfamiliar territory in making even informed guesses about the present, but it is unlikely that Tawney would have welcomed this unreservedly. He undoubtedly favoured redistribution of income and wealth, a key theme in *Equality*, and also higher public expenditure on education in particular which was the corollary of all his work to achieve a good secondary education for all, but his socialism was ethical rather than distributive, spiritual rather than material. His focus was always on the education and socialization of men and women to encourage their generosity and social conscience. For the past two generations Labour governments have enlarged the competence of the state and multiplied its agencies, but neglected the 'education of socialists', the theme of Tawney's speech at the celebratory dinner in the House of Commons to mark his 80th birthday.[59]

There is plenty of evidence that Tawney appreciated the duality in his position, the contradiction in fact, between two different types of politics which he was espousing from the 1920s. But he did not bring himself to confront that contradiction, or even just to write about it as an issue in socialism and political commitment more generally. This may be one reason why, though Tawney inspired his contemporaries, he was not a truly great writer on politics. Too much was taken for granted; too many assumptions were deployed without self-scrutiny. Equality might well be a moral requirement as well as a functionally more efficient way of organizing a society, but that must be argued through rather than assumed. As Raymond Williams suggested, it is difficult 'to disagree with the humanity of his arguments'. But there are grounds for scepticism about Tawney's methods. Williams questioned whether men could be persuaded to make 'a moral choice' as Tawney hoped, and questioned also just how easy it would then be to reform society in practice along lines laid down by these beneficent choices: 'the analysis, while decent, is likely to seem lacking in depth.' Tawney 'sought to humanize the modern system of society on its own best terms'. This involved an assumption that men and women could be persuaded to see the world through Tawney's eyes and would comply with the principles of the moral reformation that he sought. This, as Williams noted with some justice, was a mark of his limitations as a political thinker.[60] Tawney tended to assert rather than to argue; to lay down rather than to offer. When, in the *Commonplace Book*, he states that

> the merits or demerits of an industrial system are not to be measured solely, or even principally by the success with which wealth is distributed among the parties involved in it, but by the extent to which the relation existing between [them] are such as to develope (sic) self-respect, self-reliance, mutual confidence and enterprise[61]

we may well want to contest the assumption that spiritual content and good fellowship are more important than production and material comfort. But Tawney doesn't give us the opportunity to demur, though in his defence it must be remembered that this is taken from a notebook compiled for his own purposes and not for publication. But that sense of infallibility, of confidence in one's own moral judgements, of being right and possessing the truth, which, it has been suggested, disqualified him for the dialectic of parliamentary politics, is a weakness in a philosopher quite as much as a candidate for a seat in the House of Commons.

For this reason it is probably more appropriate to think of him in the line of social prophets that Raymond Williams traced in *Culture and Society*. Tawney belongs with Carlyle, Ruskin and Morris among others in a tradition of ethical anti-capitalism. He read and revered Morris. He made many of the same arguments as Ruskin about economics and politics, and was learning his socialism in an era, roughly the first decade of the twentieth century, when Ruskin's ethical denunciations of Victorian business and political economy were the most potent influence on the middle-aged, autodidact working men who had read him in cheap editions in their youth and went on to make the Labour

Party. Like these social prophets Tawney was a public figure and controversialist; like them he published on many different subjects and in several different genres; like them he built a large and devoted public following which endured for at least a generation after his death. And like them he was enabled to exploit and deploy a rich language and style which is no longer part of our culture.

Tawney could write and speak without embarrassment about morality, spirituality and transcendence because he had the linguistic resources within himself to do so, based on the Bible and classical texts which he knew intimately, the pamphlets of the Civil War and the writings of such secular prophets as Ruskin and Morris. During the early decades of the twentieth century his audiences, of any class, would have shared all or some of this linguistic heritage, and been used to a language of acclamation and condemnation. As T. S. Ashton wrote,

> Tawney was a master of style. In his propagandist pamphlets the short, direct sentences beat on the ear like successive cracks of a whip; in his historical, and even more in his prophetic works, the periods are Miltonic. Steeped, as he was, in the language of the Authorised Version and the Book of Common Prayer, he had resources of invective and exhortation denied to his adversaries. He could be violent in controversy. Those who opposed the raising of the school leaving age were castigated as "blind adders" and the irresponsible rich as "thriving earthworms".[62]

To Tawney, culture was 'not an assortment of aesthetic sugar-plums for fastidious palates, but an energy of the soul'.[63] The argument that it is vain to pursue social equality because it can never be achieved 'is like using the impossibility of absolute cleanliness as a pretext for rolling in a manure heap'.[64] To show undue deference to economic and social theory was 'to dance naked, and roll on the ground, and cut oneself with knives, in honour of the mysteries of Mumbo-Jumbo'.[65] Nations may go wrong, explained Tawney: 'It is possible, we know, for a society to be heir to the knowledge of all the ages, and to use it with the recklessness of a madman and the ferocity of a savage . . . It may master the means to harness nature to its chariot, and then employ them to drive with greater speed to the precipice'.[66] The English class system was 'as businesslike as Manchester and as gentlemanly as Eton; if its hands can be as rough as those of Esau, its voice is as mellifluous as that of Jacob. It is a god with two faces and a thousand tongues . . .'[67] As for Labour governments, they 'walk as delicately as Agag, like cats on ice'.[68]

His rich and allusive style worked just as well when writing History as when engaging in political disputation. Erasmus was described as 'a prophet without sackcloth and a reformer untouched by heat or fury, to the universal internationalism of whose crystal spirit the boundaries of States were a pattern scrawled to amuse the childish malice of princes'.[69] In contrast, Luther's 'utterances on social morality are the occasional explosions of a capricious volcano, with only a rare flash of light amid the torrent of smoke and flame'.[70] Few historians have ever written British economic history in this manner:

> The mighty forces of capital and competitive industry and foreign trade are beginning to heave in their sleep – forces that will one day fuse and sunder, exalt and put down, enrich and impoverish, unpeople populous counties and pour Elizabethan England into a smoking cauldron between the Irish Sea and the Pennines.[71]

Tawney was at his majestic best when writing about Puritanism, perhaps because, as many remarked during his life, his personal asceticism, devotion to principle, Christian commitment and capacity for hard work led him to understand the Puritans as only one of their own could. Tawney, like the Puritans, was militant, godly, infallible, devout, though if they were humble before God only, he was humble before God and man as well. Puritanism was a 'tremendous storm', he wrote:

> The forests bent; the oaks snapped; the dry leaves were driven before a gale, neither all of winter nor all of spring, but violent and life-giving, pitiless and tender, sounding strange notes of yearning and contrition, as of voices wrung from a people dwelling in Meshec, which signifies Prolonging, in Kedar, which signifies Blackness; while amid the blare of trumpets, and the clash of arms, and the rending of the carved work of the Temple, humble to God and haughty to man, the soldier-saints swept over battlefield and scaffold their garments rolled in blood.

Tawney admired and celebrated the cultural and political achievements of individual Puritans even as he condemned Puritanism's social teaching:

> In the mysticism of Bunyan and Fox, in the brooding melancholy and glowing energy of Cromwell, in the victorious tranquillity of Milton, "unshaken, unseduced, unterrified," amid a world of self-seekers and apostates, there are depths of light and darkness which posterity can observe with reverence or with horror, but which its small fathom-line cannot plumb.

Tawney could plumb these depths of devotion, passion and reverence, however. He understood the psychological tensions inherent in the creed that individual Puritans struggled constantly to master and control.

> The Puritan is like a steel spring compressed by an inner force, which shatters every obstacle by its rebound. Sometimes the strain is too tense, and, when its imprisoned energy is released, it shatters itself.

But when the act of control was successful, and their energy could be channelled towards worldly success, the Puritans were

> an earnest, zealous, godly generation, scorning delights, punctual in labour, constant in prayer, thrifty and thriving, filled with a decent pride in themselves and their calling, assured that strenuous toil is acceptable to Heaven.

In his remarks on the inner life and motives of Puritanism, a social and religious category which is now treated with some caution by historians, but which Tawney understood as few others have, he reached the very summit of his style and wrote some of the most memorable pages in modern English historiography.[72]

It was not to all tastes. Arnold Plant commended 'memorable Miltonic sections' but convicted Tawney of an excess of stylistic 'self-consciousness'.[73] W. H. B. Court admired his later 'rational persuasive prose' but found his earlier essays 'marred by rhetoric'.[74] But whether admired or not, by the 1950s this linguistic heritage was in decline and politics were being conducted in a different, undemanding and less exciting idiom. Tawney reads so well now because his language and expression are so unfamiliar – and because we no longer have the words with which to express a personal and moral commitment in our politics. Indeed, to a great extent it is because we lack the words that our politics are reduced to barter and exchange, where once Tawney could inspire commitment and spiritual transcendence. There can be no prophets without a prophetic language. According to Tawney, 'Institutions which have died as creeds sometimes continue, nevertheless, to survive as habits'.[75] Our political discourse has lost the capacity to instil belief and become a matter of routine; without the words to inspire and uplift we are unable to imagine a different future.

Tawney was the most representative of Labour's twentieth-century intellectuals. His life spanned the origins, rise and consolidation of the Labour Party almost exactly. He was educated in late-Victorian idealist ethics which provided a philosophical basis for the transition from individualism to collectivism. His religious faith linked him to earlier and continuing traditions of Christian socialism in Britain. His democratic spirit evoked the nineteenth-century struggles of working people to secure the franchise. His experience in workers' education gave him intimate knowledge of the working class so that, unlike other intellectuals, he knew the people he spoke for and led. His aversion to the spiritual void in industrial capitalism echoed the formative influence of Ruskin over the British labour movement. His love of fellowship and his faith in the fundamental decency of men and women is reminiscent of William Morris. He takes his place with the many historians, from Thomas Carlyle to E. P. Thompson, who have had such influence over the imagination and political commitment of the British left, a movement whose inspiration has generally come from the past. Tawney synthesized all these elements into an ethical socialism that should be accounted the distinctive British contribution to the wider history of socialism itself.

His own individual contribution to that tradition was the interpenetration and interconnection of past and present in all his writing and thinking, whether political or academic. This melding of history and politics was a product of the remarkable coherence in all that he did. In politics he wanted to understand, reform, humanize and overturn industrial capitalism which exploited workers and created an unequal and hence an ungodly society. This prompted him to study the historical origins of capitalism in Britain, always the central theme in his scholarship whether he was investigating sixteenth-century enclosures, the puritan mentality, the decline of an economic morality within early-modern religion or the commercial ruses of a Jacobean merchant-cum-official. 'He saw the acquisitive society of his own day as the culminating point in a very long drawn-out historical process, whose stormy passage he charted from the class struggles of late medieval Europe to the homiletics of Archdeacon Paley.'[76] The syntheses which emerged – a politics grounded in the historical struggles of working people since the Reformation, and a history focused on understanding the present through the investigation of the past – were immensely stimulating and inspiring. Scholars may blench, but Tawney gave his generation a usable past that made sense in the here and now of the society Britain had become. He also gave to fellow socialists the comfort and fortitude that flows from the identification of present political campaigns with prior struggles in history: cottagers fighting enclosures, agricultural labourers forced to take work in the new factories, eighteenth-century miners underpaid and overworked in atrocious conditions were figures evoking a sympathy which fed back into the political consciousness of the 1920s and 1930s. His was not strictly academic history and nor was it ever intended by Tawney that it should be. He was never attracted to scholarship for its own sake. Nevertheless, by relating past to present so intimately he generated powerful and structuring historical ideas which fascinated a generation and which have had an influential and controversial after-life.

When Tawney reflected on the many contributions of the Webbs, he focused on their 'intellectual ardour, disinterested devotion and unflagging public spirit' in words that could easily have been applied to himself.[77] He spoke his own epitaph at a sorrowful occasion in September 1948 when he gave the address at the memorial service in St Margaret's, Westminster, for his friend and younger colleague at the LSE who had been elected to the House of Commons in 1945, Evan Durbin. Durbin, it had seemed, was destined to be Chancellor of the Exchequer to Gaitskell as Prime Minister in a future Labour government, and Tawney had been mentor to them both. In the event, both died before their time, although Gaitskell lived long enough to give the address at Tawney's memorial service. Durbin died in heroic circumstances saving his daughter and another child from drowning off the Cornish coast, but in doing so he was pulled under. Befitting such a sad occasion, Tawney did not speak for long or reminisce, but found words that may be applied to his own life as well:

> Both in the nobility of the ends which he pursued, and in the humanity of spirit which he brought to the service of them, he lives after his death as an inspiration to his fellows.[78]

Post Script: Tawney Fifty Years on

In the course of researching and writing this book many people have discussed with me the contemporary relevance of R. H. Tawney and encouraged me to write on this theme. Once so central to conceptions of British socialism and the good society, and the subject of a public struggle to appropriate his name and reputation on the formation of the Social Democratic Party in 1981–2, what is left of Tawney's work that might form a legacy more than 50 years after his death? To answer this question is to speculate, and speculation makes readers as well as historians uncomfortable. Thus I have reserved this discussion for a separate and final section of the book, one that may be ignored or disputed without, I trust, casting doubt on the biography which precedes it. Readers will likely disagree with me, which is as it should be. I make no claim to possess Tawney or to have special insight into his legacy. Figures as protean as Tawney provide evidence to support many different viewpoints and ammunition for many different arguments.

Pinning Tawney down when he changed his ideas over time and was such a prolific contributor to public debate is no easy task. Indeed, it may be contended legitimately that a writer on politics who was always interested in the particular challenges of his own era, be they the setting of minimum wage rates, the nationalization of the mines or the extension of the school-leaving age, must, by definition, be irrelevant to succeeding periods where outstanding issues and tasks have changed. Tawney grew up in a late-Victorian world where poverty was ubiquitous, educational provision merely elementary for the great majority, public services in their very infancy and capitalist enterprise largely unregulated. The relative affluence that Britain has enjoyed since Tawney's death in 1962, the subsequent privatization of industries which had been brought into public ownership and control during his lifetime, the decline of the organized working class as a force in politics, and the development of new social identities and ethnic communities requiring political representation of a different type, have all so changed the political landscape that it would be easy enough to argue that Tawney has no very obvious relevance today.

New Labour, the slogan of the 1990s, was designed to supplant the old Labour movement to which Tawney belonged and to which he devoted his life. To mention his name is to conjure memories of a former era when socialism was the acknowledged goal of millions and the Labour Party its supposed servant and agent. We are far from that age now. After the First World War Tawney became a public advocate for, and advisor to, a union of mineworkers with hundreds of thousands of members who enjoyed so much public sympathy that the rest of the trade union movement was willing to strike in solidarity with them in 1926. That industry barely exists today. Through support for the miners Tawney also came to endorse wholesale public ownership of British industry as a means to the achievement of both equality and efficiency, though he worried over the form that nationalization would take and never overlooked the matter of the spirit which workers would have to develop if public corporations were to prosper. They did not prosper and the social experiment of public ownership was concluded inside half a century: even before he died Tawney could see that nationalization was falling back into the traps he had diagnosed in the 1920s.

We can only guess at Tawney's attitude to developments in Britain since 1962. He welcomed the expansion of health and social services, but his lifelong interest, in line with his late-Victorian roots, was in individual and collective self-improvement (understood as moral rather than material improvement) rather than the politics and mechanics of redistribution and welfare. For this reason we can be sure that the growing instrumentalism and vocational focus of secondary education in Britain would have pained a man who fought so hard to give children more years for learning, creativity and self-expression. Tawney believed that each child should have an equal chance, but he did not believe that meant that each child should study the same curriculum or attend a single type of school. He also remained attached to achieving the highest academic standards, an article of faith among the pioneers of liberal adult education whose aim was to give their worker scholars the very best education possible, every bit as good as the education provided within universities. Almost all the evidence suggests that Tawney would have questioned the subsequent development of the secondary education system after his death: as he argued in pamphlet after pamphlet in the interwar period, equality of educational opportunity does not require – and may even be undermined by – uniformity. In Tawney's view the challenge was to design an educational system capable of recognizing and nurturing the diverse talents of all children, something best achieved by the specialization of provision rather than its homogenization.

This book has argued that Tawney's Christianity was a more personal aspect of his life than many will have imagined when encountering the oft-used descriptor in his case, 'Christian Socialist'. Nevertheless, it was a formative influence and an enduring presence, shaping Tawney and his values at every stage. The argument of *Religion and the Rise of Capitalism* pivoted around the retreat of Christianity from pre-eminent cultural influence before the Reformation to a private religion for individuals after it, a retreat that evidently saddened Tawney and which he wished to reverse. His reaction to the further decline of Christianity in Britain since the 1960s and to mounting opposition to its playing any role at all in the public sphere could only have been further sadness at more evidence of the destructive impact of individualism and materialism. On the other hand, two developments since the 1960s, the transformation in the status of women in Britain, and the development of feminism as a new and vital approach to social organization and its reform, must remind us of Tawney's personal failings. His unfamiliarity and clumsiness with women, especially with his own wife whose quiet suffering and loneliness were never appreciated, is a reminder of a type of masculinity without contemporary relevance best left behind in Edwardian England.

Tawney's recognition that *Equality*, published in 1931, could not be updated but represented his best effort to capture the essential social questions at that moment only, suggests that we are unlikely to discover his continued relevance merely by reading his most famous book. It can do much, for sure, to inspire readers as a guide to the spirit and principles which should pervade the good society, but it is now an historical document rather than a handbook for our own dilemmas. Tawney's discussion was largely about economic and social equality; to these categories we have added more recently race, gender and sexuality, and expanded the context of the discussion as well to consider the inequalities dividing citizens living in wealthy states from those in developing countries. The insistence in *Equality* on the public ownership of the major industries and services as a solution to the specifically British inequalities of the interwar period has been surpassed by events.

Equality embodied the evolution of Tawney into a state socialist after the First World War at a time when many socialists were converted to this strategy. But as this book has argued, before 1914 Tawney's outlook was rather different. In and through adult education he believed in voluntarism and self-improvement rather than statism, in a spiritual socialism rather than the mechanistic collectivism espoused by the Fabian Society, and in moral rather than material advance. This is easily dismissed because, though it offered individual worker-scholars the spiritual sustenance they craved, it could not put food on the tables of the remaining mass of the working class – and Tawney knew that. But it may nevertheless be relevant today when reversion to state action is, with different degrees of complaint and enthusiasm, the instinct and reflex of all political parties and the majority of the electorate. Tawney reminds us that there was once a socialism that aspired to 'the higher life' which his students tried to reach through their studies and as members of a movement that was organized collaboratively. This movement had formed and was largely sustained outside the structures of the state. As his *Commonplace Book* shows, in his private reflections at this stage the young Tawney was seeking an informal and democratic socialism with ethical rather than material objectives, and he was living out these ideas in the service of workers' education.

It is the example of the early Tawney, therefore, spreading fellowship, enlightenment and socialism through education which may have lasting effect and relevance. As his students attested, it wasn't just his ethical message that inspired them, but the generous and just spirit in which it was conveyed, assisted by Tawney's remarkable use of uplifting language. A second and related legacy derives from the way he lived his life. The engagement of the scholar in the reform of society, using his analytical skills to both write history and to change it; the sharing of his life with his students as with his comrades in the trenches; his devotion to public enlightenment; his unfailing honesty of approach in dealing with public affairs; his fundamental decency – these aspects of his biography may be the most influential when the minutiae of interwar social policies have long been forgotten. We have been drawn naturally to the analysis of Tawney's ideas as a first priority, but as their relevance fades, it is his life itself which contains the most important lessons and the elements of enduring relevance. That is the justification of biography in Tawney's case and in the case of many others. To know Tawney's life is not only to understand the man but to carry forward the most powerful element of his legacy, his example.

Notes

Acknowledgements

1 Lawrence Goldman, *Dons and Workers. Oxford and Adult Education Since 1850* (Oxford, 1995).
2 'Tawney, Richard Henry (1880–1962)', *Oxford Dictionary of National Biography* (Oxford, 2004).
3 R. Rees to Arthur Creech Jones, 29 May 1964, Creech Jones papers, Rhodes House Library, Oxford, ACJ 6/10, f. 69.

Introduction

1 Noel Annan, quoted in David M. Fahey, 'R. H. Tawney and the Sense of Community', *The Centenniel Review*, vol. xii, no. 4, Fall 1968, 455.
2 G. R. Elton, *The Future of the Past* (Cambridge, 1968), 16.
3 A. J. P. Taylor, 'A Socialist Saint', in A. J. P. Taylor, *Politicians, Socialism and Historians* (London, 1980), 163. (A review, first published in *The Observer* newspaper in 1974, of Ross Terrill, *R. H. Tawney and His Times. Socialism as Fellowship* (Cambridge, MA, 1973).
4 Sir Stanley Unwin to R. H. Tawney (hereafter RHT), 14 Nov. 1949, Tawney Vyvyan Collection, BLPES, London School of Economics, TV12/2. *Equality* was published in 1931 and a second edition appeared in the same year. A third edition followed in 1938.
5 RHT to Unwin, 20 Nov. 1949, TV12/2.
6 R. H. Tawney, *Equality* (1931), 'Preface to 1951 Edition' and Ch. VII, 'Epilogue, 1938–50'.
7 R. H. Tawney, *The Webbs and Their Work* (London, 1945), 14.
8 RHT, 'British Socialism Today', lecture given to the University of London Fabian Society in 1952, f. 3. This was the original version of a lecture subsequently published in three different versions in 1952, 1960 and 1964.
9 Tawney, *The Webbs and Their Work*, 3.
10 I owe this piece of local lore to Sue Donnelly, the Archivist at the LSE.
11 R. H. Tawney, *The Attack and Other Papers* (London, 1953); idem, *The Radical Tradition* (ed. Rita Hinden) (London, 1964).

12 Stefan Collini, *Absent Minds. Intellectuals in Britain* (Oxford, 2006); Lawrence
    Goldman, 'Intellectuals and the English Working Class 1870–1945: The Case of
    Adult Education', *History of Education*, vol. 29, no. 4, 2000, 281–300.

13 Richard Pipes, 'The Historical Evolution of the Russian Intelligentsia' and Martin
    Malia, 'What is the Intelligentsia?' in Richard Pipes (ed.), *The Russian Intelligentsia*
    (New York, 1961), 1–18, 47–62.

14 Noel Annan, 'The Intellectual Aristocracy', *Studies in Social History: A Tribute to
    G. M. Trevelyan*, ed. J. H. Plumb (1955), 241–87.

15 Edward Shils, 'The Intellectuals. I. Great Britain', *Encounter*, iv, 4, April 1955, 8.

16 Christopher Lasch, *The Agony of the American Left* (New York, 1966); Fritz
    Ringer, *The Decline of the German Mandarins. The German Academic Community
    1890–1933* (Cambridge, MA, 1969).

17 Royden Harrison, 'Sidney and Beatrice Webb' in Carl Levy (ed.), *Socialism and the
    Intelligentsia 1880–1914* (London, 1987), 54.

18 See below, 297–300.

19 Adam Seligman, 'Tendentious Debunking', a review of Gary Armstrong and Tim
    Gray, *The Authentic Tawney. A New Interpretation of the Political Thought of R. H.
    Tawney* (Exeter, 2011), *Review of Politics*, vol. 73, no. 4, 2011, 665–6.

20 W. H. B. Court, *Scarcity and Choice in History* (London, 1970), 128.

21 J. M. Winter, 'A Bibliography of the Published Writings of R. H. Tawney', *Economic
    History Review*, vol. 25, Feb. 1972; idem, 'R. H. Tawney's Early Political Thought',
    Past and Present, vol. 47, May 1970, 71–96.

22 Ross Terrill, *R. H. Tawney and His Times. Socialism as Fellowship* (Cambridge,
    MA, 1973).

23 Anthony Wright, *R. H. Tawney* (Manchester, 1987).

24 Norman Dennis and A. H. Halsey, *English Ethical Socialism: Thomas More to
    R. H. Tawney* (Oxford, 1988).

25 Marc Stears, *Progressives, Pluralists and the Problems of the State. Ideologies of
    Reform in the United States and Britain, 1909–1926* (Oxford, 2002); Ben Jackson,
    Equality and the British Left. A Study in Progressive Political Thought, 1900–64
    (Manchester, 2007).

26 Gary Armstrong and Tim Gray, 'Three Fallacies in the Essentialist Interpretation
    of the Political Thought of R. H. Tawney', *Journal of Political Ideologies*, vol. 15,
    no. 2, June 2010, 161–74; idem, *The Authentic Tawney. A New Interpretation of the
    Political Thought of R. H. Tawney* (Exeter, 2011).

27 J. R. Brooks, 'R. H. Tawney and the Reform of English Education' (unpublished
    PhD dissertation, University of Wales, Bangor, 1974).

28 This episode is discussed in more detail below, 305–8.

29 Said by Secretary of War, Edwin Stanton, as Abraham Lincoln died.

Chapter 1

1 Lawrence Goldman, 'Tawney, Richard Henry', *Oxford Dictionary of National Biography* (ODNB).

2 Brigid Allen, *Morrells of Oxford. The Family and their Brewery 1743-1993* (Oxford, 1994), pp. vii, xiii, xvii–xviii, 6, 7, 17–18, 21, 23, 46, 147.

3 L. S. Presnell, *Country Banking in the Industrial Revolution* (Oxford, 1956), 34–6, 56, 390.

4 http://www.oxfordhistory.org.uk/mayors/1714_1835.

5 'Charles Henry Tawney', *Journal of the Asiatic Society of Great Britain and Ireland*, VOL. 1, 1923, 152–4; *The Times*, 31 July 1922.

6 Bart Schultz, *Henry Sidgwick: Eye of the Universe. An Intellectual Biography* (Cambridge, 2004), 33. E. Sidgwick and A. Sidgwick (eds), *Henry Sidgwick. A Memoir* (1906), 4.

7 Schultz, *Henry Sidgwick*, 94–5.

8 C. H. Tawney (CHT) to Mrs Henry Sidgwick, 31 Aug., 15 Sept. 1900; 27 Feb. 1906, Trinity College, Cambridge, Add. Ms. c. 101/76; 103/123; 103/124.

9 'Charles Henry Tawney 1837–1922' in *The Ocean of Story, being C. H. Tawney's Translation of Somadeva's Kathā Sarit Sāgara (or Ocean of the Streams of Story)* (ed. N. M. Penzer) (10 vols., London, nd) (1924), vol. 1, pp. vii–x.

10 CHT to Cecil James Munro, nd (1869?), Munro Family Papers, London Metropolitan Archives (LMA) Acc. 1063/2198. 'I have seen Maine once or twice . . . but I think he rather wishes to snub me.'

11 'Charles Henry Tawney 1837–1922', vii.

12 Ross Terrill, *R. H. Tawney and his Times. Socialism as Fellowship* (Cambridge, MA, 1973), 22–3.

13 J. M. K. Vyvyan (hereafter JMKV) complained about one author 'imagining a discontented boyhood and youth in Tawney's case and trying to show that Tawney's social and political ideas were a reaction against the injustice of British imperialism with which his father's life had been identified. This would have been absolute rubbish . . . I feel strongly about attempts to politicise Tawney's background and life in a tendentious way.' Vyvyan to James Brooks, 21 May 1974, Tawney Papers, BLPES, London School of Economics (hereafter T), T27/20/1.

14 Cecil James Munro to CHT, 13 Aug. 1868, Munro papers, Acc. 1063/2154.

15 CHT to Munro, 14 Apr. 1869, 20 Apr. 1870, Munro papers, Acc. 1063/2196, 2202.

16 Ibid., 29 Aug. 1870, Acc. 1096/2203.

17 Ibid., 28 Dec. 1879, Acc. 1096/2232. See 'Roberts, Frederick Sleigh, first earl Roberts (1832–1914)', ODNB.

18   Munro to CHT, 6 Feb. 1880, Munro papers, Acc. 1096/2177.

19   'Charles Henry Tawney 1837–1922', ix.

20   Charles Henry Tawney, *The Kathákoça : or, Treasury of Stories* (transl. from Sanskrit manuscripts by C. H. Tawney. With appendix, containing notes by Ernst Leumann) (London, Royal Asiatic Society, 1895).

21   Solicitors' letter to JMKV, 1 Feb. 1962, T27/19/1.

22   CHT to Mrs Henry Sidgwick, 27 Feb. 1906, Add. Ms. c. 103/124. The identity of these two daughters is not clear from the letter.

23   Transcript of an interview with J. M. K. Vyvyan conducted by Signorina Capodivento of Barletta, Bari, 1982 (hereafter Transcript 1982), T/27/21.

24   Michael Postan, 'D. M. Joslin 1925–70' in *R. H. Tawney's Commonplace Book* (eds J. M. Winter and D. M. Joslin) (Cambridge, 1972) (hereafter CB), ix.

25   RHT to Mr F. W. Parrott, 23 Jan. 1961, Tawney-Vyvyan papers, BLPES, London School of Economics (hereafter TV), 16.

26   Michael Sadleir, *Michael Ernest Sadler. A Memoir by his Son* (London, 1949); Linda Grier, *Achievement in Education: The Work of Michael Ernest Sadler 1885–1935* (London, 1952).

27   'Percival, John', ODNB.

28   Frank Fletcher, *After Many Days* (London, 1937), 86–7.

29   Ibid., 69. 'Fletcher, Frank', ODNB.

30   H. C. Barnard, 'A Great Headmaster: John Lewis Paton (1863–1946)', *British Journal of Educational Studies*, vol. 11, no. 1, Nov. 1962, 6. 'Paton, John Lewis Alexander (1863–1946)', ODNB.

31   C. P. Scott to RHT, 20 Jan. 1908, TV/30: 'Mr Paton has mentioned that he told you that we have a post vacant & that you wished to know about it.' . . .

32   *The Meteor*, 23 Mar. 1962, 164.

33   'House Annals. R. Whitelaw Esq., 1892–1900', The Library, Rugby School.

34   Ibid., 'Summer 1899.'

35   *The Meteor*, 1 Aug. 1899, 97.

36   Handwritten memoir of Temple by Tawney, T Add Mss 0005, LSE, f. 1.

37   RHT to Ida Gandy, 3 Feb. 1961, TV16.

38   Mabel J. Scott (wife of Ted Scott) to RHT, 28 Nov. 1960, TV16.

39   R. A. Butler to Arthur Creech Jones, 15 Nov. 1960, Creech Jones papers, Rhodes House, Oxford, ACJ 6/6/67.

40   Ransome to RHT 26 Nov. 1960; RHT to Ransome 14 Feb. 1961, TV16.

41   RHT to Keith S. Fox, 1 Mar. 1961, TV15.

42   Letter to RHT, 29 July 1957, T/27/17/1.

43   RHT to W. A. Pickard-Cambridge, 24 Mar. 1902, Beveridge Papers (hereafter 'Bev'), 2B/2/2.

44 'Smith, John Alexander (1863–1939) and 'Davis, Henry William Carless' (1874–1928), ODNB. Fletcher, *After Many Days*, 51.

45 Balliol College Register.

46 Jose Harris, *William Beveridge. A Biography* (1997) (2nd edn., 2003, Oxford).

47 Ibid., 9–12.

48 William Temple (hereafter WT) to RHT, 'Nov 27' (no year, 1903?), TV/34 and 'Nov 8' [1903], TV31.

49 Harris, *William Beveridge*, 12.

50 R. H. Tawney, 'William Temple – An Appreciation', *The Highway*, Jan. 1945, 44.

51 WT to RHT, 24 Jan. 1905, TV/31.

52 Jeanette Beveridge (hereafter JB) to RHT, 13 Mar. 1907, TV34.

53 RHT to JB, 21 June 1908, TV1.

54 JMKV to James R. Brooks, 21 May 1974, T27/20/1.

55 'Stocks, John Leofric (1882–1937)', ODNB; Drusilla Scott, *A. D. Lindsay. A Biography* (Oxford, 1971).

56 JMKV, 1981 interview, f.2.

57 WHB to ASB, 24 Feb. 1902, Bev 2/A/49.

58 Ibid., 8 June 1902.

59 Jeanette Tawney, Mss Autobiography, BLPES, London School of Economics, TV/21, ff. 269–74.

60 Matthew Grimley, *Citizenship, Community, and the Church of England. Liberal Anglican Theories of The State between the Wars* (Oxford, 2004), 39.

61 RHT to Richard Denman, 27 Feb. 1901, Henry Beveridge collection (hereafter HBC), British Library, BL MSS EUR.C.176/193A, f. 3–4.

62 RHT to Denman, 12 Feb. 1902, HBC, ff. 14–15.

63 S. E. Tawney to Denman, 5 Mar. 1902, HBC, ff. 18–19. See also S. E. Tawney to Denman, 11 June 1902, ff. 26–7.

64 RHT to Denman, 2 June 1902, HBC, ff. 24–5.

65 RHT to Denman, nd [1905 or 1906], HBC, f. 103.

66 RHT to Denman, 2? Dec. 1900, HBC, f. 2 (precise date unclear).

67 Fletcher, *After Many Days*, 69.

68 'Webb, Clement Charles Julian (1865–1954)', ODNB. Webb was later appointed the first holder of the Nolloth Chair in the Philosophy of the Christian Religion in Oxford.

69 E. M. Walker, classics tutor at Queen's.

70 A. E. Cowley, fellow of Magdalen.

71 P. V. M. Benecke, classics tutor at Magdalen.

72 Clement Webb Journal, 16 Oct. 1903, Bodl Ms Eng Misc e 1149, fo. 139, Bodleian Library, Oxford. I am grateful to my colleague Mark Curthoys for digging this out of the archives.

73 RHT to WHB, 16 July 1903, Bev 2A/106. See also RHT to Dick Denman [July 1903], HBC, ff. 47–8, where he made similar remarks and described the examiners' task as 'unenviable'.

74 RHT to WHB, 'Aug 1903', Bev/2A/106.

75 RHT to WHB, 13 Sept. 1903, Bev/2A/106.

76 RHT to WHB, 'Aug 1903', Bev/2A/106.

77 RHT to WHB, 20 Oct. 1903, Bev/2/A/106.

78 RHT to Dick Denman, 11 May 1902, HBC, ff. 23.

79 RHT to Dick Denman, 15 Nov. 1903, HBC, ff. 52–5.

80 RHT to WHB, 7 Nov., 15 Dec. 1903, Bev/2A/106.

81 WT to RHT, '12 Aug' [1905?], TV/30.

82 WT to RHT, nd (1904?), TV/31.

83 JMKV, 1981 transcript, f. 2.

84 Sir Arnold Plant, Transcript of interviews made by the BBC for a radio biography of RHT broadcast on the Home Service in 1963, (hereafter BBC Transcript 1963), Lena Jeger papers, 1/8/1, LSE.

85 E. J. Urwick to Tawney, 24 Aug. 1913, R. H. Tawney: Correspondence and Various Papers, WEA Archive, London Metropolitan University: Trades Union Congress Library Collections, WEA RHT/3/1.

86 Children's Country Holiday Fund (hereafter CCHF), Annual Report 1903.

87 Ibid. See also Toynbee Hall, 22nd Annual Report, 1906, p. 12.

88 Toynbee Hall, 21st Annual Report, 1905, p. 16.

89 'The Children's Country Holiday Fund', leaflet enclosed with letter from RHT to W. A. Pickard-Cambridge, 19 July 1904 (catalogued as 1902), Bev/2B/2/2, item 73.

90 CCHF, Annual Report, 1904.

91 Printed letter from Samuel Barnett enclosed with letter from RHT to W. A. Pickard-Cambridge, 19 July 1904 (catalogued as 1902), Bev/2B/2/2, item 73.

92 *The Times*, 7, 12, 16, 18, 28 Sept. 1905.

93 *Toynbee Record*, vol. xviii, Oct. 1905, p. 4.

94 *Toynbee Record*, July–Sept. 1905, vol. xvii, p. 166.

95 Harris, *William Beveridge*, 84–6. Stuart Eagles, *After Ruskin. The Social and Political Legacies of a Victorian Prophet, 1870–1920* (Oxford, 2011), 131.

96 *Toynbee Record*, Jan. 1905, vol. xvii, 66.

97 Alon Kadish, *Apostle Arnold: The Life and Death of Arnold Toynbee 1852–1883* (1986).

98 R. H. Tawney, *The Webbs and Their Work* (Webb Memorial Lecture, No. 1, 1945), 4.

99 *Toynbee Record*, Jan. 1905, vol. xvii, 66.

100   Sheila Blackburn, 'Ideology and Social Policy: The Origins of the Trade Boards Act', *The Historical Journal*, vol. 34, no. 1, 43–64.

101   'Mallon, James Joseph (1874–1961)', ODNB.

102   CB, 48.

103   Sheila Blackburn, 'Curse or Cure? Why was the Enactment of Britain's 1909 Trade Boards Act so Controversial?', *British Journal of Industrial Relations*, vol. 47, no. 2, June 2009, 231. Blackburn writes as a declared supporter of the statutory minimum wage today. Her argument against Tawney is based on the assumption that a minimum wage would have been better for British workers through the twentieth century than trade boards and the later wages councils. But in the long absence of a minimum wage it is impossible to know if that really would have been the case.

104   Sheila C. Blackburn, 'A Very Moderate Socialist Indeed? R. H. Tawney and Minimum Wages', *Twentieth Century British History*, vol. 10, no. 2, 1999, 136.

105   R. H. Tawney, 'The Theory of Pauperism', *The Sociological Review* (Manchester), Oct. 1909, 361–74.

106   Gareth Stedman Jones, *Outcast London* (Oxford, 1971).

107   David Marquand, 'R. H. Tawney. Prophet of Equality', *The Guardian* 26 Nov. 1960.

108   CB, 10 June 1912, 13.

109   R. H. Tawney, *Poverty as an Industrial Problem* (London, 1913), 16.

110   *The Observer*, 25 Jan. 1953.

111   RHT to WHB, 20 Sept. 1905, Bev/2a/106.

112   WHB to RHT, 21 Sept. 1905, TV 30.

113   WHB to RHT, 13 Sept. 1905, TV 30.

114   RHT to WHB, 22 Oct. 1906, Bev/ 2/A/106.

115   W. Smart to RHT, 21 Oct. 1906, TV/30.

116   'Smart, William (1853–1915)', ODNB.

117   RHT to WHB, 13 Apr. 1907, quoted in J. R. Brooks, 'R. H. Tawney and the Reform of English Education', 31.

118   Nathan Adler and R. H. Tawney, *Boy and Girl Labour* (Women's Industrial Council, London, 1909). See also R. H. Tawney, 'The Economics of Boy Labour', *The Economic Journal*, vol. 19, no. 76, Dec. 1909, 517–37.

119   R. H. Tawney, 'Unemployment and Boy Labour in Glasgow' and 'Labour Exchanges and Relief Work in Strassburg', *Royal Commission on the Poor Laws and Relief of Distress*, vol. xlix, 1910, 329–48, 96610–96619.

120   Ibid., 332.

121   Ibid., 346, 96836–46.

122   RHT to JB, 10 Aug. 1908, TV1.

123   See below, 286–7.

124   Sir Richard Rees, BBC transcript 1963, LJP.

Chapter 2

1 Ross Terrill, *R. H. Tawney and His Times. Socialism as Fellowship* (Cambridge, MA, 1973), pp. 108–11.

2 Vyvyen Brendon, *Children of the Raj* (2005) (2006 edn., London), pp. 120–2.

3 'Beveridge, Annette Susannah 1842–1929', ODNB.

4 Jose Harris, *William Beveridge. A Biography* (Oxford University Press, Oxford (1997), 2nd edn., 2003), p. 45.

5 Jeanette Tawney [pseudonym 'F.N.Smith'], Mss autobiography, 'I Learn to Live', TV21, BLPES, London School of Economics, ch. 19, ff. 192–6.

6 Ibid., ch. 22, f. 1.

7 JB to RHT, 'Wednesday', TV35/2.

8 JB to RHT, 7 Dec. 1903, TV35/2.

9 Rt Jenner Hoskin to Dr A. C. Gemmell, 21 May 1937, T27/6. JT, 'Autobiography', ch. 23, f. 239.

10 RHT to JT, 27 June 1908, TV1.

11 RHT to JT, undated but from Balliol College, so before RHT went down in the summer of 1903. TV1.

12 RHT to JT, 11 Dec. 1903, TV1.

13 JT, 'Autobiography', ch. 23, ff. 241–2.

14 Ibid., f. 247.

15 Ibid., f. 242.

16 JB to WB, 'April 1905', Bev 2/A/96.

17 JT, Mss Autobiography, ch. 22, f. 6.

18 Ibid., ch. 22, f. 9.

19 Ibid., f. 242.

20 Ibid., ch. 19, f. 194.

21 Ibid., f. 239.

22 Harris, *William Beveridge*, 103.

23 JT, 'Autobiography', f. 236.

24 RHT to JT, 29 Aug. 1908, TV1.

25 RHT to JT, 14 May 1908, TV1.

26 JT to RHT, 'Sunday', Haslemere TV40/1.

27 JT to RHT, 'Thursday 11.30' TV40/2.

28 JT to RHT, 'Tuesday', TV40/2.

29 JT to RHT, 8 June 1908, TV42/2.

30 RHT to JB, 29 May 1908, T27/8.

31 RHT to JB, 9 June 1908, TV1.

32 RHT to JN, 30 May 1908, TV1.

33 Ibid.

34 RHT to JB, nd (probably late June 1908), TV1.

35 RHT to JB, nd (probably early autumn 1908), TV1.

36 JB to RHT, 'III', nd (probably early 1909), TV35.

37 RHT to JB, 17 June 1908, TV1.

38 RHT to JB, 19 June 1908, TV1.

39 RHT to JB, 29 Aug. 1908, TV1.

40 RHT to JB, 20 Sept. 1908, TV1.

41 RHT to JB, 16 Aug. 1908, TV1.

42 RHT to JB, 21 June 1908, TV1.

43 RHT to JB nd (probably late June 1908) See fn 33 above.

44 RHT to JB, 21 Nov. 1908, TV1.

45 RHT to JB, 27 June 1909, T27/7.

46 RHT to JB, 16 Aug. 1908, TV1.

47 JB to RHT, 'Wednesday', Haslemere, TV1.

48 Beatrice Webb, *Our Partnership* (London, 1948).

49 At the end of Ch. 29 of her typescript autobiography, which is largely on the
    subject of marriage and divorce, Jeanette wrote of Tawney's habits and compared
    marriage to her previous home life. She mentioned Marie Stopes and sexual
    knowledge in slightly obscure paragraphs which seem to be about sexual
    problems: 'At best', she wrote 'knowledge has only acquired the art of controlling
    sex impulses and not of producing them' (f. 293).

50 JB to ASB, 24 June 1908, Bev/2/A/90.

51 JT, 'Autobiography', f. 51.

52 WB to ASB, 23 June 1908, Bev/2/A, quoted in Harris, *William Beveridge*, p. 103.

53 RHT to JB, 18 May 1908, TV1.

54 RHT to JB, 27 June 1908, TV1.

55 ASB to JB, 24 June 1908, TV42; Greta Jones, *Social Darwinism and English
    Thought. The Interaction between Biological and Social Theory* (Brighton, 1980).

56 RHT to JB, 5 Jan 1910, T27/7; JB to WB, 10 March 1909, Bev/ 2A/96.

57 ASB to RHT, 12 July 1908, TV42.

58 HB to RHT, 13 July 1908, TV42.

59 ASB to RHT, Mar. 25, 1909 and 'Pitfold, Sunday', TV30.

60 RHT to JB, 9 Oct. 1908, TV27/8.

61 CMT to RHT, 13 July 1908, TV/29/1.

62 JB to RHT, 29 Apr. 1909, TV35.

63 JB to RHT, II, nd (early 1909), TV35.

64 RHT to JB, 13 June 1909, TV1.

65 JT, 'Autobiography', f. 252.

66 RHT to Jimmy Palmer, 21 Nov. 1909, MS 3010, f. 77, Papers of Bishop E. J. Palmer,
    Lambeth Palace Library.

67   Speech to a WEA meeting in the University of Manchester, 1953, T18/9.

68   JT, 'Autobiography', ch. 25, ff. 253–6.

69   Ibid., f. 300.

70   Ibid., f. 293.

71   Ibid., f. 273.

72   JT to RHT, 22 Dec. 1910, TV38; JT to ASB, 13 Oct. 1910, Bev/2/A/91.

73   JT to HB, 3 June; 16 Sept., 22 Sept. 1912, Bev/ 2A/82.

74   JT to Will Beveridge (WHB), 17 Sept. 1912, Bev/ 2A/96.

75   Ibid.

76   JT to RHT, 19 Feb. 1911.

77   JT to RHT, 31 Mar. 1911.

78   Sir Richard Rees, BBC Transcript 1963.

79   RHT to Lawrence Hammond, 16 Oct. 1915, Papers of J. L. and Barbara
     Hammond, Bodleian Library, Oxford SC 47412, f. 54.

80   RHT to Richard Denman, 27 Dec. 1902, H. Beveridge Collection, British Library,
     BL MSS EUR. C. 176/193a, f. 34.

81   Anthony Arblaster, *Bulletin of the Society for the Study of Labour History*, vol. 54,
     pt. 1 (1989), 99.

Chapter 3

1   R. H. Tawney, 'Introduction', in T. W. Price (ed.), *The Story of the Workers'
    Educational Association from 1903 to 1924* (London, 1924), 7–8.

2   *Oxford and Working-Class Education: Being the Report of a Joint Committee of
    University and Working-Class Representatives on the Relation of the University to
    the Higher Education of Workpeople*, 2nd edn. (Oxford, 1909), 58.

3   Ibid.

4   Arthur Greenwood, 'Labour and Adult Education', in R. St John Parry (ed.),
    Cambridge Essays on Adult Education (Cambridge, 1920), 120.

5   L. V. Gill, 'What can we learn from History?', *The Highway*, vol. 40, Oct. 1949, 257.

6   Harold Begbie, *Living Water: Being Chapters from the Romance of the Poor Student*
    (London, 1918), 182.

7   Bernard Jennings, *Albert Mansbridge and English Adult Education* (Hull, 1976),
    3–7.

8   T. W. Price, The Story of the Workers' Educational Association, 16. See also *The
    Higher Education of Working Men, Being the Official Report of the Joint Conference
    Between Co-operators, Trade Unionists, and University Extension Authorities, Held
    at Oxford, on Saturday, August 22nd 1903* (London, 1903).

9   Bernard Jennings, *Albert Mansbridge* (Leeds, 1973), 23.

10 Werner Picht, *Toynbee Hall and the English Settlement Movement*,(trans. L. A. Cowell) (London, 1914), 187.

11 H. P. Smith, *Labour and Learning: Albert Mansbridge, Oxford and the WEA* (Oxford, 1956), 36; W. E. Styler, 'The Report in Retrospect' in S. Harrop (ed.), *Oxford and Working-Class Education*, rev. 2nd edn. (Nottingham, 1987), 52.·

12 Henrietta Barnett, *Canon Barnett. His Life, Work and Friends* (London, 1921 edn.), 503.

13 'Livingstone, Richard Wynn (1880–1960)' *ODNB*. Richard Livingstone, *The Future in Education* (London, 1941).

14 'Fyfe, Sir William Hamilton (1878–1965)', *ODNB*.

15 'Myres, Sir John Linton (1869–1954)', ODNB.

16 'Zimmern, Sir Alfred Eckhard (1879–1957)', *ODNB*.

17 The documents are preserved in T21/1, 2, 3.

18 See G. L. Prentice, *The Life of Charles Gore: A Great Englishman* (London, 1935).

19 RHT, Handwritten memoir of William Temple, T.Add 0005, BLPES.

20 'Lambda', 'The University and the Nation', *Westminster Gazette*, 15 Feb., 16 Feb., 17 Feb., 23 Feb., 24 Feb., 2 Mar., 3 Mar., 10 Mar. 1906. Barnett, *Canon Barnett*, 502.

21 [Anon] 'Some Principles of University Reform', *Westminster Gazette*, 22 Feb., 23 Feb., 1 Mar., 2 Mar., 8 Mar., 9 Mar. 1907. See Janet Howarth, 'The Edwardian Reform Movement' in M. G. Block and M. C. Curthoys (eds), *The History of the University of Oxford, vii, The Nineteenth Century*, pt. 2 (Oxford, 2000), 832.

22 'Oxford and the Nation', *The Times*, 3 Apr. 1907, p. 6; 5 Apr., p. 6; 9 Apr., p. 8; 13 Apr., p. 9; 16 Apr., p. 4; 20 Apr., p. 14; 29 Apr., p. 7; 11 May, p. 20.

23 'Lambda', 'The University and the Nation'. I Introductory', *Westminster Gazette*, 15 Feb. 1906, 1–2.

24 'The Limitations of the College System', *Westminster Gazette*, 2 Mar. 1906, p. 2.

25 Zimmern to RHT, 'Feb 14' [1906], TV/30.

26 Zimmern to RHT, 'March 1' [1906], TV/30.

27 W. Markby to RHT, 28 Feb. 1906, TV/30.

28 JB to RHT, 7 Dec. 1906, TV/36.

29 'Introductory', *The Times*, 3 Apr. 1907, p. 6.

30 Parliamentary Debates (PD) 4th series, clxxviii, 24 July 1907, 1526. See also Jennings, *Albert Mansbridge*, 12–13; Iremonger, *William Temple*, 89; Peter Gordon and John White, *Philosophers as Educational Reformers: The Influence of Idealism on British Educational Thought and Practice* (London, 1979), 126–8. Prentice, *Life of Charles Gore*, 290.

31 PD, 24 July 1907, 1527.

32 'The Need of Reform at Oxford', *The Times*, 24 July 1907, p. 10.

33 Howarth, 'Edwardian Reform Movement', passim.

34 A. E. Z[immern], 'The Workers At the Summer Meeting', *Oxford Magazine*, 24 Oct. 1907, 23–4.

35 Sidney Ball to Revd Samuel Barnett, 21 Mar. 1907, R. H. Tawney, Correspondence re Early Tutorial Classes 1907–8, WEA Archive, Trades Union Congress Library Collections, London Metropolitan University (LMU), WEA Central/3/6/1. See also *Papers Submitted to the National Conference of Working Class and Educational Organisations, held in the Examination Schools, High Street, Oxford, on Saturday, August 10th, 1907* (London, 1907).

36 W. Nield, 'What Workpeople Want Oxford to Do' and S. Ball, 'What Oxford Can Do for Workpeople', Ibid. 7, 14.

37 *Oxford and Working-Class Education*, preface.

38 Quoted in Jennings, *Mansbridge*, 19.

39 RHT to JB [nd, probably late June 1908], TV1.

40 A. E. Zimmern to RHT, 9 Oct. [1908], TV29/1.

41 *Oxford and Working-Class Education*, ch. 8, 'Summary of Recommendations'.

42 Ibid., 58.

43 Ibid., 88.

44 RHT, Memoir of William Temple, f. 6, Tawney Add 0005.

45 J. A. R. Marriott to R. H. Tawney, 30 Nov., 20 Dec. 1907, R. H. Tawney. Correspondence re Early Tutorial Classes 1907–8, WEA Central/3/6/1, LMU.

46 RHT to JB, 27 June 1908, TV1.

47 'Tutorial Classes Committee: Minutes of First Meeting', 'Extra Mural Work 1907–9', A. L. Smith Papers, Balliol College, Oxford. WT to RHT, 25 Nov. 1908, TV/29/1.

48 See a series of letters from Mansbridge trying to soothe Tawney's anxieties over his position and career. Mansbridge to Tawney, 10, 28, 29, 30 Jan.; 27 Mar.; 6 Apr. 1908, 'R. H. Tawney: Correspondence re Early Tutorial Classes 1907–8', WEA Central/3/6/1, LMU. See also Mansbridge to A. L. Smith, 29 Jan. 1908, 'Extra-Mural Work 1907–9', A. L. Smith Papers, Balliol College, Oxford.

49 RHT to Mansbridge, 6 Apr. 1908, 1907–8 Joint Committee on Tutorial Classes, DES/F/14/1, Oxford University Archives. During the Hilary and Trinity terms 1909, Tawney lectured in Balliol on 'The History of the English Poor Law'.

50 W. R. Anson, Warden of All Souls, to RHT, 21 Dec. 1909, TV34.

51 Zimmern to RHT, 9 Dec. [1908], TV29/1.

52 RHT to JB, 12 Nov. 1908, T 27/7.

53 Mary Stocks, *The Workers' Educational Association. The First Fifty Years* (London, 1953),40.

54 Ibid., 46.

55 R. H. Tawney, 'Introduction' in W. H. Warburton (ed.), *The History of Trade Union Organisation in the North Staffordshire Potteries* (London, 1931), 16.

56 *Board of Education: Report by H. M. Inspectors upon University Tutorial Classes under the Supervision of the Joint Committee of the University of Oxford, for the period ending 3Ist July, 1924* (n.d.), 'Copies of Special Reports, Memoranda etc.', Oxford University Archives (hereafter OUA) DES/F2/1/8, folder 3, p. 5.

57 R. H. Tawney, 'An Experiment in Democratic Education', *The Political Quarterly*, May 1914, 74–5.

58 L. V. Gill to RHT, 10 Dec. 1907, 'R. H. Tawney: Correspondence re Early Tutorial Classes 1907–8', WEA Central/3/6/1, LMU.

59 'The Rochdale Tutorial Class', MSS article [by T. W. Price] dated '1908' with Mansbridge's comment 'by a student who works in the bleaching works', 'Rochdale Tutorial Class', WEA Central/3/6/7, LMU.

60 L. V. Gill to A. Mansbridge, 26 Jan. 1908, 2 Feb. I908, 'Rochdale Class' (an exercise book comprising letters sent to Mansbridge from the first Rochdale class which he transcribed in his own hand), WEA Central/3/6/4, LMU.

61 T. W. Price to A. Mansbridge, 2 Feb. 1908, Ibid.

62 J. W. Henighan to A. Mansbridge, 2 Feb. 1908, Ibid.

63 Fred Hall to A. Mansbridge, 7 Mar. 1908, Ibid.

64 J. W. Henighan to A. Mansbridge, 14 May 1908, Ibid.

65 A. W. Wilkinson to A. Mansbridge (n.d.), Ibid.

66 'Tutorial History Class. Mr R. H. Tawney's Report on the First Session' (press cutting, Rochdale source unknown), Ibid. See also Tawney's report to the Oxford Delegacy on the class, 'Oxford University Extension. Reports of Lecturers, Examiners and Local Committees 1907–8', OUA, DES/R/3/37 f. 739.

67 Ibid., f. 740.

68 'Tawney on Wadsworth', *The Highway*, 48, Jan. 1957, 82. See also R. H. Tawney, 'A Fifty Year's Memory', *Manchester Guardian*, 5 Nov. 1956, 4.

69 A. Wadsworth to RHT, 25 Nov. 1912, T 14/1.

70 A. L. Smith to Lord Balfour of Burleigh, 30 June 1908, A. L. Smith Papers, 'Extra-Mural Work 1907–9'.

71 A. E. Zimmern to A. Mansbridge, 8 Apr. 1908, '1907–8 Joint Committee on Tutorial Classes', DES/F/14/1, OUA. See also 'Report by Mr Zimmern on the Rochdale Class', Apr. 4 [1908], Cartwright Papers, 'Records of Work in North Staffordshire', OUA.

72 Oxford University Extension. Reports of Lecturers . . . 1907–8, OUA, DES/R/3/37, f. 731. See also Linden West, 'The Tawney Legend Re-examined', *Studies in Adult Education*, vol. 4/2, Oct. 1972, 112–13.

73 On the socially-mixed nature of Cambridge tutorial classes and their recruitment from the ranks of clerks, teachers and the lower middle class generally, see Edwin Welch, *The Peripatetic University: Cambridge Local Lectures 1873–1973* (Cambridge, 1973), 112.

74 Report of the Local Secretary, W. T. Cope, in Oxford University Extension. Reports of Lecturers . . . 1907–8, OUA, DES/R/3/37, f. 735. See also 'Reports on Tutorial Classes', *Oxford and Working-Class Education*, 105. For a slightly later social breakdown of a Longton class, dating from 1912 to 1913, see the class register in TV 27/10.

75 A. Emery, 'In the Early Tutorial Classes, (I) Longton', *The Highway*, vol. 44, Apr. 1953, 253.

76 Ibid.

77 Oxford University Extension. Reports of Lecturers . . . 1907–8, OUA, DES/R/3/37, f. 732.

78 Mansbridge and Temple, 'Report of the First Year's Working', f. 4.

79 RHT to JB, 22 Oct. 1908, TV1.

80 RHT, Address to 'a gathering at [Manchester] University', 1953, T18/9. H. P. Smith, 'A Tutorial Class Makes History', *Adult Education*, vol. 31, no. 4, spring 1959, 271–3.

81 *Portrait of R. H. Tawney*, 1963.

82 Report of the Local Secretary, W. T. Cope, in Oxford University Extension. Report of Lecturers . . . 1907–8, OUA, DES/R/3/37, f. 735. See also 'Reports on Tutorial Classes', *Oxford and Working-Class Education*, 105.

83 BBC Transcript 1963, f. 15, identity unknown.

84 Cartwright to A. Mansbridge, 9 Nov. 1909, OUA, DES/F/2/1/4.

85 Oxford University Extension. Reports of Lecturers . . . 1907–8, OUA, DES/R/3/37, f. 732.

86 'Longton Tutorial Class. Report for Session 1909–10', p. 3, Cartwright Papers, 'Records of Work in North Staffordshire' (Box), Oxford University Archives. See also Cartwright's report as local secretary for 1908–9 in Oxford University Extension. Reports of Lecturers . . . 1908–9, OUA, DES/R/3/38, f. 564.

87 A. Zimmern, 'Education and the Working Class', *The Round Table: A Quarterly Review of the Politics of the British Empire*, vol. 14, March 1914, 264.

88 Frank Emery, BBC Transcript 1963, f. 14.

89 C. B. Caldecott to A. Mansbridge, 26 Dec. 1909, Tutorial Classes Committee Correspondence, Oxford University Archives DES/F/2/l/l0. For Mansbridge's less than sympathetic response, see A. Mansbridge to C. B. Caldecott, 30 Dec. 1909, OUA DES/F/2/1/10.

90 J. Walker to RHT, nd (1909?), TV 29/1.

91 John Bailey to RHT, 5 June 1911, TV29/1.

92 Ibid., 4 July 1911.

93 R. H. Tawney, *Secondary Education for All. A Policy for Labour* (Labour Party, 1922) (London, 1988 edn.), 88.

94 Mansbridge and Temple, 'Report of the First Year's Working', f. 7.

95 Oxford University Extension Delegacy: Tutorial Classes Committee: Annual Report 1909–10, 8.

96 Mansbridge and Temple, 'Report of the First Year's Working', f. 5 n.

97 RHT to JB, 16 Jan. 1909, TV1.

98 Frank Emery, BBC Transcript 1963, f. 12.

99 Lena Jeger, 'Preface' to the *First Tawney Memorial Lecture* by Stanley G. Evans (1964, Christian Socialist Movement).

100 Price, *Story of the WEA*, 33–4.

101 [E. S. Cartwright] 'Looking Backwards: A Tutorial Class Anniversary. By an Old Student', *Rewley House Papers*, vol. 2, 1929, 72–3.

102 E. S. Cartwright, 'Longton Tutorial Class: Report on the Work of the Past Session and also Since the Commencement', 10 Apr.1911, p. 2, Cartwright Papers, 'Records of Work in North Staffordshire' (Box), OUA.

103 E. S. Cartwright to RHT, 9 Jan. 1911. For similar expressions, see also ESC to RHT, 30 Apr., 6 June 1910, TV 29/1/2.

104 'Tomlinson' to RHT, 22 Sept. 1910, TV 29/2.

105 Ibid.

106 Signature indecipherable, from 34 Holme Road, Burnley, 23 Feb. 1914, TV 29/1.

107 F. Rudge to RHT nd (Nov/Dec. 1960); RHT to F. Rudge, 23 Jan. 1961, TV16.

108 RHT to Bill Flower, 27 Jan. 1960, TV15.

109 Emery, BBC Transcript, f. 12.

110 Price, *Story of the WEA*, 45.

111 Leonard [surname unknown] to RHT, 2, 12 July 1910, TV 29/1.

112 H. Jenkins and W. Morries to the Oxford Tutorial Classes Committee, 21 Feb. 1913, in 'Report on University Scholarships Held by Tutorial Class Students', Nov. 1916, p. 1, OUA DES/F/2/2/3.

113 Howarth, 'Edwardian Reform Movement', 849.

114 See A. E. Zimmern to A. Mansbridge, 19 Aug. 1913, Mansbridge Papers, British Library, London, lxiiiA, Add. MS 65257, f. 34.

115 See R. A. Lowe, 'The North Staffordshire Miners' Higher Education Movement', *Educational Review*, vol. 22, no. 3, June 1970, 263–77. See also 'Adult Education in North Staffordshire', *Ministry of Reconstruction: Adult Education Committee: Final Report*, (London, HMSO, Cmd. 321, 1919), 296–309.

116 Zimmern, 'Education and the Working Class', 267.

117 H. P. Smith, 'Edward Stuart Cartwright. A Note on his Work for Adult Education', *Rewley House Papers*, vol. 3, no. 1, 1949–50, 20.

118 Cartwright, 'Looking Backwards', 69–70.

119 Lowe, 'North Staffordshire Miners', 267–8.

120 Zimmern, 'Education', 263–4.

121 'Oxford Joint Committee. Minutes of the Meeting held on December 27th and
     28th 1907', A. L. Smith's Letters, Box 14, 'WEA', 3.

122 Beatrice Webb, *Diary of Beatrice Webb*, iv, 1924–43, eds N. and J. Mackenzie
     (London, 1985), 360 (entry for 8 Dec. 1935).

123 RHT to Mansbridge, 21 Sept. 1912, Mansbridge Papers, xxii, Add. MS 62516, ff. 89–93.

124 Zimmern to RHT, 9 Oct. 1908, TV/29/1.

125 RHT to Mansbridge, 10 Oct. 1912, Mansbridge Papers, xxii, Add. MS 62516,
     ff. 79–82.

126 Ibid., 15 Oct. 1912, f. 98.

127 Ibid., 21 Sept. 1912, f. 92.

128 Ibid., f. 90.

129 Howarth, 'Edwardian Reform Movement', 848.

130 Paul Yorke, *Ruskin College 1899–1909. Ruskin Students' Labour History Pamphlets,
     no. 1* (Oxford, 1977); Bernard Jennings, 'Revolting Students: The Ruskin College
     Dispute 1908–9', *Studies in Adult Education*, vol. 9, no. 1, Apr. 1977, 1–16;
     J. P. M. Millar, *The Labour College Movement* (London, 1979). Goldman, *Dons and
     Workers*, 163–90.

131 R. H. Tawney, 'The WEA and Adult Education' in idem, *The Radical Tradition:
     Twelve Essays on Politics, Education and Literature* (London, 1964), 89–90.

132 Jonathan Rée, 'Socialism and the Educated Working Class' in Carl Levy (ed.),
     Socialism and the Intelligentsia 1880–1914 (London, 1987), 214.

133 RHT to JPM Millar, 23 Jan. 1961, TV16.

134 A. Mansbridge to G. Lansbury, 27 Sept. 1907, in 'R. H. Tawney, Correspondence
     re Early Tutorial Classes 1907–8', WEA Central/3/6/1, LMU.

135 RHT to G. Lansbury, 9 Dec. 1910, Lansbury Papers, 4, LSE Archives.

136 RHT, *Commonplace Book (CB)*, 7 (29 April 1912).

137 Norman Dennis and A. H. Halsey, *English Ethical Socialism: Thomas More to R. H.
     Tawney* (Oxford, 1988), 155.

138 Jay Winter, 'R. H. Tawney's Early Political Thought', *Past and Present*, vol. 47, May
     1970, 74–5. See also A. W. Wright, *R. H. Tawney* (Manchester, 1987), 6.

139 Tawney, *CB*, 43 (30 Oct. 1912).

140 J. M. K. Vyvyan, Transcript 1982, f. 10.

141 See letters from his student Joseph Nuttall of Littleborough, responding to
     Tawney's requests for information and weekly budgets: J. Nuttall to RHT, 26 Aug.
     and 6 Sept. 1910, in R. H. Tawney: Correspondence and Various Papers, WEA
     RHT/3/1. See also a file of material in 'Essays of Students of Early Tutorial Classes,
     including Rochdale and Longton', WEA Central/3/6/2, LMU.

142 Henry Clay, *Economics: An Introduction for the General Reader* (London, 1916), x.

143 R. H. Tawney, 'The WEA and Adult Education', 82.

144 Tutorial Classes Committee Annual Report 1909–10, 2.

145 *Oxford and Working-Class Education*, 85.

146 'Workers and Education: Mr Tawney's Appeal to Organised Labour', *Rochdale Observer*, 14 Apr. 1910, quoted in Sheila Rowbotham, '"Travellers in a Strange Country"; Responses of Working-Class Students to the University Extension Movement 1873–1910', *History Workshop Journal*, vol. 12, autumn 1981, 88.

Chapter 4

1 C. P. Scott to RHT, 12 Jan. 1912, TV 29/1.

2 R. H. Tawney, *Equality* (1931) (1951 edn.), 198.

3 'University of London. Regulations for the Administration of the Ratan Tata Fund', Minutes of the LSE Finance Committee, 31 May 1912; 'Report of the Director, presented to the Sociological Benefactions Committee', 18 Feb. 1913, LSE Central Filing Registry, 652/A, BLPES.

4 Ralf Dahrendorf, *A History of the London School of Economics and Political Science 1895–1995* (Oxford, 1995), 124–6.

5 Arthur Greenwood, *The Health and Physique of Schoolchildren* (London, 1913).

6 M. E. Bulkley, *The Feeding of Schoolchildren* (London, 1914); *The Establishment of Legal Minimum Rates in the Boxmaking Industry Under the Trade Boards Act of 1909* (London, 1915).

7 A. L. Bowley and A. R. Burnett-Hurst, *Livelihood and Poverty. A Study in the Conditions of Working-Class Households in Northampton, Warrington, Stanley and Reading* (London, 1915), 46.

8 V. de Vesselitsky, *The Homeworker and her Outlook. A Descriptive Study of Tailoresses and Boxmakers* (London, 1916).

9 R. H. Tawney, *The Establishment of Minimum Rates in the Chain-Making Industry under the Trade Boards Act of 1909* (London, 1914); idem, *The Establishment of Minimum Rates in the Tailoring Industry under the Trade Boards Act of 1909* (London, 1915).

10 R. H. Tawney, *Poverty as an Industrial Problem* (London, 1913).

11 R. H. Tawney, 'Foreword' to Carter L. Goodrich, *The Frontier of Control. A Study in British Workshop Politics* (London, 1920), vii.

12 R. H. Tawney, 'Mr E. S. Cartwright', *The Highway*, Oct. 1950, p. 14.

13 Jeanette Tawney, Draft chapters of an unpublished autobiography, TV21/22, Ch. 1.

14 Annette to William Beveridge, 8 Sept. 1914, Bev 2/A/97.

15 A. E. Bland, P. A. Brown and R. H. Tawney (eds), *English Economic History – Select Documents* (1914).

16 JT, Mss autobiography, Ch. II, f. 1.

17 JT to WB, 26 Nov. 1914, Bev 2/A/97.

18 'The Manchester Regiment in 1914–18', *The Long, Long Trail. The British Army in the Great War*, http://www.1914-1918.net/mancs.htm.

19 John Keegan, 'Pals to the Death', *Daily Telegraph*, 1 July 2006.

20 Michael Stedman, *Manchester Pals* (Barnsley, S. Yorks, 2004), 231.

21 J. L. Hammond to RHT, 29 Nov. 1914, TV/41.

22 *The Times*, 18, 22 Sept. 1914. On Unwin, see below, 223–4.

23 RHT, *Some Thoughts on Education and the War* (1917) (WEA), pp. 7–8. Originally published in *The Times* and then as a pamphlet by the WEA, it was later known and republished as 'A National College of All Souls'.

24 Jenkins to Tawney, 30 Nov. 1914, TV/41.

25 J. M. Winter and D. M. Joslin (eds), *R. H. Tawney's Commonplace Book* (Cambridge, 1971), 'Introduction', xxi.

26 Ibid., 28 Dec. 1914, 82–3.

27 RHT to JT, nd (late 1914), TV/1.

28 JT, Mss autobiography, Ch. II, f. 1.

29 RHT to JT, 26 Dec. 1915, TV 1.

30 J. W. Ramsbottom to RHT, 29 Nov. 1960, TV16.

31 RHT to JT, 1 Jan. 1915 (RHT wrote date as 1914), TV/1.

32 Alastair Cowan, *The 22nd Battalion Manchester Regiment. The Western Front, Italy, Austria, Egypt* (Knutsford, Cheshire, 2011), 4.

33 'The Manchester Regiment 1899–1958', http://www.themanchesters.org/22th%20batt.htm.

34 Ibid.

35 RHT to JT, 8 Mar. 1915, T27/8.

36 RHT to JT, 1 Apr. 1915, T27/8.

37 RHT to JT, 22 Sept. 1915, TV/1.

38 RHT to JT, 21 Apr. 1915, T27/8.

39 JT to HB (father), 22 Mar. 1915, Bev/2A/82.

40 Lena Jeger, Speech on the unveiling of a blue plaque to Tawney in Mecklenburgh Square, London, 30 Nov. 1980 in Jeger Papers, BLPES, Jeger 1/8/1.

41 JT, Mss autobiography, Ch. II.

42 Regimental Paymaster, Preston to JT, 26 Feb., 22 Mar. 1915, Bev/9A/36/7.

43 JT to WB, 5, 23 Mar. 1915, Bev/2A.97; JT, Mss autobiography, ch. VII.

44 JT to ASB, 11 Mar. 1915, Bev 2/A/93.

45 RHT to ASB, 31 May 1916, Bev/2/A/105.

46 JT, Mss autobiography, Ch. X. *Surrey Advertiser*, 28 Aug. 1915.

47 JT to ASB, 22 May 1915, Bev/2/A/93.

48 RHT to JT, 3, 5 Oct. 1915, T 27/8.

49 RHT to Lawrence Hammond, 16 Oct. 1915, Papers of J. L. and Barbara Hammond, Bodleian Library, Oxford SC 47412, f. 54.

50 RHT to JT, 2 Nov. 1915, T27/8.

51 RHT to JT, 8 Mar. 1915, T27/8.

52 RHT to JT, 2 Oct. 1915, T27/8; 23 Jan. 1916, TV/1.

53 RHT to Mil (sister), 9 Dec. 1915, TV45.

54 RHT to JT, 22 Dec. 1915, TV/1.

55 RHT to Mil, 22 Nov. 1915, TV/45.

56 Ibid.

57 RHT to Mil, 9 Dec. 1915, TV/45.

58 RHT to JT, 'Apr. 1916', TV/1.

59 'A Talk on War Conditions & Policy in G. Britain, probably given in USA 1941–2', T16/3, f. 4.

60 Ibid.

61 RHT to JT, 10 Feb. 1916, T27/8.

62 RHT to WB, 24 Dec. 1915, Bev/2A/106.

63 RHT to JT, 29 Mar. 1916, TV/1.

64 RHT to WB, 24 Dec. 1915, Bev/2A/106.

65 RHT to JT, 14 Apr. 1916, TV/1. There is no evidence that the poem was ever published.

66 RHT to JT, 22 Apr. 1916, TV/1.

67 RHT to JT, 26 Dec. 1915, TV/1.

68 Thomas Jones, *Whitehall Diary*, vol. 1, 1916–25 (London, 1969), 24. The account of this meeting given by J. D. Chambers in which Tawney apparently met General Sir Douglas Haig and Arthur Henderson and refused to help is almost certainly incorrect. See J. D. Chambers, 'The Tawney Tradition', *Economic History Review*, vol. 24, 3, 1971, 359.

69 R. H. Tawney, *The Sword of the Spirit* (London, 1917), 14.

70 R. H. Tawney to A. L. Smith, 27 Dec. 1917, A. L. Smith papers, Balliol College, Oxford, Box 12 (T).

71 RHT to WB, 24 Dec. 1915, Bev/2A/106.

72 RHT to JT, 'Apr. 1916', TV/1.

73 RHT to JT, 23 Jan. 1916, TV/1.

74 Cowan, *The 22nd Battalion*, 7.

75 RHT to Mil, 5 May 1916, TV45.

76 RHT to JT, May 1916 (the first page is missing so the precise date is unknown)

77 'The letters from which the following extracts have been taken were written to his wife by a well-known student of social economics, who is now a sergeant in one of the New Army battalions'.

78 Cowan, *The 22nd Battalion*, 10.

79 RHT to JT, 26 June 1916, T27/8.

80 RHT to JT, 20 June 1916, T27/8.

81 RHT to JT, 23 June 1916, T27/8.

82 RHT to JT, 29 June 1916, T27/8.

83 Martin Gilbert, *Somme. The Heroism and Horror of War* (2006) (London, 2007 edn.), 48.

84 Stedman, *Manchester Pals*, 116–7.

85 Ray Westlake, *Tracing British Battalions on the Somme* (1994) (Barnsley, S. Yorks, 2004 edn.), 239.

86 Cowan, *The 22nd Battalion*, 14.

87 Sir Stanley Unwin, 1963 BBC Transcript, f. 8; CHT to JT, 26 Oct. 1916, T27/6.

88 RHT to J. W. Ramsbottom, 12 Jan. 1961, TV16.

89 J. W. Ramsbottom to RHT, 29 Nov. 1960, TV16.

90 'The Somme', Channel 4, 14 Nov. 2005, 9.00 p.m.

91 'The Attack' in RHT, *The Attack and Other Papers* (London, 1953), 11–20.

92 Cowan, *The 22nd Battalion*, 10.

93 Stedman, *Manchester Pals*, 119 and n.

94 Ibid., 117.

95 Martin Middlebrook, *The First Day on the Somme* (1971) (London, 2001 edn.), 210–11. 'Webmatters: Mametz 1st July 1916'; http://www.webmatters.net/txtpat/index.php?id=129.

96 Stedman, *Manchester Pals*, 119.

97 Cowan, *The 22nd Battalion*, 17.

98 Ibid., 18.

99 'This plaque commemorates the everlasting memory of the 20th, 21st, 22nd and 24th Battalions of the Manchester Regiment who, as part of the British 7th Division, successfully freed this village on the morning of 1st July 1916.'

100 Tonie and Valmai Holt, *Major and Mrs Holt's Battlefield Guide to the Somme* (1996) (Barnsley, S. Yorks, 2008 edn.)

101 Malcolm Brown, *The Imperial War Museum Book of the Somme* (1996) (London, 1997 edn.), 77. Martin and Mary Middlebrook, *The Somme Battlefields* (1991) (1994 edn., London), 149. 'Dantzig Alley British Cemetery, Mametz (Somme)', http://silentwitness.freeservers.com/cemeteryd/dantzig.htm. Bland's grave is in Plot IX, Row B, Grave 6. Stedman, *Manchester Pals*, 119.

102 Tawney, 'The Attack', 13. It is possible, though less likely, that Tawney was referring to the other Captain in the battalion who was killed that day, Charles May.

103 Bev/2/A/98.

104 WB, diary entry, 29–30 Dec. 1934, Bev/1/C/50.

105 William Beveridge, *Power and Influence* (London, 1953), 137.

106 JT to WB, Bev 2/A/98.

107 JT to ASB, 17 July 1916, Bev/2/A/93.

108 RHT to JT, 18 July 1916, T27/8.

109   CHT to JT, 22 July 1916, T27/6.

110   RHT to JT, 1 Aug. 1916, TV/1.

111   JJ Mallon to RHT, 29 July 1916, TV/41.

112   Powicke to RHT, 30 July 1916, TV/41.

113   Wadsworth to RHT, 24 Sept. 1916, TV/41.

114   A. Townend to RHT, 27 Oct. 1916, TV41.

115   TV41 (There is no date and Jack's surname is indecipherable).

116   R. G. Garside to RHT, TV/41 (nd, but almost certainly late July 1916).

117   George Horwill to RHT, 'June 16'. This letter was actually written in June 1917.

118   M. Sadler to RHT, 15 July, 26 Aug. 1916, TV41.

119   J. Mallon to RHT, 29 July 1916, TV41.

120   H. Barker to RHT, 2 Nov. 1916, TV41.

121   'Some Reflections of a Soldier' in RHT, *The Attack and Other Papers*, 21–8.

122   R. H. Tawney, 'Democracy and Defeat', *The Welsh Outlook*, Jan. 1917, reprinted by the WEA (nd), 2.

123   CHT to JT, 26 Oct. 1916, T27

124   RHT to WB, 27 Oct. 1916, Bev/2A/106.

125   RHT to JT, ND (early Nov. 1916), T27/8.

126   RHT to JT, 7 Nov. 1916, T 27/8.

127   RHT to JT, 15 Nov. 1916, TV/1.

128   JT to WB, ND, Bev 2/A/98.

129   Duncan Crow, *A Man of Push and Go. The life of George Macaulay Booth* (London, 1965), 60.

130   Sir Arnold Plant, BBC Transcript 1963.

131   Colin Welch to RHT, 24 June 1958, T27/17/1.

132   J. M. K. Vyvyan, 1982 Transcript, f. 13.

133   'In the Early Tutorial Classes (2) Rochdale', L. V. Gill, *The Highway*, Jubilee issue, Apr. 1953, 258.

134   RHT to E. Durbin, 24 May 1938, Durbin papers, BLPES, 7/4. See E. F. M. Durbin and George E. G. Catlin (eds), *War and Democracy* (London, 1938).

135   J. M. K. Vyvyan to J. M. Winter, 15 Nov. 1977, Tawney 27/20/1.

136   RHT to J. W. Ramsbottom, 12 Jan. 1961, TV16.

Chapter 5

1   E. Hobson to RHT, 6 Apr. 1917, TV41.

2   Duncan Crow, *A Man of Push and Go. The Life of George Macaulay Booth* (London, 1965), 60.

3   'New Fellow of Balliol', *The Times*, 30 Apr. 1918, 9.

4 Thomas Jones, *Whitehall Diary* (3 vols, London, 1969), vol. 1, 28 Nov. 1916, 2–5.

5 Quoted in A. D. Lindsay, 'R. H. Tawney', *The Highway*, Jan. 1945, 51.

6 *Christianity and Industrial Problems. Being the Report of the Archbishops' Fifth Committee of Inquiry* (London, 1918), xii.

7 RHT, 'A National College of All Souls', *Times Educational Supplement*, 22 Feb. 1917.

8 20 Mar. 1918, *The Diary of Beatrice Webb* (eds. Norman and Jeanne Mackenzie), vol. 3 (London, 1984), 303.

9 Minutes of the [foundation] Meeting of the TT Club, 21 Oct. 1919 'in Mr Lindsay's rooms in Balliol', Tawney 21/4.

10 RHT, 'Draft memorandum on the Royal Commission on Oxford and Cambridge', Tawney 21/5.

11 Philip Abrams, 'The Failure of Social Reform 1918–20', *Past and Present*, vol. 24, 1963, 43–64.

12 Ministry of Reconstruction: Adult Education Committee, Final Report, *Parliamentary Papers 1919*, vol. xxviii ('The 1919 Report'), 453–867.

13 [R. H. Tawney], Ministry of Reconstruction: Adult Education Committee: Interim Report on Industrial and Social Conditions in relation to Adult Education, *Parliamentary Papers 1918*, vol. ix, 319–49.

14 RHT to George Bell, Bell Mss, Lambeth Palace Library, vol. 190, ff. 343–9, 351–6.

15 'Methods of Censorship', *The Times*, 19 Apr. 1919.

16 RHT, *The Sword of the Spirit* (London, 1918), originally published in *The Athenaeum*, Dec. 1917.

17 COLL MISC 302/13/1, 'Tawney Coal Commission', BLPES.

18 B. Webb, *Diaries*, vol. 3, 22 Feb. 1919, 332–6.

19 Barry Supple, *The History of the British Coal Industry. Volume 4. 1913–1946: The Political Economy of Decline* (Oxford, 1987), 126–7.

20 Ibid., 343.

21 Ibid., 337.

22 See, for example, R. H. Tawney, 'The British Coal Industry and the Question of Nationalization', *Quarterly Journal of Economics*, vol. xxxv, no. 1, Nov. 1920, 61–107; idem, 'The Recent Proposals for the Nationalization of the British Coal Industry', *Clark College Record*, vol. 15, no. 4, Oct. 1920, 233–56; idem, 'The Coal Problem', *The Contemporary Review*, vol. cxix, June 1921, 727–37; idem, *The Nationalization of the Coal Industry* (The Labour Party, London, 1922).

23 R. H. Tawney, 'The Abolition of Economic Controls, 1918–21', *Ec. H. R*, vol. xiii, 1943, 1–30. The quotations here are taken from the full version of Tawney's report, a copy of which is in the Durbin papers (3/10) in the LSE. 'The Abolition of Economic Controls', f. 41.

24 R. H. Tawney, *The Acquisitive Society* (London, 1921), 174.

25 Tawney, 'Recent Proposals for the Nationalisation of the British Coal Industry', 244.

26 Tawney, 'The British Coal Industry and the Question of Nationalization', 84.

27 'Pease, Joseph Alfred, first Baron Gainford', ODNB.

28 *Coal Industry Commission, vol. II. Reports and Evidence on the Second Stage of the Inquiry*, 20,358–20,438 (quotation at 20,438), *Parliamentary Papers*, 1919, XII.

29 Ibid., p. 81.

30 Tawney, *The Nationalization of the Coal Industry*, 7–8.

31 R. H. Tawney, *The British Labor Movement* (New Haven, Ct., 1925), 72.

32 JT to ASB, 22 June 1919, Bev/2/A/94.

33 'The Recent Proposals for the Nationalization of the British Coal Industry', 246.

34 RHT to Bell, Bell Mss, Lambeth Palace Library, ff. 325–53.

35 'The Recent Proposals for the Nationalization of the British Coal Industry', 249.

36 Ibid., 250.

37 RHT to Bell, f. 331.

38 Ibid., f. 333.

39 Ibid., f. 340.

40 'The British Coal Industry and the Question of Nationalization', 91–3.

41 Tawney, *The British Labor Movement*, 86.

42 Tawney, *The Acquisitive Society*, 137–8.

43 Tawney, *The British Labor Movement*, 93.

44 Viscount Haldane of Cloan, *The Problem of Nationalization. With an Introduction by R. H. Tawney and Harold J. Laski* (London, 1921).

45 'Haldane, Richard Burdon, Viscount Haldane (1856–1928)', ODNB.

46 Haldane, *The Problem of Nationalization*, 6–12.

47 RHT, Lecture II, Chicago 1948, Tawney 16/5, ff. 27–8.

48 R. H. Tawney, *The Webbs in Perspective* (London, 1953), 16.

49 'Wallas, Graham', ODNB.

50 Matthew Grimley, *Citizenship, Community, and the Church of England. Liberal Anglican Theories of the State Between the Wars* (Oxford, 2004), 116.

51 *The Nation*, 11 June 1921, 401.

52 RHT, *The Webbs and Their Work* (London, 1945), 12.

53 For further discussion of this point, see Chapter 7, 194–6.

54 Tawney, *The British Labor Movement*, 34.

55 Ibid., 32.

56 Ibid., 49.

57 See Chapter 7, 170–2.

58 Tawney, *The British Labor Movement*, 24.

59 Supple, *History of the British Coal Industry*, vol. 4, 226–37.

60 *Royal (Samuel) Commission on the Coal Industry 1925 (hereafter Samuel Commission). Minutes of Evidence* (London, HMSO, 1926), 14 Jan. 1926, 1–40, paras. 16941–3.

61 Memorandum of Evidence by Mr R. H. Tawney on behalf of the Miners' Federation of Great Britain: No.4. 'The Future of the Coal and Power Industries' and No. 5 'Proposals for the Reorganisation and Development of the Coal and Power Industry', *Samuel Commission*, 1–10. Quotation at 4.

62 Samuel Commission, para. 17057.

63 Ibid., para. 17043.

64 Ibid., para. 17119.

65 Ibid., para. 17163.

66 Ibid., para. 16992.

67 Ibid., para. 17266.

68 Ibid., para. 17286.

69 RHT to G. Woledge (Deputy Librarian, BLPES), 29 Aug. 1951, Tawney Mss, LSE, Accession File. R. H. Tawney, 'Diary of Negotiations between the government and the Miners' Federation of Great Britain 10 March–3 May 1926', COLL MISC 0358, BLPES.

70 Cliff Tucker to Lena Jeger, 30 Jan. 1962; Lena Jeger to Bob Pocock (BBC) (nd, probably 1962), Lena Jeger papers, 1/8/1, BLPES. The anecdote may well have been inaccurate as no letter from Thomas seems to have been published in *The Times* during the General Strike. Lena Jeger suggested that it might have been sent to a railway magazine.

71 'Davidson, Randall', ODNB.

72 RHT to WT, Temple Papers, Lambeth Palace Library, vol. 46, ff. 228–59.

73 J. M. K. Vyvyan, Transcript 1982, f. 15.

74 Thomas Jones, *Whitehall Diary*, vol. II, 1926–30 (Keith Middlemas, ed.) (London, 1969), 65–6 (25 Aug. 1926).

75 Ibid., 84–5 (21 Sept. 1926).

76 W. A. Frith to RHT, 16 Nov. 1918, TV/41.

77 ILP election ephemera, ILP/6/20/5, BLPES.

78 'Portrait of R. H. Tawney', 1963.

79 A. J. Lynch, secretary of the S. Tottenham branch, to RHT, 26 Sept. 1922, TV3.

80 RHT to Mr G. Hill, 27 Jan. 1961, TV15.

81 I am grateful to Dr A. C. Lynch of Potters Bar for providing extracts from the unpublished autobiography of his father, Mr A. J. Lynch, written in 1943 on which this brief account is based. Mr A. J. Lynch was the liaison officer between Tawney and the South Tottenham Labour Party in 1922–3.

82 RHT to Gilbert Murray, 28 Nov. 1922, Gilbert Murray Papers, Bodleian Library, Oxford, reel 46, f. 47.

83 G. B. Shaw to R. H. Tawney, 22 Sept. 1922 in the possession of Dr A. C. Lynch.

84 JT to ASB, 25 July 1925, Bev/2A/94.

85 RHT to JT, 4 Oct. 1931, TV/2.

86 B. Webb, *Diaries*, vol. 4, 8 Dec. 1935, 360–1.

87 Tawney, *The British Labor Movement*, 6–7.

88 *The Times*, 17 Jan. 1962.

89 Vyvyan, 1982 Transcript, f. 14.

90 BBC Transcript 1963.

91 Philip Snowden to RHT, 16 Nov. 1918, TV41.

92 JT to HB, 23 July 1919, Bev/2A/82.

93 Ibid., nd (summer 1919?).

94 *The Saturday Review*, 26 July; 9, 16 Aug; 20 Dec. 1919.

95 *The Highway*, October 1922, 2. (An insert dated 29th September 1922: 'Serious Illness of Mr R. H. Tawney'. 'As we go to press Mr R. H. Tawney, whose name is a household word to all associated with our movement, lies seriously ill, and there are grave fears of the issue').

96 Mark De Wolfe Howe (ed.), *Holmes-Laski Letters. The Correspondence of Mr Justice Holmes and Harold J. Laski, 1916–1935* (Cambridge, MA, 1953), 22 Sept. 1922, 450.

97 See the letters in the file TV/3.

98 Mary E. Pumphrey to JT, 28 Sept. 1922: 'It is with very deep regret that I see from the *Daily News* this morning that your husband is seriously ill'.

99 W. H. B. Court, *Scarcity and Choice in History*, 17–18, 132.

Chapter 6

1 JT to ASB, 13 Apr. 1920, Bev/2A/94.

2 JT to ASB, 11 July 1920, Bev/2A/94.

3 Harold Laski to Graham Wallas, 2 May 1920, Wallas Papers, BLPES, London School of Economics, 1/64.

4 The following material on Tawney's career at the LSE is based on his three staff files in the LSE archives.

5 RHT to WB, 25 May 1926; WB to RHT 22, 27 June 1926, Tawney Staff Files (TSF), BLPES.

6 R. H. Tawney, *Eileen Power* (1940). For obituaries and other material on Power collected by RHT, see T11/1. See also Maxine Berg, *A Woman in History: Eileen Power 1889–1940* (Cambridge, 1996).

7 RHT to WB, 11 June 1929, TSF.

8 WB to the Academic Registrar, University of London, 19 May 1931, TSF.

9 RHT to the Director of the LSE, W. S. G. Adams, 13 Sept. 1938, TSF.

10 'Extract from the Appointment Committee Minutes', 22 Jan. 1945, TSF.

11 Sir Arnold Plant, BBC Transcript 1963.

12 *The Times*, 17 July 1934.

13 Jose Harris, *William Beveridge. A Life* (2003 edn.), 283–95.

14 Elizabeth Durbin, *New Jerusalems. The Labour Party and the Economics of Democratic Socialism* (London, 1985), 103.

15 'Extract from the Appointment Committee Minutes', 22 Jan. 1945, TSF.

16 BBC Transcript 1963.

17 Ibid.

18 Ronald Preston, 'R. H. Tawney as a Christian Moralist', *Theology*, vol. lxix, Apr. 1966, 160. See also Preston's letter to *The Times* after Tawney's death, 29 Jan. 1962.

19 W. H. B. Court, *Scarcity and Choice in History* (London, 1970), 19.

20 BBC Transcript 1963.

21 Frank Bongiorno, *British to their Bootheels too: Britishness and Australian Radicalism*, Trevor Reese Memorial Lecture 2006, King's College, London, 4. I am grateful to Dr Bongiorno for this anecdote.

22 Sir Arnold Plant, BBC Transcript 1963.

23 Frank Emery, BBC Transcript 1963.

24 Postan, BBC Transcript 1963.

25 Rees, BBC Transcript 1963.

26 Ved Mehta, *Fly and Fly-Bottle. Encounters with British Intellectuals* (London, 1963), 167.

27 Green, BBC Transcript 1963.

28 Rees, BBC Transcript 1963.

29 Mehta, *Fly and Fly-Bottle*, 168.

30 Plant, BBC Transcript 1963.

31 WHB to HB, 3 Jan. 1903, Bev 2/A/37.

32 RHT to Richard Denman, 27 Dec. 1902, H. Beveridge Collection, British Library, BL MSS EUR.C.176/193a, f. 36.

33 RHT to ASB, 13 Jan. 1914, Bev/2A/105.

34 RHT to JT, 9 May 1916, T27/8.

35 BBC Transcript 1963.

36 Ibid. (a member of the original Longton Class, name unknown, f. 19).

37 Ibid.

38 Ibid.

39 Ibid.

40 Lena Jeger, 'Speech at the unveiling of the blue plaque in Mecklenburgh Square in Tawney's honour', 30 Nov. 1980, Jeger papers, BLPES, 1/8/1.

41 John Kenyon, 'The Great Historians: R. H. Tawney', *Observer Magazine* 12 Dec. 1976, 38.

42 BBC Transcript 1963.

43 Ibid.

44 Ibid.

45 John Freeman, 'Portrait of R. H. Tawney', BBC Home Service, 12 May 1963; Mehta, *Fly and Fly-Bottle*, 168.

46 *The Times*, 1 Dec. 1980.

47 'Portrait of R. H. Tawney', BBC 1963.

48 *The Times*, 6 Dec. 1980.

49 Preston, 'Tawney as Christian Moralist', 160.

50 BBC Transcript 1963.

51 Ibid.

52 Cliff Tucker, 'Speech at the unveiling of the blue plaque in Mecklenburgh Square in Tawney's honour', 30 Nov. 1980, Jeger papers, BLPES, 1/8/1.

53 BBC Transcript 1963.

54 RHT to W. A. Pickard-Cambridge, 24 Mar. 1902, Bev/2B/2/2.

55 BBC Transcript 1963.

56 RHT to JT, 5 May 1916, T27/8.

57 RHT to M. Vyvyan ('Mil'), 9 Dec. 1915, TV45.

58 Clara Rackham, 'Tawney at Home. Memories of an old friendship', *The Fenland Bulletin* (WEA) nd [1960], WEA archives, LMU, WEA RHT/3/1.

59 JT to WHB, 29 Nov. 1933, Bev/2A/101; Ashton, BBC Transcript 1963.

60 BBC Transcript 1963.

61 Rees, BBC Transcript 1963.

62 J. M. K. Vyvyan to James Brooks, 21 May 1974, T27/20/1.

63 RHT to JT, 3 Apr. 1928, TV2.

64 RHT to JT, 17, 27 Sept. 1931, TV2.

65 RHT to JT, 5 Dec. 1939, TV/2.

66 BBC Transcript 1963.

67 JT to WHB, 12 Sept. 1933 and 22 Oct. 1933, Bev/2A/101.

68 WHB, handwritten note about their parents' deaths, 31 July 1933, Bev/2A/99.

69 RHT to Miss P. Smith, 8 Feb. 1961; Prof. B. Thomas, 27 Jan. 1961, TV16.

70 'A Talk on War Conditions & Policy in G. Britain, probably given in USA 1941–2, 3–4, T16/3.

71 Clara Rackham, 'Tawney at Home'. Rackham repeated this in her comments in 'Out of the Wilderness: R. H. Tawney', BBC Radio 4, 1983.

72 *Manchester Guardian*, 17 Jan. 1962.

73 JT to WHB, 28 Sept. 1944, Bev/2A/103.

74 RHT to William Temple, 29 Feb. 1928, Temple Mss., v. 46, f. 266, Lambeth Palace Library.

75 RHT to JT, 16, 19 Nov. 1931, TV2. JT to WHB, 4 Mar. 1932, Bev/2A/100.

76 Dr J. Hoskin to Dr A. C. Gemmell, 21 May 1937, T27/6.

77 RHT to Bishop E. J. Palmer, 30 Dec. 1944, Papers of Bishop Palmer, MS 3010, ff. 261–2, Lambeth Palace Library.

78 Ibid.

79 JT to Dr Gemmell,19 May 1937, T27/6.

80 Tawney was certainly in Germany in 1906 when Jeanette corresponded with him there. He recalled after Temple's death that they had gone to Germany together 'possibly – though I am not certain – in 1905'. The suspicion is that Tawney confused the years and they were together in Germany in 1906. RHT, Handwritten memoir of William Temple, f. 5, T Add 0005.

81 RHT to JT, 27 Aug. 1922, TV2.

82 J. M. K. Vyvyan to D. M. Joslin, 20 Nov. 1966, T27/20/1.

83 JT to WB, 19 Feb. 1931, Bev 2/A/100.

84 RHT to JT, 11 June 1945, T27/7; Christopher Hill to RHT, 30 May, 6 June, 21 July 1945, T II/97.

85 JT to WB, 5 Aug. 1951, Bev/2/A/103.

86 JT to WB, 4 July 1948, Bev/2A/103.

87 Beatrice Webb, *Diaries*, vol. 4, 21 Jan. 1939, 427.

88 RHT to Beatrice Webb, 6 Dec. 1942, ff. 253–5, Passfield Papers 2/4/M, BLPES.

89 RHT to Mrs A. Huws Davies, 27 Jan. 1961, TV/15.

90 RHT to Prof. Dorothy Emmet, 3 Feb. 1961, TV/15.

91 RHT to JT, 26, 29 Mar., 3 Apr. 1928, TV/2.

92 RHT, 'A Missionary Council: Meeting at Jerusalem, Younger Christian Churches: Arguing With Western Christianity', *Manchester Guardian*, 12 Apr. 1928.

93 JT to WB, 19 Feb. 1931, Bev/2/A/100.

94 RHT to WB, 17 June 1931, TSF.

95 RHT to George Bell, 24 July 1931, Bell Papers, vol. 215, f. 106, Lambeth Palace Library.

96 RHT to JT, 6 Sept. 1931, TV2.

97 RHT to JT, 10 Sept. 1931, TV2.

98 *The Reorganisation of Education in China*. By the League of Nations' Mission of Experts (League of Nations' Institute of Intellectual Co-operation, Paris, 1932), 11–15.

99 RHT to JT, 5 Oct. 1931, TV2.

100 RHT to JT, 4 Oct. 1931, TV2.

101 RHT to JT, 27 Sept. 1931, TV2.

102 RHT to JT, 19 Nov. 1931, TV2.

103 RHT to JT, 4 Oct. 1931, TV2.

104 RHT to JT, 16 Nov. 1931, TV2.

105 RHT to JT, 19 Nov. 1931, TV2.

106 RHT to JT, 23 Nov. 1931, TV2.

107 RHT to JT, 14 Oct.; 23 Nov. 1931, TV2.

108 RHT to JT, 23 Nov. 1932, TV2.

109 RHT to JT, 19 Nov. 1932, TV2.

110 RHT to JT, 16 Nov. 1931, TV2.

111 RHT to JT, 19 Nov. 1931, TV2.

112 RHT to JT, 23 Nov. 1931, TV2.

113 J. M. K. Vyvyan, 1982 Transcript, f. 11.

114 'Prefatory Note' in R. H. Tawney, *Land and Labour in China* (London, 1932).

115 Ibid., 18.

116 Ibid., 18, 166.

117 Ibid., 167.

118 Ibid., 169.

119 Ibid., 78–82.

120 Ibid., 194–5.

121 Ibid., 26.

122 Ibid., 44.

123 Ibid., 49.

124 Ibid., 72.

125 Ibid., 138–9, 182.

126 Ibid., 99.

127 Ibid., 108.

128 Ibid., 172.

129 Ibid., 69, 74.

130 Ibid., 130.

131 Ibid., 182–93.

132 Ibid., 32.

133 'Conclusions and Suggestions for Preparatory Measures of Reform submitted to the Ministry of Education of Nanking by the Mission before its departure from China' in *The Reorganisation of Education in China*, 197–200.

134 *The Reorganisation of Education in China*, 21.

135 Ibid., 38–9.

136 Ibid., 188.

137 Ibid., 192.

138 RHT to Gilbert Murray, 16 Nov. 1932, Gilbert Murray Papers, Bodleian Library, Oxford, reel 297, f. 26.

139 Ibid. See also letters between Tawney and Murray on 14 and 19 Nov. 1932; 7, 12, 20 Jan. and 2, 15 Feb. 1933.

140 *The Times*, 17 Feb. 1933.

141 *The Times*, 21 Mar. 1932.

142 *The Times*, 26 Aug. 1938.

143 John Saville, *Memoirs from the Left* (London, 2003), 4.

144 RHT to JT, 26 Oct., 16 Nov. 1931.

145 RHT to JT, 16 Nov. 1931.

146 RHT to JT, 26 Oct. 1931.

147 RHT to JT, 16 Nov. 1931.

148 Ross McKibbin, 'The Economic Policy of the Second Labour Government 1929–31', *Past and Present*, vol. 68, Aug. 1975, 95–123.

149 RHT to JT, 23 Nov. 1931.

150 Ibid.

151 RHT, Lecture II, Chicago 1948, T16/5.

152 R. H. Tawney, 'Labour Party History. Preparation and Achievement', *Times Literary Supplement*, 10 Mar. 1950, 1–2.

153 Durbin, *New Jerusalems*, 60.

154 Lena Jeger, letter to the *Sunday Times*, 19 June 1983.

155 R. H. Tawney, *The Choice before the Labour Party* (The Socialist League, 1934), p. 11. First published in the *Political Quarterly*, 3 July–Sept. 1932.

156 Thomas Jones, *Whitehall Diary,* vol. II (1926–30) (ed. Keith Middlemas), 267 (23 June 1930).

157 R. H. Tawney, *Equality* (3rd edn. 1951), pp. 197–200.

158 RHT to Beatrice Webb, 8 Nov. 1933, Passfield papers, ff. 51–3, 2/4/J.

159 Ibid.

160 *Manchester Guardian*, 17 Jan. 1962.

161 *The Choice Before the Labour Party*, 14.

162 Jones, *Whitehall Diaries*, II, 187 (11 June 1929).

163 Lena Jeger, Speech on the unveiling of a blue plaque to Tawney in Mecklenburgh Square, 30 Nov. 1980, Jeger 1/8/1.

164 Lena Jeger, *New Statesman*, 19 Jan. 1962, 2. Ernest Green claimed to have lunched with Tawney 'on the day Ramsay MacDonald offered him a peerage' and that his reply then and there was 'what harm have I ever done to the Labour Party?' Ernest Green, 'A Gentle Rebel', *Man and Metal*, Feb. 1962, 23.

165 Ernest Green, BBC Transcript 1963.

166 Vyvyan 1982 Transcript.

167 Durbin, *New Jerusalems*, 110.

168 Philip M. Williams, *Hugh Gaitskell. A Political Biography* (London, 1979), 18.

169 Ibid., 189–94.

170 Ibid., 109.

171 RHT, Lecture I, Chicago 1939, ff. 22–3.

172 CB, 29 June 1914, 77.

173 See above, 78–9.

174 'German Claim to Equality', *The Times*, 12 Oct. 1932.

175 J. M. K. Vyvyan to J. M. Winter, 15 Nov. 1977, T27/20/1.

176 RHT, Lecture III, Chicago, 1939, ff. 10–14, T15.

177 JT to WB, 5 May 1933, Bev 2/A/101.

178 RHT to WB, 24 Apr. 1933, Bev 2/A/107.

179 JT to WB, 29 Dec. 1933, Bev/2/A/101.

180 Dorothea Oshinsky to RHT, 29 Nov. 1960; RHT to Dorothea Oshinsky, 31 Jan. 1961, TV16.

181 RHT to Mrs H. J. Benedictus, 16 Jan. 1961, TV15.

182 *The Times*, 8 Feb. 1934.

183 *The Times*, 22 Nov. 1938.

184 'A Peace Plan', *The Times*, 1 Aug. 1936.

185 *The Times*, 19 Aug. 1936.

186 *The Times*, 11 Mar. 1936.

187 RHT to Arthur Creech Jones, 25 Mar. 1938, Creech Jones papers, Rhodes House, Oxford, ACJ 6/2/19-12.

188 RHT to Creech Jones, 30 Sept. 1938, ACJ 6/2/23.

189 JT to WB, nd., Bev/2/A/102.

190 *Manchester Guardian*, 17 Oct. 1938.

191 JT to WB, 13 Nov. 1938, Bev/2/A/102.

192 JT to WB, 7 Jan. [1940], Bev/2/A/102. (Jeanette had written '1939', but this letter is clearly written with a war on).

193 Terrill, *R. H. Tawney and His Times*, 229. See also A. Arblaster, *Bulletin of the Society for the Study of Labour History*, vol. 54, pt. 1 (1989), 100.

Chapter 7

1 *R. H. Tawney's Commonplace Book* (hereafter CB), (eds J. M. Winter and D. M. Joslin), xxiii.

2 William Morris, 'How I became a Socialist' (1894) in (ed. Clive Wilmer), *William Morris. News from Nowhere and Other Writings* (London, 1993), 379–83.

3 P. F. Clarke, *Liberals and Social Democrats* (Cambridge, 1978).

4 R. H. Tawney, 'Introduction' to Max Beer, *A History of British Socialism* (London, 1919), p. xv.

5 David Marquand, 'R. H. Tawney. Prophet of Equality', *The Guardian*, 26 Nov. 1960.

6 Gary Armstrong and Tim Gray, 'Three fallacies in the essentialist interpretation of the political thought of R. H. Tawney', *Journal of Political Ideologies*, vol. 15, 2 June 2010, 171–2. If Armstrong and Gray's strictures are applied to unpublished correspondence as well, almost all biographical writing would have to be discounted.

7 CB, 9.

8 CB, 12.

9 CB, 33.

10 CB, 18.

11 CB, 30–1, 56.

12 CB, 61.

13 A. M. McBriar, *Fabian Socialism and English Politics 1884–1918* (Cambridge, 1962).

14 RHT to JB, 21 June 1908, TV1.

15 Ibid.; JT, Mss autobiography, ch. 27, ff. 269–74.

16 CB, 45–6.

17 CB, 51.

18 CB, 70.

19 CB, 11.

20 'Conference on the Provision of a Genuine System of Adult Education, Corpus Christi College, Oxford, 11–12 Jan. 1944' (known as the 'Archbishop's Conference on Adult Education'), Temple Papers, Lambeth Palace Library, vol. 22, ff. 230–350.

21 WT to RHT, 6 Apr. 1944, Temple Papers, Lambeth Palace Library, vol. 22, f. 328.

22 RHT to William Temple, 17 Feb., 10 Aug. 1944, Temple Papers, vol. 22, ff. 308, 330.

23 Ibid., ff. 349–50.

24 RHT, 'Adult Education for the New Community', TV 48/1, f. 4 (A manuscript address given in wartime.).

25 R. H. Tawney, *Equality*, Preface to the 1938 edn, 30. See the same quotation used later in 'Handwritten notes from lectures given by Tawney in the United States on current affairs (1941–2)', T/16/2/18.

26 Ibid.

27 Alfred Ollivant to RHT, 28 Aug. 1910, TV 29/2.

28 Private knowledge.

29 CB, 62–3.

30 CB, 64.

31 Ibid.

32 CB, 80.

33 CB, 70.

34 CB, 22 Oct. 1912, 41.

35 CB, 30 June 1912, 19.

36 CB, 79–80.

37 R. H. Tawney, *The Agrarian Problem in the Sixteenth Century* (London, 1912), 4.

38 T. S. Ashton, BBC Transcript 1963, Lena Jeger Papers, BLPES.

39 CB, 69.

40 'Some General Remarks on the Historical Theory of Karl Marx (School of Economics)', nd, T/II/61. The lecture, running to some 47 typed pages, begins: 'It is just under forty years since the appearance of a book by a celebrated economist under the title *Karl Marx and the Close of his System*.' Tawney may have been

respectful of Marx at this stage but that is different from arguing that his historical work was influenced by Marx in the 1930s. See J. M. Winter (ed.), *History and Society: Essays by R. H. Tawney* (1978), 'Introduction', 26–8; David Ormrod, 'R. H. Tawney and the Origins of Capitalism', *History Workshop Journal*, 18, 1984, 157, n. 74.

41 'Speech to the William Temple Society, Cambridge 1949', T19/6, f. 7.

42 These quotations are drawn from five handwritten papers entitled 'The Materialist Conception of History' (two different versions) and 'Marx' (three different versions), T/II/61.

43 CB, 58.

44 Tawney, *The Agrarian Problem*, 178.

45 Ved Mehta, *Fly and the Fly-Bottle. Encounters with British Intellectuals* (London, 1963), 163.

46 John Kenyon, 'Man who hated privilege', The Great Historians, *Observer Magazine*, 12 Dec. 1976.

47 Matthew Grimley, *Citizenship, Community, and the Church of England. Liberal Anglican Theories of the State Between the Wars* (Oxford, 2004), 115.

48 Ormrod, 'R. H. Tawney and the Origins of Capitalism', 143.

49 *The Times*, 17 Jan. 1962.

50 Ashton, BBC Transcript 1963.

51 J. M. K. Vyvyan to Jay Winter, 15 Nov. 1977, T27/20/1.

52 See above, 93.

53 Ross Terrill, *R. H. Tawney and His Times* (Cambridge, MA, 1974), 61.

54 CB, 77–8.

55 The Diary of Beatrice Webb, typescript version, ff. 212, 8 Dec. 1935, LSE Digital Library.

56 Armstrong and Gray, 'Three fallacies in the essentialist interpretation of the political thought of R. H. Tawney', 162.

57 Ibid., 170–1.

58 'Speech to the William Temple Society, Cambridge 1949', Tawney 19/6.

59 T. S. Ashton, 'Annette Jeanie Tawney', *London School of Economics Magazine*, July 1958, p. 28.

60 Ashton, BBC Transcript 1963.

61 Lena Jeger to J. M. Winter, 4 June 1969, Jeger Papers, 1/8/1.

62 M. M. Postan, 'D. M. Joslin', CB, x.

63 'Gore, Charles (1853–1932)', Oxford DNB.

64 Ibid. G. L. Prestige, *The Life of Charles Gore. A Great Englishman* (London, 1935).

65 'Gore, Charles', Oxford DNB.

66 Charles Gore (ed.), *Lux Mundi. A Series of Studies in the Religion of the Incarnation* (London, 1889).

67 Gore, 'The Holy Spirit and Inspiration' in Ibid., 359.

68 Henry Scott Holland, *Henry Scott Holland. Memoir and Letters* (ed. Stephen Paget) (London, 1921), 241.

69 'Gore, Charles', Oxford DNB.

70 Gordon Crosse, *Charles Gore: A Biographical Sketch* (London, 1932), 124.

71 R. H. Tawney, 'The *Daily News* Religious Census of London', *Toynbee Record*, vol. xvi, March 1904, 87–8.

72 W. H. B. Court, *Scarcity and Choice in History* (London, 1970), 129.

73 Anthony Wright, *R. H. Tawney* (Manchester, 1987), 136.

74 Ormrod, 'R. H. Tawney and the Origins of Capitalism', 143. See the preface to Donald Soper, 'Socialism: An Enduring Creed', The Third Tawney Memorial Lecture, 1980.

75 CB, 53, 65, 67.

76 RHT, 'The New Leviathan', handwritten Mss, T/10/10, f. 6.

77 Ibid., ff. 3–4.

78 R. H. Tawney, 'Introduction' to Charles Gore, *Christianity Applied to the Life of Men and of Nations* (London, 1920) (1940 edn.), 3–4.

79 For an earlier example of this debate, see his lecture 'Christianity and Industry', 'Lectures on Christianity', T 20/7.

80 'Speech to the William Temple Society, Cambridge 1949', T 19/6.

81 RHT, 'Christianity and Industry', ff. 5–6.

82 R. H. Tawney, *Religion and the Rise of Capitalism* (London, 1926) (1943 edn.), 278.

83 R. H. Tawney, *The Acquisitive Society* (London, 1921), 237–8.

84 David Marquand, 'R. H. Tawney. Prophet of Equality', *The Guardian*, 26 Nov. 1960.

85 Lawrence Goldman, 'John Ruskin and the Working Classes in Mid-Victorian Britain' in Keith Hanley and Brian Maidment (eds), *Persistent Ruskin. Studies in Influence, Assimilation and Effect* (Farnham, Surrey, 2013), 15–31; idem, 'Ruskin, Oxford, and the British Labour Movement 1880–1914' in Dinah Birch (ed.), *Ruskin and the Dawn of the Modern* (Oxford, 1999), 57–86.

86 CB, 60–1.

87 RHT, 'Christianity and Industry', f. 6.

88 CB, 62.

89 Tawney, *Religion and the Rise of Capitalism*, 284–5.

90 CB, 34.

91 CB, 59.

92 Tawney, *Religion and the Rise of Capitalism*, 284.

93 A note at the end of the typescript reads: 'Speech prob[ably] to conference of Christian Social Movement'.

94 RHT to JB, 16 Aug. 1908, TV1.

95 R. H. Tawney, 'John Ruskin', *The Observer*, 19 Feb. 1919, reprinted in R. H. Tawney, *The Radical Tradition* (London, 1964), 40–4.

96 RHT, *The Webbs in Perspective* (1953), 6.

97 JT, Mss autobiography, 271–2.

98 E. S. Cartwright Papers, 17 Feb. 1908, Oxford University Archives, DES/F/13/7.

99 Goldman, 'Ruskin, Oxford and the British Labour Movement' passim.

100 Stephen Yeo, 'A New Life: The Religion of Socialism in Britain, 1883–96', *History Workshop Journal*, vol. 4, Autumn 1977, 5–56.

101 The Diary of Beatrice Webb, Typescript version, ff. 212, 8 Dec 1935, LSE Digital Library.

102 RHT, *The Choice Before the Labour Party* (London, 1934), 6, 12.

103 Ved Mehta, *Fly and the Fly-Bottle. Encounters with British Intellectuals* (London, 1963), 164–5.

104 'A Man for All Seasons', *New Statesman*, 19 Jan. 1962.

105 *The Acquisitive Society* appeared first as an article, which was then reprinted as a Fabian Society pamphlet. See 'The Sickness of an Acquisitive Society', *Hibbert Journal*, vol. xvii, 1919, 353–70.

106 'Moral Mind: R. H. Tawney' in Stefan Collini, *English Pasts. Essays in History and Culture* (Oxford, 1999), 187–8.

107 Tawney, *The Acquisitive Society*, 3.

108 Ibid., 184.

109 Ibid., 77.

110 Ibid., 42.

111 Ibid., 183.

112 Ibid., 30.

113 Ibid., 106.

114 Ibid., 79.

115 Ibid., 228.

116 Collini, 'Moral Mind', 190.

117 Tawney, *Equality* (1931), Preface to the 1938 edn., 29.

118 Ibid., 3rd edn., 1951, 43.

119 Ibid., 56.

120 Ibid., 182.

121 Ibid., 103–4.

122 Ben Jackson, *Equality and the British Left. A Study in Progressive Political Thought, 1900–64* (Manchester, 2007), 29–30, 168.

123 Ibid., Preface to 1938 edn., 31.

124 Ibid., 150.

125 Raymond Williams, *Culture and Society 1780–1950*, 3rd edn. (Harmondsworth, 1963), 219, 223.

126 Court, *Scarcity and Choice*, 130.

127 R. H. Tawney, *Christian Politics* (Socialist Christian League, 1954), 13.

128 Ibid.

129 R. H. Tawney, 'The Recent Proposals for the Nationalization of the British Coal Industry', *Clark College Record*, vol. 15, no. 4, Oct. 1920, 256.

130 Tawney, 'British Socialism Today' to the University of London Fabian Society, 1952, in T19/2, f. 12, subsequently published in the 1952 *Socialist Commentary*.

131 'Speech to the William Temple Society, Cambridge 1949', f. 9.

132 CB, 10 June 1912, 14.

Chapter 8

1 R. H. Tawney, *Education: The Socialist Policy* (ILP Publication Dept., London, 1924), 58.

2 Ibid., 12.

3 'Slum Clearance. Sites for Nursery Schools', *The Times*, 17 Oct. 1933.

4 R. H. Tawney, *The British Labor Movement* (New Haven, Ct., 1925), 130–1.

5 Tom Steele and Richard Taylor, 'R. H. Tawney and the Reform of the Universities', *History of Education*, vol. 37, no. 1, 2008, 1–22.

6 'Tizard, Sir Henry Thomas (1885–1959)', Oxford DNB.

7 'Memorandum on Expansion of Universities', H. T. Tizard and R. H. Tawney, 8 Mar. 1945, National Archives, UGC 2/26, cited in P. H. J. H. Gosden, *Education in the Second World War. A Study in Policy and Administration* (London, 1976), 428–9.

8 Tawney, *Education: The Socialist Policy*, 48.

9 J. F. Mountford, *Keele: An Historical Critique* (London, 1972); J. M. Kolbert, *Keele: The First Fifty Years* (Keele, 2000).

10 BBC Transcript, 1963, f. 15.

11 Jonathan Rose, *The Intellectual Life of the British Working Classes* (New Haven and London, 2001).

12 J. Floud, 'The Educational Experience of the Adult Population of England and Wales as at July 1949' in D. V. Glass (ed.), *Social Mobility in Britain* (London, 1954), 118.

13 R. H. Tawney, *Secondary Education for All. A Policy for Labour* (The Labour Party, 1922) (1988 edn., London), 22.

14 R. H. Tawney, *The Children's Charter* (WEA, 1932); Tawney, *Secondary Education for All*, 7.

15 Tawney, *Secondary Education for All*, 32.

16 R. H. Tawney, *Some Thoughts on Education and the War* (WEA, 1917), 10. See also 'A National College of All Souls', *Times Educational Supplement*, 22 Feb. 1917, reprinted in R. H. Tawney, *The Attack and Other Papers* (London, 1953), 29–34.

17 'An Educational Programme', *Manchester Guardian*, 10 Mar. 1917.

18 *The Highway*, Feb. and Apr. 1921; R. H. Tawney, 'Geddes Report on Education, I and II', *Manchester Guardian*, 21, 22 Feb. 1922.

19 'Raising of the School Age' *The Times*, 9 Nov. 1935.

20 J. R. Brooks, 'R. H. Tawney and the Reform of English Education' (unpublished PhD dissertation, University of Wales, 1974).

21 Tawney, *Secondary Education for All*, 7.

22 Ibid., 54.

23 Ibid., 27.

24 Ibid., 'Summary of Labour Party's Policy', 7–14.

25 Ibid., 70.

26 Ibid., 59, 66–7.

27 Ibid., 34–5.

28 Ibid., 132, 140.

29 Ibid., 17. R. Barker, *Education and Politics* (Oxford, 1972), 43–4.

30 J. R. Brooks, 'R. H. Tawney and the Reform of English Education', xiii–xix.

31 Ross McKibbin, *Classes and Cultures. England 1918–1951* (Oxford, 1998), 210–11.

32 RHT to Fred Clarke, 30 Sept. 1940, Tawney Papers, London University Institute of Education (hereafter IOE), TY 2/12.

33 McKibbin, *Classes and Cultures*, 211–12.

34 'Keep the Workers' Children in Their Place', *Daily News*, 14 Feb. 1918, republished in *The Radical Tradition* (London, 1953), 47–51.

35 Tawney, *Secondary Education for All*, 18.

36 RHT to Richard Denman, 6 July 1929, H. Beveridge Collection, British Library, BL MSS EUR.C. 176/193a, f. 63.

37 RHT to Richard Denman, 9 July 1929, f. 85.

38 'Trevelyan, Sir Charles Philips', ODNB.

39 R. H. Tawney and C. P. Trevleyan, 'Education Policy', Labour Party Policy no. 218, Feb. 1934. Submitted to the Local Government and Social Services Committee.

40 'The Education Bill', *The Times*, 25 May 1936. See also R. H. Tawney, 'What is Beneficial Employment? The Administration of the Education Act', *The Highway*, Nov. 1937.

41 RHT to Fred Clarke, 30 Sept. 1940, Tawney Papers, IOE, TY 2/12.

42 Tawney, *Secondary Education for All*, 30.

43 Tawney, *Education. The Socialist Policy*, 15.

44 Ibid., 32.

45 RHT, 'Typescript of a lecture given to the New Education Fellowship, Jan. 1934', T 17/1, ff. 21–2.

46 Ibid., f. 25.

47 RHT, 'On Juvenile Employment and Education', Typescript of the Sidney Ball Lecture, Oxford, June 1934', f. 21.

48 RHT, 'The Finance and Economics of Public Education', Typescript of three lectures given in Cambridge in Feb.–Mar. 1935, T17/6, Lecture II, f. 44.

49 Ibid., T17/9, Lecture III, f. 33.

50 R. H. Tawney, *Equality* (London, 1931) (1938 edn.), 27.

51 Ibid., 27–8.

52 Ibid., 39.

53 Ibid., 179.

54 RHT, 'British Socialism Today', f. 15.

55 [Lena Jeger], 'Homage to Tawney', *Tribune*, 2 Dec. 1960.

56 *New Statesman*, 19 Jan. 1962, 2.

57 Brooks, 'R. H. Tawney and the Reform of English Education', 300–4, 347, 362.

58 McKibbin, *Classes and Cultures*, 232.

59 Brooks, 'R. H. Tawney and the Reform of English Education', 304, 309; 'Norwood, Sir Cyril', ODNB.

60 R. H. Tawney, 'A Starting Point', *The Manchester Guardian*, 31 Mar. 1945; McKibbin, *Classes and Cultures*, 233–4.

61 C. D. Rackham to RHT, 7 Jan. 1939, Tawney papers, IOE, TY 2/1.

62 McKibbin, *Classes and Cultures*, 234.

63 C. H. Rolph, letter to *The Times*, 22 Feb. 1982.

64 R. H. Tawney, *British Socialism Today* (1960), 15.

65 RHT to W. H. Spikes, 29 Nov. 1960, TV16.

66 Matthew Grimley, *Citizenship, Community, and the Church of England. Liberal Anglican Theories of the State Between the Wars* (Oxford, 2004), 114.

67 *The Times*, 27 Oct. 1934.

68 R. H. Tawney, *The Problem of the Public Schools* (WEA, 1943), reprinted from the *Political Quarterly*, April/June 1943.

Chapter 9

1 G. R. Elton, *The Future of the Past* (Cambridge, 1968), 15–17.

2 *Times Literary Supplement*, 11 Feb. 1977.

3 John Kenyon, 'The Great Historians: R. H. Tawney', *Observer Magazine*, 12 Dec. 1976, 40. See Eric Kerridge, *Agrarian Problems in the Sixteenth Century and After* (London, 1969), 15.

4   See below, 296–7.

5   See above, 30.

6   Ved Mehta, *Fly and the Fly-Bottle. Encounters with British Intellectuals* (London, 1963), 164.

7   R. H. Tawney, *The Agrarian Problem in the Sixteenth Century* (London, 1912), ix.

8   Oxford University Tutorial Classes Committee minutes, 24 Apr. 1909, Oxford University Archives.

9   RHT to J. L. and Barbara Hammond, 29 June 1917, Papers of J. L. and Barbara Hammond, Bodleian Library, S C 47412, f. 106.

10 Papers relating to the writing and publication of *The Agrarian Problem* are preserved in Tawney/II/31/2, Tawney Papers, BLPES.

11 P. Vinogradoff, *Villeinage in England* (Oxford, 1892); A. Savine, 'English Customary Tenure in the Tudor Period', *Quarterly Journal of Economics*, XIX, 1904, 36–80; R. Pauli, *Drei volkswirtschaftliche Denkschriften aus der Zeit Heinrich VIII von England* (1878); G. F. Steffen, *Studien zur Geschichte der Englisher Lohnarbeiter* (1901–5).

12 Tawney, *The Agrarian Problem*, xxv.

13 David Ormrod, 'R. H. Tawney and the Origins of Capitalism', *History Workshop Journal*, 18, 1984, 142.

14 R. H. Tawney (ed.), *Studies in Economic History: The Collected Papers of George Unwin* (London, 1927).

15 Matthew Grimley, *Citizenship, Community, and the Church of England. Liberal Anglican Theories of the State between the Wars* (Oxford, 2004), 96–7.

16 'Unwin, George (1870–1925)', ODNB.

17 G. W. Daniels, *George Unwin: a Memorial Lecture* (Manchester, 1926), 2.

18 Tawney (ed.), *Studies in Economic History*, xxxvii.

19 Ibid., lxiii.

20 T. A. B. Corley, 'George Unwin: A Manchester Economic Historian Extraordinary' and 'Tawney's memoir of Unwin', unpublished papers.

21 Tawney (ed.), *Studies in Economic History*, lxxii–lxxiii.

22 Ormrod, 'R. H. Tawney and the Origins of Capitalism', 140; Tawney (ed.), *Studies in Economic History*, xviii.

23 George Unwin to Tawney, nd, file on *The Agrarian Problem*, T/II/31/2. Unwin also described Tawney's chapters in the same letter as 'constitut[ing] a most valuable addition to our knowledge and the sooner they are published the better.'

24 Tawney, *The Agrarian Problem*, 189.

25 Ibid., 14–15.

26 Ibid., 38–9.

27 Ibid., 184–5.

28 Ibid., 184.

29 RHT, Notes for an obituary of Eileen Power, 1940, TV 50, f. 2.

30 A. E. Bland, P. A. Brown and R. H. Tawney (eds), *English Economic History. Select Documents* (London, 1914).

31 R. H. Tawney and Eileen Power (eds), *Tudor Economic Documents. Being Select Documents Illustrating the Economic and Social History of Tudor England* (3 vols., London, 1924).

32 T. C. Barker, 'The Beginnings of the Economic History Society', *Ec H R*, ns, vol. 30, no. 1, Feb. 1977, 6.

33 RHT to M. Postan, 30 June 1958, TII/97.

34 RHT to Dr E. Margalit, 8 Feb. 1961, TV16.

35 Sir Arnold Plant, BBC Transcript 1963.

36 R. H. Tawney, *The Acquisitive Society* (London, 1921), 8–19.

37 Ibid., 60.

38 R. H. Tawney, *Commonplace Book* (hereafter CB) (eds J. M. Winter and D. M. Joslin) (Cambridge, 1972), 29 and n.

39 Jay Winter, 'Tawney the Historian' in idem (ed.), *History and Society. Essays by R. H. Tawney* (London, 1978), 15–6.

40 'Wilson, Thomas 1523/4–81', ODNB.

41 Max Weber, *The Protestant Ethic and the Spirit of Capitalism* (tr. Talcott Parsons). With a Foreword by R. H. Tawney (London, 1930), 1b.

42 Ibid., 7–10.

43 Ibid., 11.

44 R. H. Tawney, *Religion and the Rise of Capitalism* (London, 1926) (1943 edn.), 4–5.

45 Ibid., 61.

46 Ibid., 226–7.

47 Ibid., 135.

48 Ibid., 189.

49 Ibid., 279.

50 Ibid., 232.

51 Ibid., 280.

52 Ibid., 272.

53 W. H. B. Court, *Scarcity and Choice in History* (London, 1970), 139.

54 Mehta, *Fly and Fly-Bottle*, 164.

55 Court, *Scarcity and Choice*, 18. John Kenyon, *The History Men. The Historical Profession in England since the Renaissance* (1983) (London, 1993 edn.), 255.

56 R. H. Tawney, 'The Rise of the Gentry, 1558–1640', *EcHR*, vol. 11, no.1, 1941, 1–38.

57 Ibid., 26.

58 Ibid., 33n. The counties were: Hertfordshire, Bedfordshire, Buckinghamshire, Surrey, Worcestershire, Hampshire, North Riding of Yorkshire.

59 Ibid., 28.

60 Ibid., 4.

61 Ibid., 6.

62 Ibid., 15.

63 Ibid., 22.

64 Ibid., 25.

65 Ibid., 27.

66 Adam Sisman, *Hugh Trevor-Roper. The Biography* (2010) (London, 2011 edn.), 202–8.

67 Hugh Trevor-Roper, *Archbishop Laud* (London, 1940) and *The Last Days of Hitler* (London, 1947). Trevor-Roper's initial campaign against Stone is explained by Sisman, *Hugh Trevor-Roper*, 183–201.

68 Lawrence Stone, 'The Anatomy of the Elizabethan Aristocracy', *EcHR*, vol. xviii, nos 1, 2, 1948, 1–53.

69 Sisman, *Hugh Trevor-Roper*, 187.

70 Hugh Trevor-Roper, 'The Elizabethan Aristocracy: An Anatomy Anatomized', *Ec H R*, NS, vol. 3, no. 3, 1951, 279–98.

71 Trevor-Roper, 'The Elizabethan Aristocracy', 294.

72 Hugh Trevor-Roper to RHT, 30 Oct., 6 Nov. 1950; R. H. Tawney to Hugh Trevor-Roper, 5 Nov. 1950, TV/10.

73 Kenyon, 'The Great Historians: R. H. Tawney', 41.

74 Trevor-Roper to Bernard Berenson, 8 Nov. 1953, in Richard Davenport Hines (ed.), *Letters from Oxford* (London, 2006), 132.

75 Trevor-Roper to Wallace Notestein, 28 Jan. 1951, Ibid., 287. See also Trevor-Roper's reference to Tawney at xvii.

76 Trevor-Roper to Bernard Berenson, 30 Aug. 1952, Ibid., 96.

77 RHT to Hugh Trevor-Roper, 21 Feb. 1951, Dacre papers, Christ Church, Oxford, DP 1/2/2.

78 H. R. Trevor-Roper, 'The Gentry 1540–1640', *The Economic History Review Supplements*, no. 1 (London, 1953), 1–55.

79 Ibid., 1.

80 Ibid., 4.

81 Ibid., 5.

82 RHT to Trevor-Roper, 5 Nov. 1950, TV/10.

83 Trevor-Roper, 'The Gentry', 8.

84 Ibid., 9–26.

85 R. H. Tawney, *Business and Politics under James I : Lionel Cranfield as Merchant and Minister* (London, 1958).

86 Trevor-Roper, 'The Gentry', 51–3.

87 'Roper, Hugh Redwald Trevor-, Baron Dacre of Glanton (1914–2003)', ODNB.

88 H. Habbakuk to M. Postan, 4 Oct. 1952; Habbakuk to Trevor-Roper, 23 Oct., 6 Nov. 1952; Trevor-Roper to Habbakuk, 7 Nov. 1952, Papers of the Economic History Society (hereafter Ec Hist Soc mss) G2, BLPES.

89 Postan to Trevor-Roper, 19, 30 Jan., 9 Feb. 1953; Trevor-Roper to Postan, 24 Jan., 5 Feb. 1953; Postan to Habbakuk, 19 Jan. 1953; Habbakuk to Postan, 11, 16 Feb. 1953, Ec Hist Soc mss, G2.

90 Habbakuk to Postan, 21 July 1952; Postan to Habbakuk, 24 July 1952, Ec Hist Soc mss, G2.

91 Habbakuk to Trevor-Roper, 4 Sept. 1952, Ec Hist Soc mss, G2.

92 Postan to Habbakuk, 24 July 1952, Ec Hist Soc mss, G2.

93 Habbakuk to Postan, 28 July 1952, Ec Hist Soc mss, G2.

94 Habbakuk to Trevor-Roper 27 Aug. 1952, Ec Hist Soc mss, G2.

95 Habbakuk to Trevor-Roper 4 Sept. 1952 referring to a letter from Trevor-Roper to Habbakuk, 29 Aug. 1952, Ec Hist Soc mss, G2.

96 Postan to Habbakuk, 24 July 1952, Ec Hist Soc mss, G2.

97 Richard Rees to Trevor-Roper, 12 Oct. 1952, Dacre papers, Christ Church, Oxford, DP 9/6/1.

98 Tawney to Trevor-Roper, 14 Oct. 1952, DP 9/6/1.

99 Trevor-Roper to Berenson, 8 Nov. 1953, *Letters from Oxford*, 130.

100 R. H. Tawney, 'The Rise of the Gentry: A Postscript', *Ec H R*, ns, vol. 7, no. 1, 1954, 91–7.

101 Ibid., 91.

102 Ibid., 92.

103 Ibid.

104 Ibid., 97. As Adam Sisman points out, the Philistines were 'smitten hip and thigh' (Judges 15:8), not the Amalekites – though they were also smitten. Sisman, *Hugh Trevor-Roper*, 206n.

105 Sisman, *Hugh Trevor-Roper*, 206.

106 Ibid.

107 J. P. Cooper, 'The Counting of the Manors', *Ec H R*, ns, vol. viii, no. 3, 1956.

108 J. H. Hexter, 'Storm over the Gentry: The Tawney-Trevor-Roper Controversy', *Encounter*, vol. x, no. 5, May 1958, 31.

109 Ibid., 29.

110 Sisman, *Hugh Trevor-Roper*, 202.

111 See below, 278–9.

112 R. H. Tawney, 'Harrington's Interpretation of His Age', *The Raleigh Lecture on History, The British Academy 1941* (London, 1942), 23n.

113 Ibid., 4.

114 Ibid., 23.

115 R. H. Tawney (ed.), Thomas Wilson, *A Discourse Upon Usury* (1569) (London, 1925) (1962 edn.), 'Introduction', 41.

116 M. Vyvyan to D. Joslin, 1 Nov. 1967, T 27/9.

117 Mehta, *Fly and Fly-Bottle*, 165.

118 *Manchester Guardian*, 17 Jan. 1962.

119 T. S. Ashton, BBC Transcript 1963.

120 Ibid.

121 R. H. Tawney, *The British Labor Movement* (New Haven, Ct., 1925), 142–3.

122 Vyvyan, Transcript 1982.

123 Mehta, *Fly and Fly- Bottle*, 164, 166.

124 M. Postan, 'D. M. Joslin', CB, ix.

125 Kenyon, 'The Great Historians', 42.

126 Ashton, BBC Transcript 1963.

127 *Manchester Guardian*, 17 Jan. 1962.

128 'Tawney's Agrarian Problem 100 Years On: Landlords and Tenants in Rural England c.1400–c.1750', University of Exeter, 11–12 July 2011. I am grateful to the organizer, Dr Jane Whittle of the University of Exeter, for details of this event.

Chapter 10

1   T/15, Tawney papers, BLPES, 3rd of 3 lectures in Chicago, Mar. 1939, f. 28.

2   RHT to Evan Durbin, 9 Sept. 1939, Durbin Papers, BLPES, 3/10 f. 44.

3   JB to WB, 9 Oct. 1939, Bev 2/A/102.

4   RHT to JT, 19 May 1940.

5   *The Times*, 2 July 1940.

6   *The Times*, 18 Sept. 1941.

7   RHT to WB, 8 June 1940, Bev/2A/108.

8   RHT to JT, 31 May 1940, T27/7.

9   RHT to JT, 19 June 1940, TV/2.

10 RHT to JT, 28 June 1940, TV2.

11 Eileen Power to RHT, 3 July [1940], T11/1.

12 R. H. Tawney, *Eileen Power* (Golders Green Crematorium, 12 Aug. 1940). For a later and professional tribute, see RHT's handwritten notes, T11/1.

13 RHT to W. S. G. Adams, 11 Sept. 1939 and Adams to RHT, 11 Oct. 1940, LSE Staff File 1.

14 RHT to WB, 4 Jan. 1961, Bev/2/A/108.

15 JT to WB, 11 Nov. 1940, Bev/2/A/102. See also RHT to Fred Clarke, 30 Sept. 1940, Tawney Papers, London University Institute of Education, TY 2/12.

16 JT to WB, 14 Dec. 1940, Bev/2/A/102.

17 JT to WB, 11 Nov. 1940, Bev/2/A/102.

18 RHT to Beatrice Webb, 31 Jan. 1943, Passfield Papers, BLPES, 2/4/N.

19 Jay Winter, 'Tawney the Historian' in idem (ed.), *History and Society. Essays by R. H. Tawney* (London, 1978), 29.

20 'The Abolition of Economic Controls', f. 51.

21 Ibid., f. 53.

22 I am grateful to Prof Jose Harris for private information on the controversy surrounding Tawney's paper.

23 R. H. Tawney, 'The Abolition of Economic Controls, 1918–21', Ec.H.R, vol. xiii, 1943, 1–30. The quotation is taken from the full version of Tawney's report, in T26/1.

24 RHT to JT, 19 June 1940, TV/2.

25 R. H. Tawney, 'Why Britain Fights' in *The Attack and Other Papers* (London, 1953), 71–81.

26 Prof I. L. Kandel to RHT, 24 July 1940, TII/87.

27 Joseph E. Johnson, Dept. of History, Williams College, MA, to RHT 21 July 1940, Ibid.

28 Charlton Ogburn to RHT, 25 July 1940; J. W. Hamilton to RHT, 24 July 1940, Ibid.

29 Duff Cooper to R. H. Tawney, 17 June 1941, Foreign Office Papers (FO) 371.26185.A5521, National Archives. See also Jay Winter, 'Introduction: Tawney on Labour and Labour Movements' in idem (ed.), *R. H. Tawney: The American Labour Movement and Other Essays* (Brighton, 1979), xi–xxiv.

30 Tawney to Duff Cooper, 7 July 1941, FO 371.26185.A5521.

31 FO 371.26185.A4679. See also F. T. A. Ashton Gwatkin to Derek Hoyar Miller, 7 Aug. 1941 on Tawney's role, FO 371.26187.A6429.

32 RHT to A. M. Carr-Saunders, 26 July 1941, LSE Staff File 2.

33 *Portrait of R. H. Tawney*, 1963.

34 RHT to A. M. Carr-Saunders, 6 Aug. 1941, LSE Staff File 2.

35 RHT to JT, 19 June 1941, T27/20/1.

36 RHT, 'The War and Post-War Problems' (bearing the note in RHT's hand 'I think a talk in the USA 1941–2') T/16/3., f. 3.

37 Testimonials from the Amalgamated Weavers' Association of Accrington, Lancashire', 7 Aug. 1941, and from Walter Citrine, General Secretary of the Trades Union Congress, 8 Aug. 1941. The latter testimonial was to the President of the Trades and Labor Congress of Canada. Tawney Add 0007, BLPES.

38 Beatrice Webb to RHT, 2 Oct. 1941, Tawney Add 0007.

39 William Clark speaking in 'Portrait of R. H. Tawney', BBC Home Service, 1963.

40 Ibid.

41 RHT to Mildred Vyvyan, 31 May 1942, TV/45.

42   RHT to Carr-Saunders, 10 Mar. 1942, LSE staff file, 2.

43   RHT to Tom Jones, 22 Mar. 1942, FO371.30669.A4406. Interestingly, this letter was intercepted by the official Censor and then minuted by the Foreign Office.

44   'Handwritten notes from lectures given by Tawney in the United States on current affairs (1941–2)', T16/1/2/3. The stem lecture – the basic text – was given to a university audience in 1941 before Pearl Harbor.

45   RHT to WT, 23 Mar. 1942, Temple Papers, Lambeth Palace Library, f. 383.

46   Attlee to RHT, 14 Mar. 1942; RHT to Attlee, 7 May 1942, T Add. 0007.

47   RHT to Creech Jones, 25 Sept. 1942, T Add. 0007.

48   R. H. Tawney, 'The American Labour Movement' (FO 371.30700.A9007, 19 Sept. 1942) published in Winter (ed.), *The American Labour Movement*, 1–110. See also Jay Winter, 'Tawney the Historian' in idem (ed.), *History and Society. Essays by R. H. Tawney* (London, 1978), 30.

49   RHT, 'Labour and the Congressional Elections, 1942', Tawney Add 0007.

50   RHT, 'A Note on the Relations between the A F of L and the CIO and Between the British and American Labour Movement, 3 Sept. 1942', f. 4, Tawney Add 0007.

51   Ibid., f. 6.

52   RHT, Untitled 24-page foolscap document beginning 'The recent visit of Sir Walter Citrine.' concerning Citrine's visit to the US in May 1943, f. 23. (Hereafter 'The recent visit of Sir Walter Citrine'), Tawney Add 0007.

53   Halifax to Eden, 8 Apr. 1942, copy of telegram, Tawney Add 0007.

54   'The recent visit of Sir Walter Citrine', f. 2.

55   RHT to Attlee, 7 May 1942, Tawney Add 0007.

56   'The recent visit of Sir Walter Citrine', f. 3.

57   RHT, 'A Note on the Relations between the AF of L and the CIO', f. 9.

58   RHT, 'The visit of Sir Walter Citrine', f. 12.

59   Memo: 'Sir Walter Citrine', report of a meeting between Citrine, Tawney and Halifax at the British embassy, Washington DC, 19 May 1942, Tawney Add 0007.

60   'The visit of Sir Walter Citrine', f. 6.

61   RHT, 'A Note on the Relations', f. 10.

62   Eden to Attlee, 19 Aug. 1942, FO 371.30700.A7378.

63   'Britain Halts Anglo-US Labor Move', *Christian Science Monitor*, 14 Sept. 1942.

64   Eden to Churchill, 31 Aug. 1942, FO 371.30700.A8035.

65   *Parliamentary Debates*, 1941–2, vol. 383, 11 Sept. 1942, 530–1.

66   *Christian Science Monitor*, 14 Sept. 1942; *The Times*, 11 Sept. 1942, 2.

67   Citrine to Eden, 14 Sept. 1942, FO 371.30700.A8035.

68   'U.S. Labour and Russia', *The Times*, 7 Sept. 1942, 4; 'TUC – AFL – CIO', *The Times*, 10 Sept. 1942, 5.

69   Winter, 'Introduction' in Tawney, *The American Labour Movement*, xxii.

70 See above, 160–1. Citrine's account of these events in his autobiography is entirely unreliable, lacking reference to any critical commentary on his own behaviour. Citrine also fails to mention the cancellation of his proposed visit to the US in September 1942. Lord Citrine, *Two Careers* (London, 1967), 140–54.

71 R. J. Campbell to RHT, 11 Aug. 1942, Tawney Add 0007.

72 'Portrait of R. H. Tawney', BBC, 1963.

73 Halifax to Eden, 29 Apr. 1942, FO 371.30700.A4137.

74 Lectures given in the US, 1941–2, T16/2/ f. 18f.

75 J. L. Hammond to RHT, 7 Oct. 1940, Tawney Papers, Institute of Education Archives, University of London (hereafter IOE), TY 2/14.

76 RHT to Beatrice Webb, 6 Dec. 1942, Passfield papers, 2/4/M, ff. 253–5.

77 JT to WB, 10 Mar. 1943, Bev/2/A/102.

78 RHT to WT, 1 Aug. 1943, Temple Papers, vol. 21, ff. 41–7; William Temple to RHT, 6 Aug. 1943, Tawney Papers, IOE, TY 2/39.

79 W. O. Lester Smith, Director of Education for Manchester, to RHT, 16 Aug. 1943; P. R. Morris, Director of Education for Kent to RHT, 17 Aug. 1943, TV48/1.

80 Michael Barber, *The Making of the 1944 Education Act* (London, 1994), 8.

81 C. R. Attlee to RHT, 3 June 1943, Tawney Papers, IOE, TY 2/33. See RHT to Creech Jones, 7 Feb., 14 Mar., 18 May, 24 May 1943, ACJ 6/2/ 62-71, Rhodes House Library, Oxford.

82 George Bell to RHT, 26 Nov. 1942, Tawney Papers, IOE, TY 2/25.

83 RHT to R. A. Butler, 1 Aug. 1943, R. A. Butler to RHT, 5 Aug. 1943, Tawney Papers, IOE, TY 2/36, 38. P. H. J. H. Gosden, *Education in the Second World War. A Study in Policy and Administration* (London, 1976), 313.

84 R. A. Butler to RHT, 16 Dec. 1943, Tawney Papers, IOE, TY 2/45.

85 RHT to Douglas Miller, 30 Jan. 1943, Tawney Papers, IOE, TY 2/26.

86 Sheena, Lady Simon to RHT, 22 Dec. 1944, Tawney Papers, IOE, TY 2/48.

87 RHT to Douglas Miller, 30 Jan. 1943, Tawney Papers, IOE, TY 2/26.

88 'Fee-Charging Schools. A Reply from Mr R. H. Tawney', *Manchester Guardian*, 16 Feb. 1943.

89 RHT to Creech Jones (nd, 1944), ACJ 6/2/146. Tawney is referring to the second reading debate of the Butler Bill.

90 RHT to Creech Jones, 21 Sept. 1943, ACJ/6/2/81.

91 RHT to Creech Jones, 2 Aug. 1943, ACJ 6/2/78-9.

92 'Better Education for Every Child', *The Times*, 14 Feb. 1944.

93 'Dr R. H. Tawney's Speech at the Conference of National Organisations on Saturday 12 Feb. 1944', T18/5.

94 RHT to Evan Durbin, 30 July 1945, Durbin 3/13.

95 JT to WB, 21 July 1945, Bev/2/A/103.

96 Lawrence Goldman, *Dons and Workers. Oxford and Adult Education Since 1850*, 239.

97 Lecture II, T16/5, f. 6.

Chapter 11

1 JT to WB, 22 Apr. 1946; 30 Mar. 1947, Bev/2/A/103.

2 Letter from the LSE Governors to RHT, 31 Oct. 1940, RHT, Staff Files, LSE.

3 Extract from the Appointments Committee minutes, 22 Jan. 1945, LSE Staff File.

4 A. M. Carr-Saunders (Director) to Mr J. Henderson (Senate House), 8 Mar. 1948.

5 A. M. Carr-Saunders to RHT, 30 Apr. 1948, Staff Files.

6 *The Times*, 17 Jan. 1962.

7 T. S. Ashton to RHT, 9 Dec. 1948, T 24/2.

8 *The Observer*, 25 Jan. 1953.

9 RHT to WB, 27 Jan. 1961, Bev/2/A/108.

10 RHT to Father P. Larkin, Dept. of Economics, University of Cork, 17 Feb. 1961, TV16. See also David Ormrod, 'R. H. Tawney and the Origins of Capitalism', *History Workshop Journal*, vol. 18, 1984, 141.

11 A. M. Carr-Saunders to RHT, 2 Dec. 1948, T24/1.

12 RHT to A. M. Carr-Saunders, 8 Dec. 1948, T24/1.

13 RHT to Carr-Saunders, 22 Dec. 1948, 22 Feb. 1949, T24/1.

14 Carr-Saunders to RHT, 23 Feb. 1949, T24/1.

15 RHT to Carr-Saunders, 28 Feb. 1949, T24/1; Carr-Saunders to RHT, 15 Mar. 1949, T24/1.

16 RHT to Carr-Saunders, 25 Mar. 1949, T24/1. This letter went through many different versions before it was sent indicating both the care Tawney took and his rage over being misused in this manner.

17 Margaret Cole to RHT, 2 June 1949, T24/2.

18 Harold Laski to RHT, 23 Sept. 1949, T24/2.

19 RHT to Margaret Cole, 7 June 1949, T24/2.

20 RHT to Carr-Saunders, 19 Oct. 1949, T24/2.

21 RHT to J. L. Hammond, 25 Mar. 1949; J. L. Hammond to RHT, 29 Mar. 1949, T24/2.

22 'Typescript notes of lectures given by Tawney on the post-war Labour Government. Delivered late March and early April 1948 in Chicago,' T16/4.

23 Ibid., Lecture I, ff. 15–18.

24 Ibid., Lecture III, f. 15.

25 R. H. Tawney, *Equality* (1931) (1951 edn.), 192.

26 Beatrice Webb, *Diaries* (eds N. and J. Mackenzie), vol. 4, 8 Dec. 1935, 361.

27 Rita Hinden, 'In Debt to Tawney', *Socialist Commentary*, Feb. 1962, 11.

28 R. H. Tawney, 'Labour Party History. Preparation and Achievement', *Times Literary Supplement*, 10 Mar. 1950, 2

29 The 1952 lecture as given also includes some strictures by Tawney on the form that nationalization had taken in Britain. Not only were these absent from the 1964 version, but had been replaced by his support for an extension of public ownership, though in forms different from outright nationalization.

30 RHT, 'British Socialism Today', T19/2, f. 16.

31 Ibid., f. 17.

32 Ibid., ff. 18–19.

33 Sir Richard Acland to RHT, 25 Nov. 1953; RHT to Acland, 2 Dec. 1953, T27/16/1.

34 RHT, 'British Socialism Today', f. 17.

35 Letters to RHT from the Foreign Office: 25 July 1944, 5 Aug. 1944, 22 Jan. 1945, T/II/97.

36 Christopher Hill to RHT, 30 May 1945, 6 June 1945, 21 July 1945, T/II/97.

37 C. Hill to RHT, 27 Nov. and 27 Dec. 1950; RHT to C. Hill, 4 Dec. 1950, TV10.

38 M. Postan to RHT, 3 Jan. 1951, TV10.

39 RHT, 'Fabianism and the Fabians 1884–1914', T/6/11.

40 Eric Hobsbawm, 'The Fabians Reconsidered' in idem, *Labouring Men. Studies in the History of Labour* (London, 1964), 250–71.

41 RHT to Creech Jones, 11 Sept. 1954, ACJ 6/2/103, Rhodes House, Oxford.

42 Rita Hinden to Arthur Creech-Jones, 7 Dec. 1960, quoted in J. R. Brooks, 'R. H. Tawney and the Reform of English Education' (unpublished PhD Dissertation, University of Wales, 1974), 460.

43 RHT to Arthur Creech Jones, 27 Jan. 1961, TV15.

44 Rita Hinden, 'In Debt to Tawney', *Socialist Commentary*, Feb. 1962, 11.

45 Philip M. Williams, *Hugh Gaitskell. A Political Biography* (London, 1979), 320.

46 Ibid., 368.

47 Lena Jeger, *The Guardian*, 1 July 1983.

48 Williams, *Hugh Gaitskell*, 631.

49 Lena Jeger to Arthur Creech Jones, 9 Feb. 1962, Jeger papers, BLPES, 1/8/1.

50 RHT, 'British Socialism Today', 1952 Mss version to the University of London Fabian Society, T19/2, f. 12.

51 *The Guardian*, 25 June 1983; Lena Jeger, *The Guardian*, 1 July 1983.

52 Lena Jeger, 'Speech on the unveiling of the blue plaque to Tawney in Mecklenburgh Square, 30 Nov. 1980', Jeger papers 1/8/1.

53 Ibid.

54 RHT to W. H. Parker, 29 Nov. 1960, TV16.

55 Lena Jeger, 'Ideas and the Man', *Tribune*, 26 Jan. 1962.

56 RHT to D. F. G. Parsons, 27 Jan. 1960, TV16.

57 JT to WB, 2 Oct. 1953, Bev/2/A/103.

58 Ibid.

59 RHT to Elizabeth Lloyd, 3 Feb. 1961, TV16.

60 RHT to Ida Gandy, 3 Feb. 1961, TV15.

61 RHT to Dr C. B. Hunt, 8 Feb. 1961, TV15.

62 Jeger, 'Ideas and the Man', 7.

63 'Groser, St John Beverley (1890–1966)', ODNB.

64 BBC Transcript 1963.

65 RHT to Dr Santo Jeger, 28 May 1950, Jeger 1/8/2.

66 Jeger, 'Speech on unveiling of the blue plaque, 30 Nov. 1980', f. 1.

67 BBC Transcript 1963, f. 14.

68 Henrietta Barnett, *Canon Barnett. His Life, Work and Friends* (London, 1921 edn.), 502.

69 H. Sumner to RHT, 21 May 1950, TV6.

70 John Lowe to RHT, 12 June 1950, TV6.

71 RHT, 'Speech at the Christ Church Gaudy', TV6.

72 Frank Bongiorno, *British to their Bootheels too: Britishness and Australian Radicalism*, Trevor Reese Memorial Lecture, King's College, London, 2006, 2–5.

73 Conversation with F. B. Smith, Australian National University, Canberra, 7 Mar. 2012.

74 Eric Tams to RHT, 18 July 1951, TV10.

75 R. A. Butler to A. Creech Jones, 15 Nov. 1960, ACJ 6/6/67.

76 *The Times*, 12 Dec. 1960. File on 80th birthday dinner for RHT, Creech Jones MSS, Rhodes House, Oxford, ACJ 6/6.

77 *Fabian News*, vol. 72, no. 1, Jan. 1961, 2.

78 For details of the 'Professor R. H. Tawney Testimonial Fund', see Arthur Creech Jones papers, Rhodes House, Oxford, ACJ/5.

79 F. J. Fisher (ed.), *Essays in the Economic and Social History of Tudor & Stuart England in honour of R. H. Tawney* (Cambridge, 1961).

80 Sir George Barnes to Creech Jones, 12 Feb. 1960, ACJ 6/4/7.

81 William Taylor to RHT, 8 Mar. 1958, T27/17/1; Stephen Lukes to RHT, 29 Nov. 1960, TV16.

82 Mr J. Jackson to RHT, nd [Nov. 1960] TV15.

83 Victor Cohen to RHT, 28 Nov. 1960, TV15.

84 RHT to Mr Ian Brettell, solicitor, 31 Oct. 1956 and RHT, 'Miss A. S. Tawney. Notes on the provision made for her', T27/15/2.

85 Sheena Simon to Creech Jones, 26 Nov. 1959, Creech Jones papers, ACJ 6/4/5.

86 Solicitors letter (Van Sommer, Chillcott, Kitcat and Clark) to RHT, 5 Feb. 1959.

87 RHT, 'Estimated Income after July 1951', TV10.

88 Nuffield Foundation to RHT and RHT to Nuffield Foundation, 4, 6 July 1951, TV10.

89 Vincent Knowles (Simon Research Fund) to RHT, 18 June 1956; Sir John Stopford (Vice-Chancellor of the Univ. Of Manchester) to RHT, 19 June 1956, T27/18.

90 David Astor to RHT, 3, 9 Oct. 1956, T27/18.

91 Lord (Ernest) Simon of Wythenshawe to RHT, 9 Apr., 20 May 1958; RHT to Lord Simon, 19 Apr. 1958. Sheena Simon to Creech Jones, 26 Nov. 1959, Creech Jones papers, ACJ 6/4/5.

92 RHT to Lena Jeger, 23 Jan. 1958, Jeger papers 1/8/2.

93 RHT to Lena Jeger, 23 Mar. 1959, Jeger papers 1/8/2.

94 *The Times*, 29 Jan. 1958.

95 *The Manchester Guardian*, 23 Jan. 1958.

96 *London School of Economics Magazine*, July 1958, 28.

97 Richard Rees to J. M. K. Vyvyan, 2 Jan. 1962, T27/19/1.

98 Richard Rees, BBC transcript 1963.

99 Lena Jeger to Creech Jones, 17 Feb. 1960, ACJ 6/4/9.

100 Lena Jeger to Creech Jones, 8 Aug. 1960, ACJ 6/3/12.

101 Arthur Creech Jones to Sir Sydney Caine, 22 Feb. 1960, Tawney, LSE Staff File III.

102 Caine to Creech Jones, 25 Feb. 1960; Caine to Sir Douglas Logan, Principal of UCL and Logan to Caine, 12, 14 July 1960, Tawney, Staff Files, III.

103 Richard Rees to Creech Jones, 2 Jan. 1962, ACJ 6/3/48.

104 Rees to Vyvyan, 2 Jan. 1962, T27/19/1.

105 *New Statesman*, 19 Jan. 1962, 2.

106 'Weyman, Stanley John, 1855–1928', ODNB.

107 Jeger, 'Ideas and the Man', 7.

108 'The Death Penalty', *The Times*, 2 Jan. 1962.

109 Tawney lies in grave number 50574, square 73.

110 'London Letter: A Christian Burial', from a newspaper report found in the Lena Jeger papers, 1/8/1.

111 Order of Service, Memorial Service for R. H. Tawney, 8 Feb. 1962, LSE Staff File III.

112 Hugh Gaitskell to Sir Sydney Caine, 30 Jan. 1962, ACJ 6/9/9; Gaitskell to Arthur Creech Jones, 26 Feb. 1962, ACJ 6/9/10.

113 Lucy Rice to Arthur Creech Jones, 28 Jan. 1962, Creech Jones papers, ACJ 6/2/145.

Chapter 12

1 *The Times*, 17 Jan. 1962.

2 *The Guardian*, 17 Jan. 1962.

3 Herbert Butterfield to Sir Sydney Caine, 18 Jan. 1962, RHT Staff File, 3.

4 BBC Transcript 1963, f. 1.

5 Ibid., f. 4.

6   *The Guardian*, 17 Jan. 1962.

7   RHT to Sir Stanley Unwin, 20 Nov. 1949, TV12/2.

8   Postan, BBC Transcript 1963, f. 1.

9   Ved Mehta, *Fly and Fly-Bottle. Encounters with British Intellectuals* (London, 1963), 165.

10 'Address by the Rt. Hon. Hugh Gaitskell' in R. H. Tawney, *The Radical Tradition* (ed. R. Hinden) (London, 1964), 214.

11 See above, 122.

12 Ronald Preston, 'R. H. Tawney as a Christian Moralist. 3', *Theology*, vol. lxix, May 1966, 265–9.

13 Geoffrey Elton, *Reformation Europe* (London, 1963), 315.

14 Geoffrey Elton, *The Future of the Past* (Cambridge, 1968), 16–17.

15 See above, 33.

16 'Portrait of R. H. Tawney', BBC Home Service, 1963.

17 RHT to Gilbert Murray, 29 Oct. 1925, Gilbert Murray papers, Bodleian Library, Oxford, reel 50, ff. 86–7.

18 Colin Holmes to J. M. K. Vyvyan, 11 Dec. 1978, T/27/20/1.

19 See above, 77.

20 'Portrait of R. H. Tawney', BBC Home Service, 1963.

21 Christopher Harvie, *The Lights of Liberalism. University Liberals and the Challenge of Democracy 1860–1886* (London, 1976).

22 Janet Howarth, 'The Edwardian Reform Movement' in *The History of the University of Oxford. Vol. vii. Nineteenth-Century Oxford, Part 2* (eds M. G. Brock and M. C. Curthoys) (Oxford, 2000), 847–9.

23 'Arnot, Robert Page [Robin] (1890–1986)', ODNB.

24 Anthony Arblaster, 'Tawney in Retrospect', Bulletin of the Society for the Study of Labour History, 54, 1 (1989), 95–102.

25 'Moral Mind: R. H. Tawney' in Stefan Collini, *English Pasts. Essays in History and Culture* (Oxford, 1999), 177–94.

26 See above, 119–22.

27 Collini, 'Moral Mind', *passim*.

28 *The Times*, 18 Oct. 1933.

29 Ibid., 27 Oct. 1936.

30 Ibid., 13 Oct. 1937.

31 Anthony Wright, *R. H. Tawney* (Manchester, 1987), 146.

32 Jose Harris, *Private Lives, Public Spirit. Britain 1970–1914* (1993) (London, 1994 edn.).

33 Sir Stanley Unwin to RHT, 6 Mar. 1951, TV12/2.

34 M. Postan, 'D. M. Joslin 1925–70', *R. H. Tawney's Commonplace Book* (eds J. M. Winter and D. Joslin) (Cambridge, 1971), lx.

35 *The Guardian*, 17 Jan. 1962.

36   David Marquand, 'R. H. Tawney. Prophet of Equality', *The Guardian* 26 Nov. 1960.

37   Alasdair MacIntyre, *Against the Self-Image of the Age* (1971), 41.

38   Anthony Arblaster, *Bulletin of the Society for the Study of Labour History*, vol. 54, pt. 1 (1989), 101.

39   RHT to Merlin Thomas, 11 Jan. 1961, TV16.

40   Otto Kahn-Freund to RHT, 1 Dec. 1960, TV15.

41   J. M. K. Vyvyan, 1982 Transcript, f. 1.

42   R. H. Tawney, 'Introduction' to Max Beer, *A History of British Socialism* (London, 1919), xviii.

43   *The Times*, 2 Feb. 1982.

44   *The Times*, 5 Feb. 1982.

45   *The Times*, 3 Feb. 1982.

46   *The Times*, 8 Feb. 1982.

47   *The Times*, 4 Feb. 1982.

48   Michael Foot, 'My Kind of Socialism', *The Observer*, 10 Jan. 1982, 12–13.

49   Raphael Samuel, 'The SDP's Escape from the Christian Heritage of Socialism' and 'Tawney and the SDP', *The Guardian*, 29 Mar., 5 Apr. 1982.

50   *The Times*, 3, 6 Feb. 1982.

51   *The Times*, 9 Feb. 1982.

52   *The Guardian*, 25 June 1983.

53   Shirley Williams to Arthur Creech Jones, 9 May 1960, Creech Jones papers, ACJ 6/5/9.

54   RHT to W. H. Parker, 29 Nov. 1960, TV16.

55   Vyvyan, 1982 transcript, f. 5.

56   R. Samuel, 'The SDP's Escape from the Christian Heritage of Socialism', *The Guardian*, 29 Mar. 1982.

57   Stephen Yeo, 'A New Life: The Religion of Socialism in Britain, 1883–96', *History Workshop Journal*, vol. 4, 1977, 5–56.

58   See above, 121–2.

59   Ibid.

60   R. Williams, *Culture and Society* 1780–1950, (1961), 3rd edn. (Harmondsworth, 1963), 219, 223.

61   RHT, *CB*, 40 (22 Oct. 1912).

62   *The Guardian*, 17 Jan. 1962.

63   R. H. Tawney, *Equality* (1931) (1951 edn.), 89.

64   Ibid., 56.

65   Ibid., 54.

66   Ibid., 189.

67   Ibid., 64.

68   Ibid., 204.

69 RHT, *Religion and the Rise of Capitalism* (1926) (1943 imprint), 73.

70 Ibid., 88.

71 R. H. Tawney, *The Agrarian Problem in the Sixteenth Century* (London, 1912), 66.

72 Ibid., 197–211.

73 'Portrait of R. H. Tawney', BBC Home Service, 1963.

74 W. H. B. Court, *Scarcity and Choice in History* (London, 1970), 133.

75 Ibid., 34.

76 Raphael Samuel, 'The SDP's Escape from the Christian Heritage of Socialism', *The Guardian*, 29 Mar. 1982.

77 R. H. Tawney, *The Webbs in Perspective* (London, 1953), 21.

78 Order of Service, Memorial Service for Evan Durbin, St Margaret's Westminster, 16 Sept. 1948.

Illustrations

Figure 1 Tawney as a boy

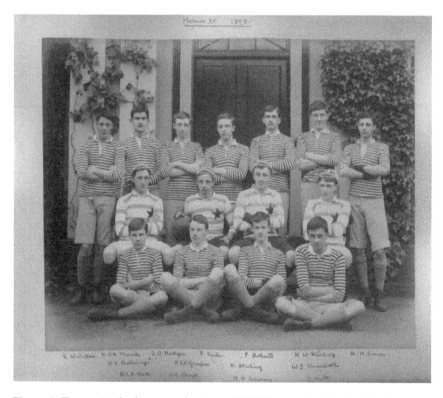

Figure 2 Tawney in the house rugby team, 1898 (Tawney is sitting in the front row, third from the left.)

Figure 3 Tawney in the house cricket team, 1899 (Tawney is sitting at the end of the line. His brother Stephen is standing behind him, also at the end of the line.)

Figure 4 House photo, 1899 (Tawney is sitting to the left of Mr Whitelaw as we see it, in the centre of the photograph.)

Figure 5 Young Man Tawney

Figure 6 Jeanette and William Beveridge

Figure 7 Jeanette Beveridge at the time of her marriage, 1909

Figure 8 Corporal Tawney, 1915

Figure 9 The Sankey Commission 1919 (Tawney is sitting, second from the extreme right of the photo. Behind him, third from the right, sits Sidney Webb.)

Figure 10 Harry, Jeanette and friend at Rose Cottage

Figure 11 Tawney receiving his honorary degree from Oxford, 1950

Figure 12 Tawney in old age

Figure 13 Lena Jeger dedicating Tawney's blue plaque, Mecklenburgh Square, London, 30 November 1980

Bibliography of Collections and Published Works Cited in the Text

Archival collections

British Library of Political and Economic Science, London School of Economics:
Tawney Collection
Tawney-Vyvyan Collection
William Beveridge papers
Lena Jeger papers
Passfield papers
Evan Durbin papers
Economic History Society papers
George Lansbury papers
Independent Labour Party collection
Graham Wallas papers
LSE Staff Files
LSE Central Registry Files

Institute of Education Archives, University of London:
Tawney Papers

London Metropolitan Archive:
Munro Family Papers (Cecil James Munro)

London Metropolitan University: Trades Union Congress Library:
Workers' Educational Association Archives

British Library:
Henry Beveridge collection
Albert Mansbridge papers

National Archives:
Foreign Office papers 1941–2, F.O. 371

Lambeth Palace Library:
William Temple papers
George Bell papers
E. J. Palmer papers

Oxford:
Papers of the Department for Continuing Education, Oxford University Archives
E. S. Cartwright papers, Oxford University Archives
Gilbert Murray papers, Bodleian Library, Oxford
J. L. and Barbara Hammond Papers, Bodleian Library, Oxford
Clement Webb Journal, Bodleian Library, Oxford
Arthur Creech Jones papers, Rhodes House Library, Oxford
A. L. Smith Papers, Balliol College, Oxford
Dacre papers, Christ Church, Oxford

Cambridge:
Trinity College, Cambridge, Additional Mss (Mrs Henry Sidgwick)

Rugby School Archives:
R. Whitelaw, House Annals 1892–1900.

Other Papers:
Mr A. Lynch, unpublished autobiography and letters

Newspapers and journals

Balliol College Register
Children's Country Holiday Fund, Annual Reports
Christian Science Monitor
Daily News
Daily Telegraph
Encounter
Fabian News
The Guardian
The Highway
London School of Economics Magazine
Man and Metal
Manchester Guardian
The Meteor (Rugby School)
The Nation
The Observer
Oxford Magazine
Oxford Tutorial Classes Committee Annual Reports
New Statesman
Political Quarterly
Rewley House Papers,
Rochdale Observer

Saturday Review
Socialist Commentary
Surrey Advertiser
The Times
Times Educational Supplement
Times Literary Supplement
Tribune
Toynbee Hall, Annual Reports
Toynbee Record
Westminster Gazette

Official publications

Parliamentary Debates, 4th series
Royal Commission on the Poor Laws and the Relief of Distress, Parliamentary Papers 1910, vol. xlix.
Ministry of Reconstruction: Adult Education Committee: Interim Report on Industrial and Social Conditions in Relation to Adult Education, *Parliamentary Papers 1918*, vol. ix, 319–49.
Ministry of Reconstruction: Adult Education Committee: Final Report, Parliamentary Papers 1919, (Cmd. 321), vol. xxviii, 453–867.
Coal Industry (Sankey) Commission, vol. ii. Reports and Evidence on the Second Stage of the Inquiry, Parliamentary Papers, 1919, xii.
Royal (Samuel) Commission on the Coal Industry 1925. Minutes of Evidence (London, HMSO, 1926)
League of Nations' Institute of Intellectual Co-operation, *The Reorganisation of Education in China. By the League of Nations' Mission of Experts* (Paris, 1932)

Unpublished theses and papers

Brooks, J. R., 'R. H. Tawney and the Reform of English Education' (unpublished PhD dissertation, University of Wales, 1974)
Corley, T. A. B., 'George Unwin: A Manchester Economic Historian Extraordinary' and 'Tawney's memoir of Unwin'

Radio programmes

'Portrait of R. H. Tawney', BBC Home Service, 12 May 1963.
'Out of the Wilderness: R. H. Tawney', BBC Radio 4, 1983.

Television programme

'The Somme', Channel 4, 14 November 2005, 9.00 pm

Books and articles

Abrams, Philip, 'The Failure of Social Reform 1918–20', *Past and Present*, 24 (1963), 43–64.

Allen, Brigid, *Morrells of Oxford. The Family and their Brewery 1743–1993* (Oxford, 1994).

Annan, Noel, 'The Intellectual Aristocracy', *Studies in Social History: A Tribute to G. M. Trevelyan*, ed. J. H. Plumb (1955), 241–87.

[Anon] 'Some Principles of University Reform', *Westminster Gazette*, 22 Feb., 23 Feb., 1 Mar., 2 Mar., 8 Mar., 9 Mar. 1907.

[Anon] 'Oxford and the Nation', *The Times*, 3 Apr. 1907; 5 Apr.; 9 Apr.; 13 Apr.; 16 Apr.; 20 Apr.; 29 Apr.; 11 May.

[Anon] (Richard Titmuss, F. J. Fisher, J. R. Williams), *R. H. Tawney: A Portrait by Several Hands* (nd, 1960).

Arblaster, Anthony, 'Tawney in Retrospect', Bulletin of the Society for the Study of Labour History, 54, 1 (1989), 95–102.

Armstrong, Gary and Gray, Tim, *The Authentic Tawney. A New Interpretation of the Political Thought of R. H. Tawney* (Exeter, 2011).

—, 'Three Fallacies in the Essentialist Interpretation of the Political Thought of R. H. Tawney', *Journal of Political Ideologies*, 15, 2 (2010), 161–74.

Ball, Sidney, 'What Oxford Can Do for Workpeople', *Papers Submitted to the National Conference of Working Class and Educational Organisations, held in the Examination Schools, High Street, Oxford, on Saturday, August 10th, 1907* (London, 1907), 9–16.

Barber, Michael, *The Making of the 1944 Education Act* (London, 1994).

Barker, Rodney, *Education and Politics 1900–1951. A Study of the Labour Party* (Oxford, 1972).

Barker, T. C., 'The Beginnings of the Economic History Society', *EcHR*, ns, 30, 1 (1977), 1–19.

Barnard, H. C., 'A Great Headmaster: John Lewis Paton (1863–1946)', *British Journal of Educational Studies*, 11, 1 (1962), 5–15.

Barnett, Henrietta, *Canon Barnett. His Life, Work and Friends* (1919) (London, 1921 edn.).

Begbie, Harold, *Living Water: Being Chapters from the Romance of the Poor Student* (London, 1918).

Berg, Maxine, *A Woman in History:Eileen Power 1889–1940* (Cambridge, 1996).

Beveridge, William, *Power and Influence* (London, 1953).

Blackburn, Sheila, 'A Very Moderate Socialist Indeed? R. H. Tawney and Minimum Wages', *Twentieth Century British History*, 10, 2 (1999), 107–36.

—, 'Curse or Cure? Why was the Enactment of Britain's 1909 Trade Boards Act so Controversial?', *British Journal of Industrial Relations*, 47, 2 (2009), 214–39.

—, 'Ideology and Social Policy: The Origins of the Trade Boards Act', *The Historical Journal*, 34 (1991), 1, 43–64.

Bland, A. E., Brown, P. A., Tawney, R. H. (eds), *English Economic History – Select Documents* (1914).

Bongiorno, Frank, *British to their Bootheels too: Britishness and Australian Radicalism*, Trevor Reese Memorial Lecture 2006, King's College, London.

Bowley, A. L. and Burnett-Hurst, A. R., *Livelihood and Poverty.A Study in the Conditions of Working-Class Households in Northampton, Warrington, Stanley and Reading* (London, 1915).

Brendon, Vyvyan, *Children of the Raj* (2005) (London, 2006 edn.).

Brown, Malcolm, *The Imperial War Museum Book of the Somme* (1996) (London, 1997 edn.).

Bulkley, M. E., *The Establishment of Legal Minimum Rates in the Boxmaking Industry Under the Trade Boards Act of 1909* (London, 1915).

—, *The Feeding of Schoolchildren* (London, 1914).

[Cartwright. E. S.] 'Looking Backwards: A Tutorial Class Anniversary. By an Old Student', *Rewley House Papers*, 2 (1929), 66–73.

Chambers, J. D., 'The Tawney Tradition', *Economic History Review*, 24, 3 (1971), 355–69.

Christianity and Industrial Problems. Being the Report of the Archbishops' Fifth Committee of Inquiry. Pt. 1 (London, 1918).

Citrine, Lord, *Two Careers* (London, 1967).

Clarke, P. F., *Liberals and Social Democrats* (Cambridge, 1978).

Clay, Henry, *Economics: An Introduction for the General Reader* (London, 1916).

Collini, Stefan, *Absent Minds. Intellectuals in Britain* (Oxford, 2006).

—, 'Moral Mind: R. H. Tawney' in Stefan Collini, *English Pasts. Essays in History and Culture* (Oxford, 1999), 177–94.

Cooper, J. P., 'The Counting of Manors', *EcHR*, ns, viii, 3 (1956), 377–89.

Court, W. H. B., *Scarcity and Choice in History* (New York, 1970).

Cowan, Alastair, *The 22nd Battalion Manchester Regiment. The Western Front, Italy, Austria, Egypt* (Knutsford, Cheshire, 2011).

Crosse, Gordon, *Charles Gore: A Biographical Sketch* (London, 1932).

Crow, Duncan, *A Man of Push and Go. The Life of George Macaulay Booth* (London, 1965).

Dahrendorf, Ralf, *A History of the London School of Economics and Political Science 1895–1995* (Oxford, 1995).

Daniels, G. W., *George Unwin: a Memorial Lecture* (Manchester, 1926).

Dennis, Norman and Halsey, A. H., *English Ethical Socialism: Thomas More to R. H. Tawney* (Oxford, 1988).

Durbin, Elizabeth, *New Jerusalems. The Labour Party and the Economics of Democratic Socialism* (London, 1985).

Durbin, E. F. M. and Catlin, George (eds), *War and Democracy* (London, 1938).

Eagles, Stuart, *After Ruskin. The Social and Political Legacies of a Victorian Prophet, 1870–1920* (Oxford, 2011).

Elton, G. R., *The Future of the Past* (Cambridge, 1968).

—, *Reformation Europe* (London, 1963).

Emery, Albert, 'In the Early Tutorial Classes, (I) Longton', *The Highway*, 44 (1953), 253–6.

Fahey, D. M., 'R. H. Tawney and the Sense of Community', *The Centenniel Review*, xii, 4 (Fall 1968), 455–65.

Fisher F. J. (ed.), *Essays in the Economic and Social History of Tudor & Stuart England in honour of R. H. Tawney* (Cambridge, 1961).

Fletcher, Frank, *After Many Days* (London, 1937).

Floud, Jean, 'The Educational Experience of the Adult Population of England and Wales as at July 1949' in D. V. Glass (ed.), *Social Mobility in Britain* (London, 1954).

Foot, Michael, 'My Kind of Socialism', *The Observer*, 10 Jan. 1982.

Gaitskell, Hugh, 'Address by the Rt. Hon. Hugh Gaitskell' in R. H. Tawney, *The Radical Tradition* (ed. R. Hinden) (London, 1964).

Gilbert, Martin, *Somme. The Heroism and Horror of War* (London, 2006).

Gill, L. V., 'What can we learn from History?', *The Highway*, 40 (1949), 255–9.

Goldman, Lawrence, *Dons and Workers. Oxford and Adult Education Since 1850* (Oxford, 1995).

—, 'Intellectuals and the English Working Class 1870–1945: The Case of Adult Education', *History of Education*, 29, 4 (2000), 281–300.

—, 'John Ruskin and the Working Classes in Mid-Victorian Britain' in Keith Hanley and Brian Maidment (eds), *Persistent Ruskin. Studies in Influence, Assimilation and Effect* (Farnham, Surrey, 2013), 15–31.

—, 'Ruskin, Oxford, and the British Labour Movement 1880–1914' in Dinah Birch (ed.), *Ruskin and the Dawn of the Modern* (Oxford, 1999), 57–86.

Gordon, Peter and White, John, *Philosophers as Educational Reformers: The Influence of Idealism on British Educational Thought and Practice* (London, 1979).

Gore, Charles (ed.), *Lux Mundi. A Series of Studies in the Religion of the Incarnation* (London, 1889).

Gosden, P. H. J. H., *Education in the Second World War. A Study in Policy and Administration* (London, 1976).

Green, Ernest, 'A Gentle Rebel', *Man and Metal*, Feb. 1962, 23.

Greenwood, Arthur, *The Health and Physique of Schoolchldren* (London, 1913).

—, 'Labour and Adult Education', in R. St John Parry (ed.), *Cambridge Essays on Adult Education* (Cambridge, 1920), 111–32.

Grier, Linda, *Achievement in Education: The Work of Michael Ernest Sadler 1885–1935* (London, 1952).

Grimley, Matthew, *Citizenship, Community, and the Church of England. Liberal Anglican Theories of The State between the Wars* (Oxford, 2004).

Haldane of Cloan, Viscount, *The Problem of Nationalization. With an Introduction by R. H. Tawney and Harold J. Laski* (London, 1921).

Harris, Jose, *Private Lives, Public Spirit. Britain 1970–1914* (1993) (London, 1994 edn.).

—, *William Beveridge. A Biography* (1997) (Oxford University Press, Oxford, 2nd edn., 2003).

Harrison, Royden, 'Sidney and Beatrice Webb' in Carl Levy (ed.), *Socialism and the Intelligentsia 1880–1914* (London, 1987), 35–89.

Harvie, Christopher, *The Lights of Liberalism. University Liberals and the Challenge of Democracy 1860–1886* (London, 1976).

Hexter, J. H., 'Storm over the Gentry: The Tawney-Trevor-Roper Controversy', *Encounter*, x, 5 (1958), 22–34.

Higher Education of Working Men, Being the Official Report of the Joint Conference Between Co-operators, Trade Unionists, and University Extension Authorities, Held at Oxford, on Saturday, August 22nd 1903 (London, 1903).

Hinden, Rita, 'In Debt to Tawney', *Socialist Commentary*, Feb. 1962, 11.

Hobsbawm, Eric, 'The Fabians Reconsidered' in idem, *Labouring Men. Studies in the History of Labour* (London, 1964), 250–71.

Holland, Henry Scott, *Henry Scott Holland. Memoir and Letters* (ed. Stephen Paget) (London, 1921).

Holt, Tonie and Valmai, *Major and Mrs Holt's Battlefield Guide to the Somme* (1996) (Bansley, S. Yorks, 2008 edn.).

Howarth, Janet, 'The Edwardian Reform Movement' in M. G. Brock and M. C. Curthoys (eds), *The History of the University of Oxford*, vii, *The Nineteenth Century*, pt. 2 (Oxford, 2000), 821–54.

Howe, Mark de Wolfe (ed.), *Holmes-Laski Letters. The Correspondence of Mr Justice Holmes and Harold J. Laski, 1916–1935* (Cambridge, MA, 1953).

Iremonger, Frederic, *William Temple, Archbishop of Canterbury. His Life and Letters*, (London, 1948).

Jackson, Ben, *Equality and the British Left. A Study in Progressive Political Thought, 1900–64* (Manchester, 2007).

Jeger, Lena, 'Homage to Tawney', *Tribune*, 2 Dec. 1960.

—, 'Ideas and the Man', *Tribune*, 26 Jan. 1962.

—, 'Preface' to Stanley G. Evans, *First Tawney Memorial Lecture* (1964, Christian Socialist Movement, London).

Jennings, Bernard, *Albert Mansbridge* (Leeds, 1973).

—, *Albert Mansbridge and English Adult Education* (Hull, 1976).

—, 'Revolting Students: The Ruskin College Dispute 1908–9', *Studies in Adult Education*, 9, 1 (1977), 1–16.

Jones, Greta, *Social Darwinism and English Thought. The Interaction between Biological and Social Theory* (Brighton, 1980).

Jones, Thomas, *Whitehall Diary*, (ed. Keith Middlemas) (3 vols.) (London, 1969–71).

Kadish, Alon, *Apostle Arnold: The Life and Death of Arnold Toynbee 1852–1883* (Durham, NC, 1986).

Keegan, John, 'Pals to the Death', *Daily Telegraph*, 1 July 2006.

Kenyon, John, 'The Great Historians: R. H. Tawney', *Observer Magazine*, 12 Dec. 1976.

—, *The History Men. The Historical Profession in England since the Renaissance* (1983) (London, 1993 edn.).

Kerridge, Eric, *Agrarian Problems in the Sixteenth Century and After* (London, 1969).

Kolbert, J. M., *Keele: The First Fifty Years* (Keele, 2000).

'Lambda' [R. H. Tawney], 'The University and the Nation', *Westminster Gazette*, 15 Feb., 16 Feb., 17 Feb., 23 Feb., 24 Feb., 2 Mar., 3 Mar., 10 Mar. 1906.

Lasch, Christopher, *The Agony of the American Left* (New York, 1966).

Lindsay, A. D. 'R. H. Tawney', *The Highway*, Jan. 1945, 51.

Livingstone, Richard, *The Future in Education* (London, 1941).

Lowe, R. A.,'The North Staffordshire Miners' Higher Education Movement', *Educational Review*, 22, 3 (1970), 263–77.

MacIntyre, Alasdair, *Against the Self-Image of the Age* (London, 1971).

Malia, Martin, 'What is the Intelligentsia?' in Richard Pipes (ed.), *The Russian Intelligentsia* (New York, 1961), 47–62.

Marquand, David, 'R. H. Tawney. Prophet of Equality', *The Guardian* 26 Nov. 1960.

McBriar, A. M., *Fabian Socialism and English Politics 1884–1918* (Cambridge, 1962).

McKibbin, Ross, *Classes and Cultures. England 1918–1951* (Oxford, 1998).

—, 'The Economic Policy of the Second Labour Government 1929–31', *Past and Present*, 68 (1975), 95–123.

Mehta, Ved, *Fly and Fly-Bottle. Encounters with British Intellectuals* (London, 1963).

Middlebrook, Martin, *The First Day on the Somme* (1971) (London, 2001 edn.).

Middlebrook, Martin and Mary, *The Somme Battlefields* (1991) (London, 1994 edn.).

Millar, J. P. M., *The Labour College Movement* (London, 1979).

Morris, William, *William Morris. News from Nowhere and Other Writings (ed. Clive Wilmer)* (London, 1993).

Mountford, J. F., *Keele: An Historical Critique* (London, 1972).

Nield, W., 'What Workpeople Want Oxford to Do', in *Papers Submitted to the National Conference of Working Class and Educational Organisations, held in the Examination Schools, High Street, Oxford, on Saturday, August 10th, 1907* (London, 1907), 3–7.

Ormrod, David, 'R. H. Tawney and the Origins of Capitalism', *History Workshop Journal*, 18 (1984), 138–59.

Oxford and Working-Class Education: Being the Report of a Joint Committee of University and Working-Class Representatives on the Relation of the University to the Higher Education of Workpeople, (1908) (2nd edn., Oxford, 1909).

Pauli, R., *Drei volkswirtschaftliche Denkschriften aus der Zeit Heinrich viii von England* (Göttingen, 1878).

Picht, Werner, *Toynbee Hall and the English Settlement Movement,* trans. L. A. Cowell (London, 1914).

Pipes, Richard 'The Historical Evolution of the Russian Intelligentsia' in Richard Pipes (ed.), *The Russian Intelligentsia* (New York, 1961), 1–18.

Postan, Michael, 'D. M. Joslin 1925–1970' in *R. H. Tawney's Commonplace Book* (eds J. M. Winter and D. M. Joslin) (Cambridge University Press, Cambridge, 1972).

Presnell, L. S., *Country Banking in the Industrial Revolution* (Oxford, 1956).

Prestige, G. L., *The Life of Charles Gore: A Great Englishman* (London, 1935).

Preston, Ronald, 'R. H. Tawney as a Christian Moralist', *Theology*, lxix, Apr., May, June (1966), 157–64; 208–15; 262–69.

Price, T. W., *The Story of the Workers' Educational Association* (London, 1924).

Rackham, Clara, 'Tawney at Home. Memories of an old friendship', *The Fenland Bulletin* (WEA) nd [1960].

Rée, Jonathan, 'Socialism and the Educated Working Class' in Carl Levy (ed.), *Socialism and the Intelligentsia 1880–1914* (London, 1987), 211–18.

Ringer, Fritz, *The Decline of the German Mandarins. The German Academic Community 1890–1933* (Cambridge, MA, 1969).

Rose, Jonathan, *The Intellectual Life of the British Working Classes* (New Haven and London, 2001).

Rowbotham, Sheila, '"Travellers in a Strange Country"; Responses of Working-Class Students to the University Extension Movement 1873–1910', *History Workshop Journal*, 12 (autumn 1981), 62–95.

Sadleir, Michael, *Michael Ernest Sadler. A Memoir by his Son* (London, 1949).

Samuel, Raphael, 'The SDP's Escape from the Christian Heritage of Socialism' and 'Tawney and the SDP', *The Guardian*, 29 Mar., 5 Apr. 1982.

Saville, John, *Memoirs from the Left* (London, 2003).

Savine, A., 'English Customary Tenure in the Tudor Period', *Quarterly Journal of Economics*, xix (1904), 36–80.

Schultz, Bart, *Henry Sidgwick: Eye of the Universe. An Intellectual Biography* (Cambridge, 2004).

Scott, Drusilla, *A. D. Lindsay. A Biography* (Oxford, 1971).

Seligman, Adam, 'Tendentious Debunking', *Review of Politics*, 73, 4 (2011), 665–6.

Shils, Edward, 'The Intellectuals. I. Great Britain', *Encounter*, iv, 4 (1955), 5–16.

Sidgwick, Eleanor Maud and Arthur Sidgwick (eds), *Henry Sidgwick. A Memoir* (London, 1906).

Sisman, Adam, *Hugh Trevor-Roper. The Biography* (2010) (London, 2011 edn.).

Smith, H. P., 'A Tutorial Class Makes History', *Adult Education*, 31/4 (Spring 1959), 271–3.

—, 'Edward Stuart Cartwright. A Note on his Work for Adult Education', *Rewley House Papers*, 3/1 (1949–50), 8–24.

—, *Labour and Learning: Albert Mansbridge, Oxford and the WEA* (Oxford, 1956).

Soper, Donald, 'Socialism: An Enduring Creed', *The Third Tawney Memorial Lecture,* (London, 1980).

Stears, Marc, *Progressives, Pluralists and the Problems of the State. Ideologies of Reform in the United States and Britain, 1909–1926* (Oxford, 2002).

Stedman, Michael, *Manchester Pals* (Barnsley, S. Yorks, 2004).

Stedman Jones, Gareth, *Outcast London. A Study in the Relationship Between Classes in Victorian Society* (Oxford, 1971).

Steele, Tom and Taylor, Richard, 'R. H. Tawney and the Reform of the Universities', *History of Education*, 37, 1 (2008), 1–22.

Steffen, G. F., *Studien zur Geschichte der Englisher Lohnarbeiter* (Stuttgart, 1901–5).

Stocks, Mary, *The Workers' Educational Association. The First Fifty Years* (London, 1953).

Stone, Lawrence, 'The Anatomy of the Elizabethan Aristocracy', *EcHR*, 18, 1/2 (1948), 1–53.

Styler, W. E., 'The Report in Retrospect' in Sylvia Harrop (ed.), *Oxford and Working-Class Education,* (1908), (rev. 2nd edn., Nottingham, 1987), 48–64.

Supple, Barry, *The History of the British Coal Industry. Volume 4. 1913–1946: The Political Economy of Decline* (Oxford, 1987).

Tawney, Charles Henry, *The Kathákoça: or, Treasury of Stories* (transl. from Sanskrit manuscripts by C. H. Tawney. With appendix, containing notes by Ernst Leumann) (London, Royal Asiatic Society, 1895).

—, 'Charles Henry Tawney', *Journal of the Asiatic Society of Great Britain and Ireland*, 1 (1923), 152–4.

—, *The Ocean of Story, being C. H. Tawney's Translation of Somadeva's Kathā Sarit Sāgara (or Ocean of the Streams of Story)* (ed. N. M. Penzer) (10 vols., London, nd) (1924).

Tawney, R. H., 'A Fifty Year's Memory', *Manchester Guardian*, 5 Nov. 1956.

—, 'A Starting Point', *The Manchester Guardian*, 31 Mar. 1945.

—, 'An Educational Programme', *Manchester Guardian*, 10 Mar. 1917.

—, 'An Experiment in Democratic Education', *The Political Quarterly*, 2, May 1914, 62–84.

—, *Business and Politics under James I: Lionel Cranfield as Merchant and Minister* (London, 1958).

—, *Christian Politics* (Socialist Christian League, 1954).

—, 'Democracy and Defeat', *The Welsh Outlook*, Jan. 1917.

—, *Education: The Socialist Policy* (ILP Publication Dept., London, 1924).

—, *Eileen Power* (Golders Green Crematorium, London, 12 August 1940).

—, *Equality* (London, 1931).

—, 'Foreword' to Carter L. Goodrich, *The Frontier of Control. A Study in British Workshop Politics* (London, 1920).

—, 'Foreword' to Max Weber, *The Protestant Ethic and the Spirit of Capitalism* (tr. Talcott Parsons), (London, 1930).

—, 'Geddes Report on Education, I and II', *Manchester Guardian*, 21, 22 Feb. 1922.

—, 'Harrington's Interpretation of His Age', *The Raleigh Lecture on History*, The British Academy 1941 (London, 1942).

—, *History and Society: Essays by R. H. Tawney* (J. M. Winter, ed.), (London, 1978).

—, 'Introduction', in T. W. Price, *The Story of the Workers' Educational Association from 1903 to 1924* (London, 1924).

—, 'Introduction' to Charles Gore, *Christianity Applied to the Life of Men and of Nations* (London, 1920) (1940 edn.).

—, 'Introduction' to Max Beer, *A History of British Socialism* (London, 1919).

—, 'John Ruskin', *The Observer*, 19 Feb. 1919, reprinted in R. H. Tawney, *The Radical Tradition* (London, 1964), 40–4.

—, 'Keep the Workers' Children in Their Place', *Daily News*, 14 Feb. 1918, republished in *The Radical Tradition* (London, 1953), 47–51.

—, 'Labour Party History. Preparation and Achievement', *Times Literary Supplement*, 10 (1950), 1–2.

—, *Land and Labour in China* (London, 1932).

—, 'Mr E. S. Cartwright', *The Highway*, Oct. 1950, 14–15.

—, *Poverty as an Industrial Problem* (London, 1913).

—, 'Raising of the School Age' *The Times*, 9 Nov. 1935.

—, *Religion and the Rise of Capitalism* (London, 1926).

—, *R. H. Tawney's Commonplace Book* (eds J. M. Winter and D. M. Joslin) (Cambridge University Press, Cambridge, 1972).

—, *Secondary Education for All. A Policy for Labour* (Labour Party, 1922) (London, 1988 edn.).

—, *Some Thoughts on Education and the War* (1917) (Workers' Educational Association). (Later known and republished as 'A National College of All Souls', *Times Educational Supplement*, 22 Feb. 1917), reprinted in R. H. Tawney, *The Attack and Other Papers* (London, 1953), 29–34.

—, (ed.), *Studies in Economic History: The Collected Papers of George Unwin* (London, 1927).

—, 'Tawney on A. P. Wadsworth', *The Highway*, 48 (1957), 82–4.

—, 'Unemployment and Boy Labour in Glasgow' and 'Labour Exchanges and Relief Work in Strassburg', *Royal Commission on the Poor Laws and Relief of Distress*, xlix (1910), pp. 329–48, 96610–9619.

—, 'Why Britain Fights' (1940) in *The Attack and Other Papers* (London, 1953), 71–81.

—, 'The Abolition of Economic Controls, 1918–21', *EcHR*, xiii (1943), 1–30.

—, *The Acquisitive Society* (London, 1921).

—, 'The Administration of the Education Act, 1936', *The Highway*, Nov. 1937, 14–17.

—, *The Agrarian Problem in the Sixteenth Century* (London, 1912).

—, 'The American Labour Movement' in J. M. Winter (ed.), *R. H. Tawney: The American Labour Movement and Other Essays* (Brighton, 1979), 1–110.

—, *The Attack and Other Papers* (London, 1953).

—, 'The British Coal Industry and the Question of Nationalization', *Quarterly Journal of Economics*, xxxv, 1 (1920), 61–107.

—, *The British Labor Movement* (New Haven, CT, 1925).

—, *The Children's Charter* (WEA, London, 1932).

—, *The Choice before the Labour Party* (The Socialist League, 1934). (First published in the *Political Quarterly*, 3, July–September 1932, 323–45.

—, 'The Coal Problem', *The Contemporary Review*, cxix (1921), 727–37.

—, 'The *Daily News* Religious Census of London', *Toynbee Record*, xvi (1904), 87–8.

—, *The Establishment of Minimum Rates in the Chain-Making Industry under the Trade Boards Act of 1909* (London, 1914).

—, *The Establishment of Minimum Rates in the Tailoring Industry under the Trade Boards Act of 1909* (London, 1915).

—, 'The Economics of Boy Labour', *The Economic Journal*, 19, 76 (1909), 517–37.

—, *The Nationalization of the Coal Industry* (The Labour Party, London, 1922).

—, *The Problem of the Public Schools* (WEA, London, 1943), reprinted from the *Political Quarterly*, April–June 1943, 117–49.

—, 'The Recent Proposals for the Nationalization of the British Coal Industry', *Clark College Record*, 15, 4 (1920), 233–56.

—, 'The Rise of the Gentry: A Postscript', *EcHR*, ns, 7, 1 (1954), 91–7.

—, 'The Rise of the Gentry, 1558–1640', *EcHR*, 11, 1 (1941), 1–38.

—, 'The Sickness of an Acquisitive Society', *Hibbert Journal*, xvii (1919), 353–70.

—, *The Sword of the Spirit* (London, 1918), originally published in *The Athenaeum*, Dec. 1917.

—, 'The Theory of Pauperism', *The Sociological Review* (Manchester), Oct. 1909, 361–74.

—, 'The WEA and Adult Education' (1953) in idem, *The Radical Tradition: Twelve Essays on Politics, Education and Literature* (George Allen & Unwin, London, 1964).

—, *The Webbs and Their Work* (Webb Memorial Lecture, No. 1, London, 1945).

—, *The Webbs in Perspective* (London, 1953).

—, (ed.), Thomas Wilson, *A Discourse Upon Usury* (1569) (London, 1925) (1962 edn.).

Tawney, R. H. and Nathan Adler, *Boy and Girl Labour* (Women's Industrial Council, London, 1909).

Tawney, R. H. and Power, Eileen (eds), *Tudor Economic Documents. Being Select Documents Illustrating the Economic and Social History of Tudor England* (3 vols, London, 1924).

Tawney, R. H., and Trevleyan, C. P., *Education Policy*, Labour Party Policy paper, no. 218, Feb. 1934.

Taylor, A. J. P., 'A Socialist Saint', in A. J. P. Taylor, *Politicians, Socialism and Historians* (London, 1980), 163–6.

Terrill, Ross, *R. H. Tawney and his Times. Socialism as Fellowship* (Harvard University Press, Cambridge, MA, 1973).

Trevor-Roper, Hugh, *Archbishop Laud* (London, 1940).

—, 'The Elizabethan Aristocracy: An Anatomy Anatomized', *EcHR*, NS, 3, 3 (1951), 279–98.

—, Letters from Oxford (ed. Richard Davenport Hines) (London, 2006).

—, *The Last Days of Hitler* (London, 1947).

Trevor-Roper, H. R. 'The Gentry 1540–1640', *The Economic History Review Supplements*, 1 (London, 1953), 1–55.

Unwin, George, *Industrial Organisation in the Sixteenth and Seventeenth Centuries* (Oxford, 1904).

—, *Samuel Oldknow and the Arkwrights: the Industrial Revolution at Stockport and Marple* (Manchester, 1924).

Vesselitsky, V. de, *The Homeworker and her Outlook. A Descriptive Study of Tailoresses and Boxmakers* (London, 1916).

Vinogradoff, P., *Villeinage in England* (Oxford, 1892).

Warburton, W. H., *The History of Trade Union Organisation in the North Staffordshire Potteries* (London, 1931).

Webb, Beatrice, *Diary of Beatrice Webb*, (4 vols.), ed. N. and J. Mackenzie (London, 1985).

—, *Our Partnership* (London, 1948).

—, The Diary of Beatrice Webb, typescript version, London School of Economics Digital Library.

Weber, Max, *The Protestant Ethic and the Spirit of Capitalism* (1904).

Welch, Edwin, *The Peripatetic University: Cambridge Local Lectures 1873–1973* (Cambridge, 1973).

West, Linden, 'The Tawney Legend Re-examined', *Studies in Adult Education*, 4, 2 (1972), 105–19.

Westlake, Ray, *Tracing British Battalions on the Somme* (1994) (Barnsley, S. Yorks, 2004 edn.).

Williams, Philip M., *Hugh Gaitskell. A Political Biography* (London, 1979).

Williams, Raymond, *Culture and Society 1780–1950*, (1961) (3rd edn., Harmondsworth, 1963).

Winter, J. M., 'A Bibliography of the Published Writings of R. H. Tawney', *EcHR* 25, (1972), 137–53.

—, 'Introduction: Tawney on Labour and Labour Movements', in idem (ed.) *R. H. Tawney: The American Labour Movement and Other Essays* (Brighton, 1979), ix–xxiv.

—, 'R. H. Tawney's Early Political Thought', *Past and Present*, 47 (1970), 71–96.

—, 'Tawney the Historian' in idem (ed.), *History and Society. Essays by R. H. Tawney* (London, 1978), 1–40.

Wright, A. W., *R. H. Tawney* (Manchester, 1987).

Yeo, Stephen, 'A New Life: The Religion of Socialism in Britain, 1883–96', *History Workshop Journal*, 4 (1977), 5–56.

Yorke, Paul, *Ruskin College 1899–1909. Ruskin Students' Labour History Pamphlets, no. 1* (Ruskin College, Oxford, 1977).

Zimmern, A. E., 'Education and the Working Class', *The Round Table: A Quarterly Review of the Politics of the British Empire,* 14 (1914), 255–79.

—, 'The Workers at the Summer Meeting', *Oxford Magazine*, 24 (1907), 23–4.

Index